"These chronicles are truly hemispheric, postmodern memories written in a ludic, singular Spanglish that encapsulates the transnational, nomad vivencias of a Jewish Chicana from Califas, a citizen of the Hispanic world. Original, powerful, and profound."　　　　　**Frances Aparicio, University of Illinois at Chicago**

# HEART

# THROB

## *DEL BALBOA CAFE*
## *AL APARTHEID AND BACK*

**SUSANA CHÁVEZ-SILVERMAN**

THE UNIVERSITY OF WISCONSIN PRESS

The University of Wisconsin Press
728 State Street, Suite 443
Madison, Wisconsin 53706-1428

uwpress.wisc.edu
Grays Inn House, 127 Clerkenwell Road
London EC1R 5DB, United Kingdom
eurospanbookstore.com

Printed in the United States of America

This book may be available in a digital edition.

Library of Congress Cataloging-in-Publication Data
Names: Chávez-Silverman, Susana, author.
Title: Heartthrob: del Balboa Cafe al apartheid and back / Susana
Chávez-Silverman.
Description: Madison, Wisconsin: The University of Wisconsin Press, [2019] |
Written in a combination of English and Spanish.
Identifiers: LCCN 2019008118 | ISBN 9780299324308 (cloth: alk. paper)
Subjects: LCSH: Chávez-Silverman, Susana. | Latin Americans—United
States—Biography. | LCGFT: Autobiographies. | Creative nonfiction.
Classification: LCC PS3603.H3889 Z46 2019 | DDC 818/.603 [B]—dc23
LC record available at https://lccn.loc.gov/2019008118

Para Montenegro, vir altyd

Waarheid is baie meer werd as werklikheid.
[Truth matters far more than reality.]
**Xavier Nagel**

# CONTENTS

## PART I

# Happy Together

Look, they say. These black signs on white paper, they are me.
My blood ran with this ink; here, where I turned the page, it
was pain to stem the flow, even for an instant, so strongly
the current ran toward you.

**Sylvia Townsend Warner**

# Happy Together

29-i-82

Late last night, pasó algo heartstoppingly beautiful, with a spirit as free and uncompromising as my own. Pero no puede ser, it seems. Can't *really* be, right now, por una serie de fortuitous, fucked-up circumstances: la distancia, vacation, moving on.

Me siento strangely calm. I'd *like* to see you so much, Roland Fraser (and wouldn't like to think I've deceived myself, que fuiste falsely ardent). Pero somehow, creo que quizás no me importaría, exactly, if I never saw you again. Quiero decir: it was perfect, encapsulated like that. Intact.

Te vi pasar, outside el Balboa Cafe. El "Club," le decimos, yo y la Trish. My heart jumped de ese modo peculiar que tiene ante las impossible (pero destino)-seeming circumstances—a definite "Montenegro" feeling— infinite longing en un quick flash. Pero no, Roland. No sabía que you also saw *me* like that. I craned around to see you go y te me desapareciste, and I allowed myself a little twinge. Le dije a la Trish: the man of my sueños just walked by the window, y se esfumó. And then Trish told me to *look*, y allí mero estabas, and I was stunned, and all I could say was *ay Dios, he's gorgeous*. Sentí ese clenching feeling, tú y yo cambiamos una long, smoky glance. Trish me dijo que you were coming over, y en vez de apprehension o ambivalencia (¿será tonto, o boring?) sentí sólo gladness. A hunger to see your face closer still, and suddenly you were upon our table de un modo tan natural, and I asked you to join us. Y la Trish habla que habla, she started her giggling, esa su famosa baby laugh. Pero no importaba: you and I were mesmerized. Tenías las cejas más hermosas, y Dios, *lips*; deep brown, large eyes. ¡Y tu acento! I loved it, pero de repente, flash of uneasy recognition. Y casi al instante, full-on dread. —*Where are you from?* te pregunté, entre suspicious y hopeful, *Australia? —Ummm, noooo. —New Zealand? —Nooo.* Allí por poco me levanto, pa' rajarme horrorizada, pero tus ojos, your hand on mine, warm, urgent, pressed me to stay. —*Just* wait, me imploraste. *Don't go.*

Emanabas charm y sensitivity, a tremendous sexy, humorous warmth. Quería estar contigo, touch your hand as we lit cigarettes. Me sentía absolutamente en casa en el aura de tu warm, steady gaze, love love *loving* your accent. A pesar de mí misma. In spite of my years of rallying for divestment.

Desde la high school, coño. My disgust about apartheid. Your friends, Ken and Steve, eran bien nice too. Pero you were the magnet.

Se sentía tan natural—why waste time? Invite you home for a while. ¡Era tan tarde! ¡Habíamos cerrado el Club! It was so good to take your hand, almost like old lovers, a la salida del Club. Everyone was teasing us as you kissed my hair familiarly; nos cantaban el theme song de *Love Story*, y el Ken te gritó, jovially, —*Rolo, hey, piss off, man. You came to America to have a good time, not to get married.*

En casa, we chatted a bit con los boys y con la Trish. The current was erotic, pero tan relaxed a la vez. You looked through my books, stacked on the floor por falta de bookshelves. Hablamos de nuestra shared fantasy: leer a Dostoevsky en la cama, nonstop, punctuated only by a cigarette, chocolates, un café quizás. Sentada detrás de ti, straddling you, my body pressed right up against your warm backside. Me tomaste el pie en la mano, gently rubbing, nuzzling my neck mientras llamaba un taxi para los boys. They left, y ayudamos (OK, *you* helped) a Patricia a sumar sus school expenditures (sí, ¡éramos así de old-time, así de relaxed!) before she went to bed.

Oh, comfortable. En mi cuerpo. Kissing you so hard, tu lengua. Besándote el cuello, hearing you moan. You biting my breasts through my fuzzy mauve angora sweater, right through the sexy red bra que me había prestado la Bizzy Bee (mi amiguísima, la Karen). Todo era tan slow, pero con una charged, overwhelming erotic urgency like never before. We were talking and talking! Discutiendo sobre el apartheid, remember? Desesperada, not wanting to believe it. —*How can you live* there? te pregunté. —*Why are you* from *there?* —*I was born there*, me dijiste, más matter-of-fact que defiant, pero not ashamed, tampoco. —*It's my country.* Then, talking about literature, our work. Yo estudiando, enseñando. Writing. Tú, un mining-engineer-in-training. Luego, riéndonos de todo ese talking cuando, como dijiste, —*We should've* long *before this consummated passionate love—several times.*

So we did. Oh, tus hombros. Wide, strong. Los músculos de tus upper arms flexing sinuous. Looking hard into one another, ojos bien abiertos, searching.

Oh, this is how love with a stranger should be. *No* extraño, otro. To be right, tiene que ser así right from the start, absolutely unabashed. Como hicimos el amor, Roland. You welded my body for your pleasure y para el mío, daring contortions. Pero nada parecía contrived. Plunging so deep into me. But never pain. Cero dolor. You loved me touching myself, touching your ass, untando todo ese slippery wetness everywhere. Sudando, just lightly sheening tu mármol whiteness, breathless, oh, when you came. Ojos abiertos.

2-ii-82

I'd like to be writing this *todo* en español, lengua que no entiendes (todavía), that we don't share (yet!), que no usamos y que, por eso, now sounds a tiny bit off in my mind's ear. In my hand. Heme aquí en el BART. Ni sé si dirigirme a ti. Pero oh *you*, Roland. I must: after spelling out with you, la primera noche, the bitter and burning reality of our deepest thoughts on love (what drives us, lo que nos asusta, lo que nos inspira cinismo, what gives us hope), todo lo que nunca he podido compartir, con esta laser precision and honesty, con nadie. After driving with you all over this city in your used and *so* LA Dodge van, siempre cogidos de la mano, gritando con los Stones on "Tattoo You."

Cuando te repetí ese line from *The French Lieutenant's Woman*—"I was lost from the moment I saw you"—I hesitated a moment, después, y de hecho intenté lograr un light, humorous tone. It's only been five days since we met! Pero me miraste unblinking, bien serious, y me corregiste: —*Not you.* You *don't get lost.*

Ah, se me olvidaba mencionarte: how spring-warm it got as soon as you left, Roland! Uf, hasta hace calor hoy. Digo, for San Francisco. Must be 70 at least. Ahora estoy en North Beach, esperando en Galletti Bros. for them to finish stitching my purse. El Caffè Puccini ha perdido su encanto, el Old World mystery de antaño. "New York, New York" en el jukebox ahora, the memory of Mauro singing it gone flat. So, es *aquí* donde escuchó ese infernal tune (vez tras vez . . .). Ahhh, my old hangouts me parecen small, lackluster. Pero si este no es "el lugar" (as Cortázar would say), then WHERE IS IT?

Roland, tú. *You* are the place. Tú, shower-wet, silky dark hair sliding into your eyes. You, imitando los pájaros de los magic, age-old names, your hands on me, looking into me, mientras nos duchamos. Making the African bush come alive for me aquí en la Marina, no less! Lion and wildebeest, leopardo, hiena, hippo. ¡Tántas aves! A desert *Green Mansions* en este warming enero en San Francisco.

3-ii-82

Hay una weighty confluencia de signos. It's the Year of the Dog, desde el sábado, 30 de enero. Everything *really* began to come together that night, después del Chinese New Year's parade. Nuestro tiny apartment transformado en passion palace, the likes of which it had never seen before! Love blooming in both rooms, unknown to each couple. Patricia con el Mr. Dicki and oh, Roland, baby, the sun is so bright now, y ¿dónde estás? One thing touching another and still another, disparando constelaciones de signos, como esos fireworks en la pyrrhic night of love de Montenegro. Remember?

9-ii-82

Oh, Roland. —*Yes, my babe*, me contestaste tan suave, when I spoke your name. We slept not at all. Y sé que anoche, our last night, *especially* won't leave you, Montenegro, amor. We had unspoken *esas* palabras, the whole time. Feeling it from the first night—desde el primer *momento*, en realidad, desde ese fated momento ("slated," as la Trish would say) cuando nuestras miradas se cruzaron, on either side of the Balboa Cafe's plate-glass window—pero never saying it. Luego, all of us amped up on a few lines of speedy cocaine, el Ken te decía que finally, *finally* you'd found someone to spar and parry with, to connect with on *all* levels. And oh, no me importa donde estés, honey, don't forget me—us. *Non ti scordar.*

Helen is here now. Regresamos en su little Honda a nuestra beautiful city, sky dark. For the first time cloudy desde que llegaste y te fuiste y volviste de nuevo. Somehow, bebé, I *do* hope you're torn up inside, espero que te dejes *sentir* estos wrenched trellises, estas tiernas enredaderas que trepan, shooting up around the tower of our shared heart, podadas a deshora, unnaturally, by the constraints that bind you: ese jodido road trip. Y mucho más ominosamente: your return home. To South Africa, tierra que aborrezco. Tu tierra.

The doorbell rang late y la Helen había vuelto. Tina nos cuidó a las dos, in the most sweet way. You left, Roland. Te vi en el "Vasbyt" van, driving away, from the window of my Berkeley classroom. Solté un grito al terminar la clase, I ran downstairs, outside Dwinelle Hall, too late for a glimpse of your beloved hair, tus hombros, tu boca suave, ancha. Oh, be strong for Helen, I commanded myself, y fui a recogerla. Fuimos a tomar un café, and already the grief of your absence se me enroscaba, bottling up a tight drum of refusal. Helen lloró y rabió, pero yo me encontraba como numb.

Tan y tan cansada, pero I must get a few words down. La Helen escribe al Steve. Regresó con un Chinese fortune que había encontrado, stuck against the windshield of her car! Who knows how long it was lodged there, o dónde coño lo encontraste, y cómo se quedó allí, not pinned under anything, for the whole long and terrible (and gusty!) ride patrás a la City de Berkeley: "Your lover(s) will never wish to leave you." Tú habías agregado esa little "s," and you'd signed it, *M*. Fuiste tú, Montenegro, my love. Y ese little fortune se había quedado allí porque it was *meant* to. Porque no te podías despedir de mí sin dejarme saber, oh my darling, that all our "no assumptions" had been for naught. We had made our mark on one another. Bien adentro. Y no el notch on the bedpost.

*14-ii-82*

Valentine's Day. Pero quizás ya intentes, maybe you've already filed and forgotten. Hoy el peor día (I guess you can tell, or I *reckon*, como dirías tú) in terms of despair. I grudgingly acknowledge it, la desesperanza: tan foreign y bitter en las venas. Rain, rain, rain. Todo el día. And in fact, este gray desde que te fuiste (the last time). So hard to keep going. I'm usually so cool; sermoneo sobre el equilibrio. Y acepto que después de la razor-edge intensity, "there *will* be some pain" (como dices). Pero, oh, la diferencia when it's actually here. Tu ausencia: unsettling all routine, lo primero en mi waking consciousness, lo último antes de caer al too-brief, comforting abyss of sleep.

15-ii-82

How empty, mi rutina diaria, anyway. So much accomplished now finally, ahora que te fuiste. Pero what *is* it, really? ¿Qué hago? Papers graded, mis Berkeley students apenas known, it seems, even at this quickly reached quarter's halfway point. My mending done, la ropa lavada, las cuentas pagadas. Roland, ¿dónde coño estás? No se te olvidó, after all (oh, you silly, impatient girl!): lovely Montenegro terse, absolutely *you* Valentine's Day card received! Pero oh, tu voz en el crackling long distance wire would be so much better . . .

Helen over after work. On and on about "the boys," intentando hacer tangible, trying to make sense of a situation whose concreteness eludes us more each hour. Fumando, huifando coca, talking and dreaming aloud hasta colapsar a las 4:30. Nuestra bedtime habitual, lately. Restless sleep entonces, limbs entwined with la Helen's sweet sleeping supineness.

We awake too early. Un café y luego las sad, soothing ablutions. Rain pours down relentless, gray, extrañamente cálida. We decide to go see Costa-Gavras's film *Missing*. Drive to Union Square, pasando todos nuestros familiar landmarks (the Presidio Theater al lado de casa, todos los little Chestnut Street Italian delis, Fillmore Hill), ahora landmines en su poder: devastador, too evocative. The damn movie sold out. Browsing in overheated stores. Luego patrás al neighborhood. Almuerzo en el Club. Boz Scaggs is also lunching. Es un shareholder. O part-owner, o algo por el estilo. Getting buzzed on too-sweet Frangelico coffees y luego mimosas, waiting and waiting for *one* solitary hamburger to share.

So much more to write. I *do* want to get the "events" down (como tú dices), the raw power, las eerie (no) coincidencias of all these days. The Last Night, as we call it. En mayúsculas. Como la Ultima Cena. I turned on la tape recorder temprano—quería poder escuchar tu voz, whenever I wanted—y luego we just forgot about it. Oh, what a pity (me di cuenta muy tarde) que nuestra hermosa conversación, yo, tú y el Ken—political, philosophical, urgent—would be buzzed over on the tape por la mushy lovebird chitchat de Steve y Helen. On and on into the night, our landlords, los Forte, golpeándonos, furiosos, el suelo (their landlord ceiling), nosotros destornillándonos de risa, trying valiantly to whisper (pero, how

8                                  Part I:  Happy Together

can we whisper about apartheid, about love?). Steve popping champagne cork ceiling-high. Tú decretaste *"total* silence," que habrá durado one stunned minute, quizás, y luego el joyous, irrepressible collapse into giggles contra el ominoso pasar de la noche . . .

Sólo supe después, after you'd gone, that the tape had clicked off heraldically justo en el momento en que el Steve nos hacía un solemne brindis. A toast to our love. And so, se quedó ese momento frozen in time: a proposition as yet unfulfilled, fecund.

Ken salió al van around 3 a.m., and we four remained talking. Tú y yo del apartheid, nuestro tema fetiche—reasoning and sparring, argumento y contra-argumento—with a thirst for each other's comments (even at that late-late hour, Montenegro, mi amor, ansiábamos esa "deeper communion," como dice Eliot). With a thirst for each other. Helen and Steve cooing at each other, llamándonos "too serious." Rajaron, *finally,* buscando private quarters en lo de Tina y Pamela.

And so at last, a solas contigo. Por un momento, *willing* the desire to come up through the wall of tears que se me formaba en la garganta. Y aquí, ahora, de nuevo, remembering your mouth, your words—*Come, cry with me now, my love, the time is near*—as you nestled between my legs and took my thighs into your hands and set your mouth firm upon my sex y me pediste que te mirara, watch you licking and nuzzling me, y se me humedecieron los ojos y el sexo and I needed coax desire no longer.

Me penetraste entonces, tan slowly, and tears poured silent, esas lágrimas que *nunca* había querido que me vieras, yet now you brushed and licked them soft from my eyes, and I tasted salt and myself on your lips mientras movíamos hacia un strange animal yearning I have never, *never.* Each intent on our own pleasure, pero sintiendo, a la vez, as if under our own skin, tanto el dolor como el tidal surge del otro. I dug my nails into your shoulders roughly, la vela roja, intensely fragrant, flameaba. Quería tenerte así, entre mis brazos, hearing esos low feline moans wrenching from me pero como de una garganta otra, you gasping wide sobs as well. Y los dos maravillados, at the strength of it: our desire welded to sorrow.

No me permitiste mirar el reloj. —*No my love, my darling. Don't measure us in time now.* Outside, el día amanecía gris. With me on top of you then, looking into you, me murmuraste ferozmente, —*I want to make love with you like no one ever has.* Sólo desistimos, finally, después de horas y horas, because it was dawning. Entonces me pediste que me quedara así, a tu lado, —*Just lie here next to me for five minutes, my babe, just* five *more minutes.* And I pressed my face into your warm, strong neck, and we held each other simply. Amados.

Y eso fue lo que le dijiste al Steve por teléfono, when we made that final morning/mourning wake-up call to them, when he asked you how you were. Le contestaste, —*Loved.* Y me duché sola, medio esperándote, yet knowing you were sleeping, dejándote dormir, ah, mi Montenegro. And then you wrote me a love note en el libro que me regalaste, Nadine Gordimer's *Burger's Daughter*, y yo hice lo mismo in the one I gave you.

17-ii-82

So much anticipation, pero no estoy como la Helen. Ayer una latter-day, blown-away Cleopatra: tipsy, hambrienta, pero not eating. No podía. Le pinté toes and fingers, I bathed and shampooed her, powdered and groomed her, ella borrachita, radiante, glowing with expectancy. I sent her off with darling Tina into the night y me preguntaba how and when it would hit me, quién me cuidaría a mí en las long waiting hours antes del vuelo, la Trish sick and at class anyhow.

After your invitation phone call ("Come with me to Mardi Gras, my love?" me propusiste), en la chamba titubeé entre half-feigned, half-real tears para una "sick cousin in Chicago." Bien crocodile-ish, pero I practically convinced *myself*, ¡coño! By 1 a.m. last night some miracle had happened: había logrado convencer a la Spanish department burocracia, encontrar subs for my classes. Lionel picks me up on campus, we lunch at Trader Vic's. We start tooting, of course—pretty mellow stuff. Compro el ticket (ida de San Francisco a Houston, vuelta de Chicago) de Marina Travel. Only trepidation comes from the pecuniary end: ¿cómo coño pagaré todo esto? Pero ni modo. I'm decided.

I am ovulating furiously now, two days late, and oh, damn, ¿qué es *esto*? Nada es casual. Right on the eve of our reunion! And so, la maleta hecha. Showered. Calm. My ticket ready. Me visto de viaje: khaki Calvins, my black tunic, silver leather disco boots. Y sólo para ti, as you requested, love, una vincha, a twist of long olive silk around the head. Lionel me lleva a un really nice restaurant, near the airport. I sip a Kir, me tomo otro Valium. Want to sleep on the plane y despertarme en tus brazos, in the city where you are. En Texas (now, just gazing out the window of the plane, catch sight of the Old and Lost rivers—¡vaya nombre!).

## 22-ii-82

On the road. Primera vez en la vida que me siento *really* on the road, like I've always dreamed it. Big ol' semi trucks rumbling by, cálida brisa de Louisiana, a straight ribbon of highway running like melted butter bajo las ruedas del Vasbyt, nuestro Dodge van-chariot.

Pero oh, este dull throb of pain medio me asusta. Ovulation was supposed to happen *last* Tuesday—hace una semana. Thought I maybe felt a twinge, pero luego nada. Then more definite, an absolute *thudding* comenzó el miércoles por la tarde, before the plane.

Baggage Claim en la cálida, húmeda Houston morning. No veo a nadie. Get on the phone to Bobbie Naughton, she checks, me asegura que you've all already left. Entonces, my beautiful darling, oh, it's *you*, Roland. You embrace me hard from behind, me levantas en tus brazos, te ves tan joven, suddenly, oh, sleepy eyes, bright rugby shirt, los cabellos sleep-mussed. So good in your arms, amor, so safe. En Texas. —*Ahhh, you* came *to me, my darling, my love*, exultas, y nos estamos besando, hard, ferocious longing. Los soñolientos, Miss Zooloo and Steve, nos esperan en el van.

Henos aquí de nuevo, together again, and it's *so* right. Houston es llano llano, concrete wide freeways. Drive out past dirt roads, coffee shops, gasolineras. Pickup trucks and cowboy hats. Hacia una could-be-anywhere suburbia, una sprawling, ranch-style house. Saludo a nuestra hostess, Bobbie Naughton y Shuga', su tiny white fluffball doggie. Hug sleeping Ken hello, charlamos un poco y un café (oh, I just *want* you, baby) hasta que la Bobbie leaves to go bowling. Read the "transcript" to you, my darling—as we call todas las diary entries, chronicling our love story—en la cama. My love who can't wait, que me desea *now, now*. Sharp popping pains continue on the left side. Me meto el diaphragm, pero we are animal naked and quick. No time for gel.

We lounge around the whole day. Toco el piano, planeamos el road trip a New Orleans. You are doing the dishes, aquí en esta Texas kitchen. We could be anywhere. Juntos. Later, te la chupo, taking my time, quiero sentir tu acrid warm cum down my throat. You loving it, estás gimiendo, pero we're edgy. Porque la Bobbie Naughton's expected home "*any* minute," nos reporta el Ken, medio paniqueado, so I impale myself on you fast, sharp (de nuevo, sin gel). And then feeling *so* tired, suddenly. La Zooloo comes in, forces vitamins on me e insiste en que duerma un poco.

We've decided to go to Gilley's that night, y partir para New Orleans in the morning. To Mardi Gras, ¡mi siempre sueño! I finally drop off to warm, brief sleep y me despierto contigo, my love. You've crept in next to me and let me sleep on. Shower. Me visto toda de negro. Conozco a Howard Naughton, your dad's friend. Tomamos para Gilley's, and here the fun *really* begins. Me siento bien, I feel so longtime with you, Roland. Good to ride by your side en el van, entrar a ese big, famous funky family dance hall agarrados de la mano, all eyes on us, foreshadowing things to come.

Lots of old-timers, smell the BBQ. Estamos todos famélicos, suddenly. A Fellini-esque dinner. Estoy en plena forma, and you are loving it. Loving showing me off. Llegan cuatro South African boys, John, Gavin, Rob, and Russ. — *Go to town on them, my babe*, me pides, con esa tu sonrisa traviesa. We are eating onions together, luego besándonos maniacally. Our three roll their eyes in mock-exasperation y en coro se quejan, "Oh shit. Here they go *again* . . ."

Los new boys atónitos. I'm fast with one-liners, sitting on your lap, tú destornillándote de risa, collapsing with lust, todo Gilley's riveted on our wild erotic circus. Russ me mira, luego a ti, y te aconseja, — *You had* bettah *not let this one get away. You'd bettah bring your guhlfriend to South Africa, Rolo.* El Steve Du Preez está de acuerdo. — *They won't know* what *to make of Chávez*, afirma. *S'th Effrica'll go crazy.*

We drink, la slide guitar calling sexy and sweet. Tú y yo bailamos apretados, loving, slow y sexy. Bañados en sudor, the pain still popping, knife-sharp, del costado izquierdo, we finally stop and rest. I'm on your lap again, swiveling my hips for the benefit of the crowd. Gavin, confundido, me guiña el ojo. A group of gringo cowboys nearly shoot their wads at the front-row view. Tú finges estar medio escandalizado, pero you are loving it. We've got eyes only for each other.

*24-ii-82*

So much to say porque tánto left unsaid for days. I want to grab the voices, las palabras, the desperation. The escape into drinking and intermittent explosions de los otros. Ken, preocupado, freaked out, exclamó, —*All I could smell was that blood!* Tus palabras tan erradas, at first: a little macho demon rearing its ugly head, dando en el blanco—bull's-eye—de la rabia, la uncertainty en mí.

Pero finally, holding your face, tears coming unwanted y ferozmente resistidas, finally, so much love. —*My darling, this is a* completely *new feeling for me*, me confiesas. Wildly unsettling lo sé, even to you—or maybe *especialmente* para ti—dizque unshakable Goat-Boy. Te veo como gun-shy colt encabritado, eyes rolling, sensing the bit. Pero yo no soy la domadora. Es sólo que no te reconoces. Pero yo veo tu (casi) reluctant joy, the relief in sensing me *knowing* you, sondeándote, señalando, mapping with sure gesture ese wild y hasta ahora untouched territory in you.

And oh, la sangre and the wonderment it caused. Polite silence de los otros, al principio. Miedo. Dolor. Tears. Fear of bonding too hard, al principio. The need to quell too much feeling in *yourself* porque me permití comentar en el milagro de esas dividing and joined cells. You perhaps sensing a mama-ness then, una bourgeois domesticidad que no me interesa. Es sólo que I refuse to deny the beauty por el untimeliness of it all.

And I shall butt up against you, "spar" with you, como dices—as you *like* it, Goat-Boy—with a charge more formidable than you have ever felt. Trust me, fair pilgrim: even here, en este papel en blanco, I shall ignite you still.

*25-ii-82*

*Non ti scordar.* Do you remember that old Italian lovers' postcard, donde leímos esa poetic phrase? ¿En aquella little shop on North Grant en North Beach, frente al Savoy Tivoli? Remember Mardi Gras?

Llevo puesta tu felt fedora. Me la dejaste. Sitting in the BART train, volviendo a casa, a la City, de Berkeley. I'm wearing your hat low (tú sonreirías, la acomodarías, I know, stroke the brim thoughtfully, adjust the top just so). There's this musty underground whistling breeze. Aquí en el BART. I would not have your hat blow off.

26-ii-82

Oh, Roland, the Club last night en el aniversario de nuestro first Thursday, now five Thursdays ago. Vaya sombra pálida de nuestro cerebral/ erotic first encounter. Pero la Trish insistió, and I went along with it. I shouldn't have had that Frangelico coffee, creo. The low pain thuds now, esta mañana, insistente. And oh, Montenegro, my love, cuando te escuché la voz al teléfono I so wanted to tell you how *much* I want you here. But even now, incluso ahora, cuando nuestro gaze, interlocked, will *always* contain the recognition and remembering of shared and lost cells, tú sabes que I won't tell you I *need* you here.

Recordando tus palabras, suddenly: —*Poor little bugger's gone and given himself up for Lent.* Oh, cómo me haces reír, Montenegro, all the way to the other side of the pain. Sabiendo que estás allí—Chicago, DC, New York, the bush, Joburg, anywhere—y te puedo pensar aquí, feel you thinking me *there*, we can be OK.

My darling, no es como lo representan. Los otros. I know Helen, Ken, and Du Preez han de cuestionar la sinceridad de tu amor por mí, if you didn't even take me to a doctor. Y supongo que it would sound selfish, lustful, demasiado twentieth century (not to mention demasiado dangerous, ¡coño!) si algún extraño nos escuchara decir, —*But my darling, I just* really *want to fuck you. I* have *to.* Especially considerando las circunstancias. Our blood loss. And Fraze, you only had to ask once (y me lo preguntaste) if I wanted a doctor. Pero it wasn't real pain anymore, ya no tenía. Así que un quick size-up told me to go ahead, follow what I wanted: you inside me. Mirándome medio hesitantly at first, almost abashed by your desire, wondering if we should, asking me wordlessly, y luego, vencido por mi yes silencioso, by all the lush wetness—some of it blood, still—you entered me, so gently. And then us, just sleeping.

Ansiaba estar encima de ti, sentada, watching you grimace and grin alternately. Necesitaba hablar, yes *talk* while we made love. Con una uncanny precisión describíamos la sensación, uno al otro; the words did not dim but instead added to our pleasure. In the van, se olía el disapproval. De ellos. Supongo que they'd chorus, "WE could smell the blood." Miffed perhaps, at our alleged "insatiability." Oh, cómo nos igualaban—si bien sólo a veces—a rutting beasts.

Well, lo hicimos anyway, mi amor. We fucked. De nuevo. Kissing long, so deep and bumping together roughly mientras la carretera de New Orleans a Chicago rolled away, *thump, thump, thump* bajo las ruedas de Vasbyt. Congratulating al Du Preez por su excellent stint at the wheel. Y de nuevo nuestros low cries, the sweat blooming on our nakedness in the approaching dusk. Y entonces, oh, Roland baby, sleep. Mientras el metal floor del van—all that lay between us and the road—even through our green sleeping bag, se helaba cada vez más, the farther north we drove. Sleep long then, right on your shoulder.

Y entonces, we were in icy Chicago. Helen, Steve, and Ken were transparently shocked que decidimos pasar todo el día in bed. Pero sí, Montenegro, my love. A bath and bed were all we wanted. Not to try and get a handle on Chicago, no tenía caso en el short, short time anyway. And as I say, F. Recuerda el Mardi Gras. Me sorprende que hayamos causado tanto stir in a town about as debauched as one could imagine. Tú y yo, strolling through the balmy, food-scented evenings . . .

27-ii-82

Too much going on. Want to sit and relish. Fortificada, exaltada, torn by your wake-up call this morning. The best. Tu maravillosa, uncompromising motivation for your immediately-upon-return trek al bushveld. I *knew* you would not fail me, R. Me aclaraste, —*No, it's* not *to forget that I go there, my love! It's to make the image of you in my arms clearer still.*

Mardi Gras. Llegaré a esto ahorita, I promise. Pero tántas distractions today. De hecho, feels like nothing *but* distractions desde que volví a casa. —*Without my half,* como dijiste. Lost vagabond girl ahora, in this city too beautiful for me to be here without you.

Oh, mi amor, my finger pushes up inside myself mientras hablo contigo por teléfono; your voice undoes me. Memory, in quick graphic flashes, de nuestro placer. We shared that same "dire feeling," as you called it, cuando nos despertamos de nuestra long Chicago nap and the time had slipped irrevocably to 5 p.m. And the need I had then to hold you eternally, *just* to hold you . . .

— *What shall you save your money for, my love?* me preguntas. — *Need you ask? For 1218 Bourbon Street.* — *Or,* me sugieres, *how about a house in Pacific Heights?* Y siguiéndote el juego, I embellish, — *With drafting tables for you, and beds* everywhere! *I can write anywhere. And fuck you anywhere, too. Tom Petty or Vivaldi or Milton Nascimento . . .* — *Rather Mick,* me corriges, *the Stones, wailing on the stereo.* El agua corre en la bañera and I leap up and cling, te rodeo la cintura con mis piernas, *Montenegro-* and Mardi Gras–style, and you will sway with me like that, juntos, besándonos, and bear me off to the divan, or to one of our zillion beds, donde nos tumbaremos, still half-clothed, fucking.

Quiero escribir, continuar el feeling de nuestro glorious morning phone call. Mi cuerpo se siente lonely, dispossessed sin ti, Rolo, dammit. Without you admiring, knowing, desiring me.

Mardi Gras. Remember Mardi Gras. *Non ti scordar!* Me loving the way you feel proud caminando a mi lado. Hungry eyes on us: negros, blancos, male, female. Un sweet comment se destaca. Mientras paseábamos por la lower Bourbon Street Sunday afternoon, bien cerca de la casa que fantaseábamos para nosotros, a dapper, middle-aged Southern homeowner took a quick look at me en tu sombrero y ese medio-outlandish atuendo safari (close-fitting grommeted black tank top y teensy, zebra-pattern shorts), luego hizo un double take at us, together, and called out to you desde su porche, "To your health, sir!" You smiled and acknowledged, and then lovingly bent down para meter un credit card slip entre los leather straps de mis Grecian wrap sandals y mi humidity-swollen, abraded ankle.

Esta mañana, roused from my reverie, después de escuchar tu voz al teléfono, heavy and catching with urgency and love, vino otra llamada. Lionel me invitó al Cliff House, y me sacó fotos afuera, right against the sea wall, ¿te acuerdas? And I pouted sexy into the lens, seeing—what do you think?—*tus* flashing dark eyes y full, boyish grin detrás de la cámara.

And yes, believe it or not, la mismísima mesa grande, the one we'd all occupied on our *Montenegro* movie Sunday, estaba libre. Nuestro *primer* domingo, remember? El día después del Chinese New Year's parade. How we drove out to the Bridge Theater, way out on la Geary, porque yo insistía en compartir mi discovery contigo: *Montenegro*, Makavejev's madcap, bizarre, ferociously erotic new film. La acababa de ver, pero I *needed* to see it with you. Anyway, I moved toward that table como en un sueño. And I could *feel* you next to me, a mi izquierda, Roland, mi amor. Me sliding bare leg onto your waiting lap, metiendo el cocktail napkin into my panties, empapándola de nuestro perfume for your pleasure and torture, metiéndome el índice, all the way up inside me entonces y luego rubbing right under your nose, allí mismo en la mesa, ungiéndote los párpados, la garganta, you with that low moan. And all of them, los otros, totally oblivious. Or so we thought . . .

Entonces, up in Lionel's Cessna. Just a tiny silvery tin can entre yo y el absoluto sky, dipping wing toward ocean, un nudo de lágrimas se me formaba en la garganta as Li took shot after shot of me. Cocaine. Merca bien chévere. Funny though, no me puse loquacious como me pasa tantas veces con la coca. Instead me volvió inward, mind humming with razor-honed lucidity. Recordando, feeling you. Una rabia repentina por tu ausencia, then a sweet longing, luego *feeling* you there, te lo juro, entre mis muslos, face wet and upturned.

Dinner at Half Moon Bay. Flying back at dusk, la luna, a new sharp crescent, se insinuaba, apenas visible en el San Francisco misty shroud. De vuelta en casa, finalmente, my little Chestnut Street apartment, and now sleep calls. You cut straight through me, Montenegro. Directo al secreto lugar donde iba, snuggled entre las twin beds in my childhood bedroom, leyendo con flashlight o sólo daydreaming, ese hidden place que nadie ha podido acceder del todo. You mined straight through me, descubriste la vena que te esperaba.

3-iii-82

My birthday month now, hoy el cumple de la Helen. She was out the whole day, con Tina. She called slightly tipsy and late; iban a salir al I-Beam,

out in the Haight. No me apetecía. Steve had called her para su cumple—
unexpected—*and* he'd written her desde su escala en Amsterdam. Well,
well. Me alegro. Maybe he *won't* capitulate without a struggle. A lo mejor—
oh, miracle—ni se rinde.

But oh, my darling Fraze, ¿te escuché bien? Did I really hear you speaking *those* words on the phone to me esta mañana? *—I love you, my precious,*
you said, a las 6:17 en punto. *—I love you, Chávez. And that's for always.*
*You can bank on it.*

4-iii-82

It's Thursday the 4th again. Today's so clear and beautiful, como el último
Thursday the 4th. Heme aquí en el 30-Stockton now, as usual, headed
through Chinatown hacia el BART. Este neighborhood que exploramos,
compartimos. I can make a place for myself, para nosotros, insular and
deep, hasta entre todo este melee—old, urban Italians talking about lunching at Dante Benedetti's New Pisa; los chinos que están de compras, eternal
orange bolsas de plástico at the ready.

Flowering plum already (los tortilla-flower trees, les digo, por su olor a
masa harina), and mimosa too. My birthday's near. Sweet, heady, dulce
perfume de New Orleans ondea en el aire on the Berkeley campus, over
Strawberry Creek bridge.

So much comes back now, even unbidden. Todo vuelve a mí cual
torrente, in precise surging waves. Ahora te escucho. Your words dropping
brittle en ese knife-edge sudden silence: astillas de hielo al corazón. You,
fearing fear (de la pérdida) in me. And I, in reaction: enraged, orgullosa,
sorrowful. Quiero asegurarte entonces, cold as ice, ahora me toca a mí: I
don't *need* you. Ni a ti, ni a nadie. Even with all the blood, puedo asumirlo,
cargarlo yo sola, as my *own* brief miracle and loss.

*—No Rolo*, te digo, *I don't think it's exactly that you don't like to be*
*trusted. It's more that you think you don't like to be "banked on," because*
*you're used to reading it as a burden, signaling weakness in the other, and it's*
*this weight makes you want to run . . . do you think I don't know?* I know.
And you look up at me; lying with your head in my lap me miras, knowing
I've got your number. You nod wordlessly and I take your head firmer in

my arms, y te acaricio el ceño y ya se acabó, the talking part. We've gone straight through to what the words never said and to what would remain hanging there, just out of reach, inefable, hasta el día siguiente—our *true* last day. Ese Tuesday (el mero Mardi Gras, de hecho. Pero us far from dreamy, balmy NoLa, already en el frozen north) en nuestro walk-in closet, en nuestro Chicago, at the airport, y de nuevo al teléfono, once I was home. Patrás en San Francisco—my city, *nuestra* city—the miles already between us pero ese telephone wire joining us, uno al otro.

—*So, Fraze, no assumptions then?* te pregunto por teléfono, medio teasing. —*No, no*, me corriges, enfático, sweet Montenegro, movie-imitation earnest fake Yugoslavian accent, *I chenge my plan. I love you. You can bank on it.*

8-iii-82

My favorite number. Hoy. Vastly different from yesterday. Hace un mes, exactly, "The Last Night." ¿Te acuerdas? I know you'll never forget. That night the catalyst. We set, esa noche, lo que marcaría el curso, la manera de nuestro amor: animal and intense the low growls came, as to a hunting or birthing lion's throat.

Tears well up, incluso aquí, días después, en La Barca restaurant en Berkeley. Yes, my darling, even *exactly* en la mismísima mesa donde estábamos todos: you, such a powerful presence, on my right. Ken, tú y yo. Talking on and on, well into our margaritas, debatiendo afiebradamente, book after book, idea after idea. Estas lágrimas son para ti, Roland, my love. Estás en el avión ahora. And it's different this time, *very*, from you being in Chicago or DC or New York. Ahora tan lejos, lejos, lejos. Really and truly, como dices tú, far away.

I've found in you what every writer needs: un lector. It's you, but somehow, de alguna manera, also *more* than only "you." Si no, we're talking epistolary. And can that, ¿podría eso ser "literatura"? You see, R., por primera vez I have a voice. Te escribo a ti, *about* you, about us, and yet you are also a touchstone for other things, otras cosas que siempre he querido decir. Pero no sabía exactamente cuáles. A quién. Or how. Hasta ahora.

Ha comenzado la sangre de nuevo. It's sweet and heartening, the way you trust me to know. Conocer mi cuerpo. When Helen and Ken interrogated you que por qué nunca habíamos ido a un médico after the miscarriage, in Chicago, les dijiste (Helen me lo contó), —*I don't know. Suzi worked at a clinic. Volunteered at Planned Parenthood. She knew what she was doing, I reckon. I mean, I* thought. *But now, I don't really know . . .*

Valientes y estoicos, the way we went about our business in Chicago: the tickets, the banks, caminando en esa endeble luz y viento helado, looking like two spies on a honeymoon. Idénticos en abrigos de azul marino, I loosely clutching your hat to my head, contra ese viento atroz, and tightly your hand. Sin prisa, we attended to the routine, and to each other. Our slow, unanxious coupling later, y entonces a dormir.

My tears then and now, ahora con esta sangre de nuevo. Rich, sudden flow again y tú tan lejos. I am angry, aplatanada por no entender estas intimate functions, su irrational schedule. ¿Por qué esta sangre ahora, de nuevo, a week after our little zygote, como le bautizamos, gave up the ghost?

Al médico mañana. Again. Fading now, light-headed. Debo dormir. Sorry to close on this note. Sabes que estaré "up" again, yo misma again, soon. I must sleep now, a tu lado. ILY (Estas initials, como tú me las escribes siempre).

*16-iii-82*

I've typed so much of this transcript for you now. Estos días, mis días, se parecen a un endless thread unraveling. A veces le agarro una sección, around the middle, y entonces los labyrinth paths reveal their contours to me con una claridad nítida. Other times, aunque esto no me desespera, there is simply too much material y veo la punta del hilo apenitas, tiny, fluttering far away. So perhaps the writing becomes as Theseus's steps: errante, searching and tentative, más que forjando un camino definitivo.

My friend Oscar Góngora me abordó hoy y me dijo, —*Susana, I have to tell you the funniest thing. ¿Sabías que you're in the movies?* —*¿Qué coño dices?* I asked him. —*Well,* explicó, *Llevé a mi clase a los film archives this* *morning, because they had a good documentary on Puerto Rico. Filmed at the Kennedy School of Government, you know, en Harvard.* And then the light came on, y me acordé de esa vez, nearly three years ago now, cuando fui a un debate, con la Frances Aparicio, my friend from Harvard. El tema era "Puerto Rico: Colony, Free Associated State or Independent Nation?" Creí que it had only been filmed for Boston Public TV, pero there was Oscar, going on, —*. . . and your hair was longer and you were even skinnier and paler than now, pero I knew it was you! You were twisting a piece of hair around your finger like you do, y tenías ese burning look in your eyes, y gritabas algo en español, about the whole debate being a farce porque what true representative party of the left would ever even show up a un debate donde la "independent nation" perspective was represented by Rubén Berríos, a known US ass-kissing reformista?*

Anyway ahora, Rolo—my mind races ahead. Esa firebrand girl aun persiste dentro de mí, her militancy quizás tempered, or redirected. Ah, I just want to live, happy together, contigo. Ay, I don't know. Pero I *do* know that when faced with the urgency of particular historical junctures (el golpe militar en Chile, the struggle in El Salvador), mi militancia, however messy—contradictions and convictions in nearly equal measure—comes roaring back, unabated.

My anger—casi desde los opening credits—that even two premovie Remys couldn't blunt. El film *Missing* una waking nightmare, aunque había anticipado que sería more or less a sellout, a capitulation to commercial viability, enfatizando lo personal, el aspecto romance. Pero hasta estas concessions a Hollywood no ofuscaron su definitely political impact. The machine guns may have only been firing en un movie set en el DF en 1981, pero para mí era raw-wound Santiago de Chile, 11th of September 1973 *real.* No pude menos que asociarlo con la concentration camp plight de mis amigos chilenos (oh, Cosme, Elbita, Walter): era su horror, right before my eyes.

Y me pregunto: ¿qué coyuntura histórica más terrible, más fraught, que el apartheid en South Africa? What am I thinking? What in God's name will prolonged exposure to that disease/paradise called Johannesburg (your hometown) *do* to me?

*17-iii-82*

St. Patrick's Day. Uf, nunca me ha gustado esta tonta fiesta. Tomorrow the one-month anniversary of our little zygote's conception. Y nada. Where the hell *are* you? Hace un mes, to the day, I was all nerves on edge, contando las horas, measuring the distance to you (en Houston, mi amor).

No aguanto esta distancia. Pero tengo que reconocer que pronto llegará un día, one with no specific resonance in our too-brief shared past. I'll consider that day, supongo, 6th of March. Oscuro para mí, sola, high on coke, having to socialize con mi hermana y la Trish, con mi primo Art y los Larsen-Feiten boys. Queriendo festejar, estar en el momento, pero craving the solace of a flood of memories too rich and immediate como para consolar, pero mine alone, at least: un painful si triunfante Walden. 6th of March: when you left my continent, Montenegro, para volver al tuyo. Al fucking underworld, it feels like . . .

Ahora cae la tarde y heme aquí, sitting in Trish's darkening room, missing you. She's gone off to work, en la California Coastal Commision. It's a real storm outside, raro para San Francisco. Más como el México de mi childhood. Lightning cracks the sky, moss-agate and opaque; el sol—esta mañana un sullen welt under paint-thick gray—ahora desaparecido. Thunder booms y luego pales to a purr that, dammit Fraze, suena gooseflesh-uncanny como tu lion imitation.

I'm going to try an exercise in memory. Esto es algo que inventé con mi hermana Sarita (you know, la que le digo Weevil), when we were very young. A game we called "Vintage." Anyway, digamos que era como la child-version of the Surrealists' Exquisite Corpse game, o un poco como la prosa de Faulkner. El objetivo era: empty your mind of all conscious thought and direction. Much harder than it sounds! ¿Has hecho algo parecido? Te juro que it becomes a necessary addiction, once you get the hang of it.

Ahora mismo, I was just drifting into it, and I got the *clearest* picture of us. Tú y yo, walking ahead holding hands, tightly clasped, on that first night, la noche que nos conocimos. El 28 de enero. Do you remember? Estaba pensando en la canción "Strangers in the Night," which I love, which always reminds me of my parents. Ken and Steve y la Trish detrás de nosotros, los boys going for a slosh en un alley (I know, my darling, yo sé que se dice *slash*; I'm just teasing you). Los otros, the three of them, poking fun at us (por andar cogidos de la mano). All of us sauntering down Chestnut Street, mi calle, a las 2:30 de la madrugada.

Anyway, con mi hermana, once our minds were suitably blank una u otra comenzaba el "vintage," o sea, she'd just start to speak lo que le viniera en mente, unencumbering, limbering up la mente del daily clutter (and/or *order*: which is worse? No lo sé . . .). Y luego la otra recogía el hilo de la unfolding narrative, y así, until sleep, or until one would draw a blank (on a blank, por así decirlo), and lie there boquiabierta en la mágica oscuridad, and in so doing, concede victory to her sister.

Bueno, esto es lo que estoy haciendo ahora mismo, bebé. Only as I grew up por supuesto que el game se volvió más sophisticated, something I could practice any time, incluso a solas. Me daba este reto: going blank and yet somehow also focusing on a particular subject or image. Es catártico: purifying and focusing a la vez. Come with me. Juega conmigo . . .

It is Canal Street. You and I, apoyados contra un muro, a slightly sleazy storefront, really. There is rubbish and moisture at our feet. Pasan negros y blancos, staring bemusedly, unabashedly, algunos snickering foul insinuations. It's Mardi Gras, after all. Apenas nos damos cuenta. Me inclino hacia ti, facing you, straddle your thigh with mine, aprieto mi sexo húmedo, expectante, en el hollow entre tu groin and thigh. Tambaleamos un poco, juntos, there is music everywhere. Apoyo la cabeza en tu hombro, acurrucada—oh, the fit—and you put your arm around my shoulders. My legs feel a bit tired, de repente. I can sense the coming of blood to my center—nuestro Mardi Gras miscarriage—aunque aun no lo sabía entonces.

Prosigo con este mi private "vintage" game. Now we're at that first jazz place, viernes el 19 de febrero. Donde cobraban $3.50 la copa pero estaban weak as water and came in plastic go-cups. Remember? Nada de eso nos importaba un carajo. I tossed my bare thigh onto yours—sighs and clucks de Ken, Steve y Helen. I was gazing at the lines of your face, thinking how just the day before te había visto por primera vez en siglos—well OK, en una semana—en Houston. And about how much it felt like I'd never left your side, digo, never *not* been at your side. Amándote con un júbilo tan wide open y delirious it felt like jazz, como el jazz y el Mardi Gras mismo.

And the jazz was conventional pero hot, no obstante. Unos vatos blancos, abueleriles, blowing cool horn. And around midnight, when our three had *hours* of carousing still in them, me miraste, y yo a ti, y le pediste la room key al Steve. Y esos tres, as always, en coro, "I can't *believe* it, man!" Thinking we were too much slaves to our passion. Nos reímos como teenagers and demurred, insistiendo que we *only* wanted a bath and to bed. And truly, me moría por darme un bath contigo en esa French Quarter Holiday Inn real hotel bathtub, more than *anything* right then.

Pero *that* wish began to change slowly, casi imperceptiblemente, as soon as we were on our own, and the soft, moist New Orleans night air hit our cheeks, y las callecitas del Vieux Carré nos pertenecían, y todos los passersby and revelers se daban cuenta de esto también. We strolled lazy-limbed hacia Royal Street. Me sentía lithe and beautiful, loving your arm around the whole of me, Montenegro. Besándonos sideways, as we walked, y luego full-mouthed, deteniéndonos en plena calle, possessing it, and each other.

And then suddenly it was there: el feroz deseo de un hot dog, a chili dog, and I (pregnant, sin saberlo) said, —*Fraze, I* must *have a hot dog!* And I knew *just* the kind I wanted—enorme, smothered in chili, cebolla y mostaza, no como aquellos little puny ones que venden en el café across from the Holiday Inn. And we rounded a corner, and lo, allí había un puesto, a hot dog stand, y compramos two GIANT hot dogs, just what I craved. Y me engullí el mío, wolfed it faster than you, a first for us. And you laughed and laughed y exclamaste, mock-freaked out, —*My darling, I can't believe it! What's got into you?*

Subimos a la habitación entonces, y el tipsiness and that chili dog took immediate effect. Nos desplomamos en esa enorme hotel bed, me lying full-length on top of you. Yo murmuraba vagamente del bath, pero no me querías soltar, you absolutely would *not* permit me to get up to draw that bath. Kissing hard, wet, yo te agarraba los cabellos, feeling the sharpness of your bones against mine. You tugging aside my panties y yo deslizándome, up and down, todo el largo de tu muslo, dejando allí un glistening, tacky trail that would dry white, emblema de nuestra furia, for all to see the next day.

Murmuring all the while, vulgar and tender things, borrachos and yet somehow, not; tú apartando el strap de mi gray Canal Jeans tank dress and taking my nipple into your mouth. I looking down and seeing the full white swell of my breast against the soft dark of your lips, aplicadamente chupando, your large hands firm on my ass. Y entonces de alguna forma we together unbuttoned those trousers, pero no nos quitamos *nada*. Sólo aflojamos el hilo en ese incongruente red nylon bikini and pulled out your hard cock and I sat on you then deep, all the way todo a la vez sheathing you decisive, watching your face go taut the way it does cuando me penetras. The sweat came then, your hair damp and dark, tú me susurrabas urgente, —Don't *hold back now my babe, just let it, let yourself* . . . Y no habría podido hold back, even if I'd wanted to. And oh, my love, cómo me haces esto, alternately laughing at the futility of my last stance against your assault y gimiendo en abandono animal.

Somehow, horas después, we fell into sleep. And it was the best sleep ever. Hours later still, Ken entró a la habitación y escuché, as if from far, far away, como desde un sueño, —*Oh* Jussus! *Some bath! You know this is really rich—couldn't even get the clothes off, and there's Fraze with his* jaloga *hanging out all over the place. Jussus, man!* Y me acuerdo que le pedí, with infinite politeness, to help me get your clothes off. I wanted you in bed, junto a mí. Pero según lo cuenta el Ken, I couldn't even move off you, y él no se atrevía a separarnos, and he ended up undressing *both* of us. Me acuerdo, pequeños flashes: Ken que te quitaba, a duras penas, los pantalones, you stirring and pulling me closer, Ken medio forcejeando con los dos, struggling with our weight, con el peso de nuestra spent and remembered— even in sleep—passion.

# Under Apartheid's
# Shadow

# Inside the Northern Suburbs
# Stronghold/Stranglehold

*8-ix-1982*
*Cullinan, Transvaal, RSA*

Dearest Lee,

Te extraño tantísimo, I can't tell you. Heme aquí, en este cottage en Cullinan que Roland y yo compartimos con Cyril, otro mining engineer-in-training. Leonard Cohen is on the stereo, son las 8 de la mañana, y Roland acaba de salir. Off to work, underground. Hace sol and it's quiet outside—except for the occasional BOOM de la nearby Premier Diamond Mine. The jasmine and bougainvillea are secretly blooming away al lado de la front door. It is Africa, y me siento muy sola hoy.

Acabo de bañarme en el tiny tub with no plug (hice stopper de un shaving cream lid). The water will soon be boiling en la tetera eléctrica (todo el mundo las usa aquí) pa' tomarme un Nescafé. My existence these days seems predicated, somehow, on these "logros": insignificantes, hasta risibles en mi ex-mundo, pero herculean here, donde todo susurra en una secret foreign tongue que no poseo todavía. Ni siquiera sé si quiero.

The mourning dove coos plaintively across the road—*rrr, whoo, whoo*—al lado de la whitewashed Anglican church; un tipo de minah bird, me parece, hace *caw, caw, caw* en los fields detrás del cottage. Más bien, in the veld! Un Peugeot 504 sedan arranca, glides noiselessly down the wrong side of the road y me recuerda nevertheless—tan wrenchingly—de mi papá. A red Datsun pickup (a *bakkie*, le dicen aquí) revs its engine en el driveway de al lado, un joven pretty boy del film crew at the wheel, gritando algo en Afrikaans a los que están en el *stoep*. Así le dicen al porch.

I sit on my porche, boli en mano, escuchando, oyendo aunque I'm not really listening. En este pueblo, en este país each new noise is an epiphany, cada newspaper article (intensamente censurado, of course) revela todo un mundo, each glibly tossed editorial, los anuncios tan retrógrados y sexistas me laceran. They seem to seek out with implacable, unknowing dagger los escondites de mi corazón vulnerable, hypervigilant, extranjero. —*We must pull ourselves up with our own hands and look at the world through new eyes*, dice el Marat de Peter Weiss. So, OK then.

A sharp, urbane black man clicks by, en un pullover y city shoes. Debe ser parte del film crew, musito. Los blacks aquí en Cullinan, excepto los waiters en el Premier Hotel (where Roland y los otros vatos del Catskills Mountain Boys' Club—así apodé a los young mining engineering graduates que constituyen su, I mean *nuestro*, peer group—take their meals), responden en Afrikaans when spoken to: the language of oppresion pero también survival en este *muy* Afrikaner cuello del bosque (digo bush!). Los Cullinan blacks son muy negros, and they don't wear shoes that click. Algunos caminan bien proud and flash their teeth y hacen *click* la lengua, switching lightning-fast entre Zulu, Sotho o Xhosa, o Fanagalo (a kind of lingua franca), Afrikaans, and English. Can you imagine? Otros caminan sombríos, women con abultados bundles en la cabeza, young men and old, cuidando los small, neat gardens de los whites. Driving the white man's tractor, sitting in the back of his *bakkie*, comprando carne en el mercado para la mesa del *baas*.

Overheard conversation, ni me acuerdo dónde, I mean, si aquí en Cullinan, among Roland's miner cronies, o en Bedfordview. Oh, my head is spinning. Las secuelas de la hepatitis que me pegué, remember? In July. And the altitude. It's so high and dry here. Me canso en seguida. Pero I'm sure it's more than this. Constantly on edge, uneasy. Uneasy in my skin. Anyway, escucha, Cuz:

—*We* must *improve the black man's education, really we must.* —Ag, *we* must *acknowledge that a vast portion of the South African work force goes untapped.* —*Are blacks to be considered South Africans, then?*

Y quiero gritar, sarcásticamente, —*It's a fucking shame that blacks are only being prepared for the most menial jobs, but of course, their non-Western, tribal traditions make their education a very delicate business.*

—*Naturally we are* for *equal opportunity in education! South Africa's future as a free-enterprise system depends on the recognition of blacks as a* tremendous *untapped labor resource, and on the future implementation of such programs as would fully capitalize on this recognition.*

Pero ¿no se dan cuenta estos imbéciles, these whites, de que los negros están al tanto, they *hear* what Anglo-American corporation is prophesying "for" them? Y lo reconocen como el patronizing, simplistic, antihistorical gesto que es. Pero who could expect otherwise, really, del Harry Oppenheimer and his boys, ¿que no? Y ¿qué otra reacción—other than capitulation and compromise, digo—se podría esperar de la Buthelezi Commission de "moderate blacks"?

You who knows (esta parte la escribí para Roland): tú me dices que *the problem is a basic economic one.* Según tú, *South Africa must be a free-enterprise state.* Pero no ves que if black education were *really* reformed, pos adiós to the sovereignty de la ruling class. Oppenheimer y sus boys lo ven, otherwise why the hell would they formulate esas brazenly racist preguntas, que si los negros deben considerarse South Africans? Y una cosita más: tú hasta me dices que *human beings were not born equal,* y que temes que *you'd be held back* si un sistema de equal opportunity fuese realidad.

Pero my darling young plutocrat, ¿no ves que tus conceptos de equality, opportunity, advancement son una distortion del apartheid? No te estoy hablando de un utopian socialist state, simplemente de un futuro tan certero que los ideologues del apartheid lo ven hasta con los ojos cerrados. And this is why they maintain este sistema educativo—black education, este oxymoron—que reprime. Which only buttresses the racist infrastructure. Tú me dices que *I haven't been tested yet, I haven't paid my dues.* Que *how do I know?* Te dije que I'd maybe like to teach in Soweto, y me dijiste que *no ways.* Ahhhh, sé que tendría que escucharte, listen more, hold my tongue. Pero my head is buzzing . . .

## 10-ix-1982 (continued)

Perdona esta digression, Cuz. Pero es que tengo tanto on my mind. My mind . . . parece que it's working overtime en este wasteland. El tiempo pasa rápido, pero a la vez nothing really happens. Creo que what happens is all in my mind. Quiero hablarte de Cullinan. Just picture cualquier pueblo chiquito, organized around a single industry. En este caso, mining (una de las industrias más racistas, even for SA). Plunk it down en el corazón de reactionary Afrikanerdom—the Northern Transvaal—y voilà. Cullinan. My new home! ¿Te puedes creer que I'm living on a diamond mine? Alucino, tía.

Deja te cuente a few things about los Afrikaners. En pocas palabras, they founded this country según su racist, short-sighted interpretation del Old Testament. Son los ideologues del apartheid. Dicen que there are two Afrikaner camps: los *verligtes* (dizque enlightened) son los so-called liberal ones. O sea, willing to make some token concesiones a los negros. Pero luego están los *verkramptes*, who feel the *verligtes* are selling los blancos down the río. Los *verkramptes* are exactly like their name sounds: narrow-minded, constipated racistas. Reaccionarios. Y estos últimos—predictably—inhabit Cullinan. They are *not* fond of English speakers—mucho menos de American women, al parecer. Of which parece que I'm the only one for miles around, en todo caso. Uf.

Pero no te he contado casi nada de mi arrival. About me and Roland. Me escribió Ageliki Nicolopolou (my Greek friend, de Berkeley, remember?): —*I hope you find what you're looking for in S. Africa, at least on the personal level.* Pero Lee, I've *never* been able to separate lo personal de lo . . . político. Y ¿aquí? Even less, me temo. I must try, try, *try* not to make snap judgments. Tengo que intentar . . . recibir. Quiero decir: wait, watch, learn. O sea: la paciencia. My most difficult lesson.

Roland dice que how can I possibly "know" anything about S. Africa, que no he visto casi nada. And it's true, al nivel racional. Lo sé. Pero I'm so hypersensitized I feel I've seen enough already como para saber que I'll never fit in here. It's so dry and hot here, Cuz. Me ha sangrado la nariz, a bunch of times. I can feel, sentada aquí en el *stoep* outside the cottage, a las 3 de la tarde, a sun hotter than any I've ever felt. Mucho más que México. Estoy en el southern hemisphere al comienzo de la primavera. I'm gonna die, surely, cuando llegue el verano.

Ojalá pudiéramos hacer un road trip. Roland dice que you can't see anything by car, pero he doesn't understand my boundless joy al mirar el paisaje, the way it changes and unfurls cual enorme alfombra mágica outside a car window. La tierra suave, rojiza de los olive groves en Andalucía, por ejemplo, watching as they fade to the gray-brown flatness of Castilla, which surges, a su vez, hacia ese verde tan lush y deep-ravined de Galicia. Ay, I wish you and I could do that. Just us two, y quizás cón Helen, who wanted so much to see this country. Fucking chicken-shit Sea Lawyer (Du Preez)! I wish we could see this country, Lee, cruzarlo de cabo a rabo, jaja, so I could *know* de una puta vez what I'm in for here. Digo with no tour guide. Ningún prefacio, no explanatory native narrative.

¡Vaya vista just now! Uno de los gay Afrikaner (casi self-canceling phrase, como dice el Herb Caen) film directors stops pa' charlar con el cute 16-ish Afrikaner schoolboy que vive just across the road. Luego, he looks me up and down and waves to me, bien cheerily, as he glides off en su slick silver-blue compact. A young black guy, vestido de plaid workshirt y dark pants shiny from use, walks by, takes in la misma escena, pero no levanta la vista para saludar ni recibir saludo. A la vez, un enorme, fat, bearded Afrikaner roars by, bouncily al volante de un dusty white semi, sitting high above the road, staring imperiously straight ahead. Y Roland cree que I haven't seen anything yet! Ojalá pudieras pintar estos tableaux, Lee.

Anyway, a decir verdad, mi reunión con Roland hasn't been as . . . apocalyptic as I'd expected. ¿Capaz esto sea una good sign? Esto es weird, and paradoxical, pero nuestra copious correspondencia is proving to be algo así como una fuente de frustración. Difícil explicar. De alguna manera, it seems things are almost . . . too easy between us now. Do you think I'm crazy? Falta algo de la mágica intensidad que produce el yearning; everything seems a bit of an atajo. And yet, a la vez, nuestras cartas nos han sostenido—they sustain us and have eased our homecoming (R. prefiere esta palabra; dice que "reunion" is too chummy and soldieresque).

Roland dice, —*Let's never forget how and what we wrote, Shug. The many months when our love letters, the written word, was all we had* (y sin embargo él no capta, sometimes I think, how very much that is . . .). Me parece que he takes it as just . . . normal que yo esté aquí con él. Cual si nunca hubiésemos estado separados. Perhaps this is a good thing. And yet: how quickly one forgets, la intensidad del yearning. Anyway, it's *his* world I've come to, not the other way round, como cuando nos conocimos. It was in my territory que nos enamoramos. Lo que observo ahora, the things I notice and rage on about le son tan familiares—especie de white noise (jaja)—it's as if he takes no notice. Yo soy la que se tiene que asimilar, absorber, ajustarse.

*14-ix-1982 (continued, still!)*

Arrrgh, I shan't go on in that vein. It's now Tuesday, llevo siglos en esta carta. I want to finish and mail it. Post it, como dicen. I miss you, Sloth. Quiero que me leas esto, give me your impressions. I feel like I'm losing . . . perspective. Like I'm losing . . . *myself.* Y no sé cómo prevenir esto. Me pregunto: how strong am I, really, si sólo 3 semanas de esta new and imposed dependency me tienen tan cowed, tan despojada de mi natural balance, sexiness, sureness. I wonder if this is all in my mind.

No. It's Cullinan. It's this damn *dorp* (pueblo). Cuánto lo detesto. Being in someone else's place, lugar donde él se encaja (quizás—hopefully?—for survival in a world he was raised in y donde tiene que estar for now, oh, que sea solo for now . . .) y yo no. It's all so neat already: Roland goes to work. Yo hago brekkie, clean up, lavo alguna ropa a mano. Leo, escribo. It's so fucking hot, I'm sleeping a lot. I'm still not well (hepatitis). ¿Por qué me siento tan put-upon? Why does everything smack of role-playing? ¿Por qué soy tan sensitive? Tengo miedo. Afraid of this icy, immutable order: put up or shut up. Me temo que Rolo will get tired of all my probing and questioning. Mi constante búsqueda de la flaw in the foundation, la mosca in the ointment, jaja. Pero, isn't this what he loves about me, mi "searching intelligence," mi restlessness? So he's always said . . .

Ya no me parece que I had nothing in San Francisco. I had . . . myself. Mi independencia. I'm getting strong feelings que no debo casarme nunca.

I mean: even stronger than usual, jaja. No que el living together sea muy diferente, de facto. Pero el matrimonio would be a final surrender to convention. Más dangerous en este país, donde todo me parece mucho más convencional. Like back in the '40s. Anyway, I'm having enough difficulty as it is, trying to shake things up desde afuera.

Oh, casi se me olvidaba: UNISA (la U. of South Africa) me ha ofrecido lectureship. $15,000 a year, lo cual se considera un excellent salary here (especially for a "guhl"). De hecho, it's more than R. currently earns! How's that for ironic? Felt like I bombed la entrevista. Felt *exactly* like being back at Harvard. Era todo el depto. de Romance Langs., firing questions at me en varias lenguas, en temas que se me habían olvidado, completely. De hecho, I was preparing myself *not* to work here—y hay varios puntos a favor de esto: the time to be able to write, to read, to learn Afrikaans. To be taken care of (Roland's selling point), por primera vez en la vida. Hay otras posibles freelance chambas—traducción, private tutoring, quizás hasta teaching at a school en Soweto—pero esto implicaría ir a vivir en un apto. en Joburg. Lo cual, de alguna manera, me intriga. Pero ironically, that would mean not living with Roland. Solo verle los fines de semana. I didn't come 10,000 miles pa' tener un weekend romance con el amor de mi vida, ¡coño!

Aunque la idea de tener free time to write appeals, por otra parte, sé que me volvería loca en Cullinan. No es un idyllic small town—it's a small-minded, racist, provincial inferno! No tengo amigos, no hay nada que hacer. I'll begin to resent Roland (sé que nada de esto es su culpa); I'm beginning to resent, already, the traditional way we seem to be becoming . . . casi a la fuerza. I'm so BORED! Pero paradójicamente, this is anathema to writing. For now, everything is new, raw. I'm outraged and sad and lonely, y no he caducado esta fuente. "The horror! The horror!" (*pace* Kurtz en *Heart of Darkness*, or Brando en *Apocalypse Now*). Pero I need input. Interactions. Me siento a la vez incredibly lucid yet stagnant. Feel like I'm losing my mind.

Para abreviar (jaja): por más que quisiera combatir el sistema en mis propios términos, I've gotta admit I'm falling right into it. Mis únicas defensas, now, las despicable, archetypal female "weapons": nagging, apprehension, resentment. Y para Roland (as no male would, quizás—they have no need to question the order of things), se me hace que "just being to-gether" is fulfilling for him. Just having me here. Pero no parece entender que there *is* no "just being together" en este país surreal. Al menos not for me.

Dado este status quo, maybe my only way out, mi modo de sobrevivir, is economic. Pero la chamba en UNISA implica algunas cosas que medio me friquean. Like *permanence.* Aceptar el puesto quiere decir a *definite* (one year at least) commitment. Mi commitment to Roland está, that's not what gives me pause. Pero I mean: being in this country. Significa "pension scheme," bank accounts. La burocracia no me va, you know that. También tengo professional dudas: what'll it be like, trabajando con estos pompous-seeming, tradition-bound académicos? ¿Cómo voy a enseñar literatura por primera vez (though I've always dreamed of this) sin mis libros, mis grad school class notes? Y la tercera pega es ideológica: me inte-graré a una institution of higher education in S. Africa—hardly a well-regarded position en la comunidad académica internacional. This is, creo, lo que me hace titubear más.

After weighing all this, concluyo: it's a pretty big deal, que me hayan elegido como salaried lecturer en una foreign uni. Será un huge challenge—and I'm nothing if not *always* up for a challenge, ¿qué no? Besides, ganar mi propio salary me dará cierto . . . concrete power. Y me dará mi independencia—o al menos, the start of it. I *must* get some kind of handle en este país. Learn how to get around on my own, sin que me lleve por todas partes Roland, o sus hermanas. I must learn how to pay for things, dónde ir. En este sueldo (more than twice what I ever earned in the US, ironically), creo que podré vivir más o menos bien.

Y ahora te dejo, my darling Lee. Enjoy la City. I miss my life there. No es solo nostalgia. Aunque sé que I was sort of desperately searching for a meaning beyond the "place"—direction, vocation, passion, *algo*—ahora veo que I was happier living in SF than I'd ever been anywhere before. Keep in touch with my parents, please. Y con la Helen.

P.D. La chamba en UNISA (a "distance-tuition" uni—weird!?) means being en la ofi 8–1, todos los días. Na' que ver con ser teaching assistant! I'm *fervently* hoping que el efecto paradójico de estar superbusy y querer escribir will push me la extra milla. También estoy fervently hoping I can convince Roland to move to Pretoria (where UNISA is). Agárrate: Roland's never lived in an apartment (siempre ha vivido en casa de los padres, can you even imagine? Digo, except for his hoity-toity boys' boarding school, Michaelhouse) y según él, they're hard to find. We'll see about that! Aunque Cullinan solo queda a media hora de Pretoria (hardly a metropolis, though it's the capital city), hay un mundo de diferencia. La Premier Mine would be an easy drive for Roland, y yo podría ir en bus a UNISA.

*11-ix-82*
*Postcard with young male lion on front*

Mi querida hermana,

Call me paranoica, pero te escribo en Spanish, mostly . . . no vaya a ser que nos censuren. Either here o en Managua. Mom & Dad must be *freaking*, la verdad. Tú en la rev. sandinista y yo aquí. Te escribo hoy en el 9th anniversary de ese nefasto acontecimiento en Chile. I hope you're well, contenta en tu trabajo, in your new life en ese país extranjero y prometedor. Tan contrario al que experimento yo en estos hot, hot days de la temprana primavera africana. Don't worry, te prometo que I'm taking to heart lo que me dijiste cuando hablamos por tel: no juzgar NADA de golpe. And above all, no desesperarme. Al nivel íntimo, all is well between R. and me. ¡Muy! Pero tú sabes mejor que nadie que me cuesta separar "lo personal" de "lo político." Me ofrecieron la chamba en UNISA. I'm gonna accept, aunque es una institución reaccionaria. Escribe pronto. Letter follows.

*29-ix-82*

Dearest Eva,

It's been over a month y no he sabido nada de ti desde que llegué al Africa. Espero que estés bien, doing what you feel best doing: helping, getting involved, participando. Ojalá pudiera decir lo mismo de mí . . .

Dad wrote me de tu trabajo en el day care center en Managua. ¿Te gusta? Esta carta va para desearte happy birthday el 12. Deja te cuente de mi vida aquí. The eastern Transvaal, donde se ubican Joburg y Pretoria (y Cullinan, this hellhole of a reactionary Afrikaner mining town donde Roland trabaja y donde—for now—vivimos) has vast beautiful expanses of red earth (como Andalucía—remember ese fateful overnight train ride, de Madrid a Sevilla?). Pero it's already so hot, con un calor tan dry, relentless. And it's high—around 6,000–7,000 feet, creo.

Lo que te puedo decir sin duda: one is *never* prepared. No obstante all my reading. Las cartas de Roland. The books he got me. Mis charlas con exiled South Africans en Califas. La realidad es otra. Infinitely more shocking and, pos . . . *real*. Me pregunto si experimentas algo semejante en Nica.

About R.'s family: hay 6 kids, can you believe that? Y ni siquiera son Catholic. They're Anglican . . . ish. He's the eldest; luego una hermana de 24, Martha; un hermano de 19 (in the navy, pero home on leave el finde: cute, algo punky, a bit like our own Wiggue); otra hermana de 16; y las twins, Shirlie y Maggie, de 13. El papá, Gordon, es handsome, youthful, inteligente y refined. Bastante quiet. Me cae bien. La mother me recuerda algo de Mom (pero sin su elegancia e inteligencia, nor her looks, tampoco). Muy opinionated and outspoken, pero también butchy y bastante matronly. Me parece gossipy y convencional y no tenemos mucho en común. OK, directamente NADA—except Roland. Hmmm. Las twins me adoran and I like them best of all. Son friendly, unpretentious and open-minded—a rare virtue en este país.

Ahora es jueves 30 and we've just done the impossible: encontramos un apto. En Pretoria, in a good location. Esto representa un tipo de turning point. No way podía continuar here in Cullinan; I feel I'm going mad. Estoy rodeada de un chingo de young white mining engineers, Roland's cohort. Su entertainment runs to . . . any deporte you can imagine: soccer, rugby, golf, tennis, aplaste (jaja), ad nauseum. Este es un sport-crazed país. Pero here's a surreal twist: hay un film crew here, on location en este "typical" Transvaal *dorp* (pueblo), filmando una serie para Afrikaans TV! Los directors son un par de dizque bisexual Afrikaners (léase felices), muy famosos aquí, and they've taken a fancy to me. Franz Marx (tiene mi mismo birthday) y Hennie Smit se han proclamado my Afrikaans teachers. So, *ek kan nou baie goed Afrikaans praat!* It's *soooo* difficult! Plus, es la lengua de los oppressors. Por otra parte: es lo que me rodea y sospecho que my curiosity will win out. Afrikaans derives from Dutch, principalmente. Pero also French, English, Malay, con un smattering de portugués y lenguas africanas. Medio me fascina.

Intento seguir tu advice: not to get blown away or discouraged. Pero every day me parece cada vez más imposible. Roland and I agree politically (*mostly*—we've been hashing this out from the moment we met, en San Francisco, often con efectos muy eróticos, tee hee), pero hay una diferencia fundamental: este es *su* país. Y las cosas que él ama de Sudáfrica (mainly the wilderness, the bushveld) more or less eliminate la posibilidad de que se exilie permanentemente. And the political situation—el apartheid—no le impacta de modo suficientemente *directo* como para que . . . reaccione. De hecho (let me be blunt—para variar), le favorece. Por otra parte, I have no stake in this country. Except . . . *him*. For his sake me vine, e intento adaptarme y aprender. Pero I feel torn. Me siento cada vez más hipócrita e impotente.

Una sudafricana que conocí en SF, shortly before moving here, me dijo que I would find that *(white) S. African existence is a constant exercise in denial and sublimation.* Me pareció medio melodramatic, apocalyptic. Pero coño, touché. Plus, this is an *incredibly* machista country. Y hay una oppressive, stubborn, tense . . . *blandness* en la day-to-day white existence que me repugna. And I don't see any way out. La vida de R. está pretty determined, creo, for the next 2 years o más: De Beers ("a diamond is forever") le pagó los fucking estudios—he never mentioned this to me—so he owes them time. Primero en esta diamond mine y next year en las dreaded gold mines (hot, dangerous underground conditions) de Western Deep Levels, where I won't even be able to live with him. ¿En qué me he metido, hermana? He eventually wants to get off the minas, quizás estudiar un MBA, o MS en mineral economics (?), maybe in the US. Pero todo eso es el futuro.

For now, como te conté en la postcard, he aceptado la chamba en UNISA. Agárrate: the largest correspondence uni en el mundo. Isn't that a viaje? Y, lo que más me intriga, a diferencia de las otras S. African unis, hay muchos estudiantes negros, Indian, "colored" (a legal racial classification—corresponde a mestizo, more or less) y foreign. They can do this, a pesar de las leyes del apartheid, *precisely* because they're a correspondence uni. Crazy? Maybe I'm being ridiculous, pero esto me brinda cierta esperanza. Pretoria (the governmental capital y por ende, the heart & soul of apartheid) es una ciudad notoriamente conservative (compared to Joburg or Cape Town). Pero maybe la gente conectada con la uni tendrán intereses más parecidos a los míos. A girl can dream . . .

Anyway, me piro. Write me soon, te ruego. Oh, antes de rajarme, get this: Roland's idea of a vacation is a camel trek across los pantanos de Botswana. En serio, he's aleady introduced me to the bush. Can you imagine your sister, cara a cara (well, OK, quizás a 100 pies) con un RHINO? We're going again este finde. It *is* beautiful—in a strange, desolate way. Baboons galore, *volstruis* (avestruz en Afrikaans!), all sorts of gazelles, hippos y los hermosos rhinos blancos.

13-x-82

Dearest Sloth,

Well, I was hoping que recibir mi EPIC letter te inspirara a escribir. But as yet, solo he recibido 3 postcards. I start my new JOB el 18, y me siento medio trapped and panicky: ni puta idea en qué consiste el actual work. Ironically, ni siquiera he visto mucho de Roland these last few weeks, or so it seems. Except for los weekends, y entonces siempre regresamos a Joburg because . . . his life is there. Y allí it's one "pleasant" activity tras otra: windsurfing en el Hartbeespoort dam con sus friends, al cine, out to dinner. Todo es con sus friends, friends, friends, most of whom me parecen infantiles, sporty, apolitical. Yawn. El no es así. Or . . . he *wasn't*, in the US. Sus friends no me hablan, or not hardly. Never a question about who I am, de dónde vengo. Cero curiosity. Solo me ven como la American *guhlfriend* de Roland.

R. was rehearsing casi nightly para esta inane musical play he got himself into in Cullinan (antes de que yo llegara). Anyway, se estrenó last weekend. La familia came up el viernes to see it y ya que no me latía quedarme en Cullinan to see it *again* el sábado (y me interesaba even less asistir a la beer-swilling cast *partytjie* en la casa del General Mine Manager), me volví a Joburg con su hermana la Martha, and was very glad I had. Pero it kind of pisses me off que R. lo pueda pasar bien con esta gente tan boring y de hecho: this is maybe our major problem. He seems too complacent, accepting of a scene I find intolerable. Entiendo por qué—it's his country after all, these are people he's known for years—pero knowing this doesn't make it more tolerable for me.

No he tenido noticias de Miss Weevil (aka Sarita) since I arrived, which worries me. Ayer cumplió 25—I can hardly believe it. She wrote Mom &

Dad que se casa con Gary en Managua en diciembre, pero . . . we'll see. Helen's been writing me a lot. Get this: hasta me mandó revolutionary newspapers de la U. de El Salvador (bless her daring corazoncito)—which she picked up attending a lecture en la SF State! My darling former roomie la Trish me ha escrito. And I just got a letter and photos from Riet Tramèr y una carta (aparte) del James, cada uno dándome su versión del breakup. No me gusta admitirlo, pero my interpretation is that James left Zurich por las mismas razones que me tientan a abandonar este país. "It's so old and cold and settled in its ways there," como canta la Joni Mitchell (about Europe) en "California." Of course, it's more than that here—agréguele un dash of apartheid (grim little jaja). But it *is* also that. Anyway, James ahora está en París. He plans to return to SF en enero—esa city that has touched each of us and brought us all together.

I've been on the verga (jaja) of going over the edge here in Cullinan esta últimas semanas: aburrida, restless, lonely. Estoy leyendo un chingo. You know I've always been a voracious lectora pero now it's like . . . me ayuda a viajar en la cabeza, helps me get out of my own *kop* (cabeza) a bit, soar above this desolate, bone-dry highveld hacia latitudes más afines. I'm devouring Jorge Luis Borges, Simone de Beauvoir, John Fowles, siempre Julio Cortázar (JC)—even Spanish grammar books! And Roland turned me onto a chévere Afrikaner writer, André Brink.

A veces me siento tan enamorada de Roland. Pero other times I feel engulfed by a great distance. Es todo tan raro. He's been, in a way, so *incredibly* patient. We talk and talk, sometimes for hours, y él intenta convencerme de que I don't have to either go stark raving mad o rajar inmediatamente. El está convencido de que we'll be able to find a solution. Some middle ground. Pero I'm so stubborn and intransigent. I feel myself reacting strangely, Cuz, de un modo tan . . . exagerado pero me siento powerless to rein myself in. Things I wouldn't give a second thought to, normally, me friquean aquí: sus friends (wouldn't bug me so much if I had my own), su laconismo (I found that "strong silent type" vibe of his sexy, alluring en mi país), y sobre todo, quizás, su constant . . . cheerfulness o digamos, *optimismo* (complacency?) ante una situación que me parece inaguantable.

And how's this for bizarre: Roland me jura, over and over, que la verdad—*the very essence of his love, his commitment to me, his conviction*—is contained in his letters. Esto salió cuando le dije el otro día (cruelly, I admit it) que a veces I can hardly remember all the things he'd said to me en esas cartas. Even *more* bizarre: that same day me dijo que todos estos feelings están *inside him, in his heart*, pero que tiene *difficulty articulating it to me—now that I'm here*. Huh? Ironic? Pero that's exactly what I desperately *need* him to do! Y es más: he had no problem "articulating it to me" in my bed o en las calles de San Francisco. Or in New Orleans. Uf . . .

Anyway, encontramos un piso en Sunnyside (Pta). Close to shopping y en el bus line a UNISA. Se ve bare and impersonal, pero al menos it's a start. And it's our own. I'll close now. Hace un calor de 4,000 demonios por la tarde, and the residual exhaustion (hepatitis) is still with me. Salute my tíos Phyl and Shell, y tu darling hermano, TB. And if you get the urge to make me some tapes, *don't* hold back. I miss good music, fuck! Rolo te quiere poner unas palabras, so I'll let him close. Love you, Cuz.

*Dearest Lee,*

*We are missing you! S. is looking forward and is also afraid for what UNISA might hold in store. We've ascertained that Cullinan doesn't hold much at all—I knew that already. I've done my time in this hick town—but S. has had to go through all that now.*

*We are moving into an apartment in Pretoria this week, which will make things more workable. I'll drive to work and S. will have a short bus trip to UNISA. She's seducing me while I'm writing this to you and I am having difficulty in retaining this pen! I am hoping that working at UNISA will give S. a feeling of worth and recognition—something she lacks and keenly feels being a foreign woman in a VERY MACHO, VERY SEXIST Cullinan. Politically S. feels I am too placid and accepting. She thinks revolution is the* only *answer. I hope it is not. It may well be. I don't know.*

*We miss taking you out to dinner. Remember Hamburger Mary's? Love, R.*

*12-xi-82*
*Postcard. "Skemer in die veld / Dusk on the veld"*

Dear Weeve (o Peeve, as Sam Armistead used to call you),

Thrilled to receive your letter. Llegó bien. Creo que solo abren la correspondencia a la gente "sospechosa" y no creo que figure yo (unfortunately) en su lista. Al menos, not yet . . . Creo que si escribimos "lo que sea" en español, no se enteran. I hope not anyway. So happy que te estés encontrando allí en Nica-libre. Acá, no hay nada *concreto* que yo pueda hacer. My work is going OK. Te escribo pronto. Love to you and your future MARIDO.

*15-xi-82*

Dear Cousin Sloth,

Sorry to have taken so long pa' responder a tu phone call, which was the greatest. Ditto tu long letter, que finalmente llegó—*only* took a month, ¡coño! It's just been soooo hot here, lo cual explica, I guess, my uncharacteristic slothiness pa' escribir. I'm so tired all the time . . . weird. Last night Roland y yo fuimos a casa de Anita Wurfl en Joburg, and ended up staying till very late. Ella es otra Spanish lecturer en UNISA. Ecuatoriana, age 44, casada con un alemán, Peter. They have two lovely hijas, Astrid and Karen, ambas muy feministas. Me caen muy bien. They're all very into the bush, so tienen eso en común con R. A nice time, pero now I'm half-asleep aquí en el office.

UNISA tiene summer recess en dic./enero. Roland dice que he wants to show me a bit of the country y supongo que I should actually *see* it antes de emitir un juicio categórico. Dicen que the Cape province is beautiful, pero me importa un huevo la belleza—it's all overshadowed by apartheid. Y esto me produce constante angustia, frustración y resentimiento. Fuck. R. tiene que participar en una wedding en Durban en enero. Of course, quiere llevarme. To show me off a las ODFs (Old Durban Families?!). Durban is a sort of resort city, con world-renowned surf. Some of the best waves en el mundo, I remember que me lo decían mis surfer pals en Santa Cruz. R. says que podemos visitar al Du Preez, which would be nice. Así podría dar un full report (on his dizque fiancée) to la Helen.

You asked about UNISA. El dept. chair, Prof. Haffter, es un pompous, traditional suizo. Me cae de la patada. Los de Italian are great—two women y un 40-ish Casanova type, Piero D'Onofrio, who dresses to the hilt y habla *exactamente* como Mauro Ritucci. Dos mujeres en portugués, one young and friendly, Elisabeth Soares, y la otra una squat, middle-aged Brazilian cotilla, Mrs. Louw. In everyone's business e intenta (me cuentan) intimidar a los new arrivals. O sea: yo. Ya sabes como pongo nicknames a todo el mundo. Well, I've baptized her "la Voz," ya que sus annoying chillidos penetrantes echo up and down the corridors. My two new friends, Anita W. y Augusto Castells, crack up con mis Voz imitations. Agárrate: you'll meet Augusto en enero. He's going on long leave to the States (por eso me dieron la chamba), and plans to go look you up en San Francisco. I'm bummed he's leaving, pues me cae fenomenal.

Algo strangely positive que ha salido de este foray into el heart of *duisternis* (strangely beautiful word in Afrikaans, *nê*?): mi angustia y hasta cinismo (about academe) is sort of waning. I love to teach y me apasiona escribir. Si solo pudiera convencerme de que puedo aportar algo . . . valuable al "real world" usando estos talentos, instead of lacerating myself so much about la responsabilidad social. Ya sé que the real *revolusie* is made with guns. Pero surely hay un lugar pa' committed intellectuals and artists. Teachers fo' sho. There *must* be.

In a way, supongo que esta chamba could be considered a kind of . . . hiding out from a reality que no aguanto, pero I didn't see another choice. I'm still so lonely. La vida (doméstica) se ha vuelto bien routine: our empty flat in Pretoria durante la semana, both of us at work, y a Joburg los weekends. Estoy aburrida. R.'s friends bore me. If I can sort of create my own little world (leyendo, escribiendo), la cotidianeidad es más abordable. Pero I've never felt so enajenada en la vida, Lee. R. seems to me so . . . laconic. Tan pragmático y sobre todo, too much a part of this. Pobre de él, he tries to understand my feelings. He's convinced we belong together, that we'll make it. There's a new mine in Napa county, R. dice. Can you believe it? That would be beyond *lekker*. Hope, hope, hope . . .

21-xi-82

Dear Miss/MRS. (?) Weevil,

Recibí tu 2a carta, ex Managua. Muy slow, pero things *do* get through from there to here. Milagro. Para cuando recibas esto, I guess (I reckon, como dicen ellos) you'll be married. UnbeLIEVable, como dice la Wilhelmina Wiggins Fernández, la hermosa black protagonist of that film Lee & I are obsessed with, *Diva*. Anyway, by now you likely know que R. y yo nos mudamos a Pretoria, and I've been working at UNISA for a month. Menos mal que salimos de Cullinan, pero things aren't much better here. Para una mujer blanca (or, well, white-*looking*) y foreign, es harto difícil penetrar esta realidad. Me siento restricted, trapped. Pero . . .

He tenido una experiencia insólita y chévere. Three weeks ago, R. me llevó a un football (soccer) match en Orlando stadium en Soweto. Some conectes through his dad's law office, así pudimos ir. Creo que figuramos entre los 5–10 whites en una muchedumbre de 100,000 negros. Te lo juro (or, I *promise* you). Fueron sensaciones tan . . . powerful. They were all so polite, demasiado corteses, somehow. Hard to explain. Pero allí, suddenly, me di cuenta de que this was the first time I really felt I was in Africa. I mean, en un país con una gran mayoría negra. Oh, I wish you could've heard how people talked and shouted, cómo alientan a sus héroes de ambos teams, los Kaizer Chiefs vs. los Orlando Pirates. Entre gritos en sus varios idiomas—Zulu, Sotho, Pedi, Xhosa—salen de repente en inglés con —*Ah, geddap 'n' dance, mon. Jeezas, Jeezas, oh come* on, *Pelé, mon.* Me moría de la risa, de la maravilla. Pero later me sobrecogió esta sad, frustrating thought: toda esta fuerza en potencia . . . channeled, anesthetized in popular entertainment. Sports, los conciertos. I'm wondering if this is how you felt en Brasil. Did you?

Afterward, me sentí curiosamente drained y elated a la vez. Ya sabes que unlike you, I've never been into los deportes. Pero the crowd alone—sentirme rodeada de esa surging, electric energy—was worth it. Te juro que los aftereffects de la hep are still with me, hermana . . . and they're not just physical. He hablado con otra gente que tuvo hepatitis, and some of them hasta me contaron que felt depressed, for up to a year. Scary!

Anyway, I know R. is trying. I know, por ejemplo, que su pasión por el bushveld va más allá del mere tourism. Dice que he wants to learn as much as he can about S. African nature para luego establecer education programs for blacks, lo cual no se hace aquí. Esto me parece very noble, pero me cuesta entender cómo puede—he or any conscious person—vivir aquí sin intervenir. De modo (más) activo y consistente. I'm telling you, *todas* nuestras polémicas giran en torno a esto. I tell him, no ways puedo radicarme aquí sin intentar hacer . . . *algo,* however minimal. Y él me responde que *violence is not the solution, education is the only way forward,* y bla bla.

And: se siente hondamente *African*. His destiny is here, en este país. And mine? Ay, hermana . . . I don't know.

Pasando a otro tema: leí en *Newsweek Intn'l* lo de la projected US invasion of Nicaragua next month. Fuck! Lo que están haciendo ahora en Honduras es una mierda. I'm worried about you. Write me, please (en español). Agárrate: I have the sensation de que abrieron tu 2a carta. It's now the 22nd, y recibí la 3a (mailed from the States), last night. Pero en la anterior, I promise you, el pegamento looked . . . weird, aunque this could be paranoia mía, I freely admit it. Pero *definitely* han abierto (here) una carta que mandé al Chino (Jonathan Wong, remember). He's in China (digo, la PRC). I know what they did porque he wrote me back que mi carta le llegó with the envelope torn and resealed. Y lo más creepy: había unos slogans anti-comunistas dentro que of course yo *no* los metí allí. El Chino freaked out y obvio, it could be dangerous (para él) si los chinos think he's consorting con gente anti-comunista, especially en este nefasto país, understand? Isn't that sick? Me da miedo. I didn't tell Roland . . . not sure why, pero no se lo dije.

Estos Afrikaners son una bola de hypocrites racistas y machistas. Viven—e imponen—la total segregación, pero who do you think son los que hacen sus "dirty weekends" en Sun City (en Bophuthatswana, dizque un estado independiente, pero esto es fake) o a Mbabane (Swaziland) pa' ver los strip shows, comprar porno mags, bailar y, of course, acostarse con las hookers negras? Simón, los mismos "cristianos" que llegan a casa los domingos, right on time for church. Y la prensa aquí, what a joke. Da la impresión de que el mundo consiste en sports, beauty contests, chicas semi en pelotas (en primer plano for no reason at all)—y asesinos negros.

Ay Eva, perdóname estos melodramatic arrebatos. Pero te juro que it's mind (and soul)-warping, vivir aquí. Write me. And stay safe!

26-xi-82

My darling prima,

Gracias por la fab letter, que recibí el martes. You have immense talent. Leer tus letters es casi como estar platicando. I'm typing this en el ofi. And as soon as el Castells arrives, tenemos que comenzar el proofreading de la study guide to linguistics (uf). He's the resident experto en la ling. and is desperately trying to teach me los basics de la generative transformational grammar (triple uf) antes de rajar. No veo cómo coño voy a enseñar esto— I barely understand it myself. Pero el Castells dice que I'll do fine.

Did I tell you en la última carta que you'll meet Castells en enero? I've become very fond of him y guess what? Next Wednesday (1 de dic.) he and I are buggering off (como dice él, tan fino, jaja) to Cape Town en un road trip. It's been infernally hot in Pretoria. Plus, estoy hasta la little crown of driving back and forth to Joburg, sick of feeling like an appendage, tagging along. Harta de escuchar de las epic highveld exploits del Rolo from his tactless, provincial amiguetes. Las twins, en cambio, son tan refreshingly different. Ejemplo: el otro día la Shirlie me dijo, —*Suzanne, you have the liveliest* heh! *Rolo's former guhlfriend had straight* heh, *like eeevryone in SA. And we think it's DULL.* Cuz, me partí de risa. Isn't that adorable? (Of course, they were only talking about white people.) Creo que la Ma F., en cambio, is rather scandalized by my "heh." Le parecerá too "ethnic," supongo. "Dull" las twins picked up from me, y yo de ti.

Sabes, Cuz: being in a foreign country, sin familia ni amigos, having to rely on one person (oriundo del lugar) es como no tener historia. I mentioned this to James (in the wake of his breakup con el Riet, en Zurich)—y me entendió perfectamente.

Anyway, it's now Monday the 29th. Images and memories of a magnificent event—una boda en Soweto (I promise you!)—yesterday are fresh y te lo quiero contar. Pero el contraste con la noche del sábado, ay . . . vaya whiplash. Rolo y yo fuimos a dos DULL *partytjies* con la Martha y Paul, su little brother (home on leave de la navy—an absolute dreamboat) y un amigo de R., Tommy M., de Zimbabwe. La fiesta had a Mauritius theme (o sea, "island"), so me compré tropical fabric en la so-called Oriental Market and whipped up una especie de sarong. They were all deeply impressed pero te juro, it's just so fucking hot all I want to wear is diaperdresses! La segunda fiesta was also una mierda. So we went to Rolo's fave hangout, Cafe Casablanca (muy feliz), pa' mirar semi-alienating, seminostalgic British New Wave vids en la TV.

Pero yesterday was another matter. Este vato negro, Max, from R.'s dad's law office, nos invitó a su wedding, a semitraditional black boda. So there we were, una bola de *umlungu* (white people, en Zulu), sitting around in zooty cars en el parking de un drive-in restó just outside Soweto, awaiting our black lazarillo to give us safe passage a su boda. How's *that*? You need a permit pa' entrar a Soweto—Rolo's dad nos lo había conseguido. El Max finally rocked up, and off we went—una cavalcade de Mercs, BMWs and Jaguars—por las calles de Soweto, which looked *nothing* like what I'd been expecting. A verrr, ¿cómo te explico? As we drove in, no parecía shanty town, or . . . not exactly. Parece, más bien, una serie de *really* tiny houses, like one room, quizás. Pero houses, nonetheless. Seguro que I only saw la punta del iceberg, pero algo es algo. Obvio, la diferencia entre Soweto y Joburg—especially Rolo's white northern suburbs—es marcada, y obscena. Pero somehow it's more subtle, no tan in-your-face as I'd expected. So, quizás lo más jarring es el simple hecho de que they live *there*: over a million blacks, just beyond los southern fringes de Joburg. Segregated. Esto es el apartheid (apartness, en Afrikaans).

La boda se celebraba en un enorme school hall. The actual ceremony had been earlier, so now here we were, todo el mundo waiting around en el parking lot hasta que llegaron los novios y su wedding party. La bride vestía una fancy, poufy white gown y el Max bien dapper in a formal suit. Un chingo de bridesmaids en frilly dresses y todas las flower girls como teensy fairies. Las older women llevaban brightly colored, traditional tribal atuendo y mientras la wedding party all lined up para proceder al hall, they suddenly burst into this beautiful (very LOUD) song, con todo y una complex, layered harmony, rhythmic hand-clapping y hasta dance steps. Me sentí entranced, como si se me rompiera a batir un enorme tambor adentro.

Casi todos los white guests hung back, pero de repente un negro de la bridal party grabbed my hand, and I dragged Roland into the fray too! Agarré los dance steps bien quickly and there I was, Cuz, jiving into the hall con la bridal procession. La costumbre dicta que los whites, as their "superiors" (can you fucking *believe* this?), entren y tomen asiento primero. Pero right off the bat vimos que there weren't enough seats so Rolo y yo kind of hung back hasta que un older black man vino para preguntarnos how we were doing. —*No, fine*, le dijo Roland (nota cultural: South Africans often start sentences con un negative, bien hilarious), y allí entramos en una long, drawn-out casi ritualistic rap con este vato, Alfred, who befriended us and became our mentor throughout la ceremonia.

De hecho, through Alfred, Roland and I became los star (*umlungu*) guests! No sabría decirte, Lee, exactly why they grooved on us so much. Pero se me hace que quizás se dieron cuenta de que I felt sort of . . . at home there. I know it sounds medio weird, y tú sabes que I don't even dig weddings. Pero te juro, Cuz, I felt happier, more alive en esa black boda than at any other place en todas estas semanas en SA. I don't want to sound simplistic or naïve. Pero había algo de la energía de las fiestas en UC Irvine, con mis amigos chilenos. No quiero hablar en stereotypes, sobre el "carácter negro" (o Latino, for that matter). Pero I can't deny que había un feeling tan warm, tan open. The opposite of Bedfordview.

Había una cantidad de speeches and toasts. Gordon, el papá de Roland, gave one. Y las old mothers and aunties se presentaban entre enthusiastic screeches and shouts. Luego circularon una enorme olla de *umqombothi* (home-brewed beer) entre los hombres. Gordon, Rolo y Paul took big gulps y el Alfred insistió en que yo la probara. Ya sabes, Cuz, que NO me gusta la cerveza. At all! Pero no quería ofender, so I gamely took a sip mientras todo el mundo aplaudía y se reía. Uf, tasted a bit like sourish goat's milk . . .

Luego comimos, this *huuuuge* meal, entre mucha risa y plática. Roland hablaba con una maestra—she speaks about five African languages, plus English y Afrikaans. Meanwhile, yo charlaba con el (by now muy tipsy) Alfred, en una mixtura de English and Afrikaans. Al final, conocí a otra mujer, Yvonne Kekana, a nurse, sister of the woman R. was talking to. They were so friendly and so curious about me (quién yo era, de dónde, why was I there)—much more than any of Roland's white friends. Muy irónico. Surprised that I was American, muy chuffed I'd come to Soweto. Agárrate: muchos de los *umlungu* wedding guests me contaron que they'd lived in Joburg toda la vida and had never been to Soweto before. Me quedé helada.

I'd like to go again, pero it isn't easy. Como te dije, you need special permisos, passes, etc. Y según, it's very dangerous (for black-on-black crime especially). Anyway, I've only been in this country 3 months y ya fui dos veces a Soweto (gracias al padre de R.). Small triunfos . . .

Me he quedado pensando. Something you wrote en tu anterior carta. About how we'd done so much dream-planning about our future, pero now I'd gone off to SA for love. Es verdad, supongo, pero I'm not sorry, Lee. Como dice el Robert Palmer, "love won't take second best." Plus, how many people do what I did, tirarme right off the cliff of my life, pa' venir al Africa? A veces, it hits me with an overwhelming force, como ayer en Soweto, y me digo: here I am, in *Africa*. If I can just arrange all these (wildly conflicting) thoughts and emotions, un día, en una totalidad creative and compelling, well . . . esta rara, hermosa, lonely vivencia will have been worthwhile, ¿que no? Lo que me escribiste, "a book about being a stranger in alien territory, told through letters to a cousin" . . . Why not?

P.D. Can't believe you saw Nina Hagen and Iggy Pop—¡qué envidia! Can't believe you ran into Mauro on Polk Street (por otra parte, SF really *is* a small city) and he's going back to Italy soon. Lucky him. Give him my love, si le ves de nuevo, *va bè*?

*12-xii-82*
*Durban, Natal Province*
*Road trip Diary / carta a Roland*

What a relief it is to cry now, por fin sola, de tarde-noche, after wanting to, needing to, todo el día. Mordiéndome el labio, needing a physical restraint y aun así a solitary tear or two asserted itself (no se fijaron el Du Preez and Co., thank God) onto the beach towel here, la almohada allá. I'm writing to you again, Roland, para variar, pero what's the use?

Tiemblo de rabia, de resentimiento, de dolor. Me cuesta creer que cuando te digo que I'll be home a day early (¿cómo coño iba a saber que el Castells would need to be back a day sooner?), you tell me why don't I "pitch up" en lo de tus parents, y esperarte allí—till the next day. Para peor: I can't believe you actually accepted my "alternate sugerencia" de dejarme la llave (si te lo dije dripping with sarcasm), and you'd see me tomorrow night *after* your dinner engagement. Is this a fucking joke? You are not the man I fell in love with. Na' que ver. Where did he go? Invasión de los body snatchers.

Wake up, Roland! ¿Quién coño eres? Has every ounce of passion and spontaneity drained out of you? I can't pull this alone, no puedo. Is it selfish to want to see you right away, después de dos semanas fuera? Me siento suddenly awkward, with an excessive sense of urgency (por tu *lack* of urgency). I promise you: no me olvidaré de este outrage.

Me ha hecho bien este getaway. He leído mucho (*Song of Solomon*, por Toni Morrison), and just being on my own en un lugar desconocido casi me hizo olvidar. Where I am, y sobre todo, *why* I'm here. Al principio I missed you intensely. Graphic, disturbing dreams of betrayal reflejaban mi miedo de perderte. To someone . . . easier. More local. Pero gradually, the comfort and freedom of being . . . *me*, on my own, resurfaced. Por primera vez desde que estoy en SA, descubrí que mi every waking thought was not about you, or us. How's *that*? Vaya novedad, hey? I wasn't fretting, no me perdía en ensueños paranoicos del futuro. I just *lived*: I've been dancing, reading, hablando con la gente. Todo esto sin esa terrible . . . urgencia que me asedia contigo. I've been seeing so much, Rolo. Of your country and its people. I've been laughing. Me siento hermosa. Lithe, brown-skinned.

Es irónico: solo aquí en Durban, after some disheartening—actually quite disturbing—talks con Du Preez, comienza a asediarme la claustrofobia de mi imminent return to the highveld. This can't be good! Creo que I don't even look forward to seeing you as much as I'd anticipated I would. Digo, when Castells and I departed en este *groot trek*. Oh, I felt so in love with you. And I felt a spark of hope. I wanted this trip to work some magic. It's funny, este estar sola, your physical absence, me hizo sentirme closer to home somehow. And closer to you, too, si bien menos conectada a este infernal país. Strange, lo sé.

El Sea Lawyer "does not envy us." He really seems to harbor very little hope for us: —*Rolo won't give up the good life we all (whites) have in SA, Chávez. Eventually, he'll have to choose between you and SA and I know he'll never leave.* Oh, no sigo. I'm furious. Ya te lo contaré todo, when I see you. Pero for now, necesito aclararte algunas cosas:

—No quiero ir al farm this week. I'm just not ready (physically) for a week of nature hikes, si esa es tu idea de welcome-home fun and intimacy. Way too strenuous for me y hace demasiado fucking calor.

—No quiero acompañarte a Durban next month. I don't like weddings, y no creo en las stag parties. Besides, la gente estará trabajando, and I won't be shunted around de casa en casa. Y no me importa un pepino conocer a las Old Durban Familias. En serio, Rolo, how *could* you?

—No quiero que tú sigas decidiendo todo por mí. Programming our every waking moment. Work, leisure, toditito.

Los Spurgess, by the way, estaban totally surprised you'd even *want* to go to the farm con un huge entourage right after my return. Le chocó al Paul Spurgess que you hadn't even entertained the possibility of just us two going. O que fuéramos tú y yo a otra parte. Just us. And leave the farm pa' después. It suddenly hit me in Cape Town: how fucked in *die kop* must I be getting—¿me habré acostumbrado, already, a tu taciturn complacency? Scary!—si ni siquiera se me ocurrió sugerirte un farm trip à deux. Even scarier: didn't this "public" routine begin immediately, digo, ¿desde la noche que llegué?

Al despedirse el Du Preez (ever the die-hard romantic), me dijo, —*Just you wait, Chávez, Rolo'll surely cancel his dinner plans tomorrow night and be home when you arrive. Surely he wouldn't really leave the key out for you? Things can't be that different to how you two were in the States. You were madly in love. The perfect couple. Everybody saw it!*

What is happening to us? Mira, Rolo: things are *seriously* fucked up (ay, cracked myself up sin querer just now . . . remembering a scene from *Dog Day Afternoon*). I need us to work it out, or . . . cut me loose already (como dijera mi daddy). ¿Entiendes? Do you understand? *Verstaan jy?*

15-xii-82
Pretoria
Diario / carta a Roland

No, I don't think you do, por más que me horrorice escribirlo. I can hardly believe it, pero no creo que mis palabras te alcancen. Me siento embarrassingly trillada, como en un daytime TV show. Pero heme aquí suffocating delante tuyo and you speak of sharing las maravillas del bushveld with other people y la inconvenencia de cambiar los holiday plans. Fuck, Rolo, *listen* to yourself. Es como si te hubiera colonizado un robot, I swear.

Parece que the idea of being alone with me doesn't even occur to you. I mean: why are you not *hungering* to be alone with me? What a desolate and rocky place we've arrived at, hey Mr. Montenegro, desde los días que pasamos ALL ALONE en mi "island bed" en Chestnut Street? Or holding court en nuestro queen-sized pleasure palace, sharing a bottle of Cabernet and a loaf of sourdough con Miss Zooloo y el Sea Lawyer y Ken, all rolling their eyes and sighing at how much time we spent together, en esa cama.

— *Things can change*, me dices. — *They* will *change*. Veo que you're aware there's something wrong. Pero it's vague and formless mientras que para mí it's a specific, burning need for change. — *It's just a matter of money*, me dices. — *A temporary inconvenience*. Pero that's not it. Oh, how the hell did we get *here*, Rolo?

Estoy sola (ay, coño, I sound like Neruda en *Residencia en la tierra*). The guitar doesn't help y no me apetece escribir cartas. That ritual interrupted by my road trip. Ese viaje . . . los últimos vestigios de mí, of anything I *recognize* as me—un sentido de vitalidad, freedom, bienestar—buried somewhere en la Cape coastline. Was it after that lovely, sexy night, bailando reggae en ese club en Port Elizabeth? Or somewhere entre Cape Town y Nysna, en ese gorgeous stretch of pines and lakes tan reminiscent of my northern Califas home? A resurrected confident smile cast over sun-bronzed shoulder, hair a fluff of rizos en la briny brisa marítima. Whole and grounded después de meses tan ill and weak, tan jaundiced y mareada.

Esta es la mujer que veo en las fotos que me sacó el Castells, which he'll take to the States pa' mostrar a mis amigas. Conmemoran esa too-brief flight from time, mi fuga de estos hideous, life-denying square buildings, este searing inland heat. *Esta* soy yo, Roland. La mujer que amas. Pero you don't see her. All you see, me temo, is a sullen, antisocial woman, torpe y desconsolada. My only friend has just left. Con un new haircut and dreams of fulfillment in America. Me trajo un perfume (ah, how well he knows me already). And my heart is cold as a stone y vacío ahora que se fue el Castells.

— *I can't touch you, Shug*, me dices. — *Your pain is too great to let me in*. Pero ¿no ves que it's *you*? Your taciturn complacency has brought me here, al umbral del silencio, lugar que habito hardly ever, and badly. Why didn't I see this before? Pero perhaps it's only *here*—here in your country, entre los tuyos—que esto sea verdad. After all, has aprendido los rudiments of affection de una familia de stilted, small-talking títeres. Especially your parents! Uf, what wouldn't I give pa' ser mosca en la pared at a dinner with June & Joe, Gordy y la Ma F. Mis padres tan boisterous y warm-blooded. Pero los tuyos—they don't even feel to me like an actual couple. Kinda creepy, al pensarlo.

*Ag*, Montenegro, you shook off the burden of your history in my country, ¿que no? Viviste y expresaste conmigo algo que debe haber estado inside you, that must *still* be deep inside you. Y esto me mata. Pero it's no good to me now, here, si no lo puedo encontrar. O desenterrar. If even after months of pick-axing away no logro fracturar la piedra que te contiene. Que te escuda. From *me*, your love.

Erase una vez (in my country) me dijiste que you wanted—needed—to learn to love from me, *with* me. Pero here we are in apartheid S. Africa con tu family, en tu país. Cold and threatening and false to me, pero ejerce un tidal hold over you. I can't release you anymore, Rolo. No aquí. Mis Aphrodite powers me han abandonado. It's like . . . la diferencia entre Oz y Kansas.

*20-xii-82*
*Pretoria*
*Diary/carta a Roland*

Christmas is coming. Pero my God, it's *so* hot and oppressive. No aguanto. Tengo momentary revivals. Litle flashes of hope. Anoche en el auto, as we talked and talked for hours, my head in your lap y tú acariciándome. It seemed, ay casi, that we were getting somewhere. That we would make it, como dices tú. Pero ahora, rodeada del echoing vacío de este wretched flat (perfecto correlato objetivo, she says grimly), me siento desesperanzada.

Me he bañado. Colored my hair with some weird local potion, caught up en el deseo de estar hermosa para ti. Pero de repente I'm seized by a wave of bleakness. Me rodea: en el aire, en este flat, al recordar todas esas beautiful, passionate words que me decías en San Francisco. En tus cartas. On the phone. Words that smite me now with cold betrayal, y que no logro descongelar con estas useless girlish ablutions.

Acabo de leer un libro medio espeluznante (*The Yellow Wallpaper*) about a woman going mad, y creo sentir tal madness settling upon me. Pero surely not. Surely if I can write this, write this question, sigo en mis cabales. Sigo en mí. ¿O no?

31-xii-82

My dearest Cuz,

Thank you, thank you, mil veces, por el care package. La carta, los tapes were just the ticket, como dice mi daddy. Estas dos semanas después del road trip I've been feeling really alone y bien . . . at loose ends. Especially ya que it's "the holidays," y no tiene sentido con este fucking incessant heat. Loved your collage, especially lo que hiciste con las fotos de Mauro (with me and you y las streets of our beloved North Beach como backgound). Man, what a hunk! Weirdly, R. barely batted an eye cuando las vio. Me ha dicho que he'd throw a fit and break up with me if I "fell in love with another man," pero por lo general in terms of jealousy me parece curiously bloodless. O quizás sea wannabe hard-ass, stiff-upper-lippish. En todo caso, the polar opposite de los mostly Mediterranean dudes I've been with before—al menos on the surface. Hmmm . . .

Loooved the *Diva* soundtrack! Oooh, me hizo acordar de cuando vimos el film, and that reverie got me thinking about el protagonista, Jules, and *that* led me to Didier (aren't all those pointy-chinned, pale, languid-limbed Frenchies basically the same?)—y de esa noche tan weird y awkward. How he shattered our love-triángulo fantasies con su obstinate, inexplicable, repressed . . . Frenchness. Jaja, agárrate: I've had two cards from him! BTW: Roxy Music makes me swoon, también. Bryan Ferry forevah!

Well, hoy el último día del año, and R.'s birthday. Lleva trabajando night shift all week, and he's asleep now (11 a.m.). We probably won't do anything special tonight, ya que—brace yourself—ni siquiera tenemos phone so he wasn't able to book us a nice, romantic dinner res. Can you fucking believe *that*? Ni que estuviéramos en el 19th century! Anyway, I've flat-out refused to go party en Joburg. Estoy up to the little crown of R.'s ready-made social scene, y de sentirme out of place, sick of looking at all the white, complacent, postadolescent faces de los amigos de R. Something has risen up inside me that me insta a decir NO, without being afraid of "losing" Roland, sin temer que me juzgue misántropa, or too intellectual. Or whatever. Hoy, el último día del año, I have the keen realization that I am *here*—and no other place—y esto me hace pensar que I must be here for a reason. Digo, perhaps Roland isn't the *only* reason. Difícil explicar . . .

Anyway, tu idea de un libro basado en "letters to a cousin" me intriga. Tell me more. Porque I've been bitterly disappointed in myself lately—mis intentos de escribir ficción naufragan. I just don't seem to be cut out for that (como escritora) por más que todo el mundo fetichice la NOVELA (even *me*). Me siento una wash-out, especially with you, who's always urging me to write fiction. Pero nothing comes to me, Cuz. Digo, no outline, no shape, ningún personaje ficticio. Lo que me motiva: el ansia, unrelenting, de . . . ever-greater intensity of experience and feeling. Y poder captarlo. In writing. There: he dicho. Pero, what's this *called*? Is it literature? *Can* it be? En todo caso, what comes naturally to me is writing letters, sentir ese heartbeat at the other end. Aunque since I'm back from the Cape, casi ni eso. Roland works; I'm in recess (en UNISA) y hay ola de calor. En el mundo and inside me.

Deja te cuente del Castells. Mi único amigo—and now he's gone. Su historia es como una novela. Tiene 32 años y es de una super aristocratic familia. *Genuine*, como dicen aquí. Su papá es el lawyer del Duke of Windsor, or some duque or other. Anyway, he's Spanish y la madre una hermosa British socialite. La familia me suena bien strange, o quizás just bien British (of the posh variety). Totally cold and unaffectionate. Predictably, le mandaron a un tony public school (o sea, *private* school), Catholic, donde abundaba el abuse y el sadismo. Me pone los pelos de punta when he reminisces about his school days. Te juro que it's like a Dickens novel. —*You wrrretched little man*, me dice que les decían esos fucking pervy curas, before caning them—o peor. Su hermano mayor se casó y se hizo successful art dealer en Londres. Pero el pobre Castells didn't measure up. Los padres querían que fuera abogado, pero he was more into Latin and philosophy. Las letras. So, like it comes to pass for every segundón, they shipped him off to las colonias. En serio, lleva ocho años en SA, where he completed a uni degree in classics y un honors degree in translation. Lleva dos años trabajando en UNISA.

Agárrate: for the last couple of months (desde que le conozco) he's always running off to some doctor, pero nunca me quiso decir por qué. Finally, after much badgering de mi parte, he asked me to guess. —*Some . . . sexual thing?* me aventuré. I wish you could hear him, Lee. He's got *such* a lovely accent—pero I mean *really* posh. Anyway, I hit it on the head (jaja), porque por poco le da un telele. —*Good Lord*, he shrieked, *does it show?* —*Of course not*, le aseguré. Le dije que I'm psychic (which you know I am) y al tiro I told him about my uncle Joshua el sex therapist en UCLA, and how I'd studied psychology pa' ser therapist myself (hasta que me hizo derail esa jodida statisics class). You know me, Lee. No me friqueé para nada, y al ver mi nonchalant reacción, el Castells calmed down y me contó que he'd never told anyone before en la vida pero que se sentía tan comfy conmigo y así nos hicimos fast friends. This all came out el día antes de salir pal road trip.

Anyway, nos pusimos a tomar vino (a *nooo*-ble red, as he says) y allí le salió un relato bien sordid, espeluznante. Entre su cold-fish familia y ese boarding school—una cruza de medieval torture chamber y *Lord of the Flies* (donde muchos de los boys were involved in sexual liaisons, either by force or coercion, con los priests o unos con otros)—el vato was *really* messed up. Hasta los 18 apenas tuvo contacto con las chicks, and coming to S. Africa sealed his fate, dice. El Castells likes many things about Africa (las cosas que le gustan a Roland: the bushveld, la naturaleza, el wildlife, etc.), pero in Castells he encontrado un kindred spirit. Porque he's an articulate and astute critic de las perverse, sexist relations entre los sexos en este país. Y aunque es *uitlander* como yo, he's got credibility pues he's been here for eight years. And: he's a man.

Tuvo una novia aquí en la uni, pero antes de que follaran, she committed suicide. Isn't that *hideous?* So, eso of course le traumó. He briefly tried to go feliz, pero eso tampoco le resultó. Según él, las mujeres (blancas) aquí son casi todas una bola de brainwashed, traditional ninnies who expect the corresponding prototipo macho. Ha tenido cero suerte, romantically. Sus amigos son todos felices, girls and guys, pero he's never told anyone about all this.

Hace unos años, comenzó a buscar médicos. Pero as you can imagine, el clima para sex therapy here is hardly *verligte*! So el Castells has tried to bury the problem, para no obsesionarse. He's tried to convince himself that intimacy is overrated, que él es un tipo "independiente," etc. Pero según, conmigo is the first time he's let his guard down. About any of this. Can you imagine the *weight*? Me siento honored, pero también, un poco . . . dizzy. ¡Jamás pensé que mi career as a sex therapist comenzara a los 26 años—en South Africa! Le dije cosas que recordaba de los sex manuals de mi uncle Josh, how there's way too much emphasis en la verga, como hay muchos modos de dar y recibir placer y bla bla (which, en todo caso, is true).

He was totally chuffed al escuchar esto. Lately, un médico has been monitoring his sleep, y físicamente, no hay problema. It's all in his *kop*! The other doctor (agárrate: le acompañé al appointment, and I met him—didn't tell Roland), un urólogo, quiere que el Castells vaya a la Masters and Johnson clinic. So, *there's* the true reason for his "long leave" in the US! Yo he leído mucho de las M&J techniques, y tienen un high success rate. Pero here's where things get a bit . . . kinky. Turns out the real reason que el Castells quería que yo conociera al urólogo is . . . el good doctor me contó que su paciente tiene una "very high opinion of me" y que—agárrate—he is in addition highly attracted to me. In short: el médico creía que our road trip to the Cape could be the "perfect cure" for el Castells. Would you believe I actually contemplated it for a minute? Pero al tiro me di cuenta de que I really didn't want to feel like a sex surrogate (digo, *again*: I've sort of done a lot of that in my day, informalmente, jaja), or fuck up my amistad con el Castells—not to mention mi (already semiendangered) relación con Roland.

Pero just listen to what happened on the road: la primera noche, in the middle of the Karoo (this vast semi-desierto), en un teensy hotel de mala muerte, o "de segunda categoría" (como dijera mi mamá), de repente I'm jolted awake con un shriek triunfante del Castells, from the other bed: — *Would you* look *at this!* Prendo la luz and I'm staring at one of the biggest hard-ons que he visto en la vida. Te lo juro, Lee, it was *prodigious*. El Castells me juró pa'rriba y pa'bajo que this had never happened to him before, y quería que la "aprovecháramos." I declined. Me semi-tentó (como experimento científico), pero le dije que if it happened once, it could very well happen again. Por suerte, aunque he heralded me as his salvation y estuvo bien achicopalao, respetó mis wishes. He didn't—ejém—press the issue.

Supongo que el trust que sentía conmigo, the fact that I was OK with sleeping in the same room pero sin exigirle nada, got his guard down y su confidence (y otras cosas . . .) up. Tuvo varias más de esas humongous *ereksies* en el trip, and *begged* me to go to Master & Johnson's with him (can you just see Rolo's face, si le contara de esto?), pero I managed to talk him down. Anyway Sloth, cuando le conozcas, he may or may not allude to this. Just let him take the lead.

No te aburro con muchos travelogue, touristy detalles del viaje. A couple of hours east of Cape Town el landscape comenzó a parecerme casi familiar: greener, ¡ay, tanto verde, at last! Mountains, con pequeños vallecitos, farms, beautiful vineyards. Mientras descendíamos, de repente I smelled the ocean. It was suddenly all around me, wafting into that little orange VW bug que había sido insoportable tin can all through the desolate Karoo. De repente comencé a sentirme curiosamente casi relaxed. Almost . . . at home.

Cape Town was the first city founded, y se nota: los hermosos, chalky-white, thatch-roofed colonial buildings y los public gardens no se ven para nada en el interior. El Castells drove me all the way down the Cape Peninsula, hasta la Cape Point nature reserve, donde se juntan el mar atlántico y el Indian—isn't that mystical? There we bronzed bajo el blazing African sun—or I did, ya que el Castells es el clásico Brit paleface—blissfully unencumbered by turistas. Los colegios en el Cape estaban todavía in session, and most tourists from the Transvaal go to Durban—much closer y más comercial (home, as you know, of Steve Du Preez—suits him to a T . . . pero esa es otra). Visitamos el Malay quarter y en general just wandered around, admirando esa hilly, coastal city y su gente—tan diferente de la de Joburg y Pretoria. Me fascinó la gente colored (te juro que that's what they're called): son mestizos who look more or less like American blacks to me, pero con un toque de Chinese, or . . . *some* kind of Asian mixed in, too. Y hablan Afrikaans—la lengua del white oppressor—as their mother tongue. Coño, learning this messed with my paradigmas, en grande.

Anyway, después de tres noches en un hotel downtown con el Castells, my money started to run short (para ni mencionar que it was getting harder and harder—tee hee—to fend off his *ereksies*) y decidí llamar a unos amigos de la familia de Roland, los Spurgess. El papá, Paul, es education prof. en la UCT (incidentally, a lovely campus, no del todo unlike UCSC, overlooking the whole city bowl y el mar, con hermosos old buildings). They immediately invited me to stay, y te confieso que acepté con cierto relief. They were really hospitable y ese sojourn fue fascinante y . . . bien revealing. Porque los Spurgess y los Fraser have been friends desde hace 30 años.

They took to me en grande y me dieron un chingo de insight into the workings de R.'s clan. En primer lugar, me pasó algo weird: al instante I felt more at home con los Spurgess and their four girls than I've *ever* felt con los Fraser. Los Spurgess son una academic family, so we had that (digo, lower sueldo) in common. Y otros values, too. For one thing, no tienen "domestic" (maid), y eso es *bien* unusual en este país. Not necessarily for political reasons, me dijeron. Más bien, no quieren que sus girls sean "spoilt" (con ese exaggerated sense of privilege que tiene la white middle class en SA). Plus, son muy Christian—pero not in an irksome way. Tienen esta little custom of holding hands to say grace antes de comer, y me preguntaron if I would mind joining in. Casi lloré de gratitude—les conté que eso lo hacemos in my grandparents' house. It really hit home, then, how *starved* I've been for months. Porque estos little rituals, este afecto tan homey, are totally MIA en la familia de R. La Spurgess girl más joven, Tessie, me vino a dar goodnight kiss every night! Te juro, Cuz, I melted.

Anyway, lo que me contaron de los F. pretty much confirmed lo que había comenzado a intuir: son una classically nouveau-riche family. R.'s dad got rich in his own lifetime (I mean, no heredó la lana). And get this: he's one of the best-known abogados en S. Africa. Todo esto les trajo esa *huuuuge* house en los northern suburbs como te he dicho por tel. (con todo y su pool, tennis court y bla bla), all kinds of social commitments, comités, clubs, etc. El Gordon sent all six kids to hoity-toity private schools, se toman un sinfín de family holidays, y hasta se ha comprado un private game farm en el bushveld. Naturally, mucho de la wealth—y de la atención—se ha concentrado en el scion, Roland, the eldest. Los F. kids don't act horribly spoiled, pero según los Spurgess, they've never known want y han llevado una vida muy privileged y sheltered. Paul and Cecilia Spurgess quieren a Rolo, lo ven como responsible and mature—as much as his "situation" (or . . . station?) has permitted him to be. Pero me dijeron que he's been *groomed* for a particular way of life (usaron esa palabra, Cuz, isn't that semi-creepy?). Y que este grooming—and his own temperament— would discourage him from questioning this. Esto me inquietó bastante, I'll tell you. Como broche de oro me dijeron que after spending a few days with me, les parece que I'm "more mature than Roland."

*Ag*, Lee, perhaps I ask too much from a man . . . R. and I have been talking about expectations, nuestros temperamentos tan diferentes, etc., since I've been so obviously restive and unhappy, mucho más desde que volví del Cape. El me asegura, over and over, que he loves me. Pero I don't *feel* it. También lately me ha dicho que he's always been a loner. Y que sus ex-chicks "gave up in frustration" porque they couldn't get inside his head. Well, eso no me pareció nada comforting. Pero en the States, el vato me había atraído precisely 'cause he *was* a hard nuez to crack. No me gusta la gente mushy. And I did feel like I was getting in, y él me decía que sí. En esos long drives se me abría, we opened to each other. Y Ken, su best friend, lo comentaba. Y Rolo mismo se lo comentaba con Helen, when I wasn't around, en sus private chats. How much I'd gotten under his skin. —*You* really *messed with Rolo's head*, me decía la Helen. Pero aquí, it's completely different. Makes no fucking sense to me, pero es como si . . . *puf*—all our intimacy se hubiera esfumao.

Y todo esto arriba is the only way que te puedo explicar un little . . . incident que ocurrió en el road trip:

El Castells and I stayed about 10 days en el Cape, y vimos un chingo, como te dije. Then we headed back up to the highveld por la Indian Ocean coast, hacia Durban, donde me había invitado el "Sea Lawyer." La primera noche paramos en Port Elizabeth, una coastal city famed for its surf. Nos quedamos con una Indian journalist, Charmain Pillay, amiga del Castells de la uni (o *varsity*, like they say here—isn't that bizarre?). Me cayó re bien right from the get-go: una chica friendly, con un bawdy sense of humor. Bien warm. Al tiró la Charmain me pareció way more unpretentious e interesante que los amiguetes de R.

Esa noche salimos a cenar y el "wine steward" caught la Charmain's eye—y el mío. Era—pa' hacértela corta—un full-on Adonis. Primita, you would've passed out. En primer lugar, parecía jailbait total—la Charm y yo le calculamos between 16 and 19, tops. Remember ese boy en *Death in Venice*, ay, *what* was his name? The one el Dirk Bogarde goes crazy for? Oh yeah, Tadzio, no? Well, este efebo was a bit like him pero far more masculine: tall, lean, muscled, bronceado, con floppy beachy hair, pouty mouth y hermosos green eyes. Que how do I know? Well, le pedí un Cinzano rocas y el adorable me trajo a whole bottle of disgusting Spumanti. When I jokingly asked him, —*Did you think I'd drink a whole bottle by myself?* (porque el Castells y la Charm had ordered wine), su puso bien flustered y confesó que he'd only recently started working. Luego luego me trajo el trago correcto, bien strong!

Todo su coltish fumbling really inflamed la Charm's ardor—y el mío también, te confieso. So al rato, when he stopped by to see "how we were doing," le pregunté algo semi-lelo: if he knew what music was playing. Can you just picture me, Cuz? Todo esto encouraged by little goading patadas under the table de la Charmain. El Castells was just rolling his eyes. No, he didn't, y allí me preguntó en ese charming way S. Africans have of phrasing questions, —*Must I find out who it is for you?* —*Yes you* must, le dije teasingly. Volvió con el nombre del grupo en un little slip of paper y al tiro, la Charm dared me to ask him que qué planes tenía after work. Well, it was nearly 11 on a Thursday y yo supuse que he'd likely be heading home. Pero tú me conoces, Cuz, since when do I turn down a dare? I quickly scrawled out this little note: "You're the sweetest sight for sore eyes I've seen since coming to SA. When do you get off work?" Cuando volvió a pasar me sentí supernervous pero I made of tripe, heart y se lo di, saying, —*This is for you.* Te juro, Lee, he actually blushed.

En eso, la Charm y el Castells me dijeron que he'd probably be mortified and go hide en la cocina till we left. Que no normal South African woman would *ever* do anything like that, y bla bla. Pero la Charmain estaba enthralled conmigo, at my "boldness," dijo. Esperamos en tenterganchos, pero al rato he emerged, me dio un papelito, and carried on walking. Ponía "My name is Sean. I finish at half past 12. Would you like to go dancing at a reggae club with me? You are gorgeous." Tierra trágame, pero when he passed by, I nodded yes. Al salir, we arranged for him to pick me up later en lo de Charmain.

— *You lucky dog*, la Charm teased. Pero el Castells wasn't having any. Hasta se puso celosito, Lee. De hecho, as we all lazed on la Charm's bed esperando al teenage galán, el Castells got one of his (by-now signature) huge hard-ons, y me rogó que since I was gonna break my vow of chastity unto Roland, que por qué no lo hacía con él primero. I about *died*. Good thing que he and la Charm were old college chums, si no . . . Anyway le dije que I was doing no such thing, que all I wanted to do was dance and flirt. Let off a bit of steam. Total, the last time I danced (the *only* time, can you fucking believe this? Ya sabes como me mola bailar) was, creo, en la boda de Max, en Soweto. Y eso que R. sabe bailar, remember? Hell, la gente cleared the dance floor around us and gaped cuando bailábamos en Gilley's (en Houston), y en los clubs de New Orleans.

Anyway, el Sean llegó on time. Endearingly, se había ido a casa to change *and* he'd doused himself with Halston Z-14. Yummy. He was driving a kombi (van), lo cual me pareció surf-perfect. Me llevó al reggae club, which was appropriately dark y un pelín seedy. La gente stared as we came in: yo llevaba un black mini T-shirt dress con low-cut, crosshatched neckline. My Cape Town tan (ya sabes que soy bien paleface, pero mis Raza-roots come out al sol), pale pink lipstick, mis rizos todo wild por la coastal damp y ese gold eye shadow que me echaba pa' ir al I-Beam. Me sentí muy *me*, de golpe. Leading by the hand a ese tall, tanned local surfer boy. El saludó a una gente as we came in, y era bien Alice in Wonderland, todo el mundo staring in awe.

Me llevó a una mesita in a dark corner, y allí comenzamos a platicar. La música era sublime, the vibe mellow. Here I was on the southern edge of Africa, pero surreally, me sentí en casa. Completely. El Sean asked me de dónde era. — *From San Francisco*, le dije. *Well, actually from Santa Cruz, but no one knows where that is.* — *No, I do*, me corrigió shyly. — *I surf.* Incluso me dijo que he'd met professional surfers del Cruise en Jeffreys Bay (cerca de Port Eliz) — uno de los hottest surf spots del mundo. Tiene 18 años y además de hacer surf, he's a pharmacy student. Pero clearly, sus estudios were about the *last* thing on my mind. Tenía una low, laid-back, melodious gurgle of a voice y cada dos por tres metía surfer jerga, which, clearly, is an international language. De hecho, en una I almost cracked up, tanto me recordaba este Sean de David Vidnovic. El hermano de Nick, remember? The one I went out with first. Consummate surfer, de un guapo que te caías patrás y *muy* inteligente—si bien carefully disguised by his motero ways y su surf-drawl. Anyway, con este Sean, I could've been back on Steamer Lane or the wharf or 41st Avenue. O sea, en casa.

El Sean me tomó de la mano y me llevó a la pista. I remember thinking ay, si el Dan Dickison could see me now, porque this was very much his kind of place. Bailamos, y todo era sinuous and slow bajo esas flickering mood lights, breathing softly, sintonizados con el reggae beat, catching mesmerizing little whiffs de su Halston-y boy-sweat scent. Sexy and close. And Cuz, it was *so* weird, pero me sentí tan at home, creo, porque I felt . . . *seen* by that boy, por primera vez en mucho tiempo. Sé que suena crazy and ironic pero te juro que I've been feeling invisible. In Roland's mundo and even . . . to *him*, desde que puse pie en este país.

Después de largo rato en la pista volvimos a la mesa y pedimos drinks y el Sean me hizo un chingo de preguntas about me. Y allí, I realized something else weird: aparte del Castells y la Charmain and . . . maybe Anita (en UNISA), y la gente en la Soweto wedding, this was the first South African who seemed genuinely curious. About me. My life, de dónde venía. Y entonces (if not unxpectedly: waves of desire had been flowing entre nous desde que nos vimos en el restó) he took my face in his hands and looked at me and our green gaze melded y me besó. I mean, *truly* kissed me. It was astonishing. Nos quedamos así largo rato, kissing and inhaling each other, acurrucados, purring and nipping at each other. Hasta que miré el reloj y chingao, vi que pronto ese kombi of his was gonna have to turn back to a fucking calabaza. Yo había perdido toda noción del tiempo pero it was after 3:30, y la Charm had sternly warned me que saldríamos a primera hora. And so, with great reluctance, I disentangled myself del embrace de ese sexy y sweet teen surfer y le pedí que me llevara a lo de Charmain. Which he gallantly did, si bien también with great reluctance.

Uf, Cuz, tengo más que contarte pero I'll stop now, end this letter con esta sweet, slightly melancholy fable, antes de que despierte R. It's hot and I'm wiped out. Llevo escribiéndote *horas*. Happy New Year, darling Lee. Later, gator!

*3-i-83*

Darling Sloth,

Ahora te cuento the end of the road trip caper (as Daddy would say) y el fin de año caper. Castells and I carried on up to Durban, donde me quedé varios días con Du Preez and family. Me quedé *thoroughly* disenchanted—with muggy, tropical surf city Durbs y con el superfish hipócrita del Steve. What a difference el contexto makes, hey? Si el Sea Lawyer and I had been uña y carne en San Francisco. Anyway, I met la Judy, su dizque fiancée of 7 years (who's caused poor Miss Zooloo such angustia). Ni que fuera particularly potent rival. Oh, es bonita in a tall, sporty sort of way, and she was nice enough. Pero . . . not much substance there, me pareció. I'm sure Du Preez will end up marrying her, aunque me profesa estar "confused" and "torn." Pero I just don't see any existential angst. Instead, I saw a complacent burguesito who'll never have the balls to rebel. Y sin embargo, he took it upon himself to critique Rolo. Harshly! Y seguía repitiendo, —*I don't envy you, Chávez, I really don't.* I wanted to fucking punch him!

Al día siguiente, we finally got back to Pretoria. I'd been semi-dreading la vuelta. El opresivo calor del interior, plus tenía tantas cosas heavy pa' platicar con R. Pero he wasn't even fucking home! El Castells dropped me off en nuestro flat vacío and I cried myself to sleep. Lo que quería hablar con R. era el downer de mi visit con el Steve. And even more, de mi convo con los Spurgess: they couldn't believe I've been here over four months sin siquiera un solo fin de semana *to ourselves*. Just writing this out now, Cuz—alucino. Paul and Cecilia me dijeron que con todo el catching up we had to do they were appalled que regresáramos every week-end to the family "compound" en Bedfordview. *No privacy*, they shook their heads . . .

Oh, it all came flooding out, cuando por fin estuvimos face to face. Le dije a Rolo I *can't* go on like this. Le dije que I don't feel like I have a home at all, que estoy HARTA de estar siempre rodeada de su family y sus friends. Hasta le dije que su aceptación de esta lack of intimacy es señal de enfermedad. I couldn't believe I went that far pero to my shock, he heard me. Y no se enfogonó. Al contrario, parecía genuinely perplexed. Me dijo, — *Why didn't you tell me this before, Shug?* —*I've tried*, le respondí, *but you weren't paying attention.*

Desde entonces, we've been in somewhat of a tregua. Nos quedamos en casa last weekend, for the first time (can you believe it?). Celebramos New Year's Eve—and Rolo's *verjaar*—con nuestros neighbors, a Dutch couple. Low-key, nice. I've been practicing my destrezas culinarias. We've been having lots of sex again . . .

Pero decidí no ir con R. a esa Durban wedding, by the way. He's leaving next weekend, y se queda una semana. Va a ser una muy high-society affair y . . . I just didn't have the stomach for it. A Rolo esto le pareció bien odd at first (mi actitud), pero eventually lo aceptó. After all, me conoce. I've got nothing to wear, no conozco a nadie. Sé que me sentiría totally fish out of agua y no me va tener que fake it. R. va a estar super busy anyway— he's the best man! He'd assumed I'd go off to Du Preez's, pero . . . that bridge's burned, me temo. Not sure si el Du Preez captó lo pissed off que estoy, pero between seeing him again o tener que ir a las "hen parties" (*cluck, cluck*), no se cuál sería peor.

Tengo cosas que escribir para UNISA, things I want to read. I wanna join the gym a la vuelta de la esquina. Looks like una bola de big ol' Afri- kaner bodybuilders—hardly el feliz-heavy crowd I was used to en el Berkeley campus gym—pero ni modo. ¡Lo tomaré como social experiment! Me da un poco los heebie-jeebies quedarme sola en Pretoria. I mean . . . when I say sola, Sloth, quiero decir *completely* alone. Me siento bien brave, haber tomado esta decisión. And kinda scared. It's the first time que le digo que *no* a Roland, la primera vez que no le sigo el "plan." He must think I'm crazy! Y capaz lo estoy. A week totally alone, sin amigos, sin teléfono. Life on Mars! Pero pos ni modo: I'll try to keep myself busy reading, writing, working. Maybe I'll venture out. Quizás vaya al cine, aunque I'm not like you, Cuz. Not used to going by myself and they never show anything good here—besides, está todo censored.

Write me soon, primita. You know where to find me . . . jaja. Y dime lo que piensas de todo esto, OK?

2-ii-83

Querida Lee,

So happy to hear from you por fin. Estaba a punto de escribirte—tengo muchas noticias. Some pretty strange stuff's been happening. Can't believe you were actually working in my fave shop, Fillamento—or that you've quit already. Really, Cuz? Pero pos, if you hated it that much . . . how did Phyl and Shell take it? Espero que encuentres algo más . . . I dunno. Bearable, al menos. So you can keep painting y también pay the rent.

Glad things are good con tu James. So amusing, lo del reading aloud in bed. Agárrate, cuando fuimos al farm (Rolo's dad's property en el bush), me puse a leer *To Kill a Mockingbird* aloud, al Rolo. En un abrir y cerrar de ojos, the whole group was gathered around me, hechizados. They couldn't believe que "in this day and age" someone would have the patience. Pero it's fun, and intimate. A R. le fascina. We started doing that, reading to each other en la cama, right from the get-go. Digo, en San Francisco. Odd, hey? Pero, well, our whole courtship was back-assward, al pensarlo. Jaja. We'd fuck for hours, y luego just . . . lie around, de un modo bien 19th century, romantic. Fumando, tomando vino o café, charlando (o "sparring," as he would say), reading aloud to each other. In fact, lo que me choca es lo poco que lo hemos hecho, ever since I got here.

Anyway, tu reading list me fascina. Didn't I recommend *The Moviegoer* to you? I loved that novel cuando la leí hace unos años, en esa contemporary American fiction class que siempre te comento, con mi undergrad ídolo el John Carlos Rowe. Y hablando de moviegoing, qué envidia que hayas visto *Blade Runner* con mi NOVIO el Rutger Hauer. Sounds divine. You know how obsessed I am with movies, pero aquí o ponen commercial *kak* (tipo *ET*, *Grease II*) or they censor the hell out of it. Lo último que vi fue *Tre Fratelli*, again. Remember, we saw it with Mauro? So beautiful.

Vivimos al lado mero de un movie house, and close to about three more. I believe you, about *Gandhi*. Lydia V. saw it y también pensó en mí, bien worried. No ha llegado aquí. To answer your questions, yes, blacks and Indians ahora pueden caminar por las sidewalks! Pero: they usually move out of the way, casi siempre eyes downcast. No hay tantos Indians up here en el highveld (Pretoria-Joburg). Se concentran mainly in Natal, aunque I saw quite a few en el Cabo. And of course, el Castells introduced me to Charmain. Their situation isn't good either—pero según R. they're closer "in spirit" to whites. Whatever *that* means!? I think he means they'd rather be white, o que intentan "pass white." O que les tratan *marginally* better than the blacks. Anyway, here's a little something que escribí esta mañana:

Son las 7:30 de la mañana. Already searingly hot. Hottest summer in 10 years, dicen. Ya apenas me acuerdo de la cool San Francisco sea breeze. Intento recordar estos mismos días, last year: nuestro amor fresh, sharp, rebozante de early bloom. Pasaba los late-winter días riding the 30-Stockton y el BART en un love-haze, escribiendo en mi Chinese journal con mi fat fuchsia calligraphy pen, wide-open to that particular bright, soft North Beach light, abierta y engullendo los scents of Chinatown, los tortilla-flower trees en Berkeley, los mimosa sprigs for sale al lado de Macy's en Union Square, the pungent, bitter beans roasting en Cafferata, on Columbus. Me sentía poor yet elated, ferozmente independiente pero happy. Loved.

Ahora, esa foto está blurry. Solo está este calor, this incongruous February summer. Y nuestra equally incongruous pero innegable distancia. Y no obstante, me parece que I'm beginning to awaken—no sé por cuál milagro (*pace* Alfonsina Storni)—por más que no quiera, to the strange, particular, contradictory beauty here, even here, en Pretoria: la capital del apartheid. Sleepy side streets overhung with las lacy green frondas del jacaranda; blond, pecosos Afrikaner schoolkids dragging heavy satchels, arrastrando sus pale bare feet en la tierra roja, trailed—a half step behind— por la smiling, aproned family maid. Hasta saludo a algunos acquaintances en la Sentraal Swembad del barrio y en las shops.

Me estoy permitiendo (¿obligando?) sentir placer ante cosas tan silly, tan ínfimas: being able to bear up a little bajo este infernal calor, estas heavy, mosquito-plagued nights. Y por fin: human contact, wrought by *me*, Roland, while you were away. Un almuerzo con Etienne en Sir Loin (I promise you, así se llama el local steakhouse), donde sirven esa meltingly delicious meat, hasta más rica que la carne más delish del mundo, en "El cerdo que ríe," donde me llevaron Mom and Daddy esa vez en las Canary Islands, pa' mi cumple. Chilled white wine at noon, tan decadente, wearing Etienne's three-part faux-Cartier ring, como el tuyo, Lee. O sentada en la terraza de Giovanni's pizzería con Rolo y Peter R., our thighs rubbing in easy, electric familiarity bajo la mesa. Me doy cuenta de que I'm inhabiting a Truffaut film y me siento agitada y slighty guilty. Pero no me muevo la pierna.

Cuz, seguro que tienes mil preguntas. Deja te explique. Remember about la boda en Durban, como decidí no ir con Rolo? Well, el día que salió (8 Jan.) it rained and rained, todo el santo día, y me quedé en la cama, crying. Pero finally, hacia la tarde, hice de tripe heart (jaja) y me dije look *meisie*, all this moping's getting you exactly nowhere. Five months of pan y agua is enough! Nunca he sido la depressive sort, tú lo sabes, Lee. So me levanté, me vestí (my black leather pants from Riet, remember?), determined to hit the calle and find some *aksie*. Ay, Sloth, if you could only know how ridiculous this idea was. Las mujeres simplemente no salen solas en este país, especially not in Pretoria. Pero there's this little open-air café just down the street, Tivoli Gardens. Se queda abierto hasta tarde—the *only* place in Pretoria that does. So, there I headed.

Before the night was up, había conocido a varios de los waiters (casi todos gay—otro miracle here). Mientras pasaba por el café, uno de ellos, slim, guapo, dark-haired, called out, —*You're not from here, hey?* —*No shit*, le contesté. To my horror, it just slipped out! Por suerte, he just laughed. —*Come in here, sit down*, he commanded. That was Etienne, un chévere, feliz Afrikaner. Blew my mind—ni sabía que existiera esa posibilidad. Another waiter, Victor, había viajado por todo el mundo "including Texas" (me morí de risa), and was recently ejected del army on grounds of "mental instability" (code for feliz, se me hace). Before I knew it, había pasado horas allí, just chatting. Lee, it was the first time that had happened (aparte esa reggae night con el Sean—pero eso era otra cosa) desde que estoy en SA.

Lo pasé pipa y el Victor invited me to a *braai* (indigenous term for BBQ: la national obsession) al día siguiente en lo de sus parents.

What have I got to lose? pensé. Y fui. Again, lo pasé divino. *Lekker* fun, como dicen. Había un chingo de gente, little kids, varias familias Afrikaner medio nerdy y dull. Pero Etienne estaba, and Victor's brother Mark, quien es arqueólogo, varios artistas, y un vato del UK, Peter R. He'd come out here to work, como mecánico técnico. Hay muchos blue-collar immigrant workers en SA, porque no hay trabajo en el UK y lo hay aquí. For whites, obvio. Anyway, he'd come out con su wife, pero she'd hated SA y rajó last July. Filed for divorce y se volvió a Essex.

Everyone was *so* friendly, Lee. Funny, era la primera vez que me sentí tan at home in the company of S. Africans, y fíjate que most of them were Afrikaners—the mortal enemy, al menos so I thought. Los arquitectos del apartheid. Pero they asked so many questions: where was I was from, what was it like there, cuáles eran mis impressions of S. Africa? Parecían genuinely interested in *me*—y no porque yo fuera Roland's guhlfriend. Obvio, R. no tenía nada que ver. Y me sentí curiously proud, that I'd made these connections on my own.

Los padres de Victor son bastante wealthy, pero they're nothing like los Fraser. Nada snobby. We swam, ate a *braai* y luego jugamos interesting, weird word games, a bit like Dictionary, ¿te acuerdas? How we used to love to get high y jugar al Diccionario con Dan Dickison y la Marianne Breidenthal y el Schweggie y mis Berkeley pals? Anyway, it's been really strange, porque después de meses de total loneliness y aislamiento, de repente I went from 0 to 60 en un heartbeat: I was hardly alone at all toda la semana que estuvo fuera Rolo. Con Etienne and Vic y Peter y otros new friends fui al cine, for coffee en el Tivoli Gardens, or just over to their flats pa' charlar y escuchar música. Lee, me sentí otra. I mean, yo misma. Como si hubiese estado muerta y ahora resucité.

Lo más importante fue la b-day fest de Etienne (10th Jan.). Hizo un champagne buffet en el Tivoli, con guests eccéntricos y fascinantes. Mucha gente feliz, ballet y hasta flamenco (?) dancers, clothing designers. Casi todos Afrikaners. Ya te puedes imaginar el culture shock. Since I've been here, solo he conocido a los English. All R.'s friends, y su familia, of course. Etienne había invitado al Peter R., el vato británico del *braai*. Me había caído bien allí—he was hilarious y bien witty en el Dictionary game. Y en la fiesta de Etienne we chatted a lot. It was noisy and hot and crowded en el Tivoli, so nos sentamos al bar y tomamos vino y hablamos. Era interesante— comforting—hablar con otro expatriate pero no-americano. No es, para nada, el typical cold, bumbling "Pommie" (así les dicen a los del UK aquí—derogatory). Los Afrikaners also call them (and English S. Africans) Engelsman or *soutie*, which literally means salty, y se refiere (super vulgar-mente) a que según, tienen one foot in S. Africa, el otro en England y la polla dangling in the deep blue sea! Isn't that hilariously insulting? Pero anygüey este Peter británico es earthy y funny, bien warm.

De repente, don't ask me how, el Victor organized an impromptu mini-fest—*en mi casa.* ¿Te lo imaginas? Roland would have freaked out. Y yo alucinaba, pero we'd been at the Tivoli for hours, y yo vivo al ladito mero. All of a sudden my lonely, barren flat blossomed with about 50 people, casi todos Afrikaners y strangers. Era tan surreal, Sloth. All these people sitting around my nearly empty flat tomando whiskey y escuchando los cassettes you'd (thank God) sent me, en un ridiculous, tiny tape re-corder. And it didn't matter at all. Me sentí tan aceptada, tan relaxed. Tan at home! Fumamos mota (yo no lo había hecho en siglos, as you know; plus, it's mega illegal here, digo, lock you up y tirar la llave illegal)—yo temía ponerme paranoica, pero I swear, Cuz, esa mota (*dagga*, le dicen) fue espectacular. Mellow y trippy. Algunos comenzamos a bailar, whirl-ing around el bare living room (lounge, le dicen) con esa inspired sound-track que me mandaste—Talking Heads, Laurie Anderson, Roxy Music, the English Beat, Peter Gabriel. Luego, one of the guys played flamenco guitar—beautifully.

A todo esto, el Peter R. había traído unos candies de la birthday party de Etienne, y mientras bailábamos, somehow me parecía lo más natural del mundo que él me metiera uno en la boca. I mean, con un beso, obvio. I'm sure you can see where this is headed, Cuz . . .

*(next day)*

I'm at work now, y te tengo que contar algo raro y bien unpleasant. Last night, resulta que Roland was spying on this letter, mientras yo te escribía.

Not quite sure cuánto leyó before I caught on, and snatched the paper back. Pero puso el grito en el sky. He acted all medieval y machista—hasta me dijo que se sentía "cuckhold." Aunque he'd be loathe to admit it, me parece que he's jealous of Peter. Muy. In fact, te diría que he's rattled by my having made friends (on my own).

De alguna manera, aunque me carga que me espíen, it was kind of a good thing that he saw part of this letter. Nos ha servido de catalyst. I'd already put my foot down al no acompañarle a Durban, para esa snob-fest boda. Y antes de eso, cuando le leí el riot act about going to his parents' every fucking weekend. Pero this was different. Roland went on and on about morality y de que one can't just give up and succumb to infidelity cuando las cosas ya no están quite as exciting as in the beginning y bla bla. Barajó una bola de traditional, boring ideas que me dejaron anonadada. Y furiosa. Le recordé que de hecho, he'd had a girlfriend cuando nos conoci-mos. Pero eso no contaba porque according to him, I somehow magically bewitched him. That's rich—besides, yo no tenía idea de que tuviera "steady guhlfriend" when we met. I only found out later. Le dije que he's twisting morality around pa' acomodar sus conservative, sexist views. Ay, Lee. You get the idea. Entre otras cosas, me sentí bien sad. Toda achicopaladita.

Anyway, la convo went on and on, we argued casi toda la noche. About the gradual waning de nuestra formerly legendary sex life. Pero I mean, come on, *what* sex life? Si desde que llegué, last August, consiste en me sneaking down to his childhood bedroom to fuck surreptitiously en la casa de sus padres. ¿Quién se pone cachonda under these circumstances? Or, Rolo comes home "finished" (o sea, exhausto) de la diamond mine o duerme de día y nuestros schedules totally out of sync. También están los money problems. Obvio, these two topics are fatally intertwined, al menos para mí. Ironic, hey? His family's filthy rich, pero Rolo tiene tanta deuda con su dad (quien le pagó el overseas "holiday") que he's unable to come up with even half the rent, la comida, los gastos domésticos. ¿Te parece fair?

También hablamos (in a less heated way, al menos) del futuro y te confieso, Cuz, lo veo bastante turbio. ¿Te acuerdas que a few months ago Roland mencionó la posibilidad de ir a trabajar a una mina en Napa? I think I wrote you about that. It sounded like a dream to me then, y ahora . . . creo que that's all it was. No te digo que he *deliberately* deceived me. Pero I can't help but feel que now he's got me here, the truth is coming out. And it's all him, him, *him*. ¿Y para mí? Adapt or die. Lately me está diciendo que he'll probably have to stay in SA another 3–5 years MINIMUM, porque he needs "experience underground." Y ahora me viene a confesar que ni sabe qué tipo de mining chamba he could "realistically" get in the US. Que he might need an advanced degree, que esto que lo otro.

It's all beginning to feel . . . incoherente, fuzzy, norteado. To think: we'd even talked about getting married in the States en julio. Pero ¿pa' qué? What would that solve? Parece que R. wishes I could just . . . be fulfilled en mi UNISA job, and happy as his guhlfriend. Pero that's not the woman he fell in love with! Ever since I pitched up in his country, no creo que piense mucho en *mí*, much as it kills me to write that. Digo: en quién yo soy.

Strangely, I've begun to feel less urgency about returning to the US en estas últimas semanas. Algo tendrá que ver, I reckon, con mis new friends. And don't think me crazy, Lee, pero mi expat idilio con el Peter R. de alguna forma me ha renovado la pasión por Roland. Isn't that strange? Por eso escribí lo de *Jules et Jim*. No nos confundamos: I think R. and I are sort of falling apart. Vacilo entre la rabia y la desilusión. And: his mother definitely can't stand me. Es tan obvio. Every time we go there, aumenta la tensión. She infinitely preferred la anterior guhlfriend de R., who was "dumb as a post" según las twins (and even R. himself!). Yo no tengo nada en común con Mrs. F.—y me importa un pepino. Es burguesa y racista. Ironic y frustrante, porque Rolo's sisters and his dad adore me. Pero la Ma F. wears the pants—eso se ve a leguas. Anyway, agárrate: my desire for R. (menguante en los últimos meses, between our every weekend en Joburg y mi creciente resentimiento y loneliness) has come roaring back, como side effect de mi romance con Peter, este gentle, funny, sensual, working-class Brit. Perverse y confusing, lo sé. Ay, don't be too hard on me, Cuz. Me siento tan alive again . . . después de meses de sonámbula.

Haven't told anyone else about all this, ni mucho menos J2 (June and Joe)—they'd only tell me to come home y no quiero. Write me soon, Prima. Te echo de menos. Ay, ¿por qué todo siempre tan apocalyptic conmigo (*don't* answer that!)?

*15-ii-83*

Queridos Mother and Daddy,

Howzit, como dicen acá. Hablé con Lee y Helen, and with my friend Augusto Castells. Me dijeron que they were taking Augusto to visit you last Sunday, el 6. Espero que sí, y que el Castells told you about UNISA, y nuestro road trip, and showed you some foties.

I've been dreading writing you this letter. De hecho, lo postergué. I wanted to be as sure as possible antes de escribirles, pero estoy casi segura que it won't come as a complete surprise. Después de pensarlo mucho, y mucha angustia, I've decided to separate from Roland. No me pregunten si es temporary or permanent—I'm not sure. First of all: no se alarmen. Tengo buena chamba—ironically, the best job I've ever had. Tengo donde vivir, and I have friends (míos propios). Things with R. are not hostile . . . por lo general.

Tengo mixed feelings. I still love him, pero sobre todo, creo, me siento bien disappointed. And bitter at him. I do blame him for some things pero otras se me hace que son el resultado inevitable de esta sociedad y de su upbringing. Es verdad, una persona más independent (despite his friends' nickname for him, "Rough, Rugged, and Independent," no lo es en absoluto—what a laugh, she says grimly) podría haber tomado otras decisiones, otras acciones.Taken *some* action! But he hasn't, ya sea por complacencia o por miedo. Maybe both. Ha estado como . . . paralyzed. Deer-in-the-headlights. Comfortably numb, *pace* Floyd Rosa.

Desde el primer momento que puse pie en S. Africa, y vi . . . todo esto (not just the country, the glaring inequality and indignities y el racismo del apartheid, me refiero a sus propias circunstancias familiares), I sensed the deck was stacked against me. En contra de *nosotros*. Vi su mundo tan bourgeois, tan materialistic. Everything ordered, mapped out. Y también vi (to my chagrin and mounting horror) que Roland fits in well here. Nunca ha tenido que cuestionar su place and really, why would he? That he'd rise to the top of this social order parece preordained: from Head Boy en Michaelhouse (ya sé que you've never heard of it, neither had I, obvio! Pero it's the most prestigious English-speaking boys' boarding school en S. Africa) to a brilliant career en la Navy, to the top graduate en su clase en mining engineering en Wits, la U. of the Witwatersrand, la Great (White) Liberal uni. Y su job ahora: mining engineer at Premier Diamond Mine (home of the Cullinan diamond, I promise you!). All this has paved his way hacia la gloria: a top management or consulting job en la S. African mining industry, con el requisite black Mercedes y membership en el all-male (all-white, por supuesto) Rand Club. Y bla bla . . .

Mom & Daddy, I didn't see this coming. I didn't see *any* of this el año pasado, when we first met, while we were together en nuestro país. You met him—el hombre de quien me enamoré era inteligente, sensitive, funny as hell. Nature-loving y outdoorsy pero a big reader, too. ¡Y tan handsome! And passionate—or so I thought. So he *seemed*. También se expresaba contra el apartheid. Pero now, here, veo que he doesn't really feel strongly enough about it como para cuestionar el sistema radicalmente. Like . . . leaving the country, por ejemplo. Tampoco creo que tenga las destrezas—the maturity, let's say—para negociar. Accepting only *part* of it (closeness con su familia, say, sin sucumbir al stranglehold que ahora ejerce en él), or living something less mapped-out, more tenuous: una vida conmigo en la que yo pudiera sentirme coherent con mis values, both ideological and personal. ¿Entienden?

I loved—*love*—Rolo, so at first, intentaba entender y aceptar lo que le importaba tanto. Mainly, la familia (but also . . . the *familiar*, lo veo ahora). Going there *every* bloody weekend! His dad was taken with me y las twins me adoraban. They're only 13, young enough como para no haber sucumbido a las garras de Ma Fraser: the pinched, Calvinistic spirit que ella impone en su hogar, en su familia in the name of morality. Pero coño, comencé a ponerme cada vez más resentful. I couldn't believe "Mr. Rough, Rugged e Independiente" would never question my immediate and absolute . . . *incorporation* into La Familia (sorry, me doy cuenta de que this sounds like the Mafia pero I swear that's what it's felt like!), especially since it's been obvious from the get-go que su madre me teme. Y también: she doesn't value el tipo de persona que soy, ni de donde vengo. Me he sentido swept up in this nauseating wave of . . . housewifery. Lo único que habla Mrs. F. son temas banales tipo clubs and parties, recipes y la iglesia. O peor: how bad it looks cuando los domestics (black servants) cogen el teléfono en el lounge (living room) delante de los guests. Can you believe that?

She also goes on and on about the evils of working mothers y critica el living together antes del matrimonio. Obvio, this is a direct condemnation of *me* (pero su darling scion, Roland, remains unscathed).

Hace poco, R. finally me confesó que su mother no cree que él sea "old enough" to be independent. That was the limit! Anyway, llegó un punto cuando la tensión entre la Ma F. and me could no longer be ignored. —*Speak to her*, le rogué a Roland. Para aclarar de una puta vez if she actually didn't like me, or *what*, exactly, she objected to. What are her fears? Yo me sentía cada vez más nerviosa y frustrada. Todos los weekends bajo el scrutiny de esa provincial, uptight cold fish. ¿Y Rolo? He avoided the issue. Hasta que un día un family friend le dijo a Rolo que hablara con su mother porque he sensed she was "worried about him." And guess what she was so worried about? You got it: *your daughter*. La Mrs. F. le dijo a R. que I might spoil his career chances by not being "the right sort of wife." ¿Y lo que más temía? That I'd induce Roland "to give everything up and go live in America."

Well, J2 (para June and Joe, jaja), as you can imagine, cuando Roland me contó esto I hit the roof. Temblaba de indignación, de rabia. Maybe most of all at R., por no tener las agallas de enfrentar a su madre. ¿Amenaza a su illustrious future career? *How?* ¡Si tengo degree from Harvard! Plus, ironically, I'd been *especially* mindful about not alienating his mother, recordando tus consejos, Mom. —*The best way to win a man is to win over his mother.* Well, perdonen mi bluntness pero that didn't work out so well for you, ¿que no? Is that how you "won" Daddy? Let's be honest: you couldn't *stand* Grandma Edna, ni en pintura. No te culpo. I mean damn, she didn't even go to your boda y las pocas veces que nos visitó you could cut la tensión entre Uds. dos con cuchillo. Pero put your lana where your mouth is, mamá. Porque la verdad es que you pushed Daddy to choose between you—y tú ganaste. I remember . . . I can hear Daddy telling me que en una, while you were engaged, le había dado úlcera por todo el stress between you and his mother. Y que el médico le dijo, —*Look sonny, who's it gonna be, your mother or your wife?* Hubo consecuencias, anyone can see that. For all of us, de hecho. Dad gave up a lot pa' estar contigo— don't even get me started. Pero the upshot was, you put your foot down y ganaste.

Supongo que if push came to shove, I'd hoped Roland would make the same choice, aunque I honestly didn't think it would come to that. O no tan . . . pronto, y tan tajantemente. Pero hearing esas insulting boludeces de la Mrs F. precipitated a crisis. Roland dice que me ama. Over and over, *siempre* lo ha dicho. Pero from my perspective, me parecía que if the love was there, once we'd worked out los geographic details, podríamos tener una vida fulfilling, exciting, even. Ojo, no soy pendeja: I knew this would mean compromises. Pero comenzó a parecerme que los compromisos were all one-sided: de mi parte.

After this crisis, R. me ha admitido que he supposes he's been selfish, he can see that. Pero he seems compelled to proceed según una estructura determinada y leyes inmutables. No puede hablar de "marriage and children" yet, while his future is so "precarious." Pero I don't care about marriage! Si está el commitment (o sea: him putting me—*us*—before his mother), the rest can be worked out. Struggled over, quizás, pero worked out. Pero parece que él lo ve al revés: the security and position and lifestyle must be worked out *first* . . . ¿Ven el dilema?

Estoy llegando a la conclusión de que all Rolo's talk about returning to the States (hasta mencionó trabajar en una mina en Napa . . .), todas sus hermosas, románticas palabras en las cartas—all those letters!—and even afer I got here, earlier on, were just that: *words*. "Pretty lies," como dice Joni Mitchell. Me estruja escribirles esto, pero Roland is motivated by fear and security mientras que a mí me motiva la esperanza, la pasión y quizás more than anything, la curiosidad. Remember Daddy, lo que me dijo Cortázar en Berkeley? Que hay dos tipos de personas en el mundo: los *famas*, motivados por el miedo y la necesidad de los sistemas y los *cronopios*, motivados por una childlike, ludic curiosity. And by a distrust of systems! —*Y vos Susana*, he told me, *sos cronopio*. Sigh . . .

Mamá, I know you thought it was wonderful Roland was close to his family y que le gustara tanto la naturaleza, el bushveld. I know you had high hopes I'd be able to fit into this new kind of life (even if Dad and I were *never* really all that into Yosemite y el river rafting y el hiking y bla bla que a ti tanto te fascina). Well, I gave it a go, te lo juro. Pero cuanto más tiempo pasaba con su familia (OK, especially his mother) más *mi propio upbringing* me ponía los pelos de punta. They're superficial, bourgeois social-climbers; no se apasionan en las after-dinner convos de política y cultura like we do. No se apasionan—y punto. Creo que Gordon is different—there's more to him. Pero la Ma F. rules the roost. El se escapa mucho en su work, o bien just . . . into himself. He's a Libra, like Daddy. Cool-warm, más intelectual. Hidden depths, sospecho. Pero su vibe, su presencia, no predomina en la casa Fraser. Al contrario.

Mi amiga Anita Wurfl (la ecuatoriana, from UNISA) me ha dicho que obviously Roland was powerfully attracted to something in me, se enamoró precisamente, Anita thinks, de mi *diferencia*. And: he felt the confidence y sobre todo la libertad de enamorarse de mí en mi país. And he felt it strongly enough to tell me, —*You can bank on it, Chávez. I love you.* Y me pidió que viniese a Sudáfrica—about the *last* place on earth I thought I'd ever end up! Me ha dicho que I'm the most fascinating woman he's ever known—and he *still* thinks so. Anita cree (and so does Castells, y hasta la Lee W.) que si nos hubiésemos quedado en los States, the relative freedom there (especially for Rolo) y la distancia de su familia would've enabled us to flourish on our own terms.

I felt him to be . . . *different* casi casi desde que me bajé del avión, last August. I felt the *weight* of it—del apartheid, de su lugar en este mundo—pressing down on me cual lápida. Y también intuí que he wouldn't have the strength to change, to reject things que me eran intolerables. Para cuando Rolo comenzó a hablar de "alternatives"—because he could tell he was losing me, que yo me le estaba cerrando, submitting to despair and frustration (Anita cree que comenzó en el road trip al Cabo con Castells, when I was able to talk to los Spurgess, conocer a gente, ver el país desde mi propia mirada)—maybe me going back to work on my doctorate, quizás vivir separados un tiempo, him joining me later, yo ya había perdido prácticamente toda esperanza.

Like I said before, no creo que Gordon sea tan . . . supercilious e hipócrita y judgmental como la Mrs F. Lo irónico es que Roland tampoco es así. Ugh—I'd never in a million years have fallen in love with him si lo fuera. Es inteligente y hay en él una sensibilidad, the ability to *question* que no veo en su familia. Pero lo frustrante—lo trágico, if you come right down to it—es que no tenga la confianza de permitir que estas cualidades se muestren. Not in his country, not in his family home donde rige el decoro, el terror del "qué dirán" y la Gran Costumbre, *pace* Julio Cortázar.

Que qué corno voy a hacer, I know you're wondering. It's strange (y no se me escapa la ironía, don't worry) pero por primera vez en la vida I can save money. No quiero comprar bienes materiales en este godforsaken racist place—a token protest, perhaps (since my presence alone me produce un chingo de guilt), pero algo es algo. Ya sé que I came here expressly (and *only*) por Roland, pero although I can't quite say why, exactly, I'm not sorry I came here. Alan Weinberg (lecturer in English en UNISA, marido de mi amiga Grazia, a lecturer in Italian) me hablaba el otro día de un French philosophy professor que enseñó unos años en UNISA. He'd been at the Sorbonne before that. Volvió a París, pero now he's returned to S. Africa. He feels the lure, tal como yo comienzo a sentirlo, de estar inmerso en una sociedad que te obliga a vivir on the edge (*pace* Norman Mailer, gran machista pero right about some things). Al filo de uno mismo, looking inward. Y al filo del peligro, the taut, palpable sense of something about to happen. Como escribió Nadine Gordimer (in the novel *Burger's Daughter*, regalo de Roland, en cuya inscripción me pidió que viniera aquí)—citing Lévi-Strauss, creo recordar—"You are the place in which something will happen."

So, I've decided to remain at UNISA hasta fin del año. And then, veré lo de grad school. For now, me he mudado con Etienne. Remember, mi amigo feliz, del café Tivoli Gardens. He has a lovely flat, todo amueblado. Less than half the rent we've been paying en el Place Pigalle. O, digamos, *I've* been paying (pero I don't wanna get into that now) . . . Please give my new address to Granny, y mis hermanas. Les escribo pronto. I'll be OK. He aprendido un chingo. Above all: que el *amor NO vincit omnia* . . .

P.D. Llevo siiiglos working on this letter! It's *so* hot, me siento tan drenada. It's now Feb 18th. Una fecha muy meaningful for me and Roland. Exactly a year ago today estábamos en Houston (remember, mamá?). Madly in love y camino al Mardi Gras. I've read most of this letter aloud to R. y por más que le cueste, dice que he agrees with my analysis, en lo principal. Y sin embargo, somehow, he *insists* he's still in love with me and "has hope for the future." ¿Y yo? *Ek weet nie* . . .

*10-iii-83*
*Postcard, ex London*

Dearest Sloth,

   ¿Hablaste con Paq o la Bizzy B.? If so, no te sorprenderá este postmark from England. Lesotho dizque fucking "clinic" a nightmare. Peligro mortal. Scary, horrible. No se pudo. Por suerte, I had some ahorros y por embarrassing que fuera (ya que I had to explain my um . . . *delicate* condición al dept. chair, can you believe *that* primitive patriarchal BS?), got a salary advance from UNISA pa' pagar el airfare. Peter arranged my stay con su hermana Linda y su familia in their hometown, Sible Hedingham, an impossibly beautiful, teensy medieval village in Essex, a dos horas de Londres. Almost perversely happy (al menos relieved) to be here in old, comfortingly COLD Europe.

Anyway, it is done. Fue horrible, Cuz: general anaesthesia, unbearable nausea, me desperté sobbing, totalmente disoriented. Peter me ha llamado. Strangely, Roland me llamó aquí a la Rosslyn Clinic también. I even spoke with his dad, ¿ surreal, no? All this concern for my well-being AHORA . . .

   I think I *must* write a book about this en el futuro. What I had to go through pa' llegar aquí. All the way to Londres, coño. Te juro, Lee, this word will send shivers down my spine forever: Lesotho.

*10-iii-83*
*10:30 a.m.*
*Rosslyn Clinic, London*
*Diario*

Cuánto me gustaría ver mi diary entry de hace un año. Pero que yo recuerde, it wasn't important. The date emblazoned en la memoria: el 6 de marzo. Roland dejó mi país, returning to the undermundo (ella dice, con amargura). Back to la tierra del apartheid. That night, the Larsen-Feiten concert en San Francisco, mi primo el Art Rodríguez on drums. Partying con Art y el Lenny Castro y la Trish after the show, en nuestro little apartment on Chestnut Street. Holding the bereftness at bay con la coca y el cognac (my fave alliteration), la risa, el baile. Dreading la incipiente soledad, la distancia geográfica entre Rolo y yo.

And now a year later, heme aquí en Rosslyn. The Morning After. Here I sit, mirando por la frosted window estos bare London trees, gray streets, milk-pale sky. Against all odds, me siento casi hermosa this morning. No more queasy tummy—aunque se siente bien sore to the touch, tender. Los horribles mareos, my constant shadow estas últimas semanas, quelled by a metal probe in my womb. A 10-minute op, tal me dicen, anyway: no me acuerdo de nada. I only remember counting backward, terrified que no funcionara. Like when I was ten, esa horrible tooth op en el hospital. The only other time, creo, que he tenido general anesthesia. Pero this time, me desperté con una terrible angustia. Huge, heaving sobs, como si . . . out of nowhere. —*You arright, luv? Just breathe now. Easy, easy.* For a minute, el llanto made no sense to me, presa de un dolor que emanaba de antes de esa . . . blank *nada.* Then it hit me. Pero el desconcierto, that clutching sorrow, parecía ser . . . de otra. De una lejana (*pace* Cortázar). Desde muy lejos, una soothing British nurse-voice que me reconfortaba. —*S'arright, luv. Just a bad reaction to the anesthesia, innit.*

Luego, they brought me to this room. A la deriva, entre sueño y vigilia, for hours. Pesadillas all last night. I'd wake up y luego por más que batallara, ese irresistible undertow. Just like JC's moteca, ¡coño! Soñé con Lesotho. Peter's apprehensive, resolute face. Esos twisty, nausea-inducing mountain roads. Esa sordid, filthy "clínica." Dreamed of Rolo too. Yo le gritaba y gritaba and he couldn't hear me. Or, no. Sí que me escuchaba, creo, pero he didn't answer me. Lo cual viene a ser lo mismo. O peor. Must've been the fucking anesthesia . . .

*13-iii-1983*
*Sible Hedingham, Essex*
*Diario*

Mi cumple a week away. Last year en Santa Cruz, en lo de Mamá y Daddy. Eating Mom's delish chocolate chip poundcake, esperando en taut count-down tu birthday phone call desde S. Africa. Bizzy B. y el Ronnie playing the piano. Mom cantando.

My heart bleeds sorrow. Sé que esto es metáfora, medio medieval, pero I don't care: this *is* a bloodletting. Ay, I want never to return to UNISA. I need time to think and feel (and heal), y demasiado pronto el infernal calor de nuevo. Ese hot, empty flat sin fridge. Fuck. Who lives like that excepto en estado de emergency? Desde cuando have I *ever* lived like that? Sé que me vas a exigir explanations y sé que te las debo pero . . . ahhhh, Rolo. Now that I've read this beautiful, true, wrenching book, *Braided Lives* (de Marge Piercy), me gustaría decirte solo esto: I love you.

No tiene sentido, I know that. Pero neither does what's happened to us. Look at me, mira donde estoy. Insistes en mi "infidelity," para recalcar how much I've hurt you. Pero your capitulation hurt me, Rolo. Tu parálisis y tu miedo. Y sin embargo, a pesar de todo esto—y me parece tragic, *completely* avoidable a la vez que irrevocable—I love you. Our bright beginning in my land, which whispered freedom to you tal como el tuyo speaks of bondage to me. Si solo no fuésemos tan . . . proud. Si solo pudieses ver más allá de . . . tu family, Joburg every weekend. Tu fucking job. It doesn't all have to be so regimented, coño. If, if, if . . .

Esta crimson penitencia chorrea a borbotones de mi prized-open womb. Same blood as last year, ¿te acuerdas, my darling? Our little zygote. Pero this time, yo misma me sometí a esta odyssey. Lesotho, ahora Londres. Pa' que me lo extirparan. No way iba a parir yo un South African citizen bajo el apartheid. No, no y no. So now heme aquí, Rolo, wretched with fright. Rich solid scarlet me mancha las panties de noche. Me aterra que they might have . . . left something inside me. Que no haya médico que me ayude when I return to S. Africa. ¿Te preocupa esto? Do you worry about *anything* besides your fucking wounded orgullo? It's 1983, pero mi rabia y miedo, el sentido de betrayal y danger son timeless. They belong to the province of women, y esto me redobla la rabia.

*14-iii-1983*
*Sible Hedinham, Essex*
*Diario*

Me miro al espejo. It's been *so* long—semanas, months quizás. Me he sentido tan thick and formless (si bien intermittently tan *Jules and Jim* erotic, too, antes de que me comenzaran los mareos, los vómitos). Casi casi sin distinguishing features. Just a female—hopelessly stretched, exhausta, washed out. This morning, me siento beautiful. Ya no me encuentro nauseated ni bloated ni tired. Almost no pain. Me siento comfy in my long limbs. My hair a wild dark halo en este frío, esta British damp.

Pero I ache inside. No he purgado la rabia, el miedo, ni mi bitter disappointment or betrayal. My sorrow porque sé que te he hecho daño, Rolo (por más que quieras recluirte en tu pride). Hace unas semanas you admitted some stuff, finally. Cracked open (tal como hacías el año pasado en mi cama, or on our long cross-county road trips, remember?). So, no eres tan "rough, rugged, and independent" after all, Mr. (ex?) Montenegro. You need love. You just didn't calculate how big it would be, cómo te sentirías inside it. Living with it. Digo, una vez back en tu home turf, en Joburg.

Me encuentro careening entre mighty rage y leve, numb irritación. Sé que it doesn't make sense, pero es así. ¿Por qué carajo no usé better judgment? A pampered mama's boy es lo que eres, por más independiente que parecieras en tu overseas holiday last year. Pero these two irreconcilable extremes se sintetizan en una all-consuming sadness: I know it's over. Soy demasiado proud, myself, como para volver patrás. Even if you wanted to (*do* you?).

I love you, Rolo. Y me dices que me amas. Pero nuestra love story solo tiene sentido en mi país. Or in the in-between no-man's-land de nuestra correspondencia, fueled by memory y la imaginación.

*15-iii-1983*
*Ides of March!*
*Sible Hedingham, Essex*
*Diary*

I met my beloved primavera after all. Quizás por eso I felt so certain coming here would be the right thing. Ni modo que el padre de Peter repita "cheers mate" over and over, o que su mamá me pregunte que cómo se siente, living among a lot of blacks. Pa' mis adentros I'm rolling my eyes, pero de la boca pa' jucra (jaja), I just leave it. Después de meses de ratcheting-up tension con la madre de Roland, no puedo más. I'm meek as a lamb here in England, wrung out.

No tengo nada en común, really, con los padres de P., pero what does it matter? No siento esa terrible pressure: de conformar, impresionar, callarme. If they want to ask questions (about me, about me and P.) pos que pregunten nomás. Hasta ahora, no mucho. Su hermana Linda sí. Pero nada . . . heavy. Well, I take that back: cuando me llevaba a la Rosslyn Clinic, me preguntó. If the baby was Peter's. — *Of course*, le dije, sin titubeos (crossing my fingers mentalmente). She's been lovely to me. Y su hubby el Ken y el hijito, Lee, y las baby twins too. Adorables.

And their town: este pueblito medieval, Sible Hedingham. Parece picture postcard pero te juro, it *really* looks this way. Te lo voy a descibir. Lee, I'm thinking of you, now, tu ojo de artista. O mi hermana Sarita. Los bedtime tales I used to spin for her de lugares fantásticos, insólitos. O de algo o alguien bien banal pero . . . looked at de modo diferente pa' que se volviera strange, maravilloso.

Todos los villages aquí en Essex tienen stone and brick buildings, calles angostas, algunas de cobblestone. Old inns y desde luego los ubiquitous pubs (con lo que a mí me REPUGNA la cerveza, jaja), occasionally una iglesia hermosa. The earth is a soft gray-green or pale brown, mist-shrouded. Nada que ver con la red, red African dirt. Los árboles still stark-bare. Charcoal dendrites, una felicitous tun of phrase (dice ella, proudly) que acuñé una vez en Boston, cuando viví el primer true winter de mi vida. Wow. Remembering Harvard. Todo eso se siente como . . . un long-ago dream. Supongo que Mom will try to talk me into going back there, pal PhD, ahora que les confesé que I'm no longer with Roland. Uf, bregaré con todo eso later.

There are fields and barns, animales, haystacks. Blessed moisture constantemente en el aire. No ha llegado la primavera, but it's coming. La veo en las dark, opulent vainas, los delicate buds ready to burst. My body's just relinquished its fruit, conceived en una strangely revived passion (R.), or lust/confusión coupled with a sort of ex-pat mutual reconocimiento (P.). No puedo estar 100 percent segura. Pero either way, sería too unbearably sad que la English countryside estuviera in full flower.

Caminé hoy con la madre de Peter, down to the mill. —*A proper working mill*, ella me informa, pero I wouldn't know the difference. De su brick country house cruzamos el jardín, past the rabbitry (¡así se llama!). Mrs. R. me dio tour earlier. The damp, pungent rabbit-pee scent casi pleasant en su earthy insistencia, los fluffy conejos a pink and white blur en sus suspended hotel rooms. Están allí para follar (oops, "for procreation," tee hee) y luego, pa' comer. Uf, bunny *braai*? No way! We pass around the fence y salimos a los wide, fallow fields.

Our feet fall into an easy rhythm, my hips jolt, pero softly, al conectar con las irregularidades de la tierra. Caigo en cuenta de que this is the first time I *really* feel myself walking en mucho tiempo. Tiene que ver con el countryside, creo (as opposed to Pretoria). Y más que nada, con este bracing, late-winter chill. Rolo, you were right cuando me dijiste que I bloom in the cold. Remember? Me lo dijiste en Chicago, a year ago. Cuando salimos a esas bleak, snowy streets después de nuestra long winter nap (ejém) en ese enorme walk-in closet. Salimos y ya era, incredibly, casi de noche y sabíamos que nuestro chariot was turning calabaza y nos pusimos tan sad, sad, sad.

Anyway, con la Mrs. R. no hablamos mucho. No need. Caminamos nomás, side by side. My womb contracts and shakes. Me preocupa la sangre. Am I bleeding through? No he usado estos bulky pads desde la high school, ugh . . . Absorbo, por las plantas de los pies and on upward, coursing through my body hacia las fingertips, even to my scalp, the rich, tobacco-colored mulch de las hojas caídas, el olor dulce, grassy de los shoulder-high bundles of hay. Doblamos en un senderito, leading to the mill. The river is high; cubre el sendero y nos obliga a cruzar en un narrow footbridge. El dizque working mill es una tall, white clapboard structure. No me parece functional pa' nada: it's dark inside y hay plantas raras, medio *Addams Family*, pressing against the windowpanes desde adentro, buscando la pale light. Veo una cocinita en la ground floor; incongruentemente, cosmetics atop a dresser in another room. Parece más country inn que otra cosa, pero there's no sign of life.

Dusk is approaching. Es esa violet hour, la hora que más me encanta. We round the mill y caminamos por la orilla del río. De repente, doy un silly little shriek: ¡hay crocuses! Ya sé, son los classic heralds of spring pero se me hace que these are the first (nonliterary) ones que he visto en la vida. Tiny, pert florcitas, adorables en su formalidad. Pequeñas manchitas de purple and white, los únicos colores en este landscape de puro gray, palest green, brown, black.

A flock of wild Canadian geese live on the river, me dice la Mrs. R. Sería too chévere to see them, pienso, after the glorious crocuses. Pero echo una mirada upriver longingly, por si acaso. Y allí están: prenden vuelo en una ragged V, toda la bandada, flying low over bare trees. Son maravillosos, tan graceful y majestic. Me dan unas ganas tremendas de llorar, all of a sudden. Llegamos al stile. Mrs. R. ducks under the fence, girlishly, pero yo elijo cruzar la cerca por el stile—a "stile" is just . . . little steps! I'm living in a Bronte novel, me río pa' mis adentros.

Nos alejamos del río en el gathering dusk, heading home. Veo una oveja y sus dos lambs en someone's field. Veo las casas en la main road, stacked one atop the next, algo higgledy-piggledy. A lo lejos, near the horizon, veo el humo que sube de la chimenea de una lovely white house. Más cerca, two boys chase an ugly black dog y se gritan en un broad, choppyish Essex accent. No es de ningún modo beautiful, pero it does to my ear lo que esta tierra a mi cuerpo. I'm suffused with tenderness, gratitude. Me siento casi calm, hasta enchanted. Como cuando leía *The Secret Garden* o *Wuthering Heights*.

Hemos llegado. I don't want to go in, pero soon the light will be lost. I turn toward the door, veo la cozy glow adentro. —*Come on then*, me dice la mamá de P. —*Let's have tea.*

16-iii-83
Postcard, ex London

Hi Lee,

¿Te gusta esta Hockney? Te la compré en Cambridge, earlier today. La mamá de Peter took me to Cambridge, y luego nos vinimos a Londres. Cambridge me pareció just like in the movies. O sea: a *real* university. Como Harvard, pero even older. Beautiful! Crocuses y patos en el río, 16th-century cathedrals, the Bridge of Sighs. Ahhhh.

There's been *a lot* of blood, pero I'll soon be OK . . . You'll *never* guess what I got mixed up in hace unas horas: ¡una gran protesta en la S. African Embassy! P.'s mother me llevó a Trafalgar Square, and there it was. Cruzamos la calle y nos metimos en una huge demonstration. Gente que llevaba giant posters: "Fight imperialism! Fight racism! Smash apartheid!" Can you imagine? Sentí a la vez exhiliration y guilt. I felt like . . . me again. Digo the "me" que en la uni participaba en los grupos anti-apartheid, fighting for la UC to divest. Pero luego apareció la "me" de ahora: la que vive entre los enemigos y vino a London pa' abortar. Cognitive dissonance total, Cuz. Anyway, el broche de oro: la mamá de P. me llevó a un trendy salón y me hice un corte bien punky. Still long pero shortish on top, y medio pinkish-red. I'll send you foties later. Miss you!

25-iii-83
Oversized postcard (de Prince Charles)
Back in Pretoria.

My darling cousin Sloth,

Mil gracias por la gorgeous, moving (y take-no-prisoners) letter. Ya que I know you're such a big fan, te mando este signed portrait of HRH Prince Chuck! I got back OK, pero I'm swamped en el trabajo. Tengo que preparar una study guide (para el 31), a Saturday class for tomorrow y pilas de tareas pa' corregir.

Physically, I'm slowly recovering. Mentally y emocionalmente—es otra cosa. Vacilo entre anger, betrayal, sorrow y confusión (porque part of me still loves R.). Brace yourself: Roland tuvo una heart-to-heart convo con su papá (while I was in England), y ahora he swears he's seen "the error of his ways." Es más: he proposed marriage! Can you fucking believe that? Estoy en shock. How'd he summon the courage (knowing how his mother feels about me)? No estoy segura . . . te cuento más luego.

Etienne sale pa' Cape Town on April 1st, for 2 months. Voy a vivir sola, en su flat. I need breathing room now—*that* I do know. Bizzy B. y la Helen called me on my b-day, BTW. Pero la Helen only managed to upset me. Me dijo, —*You went there to be with Rolo—make it work!* Le dije, —*I just can't, at least not now.* Y me respondio, —*Oh well, easy come, easy go, I guess.* Isn't that heartless? She was with me and R. desde el get-go. Conoce quizás mejor que nadie nuestra love story . . .

*28-iii-83*

Dearest Eva,

Tan thrilled to receive your long letter, despachada por nuestro faux-primo, el Tim Golden (no puedo creer que te hayas topao con el Timo Dorado en Managua)—ex Marina del Rey. And no, you weren't "too paranoid" asking him to mail it desde Califas. Agárrate: several of my letters have been "randomly" opened by BOSS (equivalente sudafricano de la DINA en Chile), y hasta abrieron un paquete de educational materials que me mandó Dad. Grotesco, right? Pero not surprising.

Aquí respondo a lo que me cuentas en tu latest letter (about Nica dizque-libre . . .), pero just quick-quick como dicen aquí. Estoy super-atareada en UNISA y me urge traerte up to date en lo mío. *So* much has happened en estos últimos meses, no te lo vas a creer. Pero first: en cuanto al proceso "revolucionario" (in quotes porque por lo que me escribes, it seems more like proceso retrógrado o anquilosado), sadly I'm not all that surprised. I mean, about what you wrote y tu reacción. Me duele verte así, in such a state of desengaño (valga el barroquismo). Solo espero puedas usar este nuevo y ojiabierto (does this word even exist? Jaja, if not, la acuñé) realismo y objetividad (and I refuse to apologize for using this word, no obstante que los revolucionarios más card-carrying y rabiosos estén rolling their eyes in horror) para forjar tu propio activismo desengañado—in your own world. There, he dicho.

De mí . . . sigh. I've started *so* many letters to you desde enero, hermana. Lo más importante: I'm no longer with Roland. No sabes lo que me estruja escribirlo, pero it's been about a month. A verrr, ¿cómo resumírtelo? Rereading my diary se ve que sentí—almost from the start—que él no era, aquí, el mismo hombre de quien me había enamorado (in our country). Le vi trapped, cual caged beast pero a la vez creepily complacent con la jaula. Constrained por el peso inexorable de su social class, su job y su familia. Pero no matter how hard I tried, me parecía que I couldn't get through to him about this.

El siempre afirmaba que he loved me (to this day he *still* does), pero Eva, nunca llegamos a construir un mundo propio. I don't mean isolated de la realidad circundante (aunque I confess this is an overwhelming temptation, viviendo bajo este sistema que odio) sino . . . deshacernos un little hair de las fucking garras metidoras de su family (léase su mother, en particular). Te confieso que la solución que encontré wasn't constructive—más bien un escape hatch o especie de salvavidas: conocí a un vato británico en un *braai* (BBQ party). Shocking, lo sé (you can ask Lee for details, ella lo sabe todo), pero te dije que a lot has changed.

I have my own friends now, los conocí a principios de año, una semana cuando R. estuvo out of town. Y estos friends—*all* Afrikaners, lo cual es más que irónico—me presentaron a un British friend, Peter. Al principio pensé que sería un fluke, a fling. Pero luego las cosas se complicaron. To say the least. R. volvió de Durban (he'd been best man en una high-society boda—lo cual no me interesaba ni un punto, por eso I'd stayed home in Pretoria) and for a few highwire weeks I was sneaking around, viéndome con Peter pero still living with Roland—I even introduced the two. Era todo muy uncomfortable and weird y a la vez kind of . . . sexy y highly charged. Total, Rolo eventually found out. Creo que (unconsciously) I must've wanted him to. Estaba destrozado, llorando y rabiando. Pero pronto se puso bien moralistic y judgmental. Totally siglo XIX, que cuckhold this, infidelity that. Agarras la onda ¿no?

Around mid-February todo se crispó: abandoné nuestro flat y me mudé con mi new friend, Etienne, un camarero feliz super chévere. Pero la cosa se pone peor: I'd fallen pregnant, como dicen aquí. Can you believe that? Las circunstancias couldn't have been worse: viviendo bajo increíble tensión, new chamba in a foreign country, which, by the way, is a racist, authoritarian dictadura. Y, oh, the hottest summer in ten years, según dicen. Para colmo, se me estaba subiendo la bilis (according to the doctor who confirmed my embarazo, en un appointment awkward y scary, cuando supo que he couldn't call me *mevrou*, o sea Mrs.). In other words, estuve a punto de un relapse de la hepatitis.

Contemplé mi estado (ya sé: suena a Garcilaso poem. Y bueno, the desperation's the same si bien *no* el setting bucólico ni la causa), y tomé una decisión. No way was I gonna bring a baby into this world como S.

African citizen. Traumas horribles con Rolo y Peter. En cuanto le dije a R. que the baby wasn't his (I wasn't sure, y de hecho it probably *was*; pero no quería que me presionara a . . . casarme, a dar a luz aquí), predictably, se enfureció. Vaciló entre el llanto y una actitud fría, bien callous. Peter, en cambio, estaba hurt. Para más inri: él también se declaraba in love with me. *And* he wanted me to have the baby! Pero al final, we both agreed que esto sería un desastre. El no está tan politizado como yo, pero igual, he hates apartheid.

What to do? Aquí comenzó la pesadilla: in a dizque Christian country, donde "procurar" el aborto es ilegal, todo huele a traición, everything feels dangerous, sleazy, surreptitious. Médicos que alguien había "oído" que they'd performed abortions. Yo fui a verles y . . . me trataron de loca, o puta. Or worse. And all the while este nudo en la panza, growing cual fruto maligno pero (parcialmente) anhelado. El calor incesante, los ojos ya casi amarillentos (uf, now I sound like a Neruda poem). Having to go to work y que nadie se enterase. El dolor y la rabia de Roland, el dolor y la aprehensión de Peter.

Finally, alguien nos platicó de una clinic in Lesotho (look on a map: it's *completely* surrounded by SA, pero es un dizque "independent" kingdom) donde se podía, pero illegally. Ya desesperada, consulté con una acquaintance, Charmain Pillay (an Indian journalist I met thru el Castells, en nuestro road trip to Cape Town) y ella me habló de un high-ranking journalist, Norman Chandler. Trabaja donde la Charmain (Joburg *Sunday Times*) y dio la "casualidad," jaja (ya sabes que I don't believe in coincidences) que lleva trabajando una story about this *very* clínica. We wait and wait, pa' que el tal Chandler regrese de Lesotho. He gives me la luz verde: simón, they do them there. Más de 100 "casos," con "only two mishaps." Obvio, no me puede dar detalles—"press secrets." Solo me explica que you rock up there and ask for a Dr. Rudolph (quien no existe: esto es code pa' la cosa) y . . . te ayudan. Cuesta R400.

Peter y yo lo hablamos, pero by now I'm so sick y tan desperate que really, ya no hay mucho que hablar. We rent a car y emprendemos el largo y triste trip to Lesotho. Se me ocurre que it's the road to hell: lo opuesto de mi road trip to the Cape, con el Castells—tan eye-opening, liberating— just a few months earlier. Al llegar a la capital, Maseru, entramos a un hotel. Caro y sucio pero we're worn out, scared y no sabemos nada de la ciudad ni del (teensy) country. We take a room. A pesar de nuestra by-now second-nature, mal escondida guilt y "simpatía blanca," we realize the staff is horribly rude, flat-out hateful, la verdad, *and* trying to rip us off. Na' que hacerle. Yo vomito tres veces en la bathtub—can't even make it to the toilet—antes de salir para la clinic. Incongruously, me doy cuenta de que the landscape is rural and beautiful, pero casi no pongo atención. Los nervios los tengo a flor de piel, a tight little knot of terror que me ahoga. Y veo que P. tiene las manos sudorosas, aferradas al steering wheel.

Llegamos. La so-called clínica es un building low, oscuro, filthy, pequeño y cutre. We enter, y en una voz trémula, I ask for "Dr. Rudolph." They direct us por aquí y por allá. Finally, sale una médica que nos mira con desprecio y nos pregunta —*Haven't you heard the news?* Cagados de miedo le decimos que no. She tells us to go back out to the car pa' escuchar la radio: van a dar un broadcast about a South African journalist que había estado la semana pasada haciendo interviews, sacando fotos y—en pocas palabras—preparing an exposé de la clinic. Hermana, me temblaba todo el cuerpo. Me sentí a la vez helada y sweat-drenched. We didn't hear anything en la radio pero en un flash of rage, caí: —*Norman Chandler, cabrón de mierda. It's you. All you fucking wanted was a dramatic P.S. to your story.* Por poco me da un telele, I promise you. I look at P. y veo que he sees it too. Y comienzo a recordar . . . little seemingly offhand things que me había dicho el Chandler, like que le llamara "straightaway when it's all over." Ese asshole me había hecho venir a este lugar de mala muerte, he'd set me up just for the money shot: un aborto más. Y si sangriento y botched, mejor pa' él.

Totalmente deshechos, we return to the clinic. Back inside, más espera. Hot, flies, buzzing fluorescent lights, esa luz mortecina que me pone los pelos de punta. Mareos y dry heaves. P. is trying to help, me quiere coger la mano pero estoy inconsolable, burning with rage y de un terror solitario. Finally—weirdly—nos dirigen a la casa (?) del médico: a Ghanaian con un stutter tan fuerte que apenas se le entiende. No, no y no, he tells us. Que after the "betrayal of that journalist" no hay manera. We just stand there wilting, sweating, aterrados. De repente, he changes his mind. Que volvamos a la clínica, he tells us. Wait for him there. — *What for?* le pregunto a

Peter. —*He's just testin' us, darlin'*, intenta consolarme. Can you fucking *believe* this pesadilla, Eva?

We trudge back to the clínica (se me ocurre just now, mientras te escribo esto: I'm really not even sure if it *was* one) y al rato vuelve el médico. Después de mucho tense hemming and hawing (literally), nos pide los passports. He looks them over y yo me encuentro begging him to do it, jurando que we're not South African, que we've got nothing to do with the press, etc. Finalmente he relents, pero bajo una condición: we have to stay the weekend in Lesotho, y para el lunes . . . Entonces we saw the light: he wanted to wait pa' ver si salía la nota del Chandler en los Sunday papers! Me quedé de PIEDRA, hermana. Still, I pressed on. Le pregunto que how would he do it, que si sería con vacuum aspiration, D&C, con o sin anestesia. Writing this, casi no puedo creer mi brazenness, mi aplomb. Pero remember que trabajé de volunteer en Planned Parenthood? Supongo que I summoned some vestigial shred of valentía: quería que ese tipo viese que I knew what was what. Well, medio me soslaya las preguntas or maybe solo haya sido su stutter. Pero either way, no me inspira confidence en absoluto. De repente, me entra la paranoia de que he's gonna try and abscond con los passports, report us to the authorities and . . . I'll give birth in an African jail. Prácticamente se los arranco de la mano y Peter le dice que we'll call him Monday (this was on a Friday), y volvemos a ese overpriced, hostile, depressing hotel.

Hermana, una angustia y confusión total. We hadn't eaten all day pero entre los vómitos y nuestro miedo—plus, we had no idea where to go y ya era de noche—we just gave up. Huddled together all night, entre la rabia y la desesperación. For two days, we stayed in that awful room. Me sentí . . . mercancía. Pura carne. My womb—no, *toda* yo—at risk en un juego de vida o muerte. En una illegal *maybe*-clínica en Lesotho, a la merced de un *maybe*-médico de Ghana—himself caught entre el miedo (of being busted) y la codicia—y un cynical South African yellow journalist.

Well, considerando tu experiencia con los desengaños periodísticos y políticos (in Managua, I mean), you probably already guessed: el domingo a primera hora P. went out and bought the Joburg *Sunday Times*. El front page headline: "The corridor of shame." It carried on: for R400, South African women can risk their health, bla bla . . . Ese prick el Chandler hasta me aludió (sin nombrarme): que una young American university lecturer iba a ser la "next victim of these mercenary butchers."

¿Qué hacer? We got the hell out of Dodge. Emprendimos el largo viaje patrás a Pretoria friqueados, still pregnant pero al menos alive. Tú me conoces, hermana. I was livid, pero la ley no estaba de mi parte. Así que penning a diatribe contra el Chandler was a no-go: I could lose my job o . . . mucho peor. Estaba tan disgusted (as Granny Eunice would say) que I never even called el Chandler. Y eso me hizo sentirme todavía *más* disgusted—with myself. Pero igual . . . powerless. Nunca llamé a la Charmain Pillay either. Como que . . . I just didn't know who to trust.

El tiempo apremiaba, so Peter y yo decidimos que I should go to London. I borrowed R1200 y me fui. Me recogió Linda, P.'s sister (una santa). She'd arranged everything en una clínica (a *real* one). I did it el 9 de marzo, bajo anestesia general. Me quedé en Inglaterra (in a beautiful medieval village in Essex) dos semanas, con Linda y su hubby el Ken y los tres hijitos. Agárrate: P.'s parents thought I was "on holiday," aunque why I'd go stay with his family for two weeks, sin él, claro que it makes no sense. Pero they accepted it—and me. Esas dos semanas en el frío—la temprana primavera en Inglaterra—were just the ticket, como dice Dad. Brought me back to life, aunque te confieso que me siento in mourning por el pobre finadito de mi feto destrozado.

Anyway al regreso, I buried myself in work. Pero ha ocurrido algo bien strange, totalmente out of the blue: while I was away, Roland tuvo una especie de anagnórisis. A heart-to-heart talk con su padre lo precipitó, according to him. I'm not quite sure why (ya que su madre me odia) pero Roland's dad likes me y es más, seems to think I'm actually *good* for him. En todo caso: R. ahora quiere que yo vuelva con él. He loves me, he *needs* me, hasta dice que he's "seen the error of his ways." Que no entiende por qué no me lo podía mostrar antes, etc. Hermana, he even asked me to marry him! Me quedé estupefacta. Pero I don't know . . . algo en mí se ha quedado como numb. Guarded, wary, y con una fuerte carga de resentimiento. Pero sobre todo strangely numb. Creo que es por toda esa odyssey (los horribles médicos machistas en Joburg, Norman Chandler, Lesotho, London) que sufrí yo, sin él. He may have "come to his senses," pero los mismos problemas persisten: dónde vivir, his work, my career, y sobre todo, su MADRE. I'm not saying never, sé que we still love each other. Pero de momento I just can't.

Total, he decidido que I'm not going back home pa' enseñar en el Summer Language Institute (SLI) at UCSC este verano. Mom and Dad no lo comprenden. Creen que ya que rompí con Rolo debo regresar al fold, patrás a mi "niche," as la June puts it. Pero Eva, I'm not really sure any more cuál es mi niche. Mom me dijo (con desprecio) que ya tengo 27 años and I should hurry up and finish *something* de una vez, en vez de andar siempre "en algo tangencial" (verbatim). Well, that pissed me off y no sé si es pa' llevarle la contraria pero I'm not going back yet. Sacar una MA en Harvard, ¿no es "terminar algo" anyway? There's no pleasing Mamá . . .

Esta chamba en UNISA es insólita (distance-tuition university?!) pero it's hardly "tangential." Y es más: intuyo que estar aquí—bregar con el fascismo del apartheid, el tremendo dolor de mi Gran Love Story (aparentemente) tronchada, esta naciente soledad o quizás . . . independence—todo esto me enriquece. Contribuye a mi raison d'être: la creación. There, he dicho.

Por favor, hermana, write soon. I'll be OK. No he encontrado un médico aquí en S. Africa (I mean, que me revise post-op). Pero I will. Huelga decir: don't tell J2 *anything*. Ya saben que I'm not with Roland (they're *not* happy about that, especially Mamá—she took quite a shine to him el año pasado), pero that's all they need to know.

*1-iv-83*

Dearest Cousin Lee,

*Gelukkig Verjaarsdag* (para el 17)! I'm remembering your cumple hace dos años, cuando fuimos a ver *True West* de Sam Shepard en ACT, en SF, remember? Have you found another job? Not trying to bug . . . créeme, ya sé que there's little assurance out there para los que hacemos strange things y rehusamos pactar. Speaking of strange things: la idea de escribir un libro de letters to a cousin cada vez me intriga más. I write to Bizzy B. (Karen), la Helen, Trish, mis padres. Pero besides my friend Lydia Vélez (de UC–Irvine) y mi sis Sarita (aka Miss Weevil), mi correspondencia contigo feels like the most lucid, steady, reciprocal. Mis padres me brindan cierta continuidad, support, especially my dad. June sees me un poco cual si yo fuera ella, I think. Or . . . *como* ella. ¡Nada más lejos de la verdad! Mi daddy me conoce mejor—almost better than anyone.

It's been rough con la Helen. She's a link to last year, testigo y compinche de mi Gran Love Story. Pero sus cartas son casi siempre superfish, cuando no directamente insulting and hurtful (mostly sin querer . . . al menos I hope so). Creo que te conté esto ya, on a postcard. Helen called me for my birthday, el domingo que volví de Londres. La convo felt . . . strange. She went on and on about how worried about me she'd been, al punto de que she even phoned Du Preez! I've had absolutely no contact with him in months (strange, you think he'd call or write me ya que según él, I'm "one of his best friends"), desde ese medio-unpleasant weekend que pasé en su casa en Durban, en el road trip con el Castells, remember?

Get this: el Steve le dijo a Helen que he suspected my recent "trouble" might have something to do with the POLICE! Great "friend," hey? Next she called Roland (while I was in England) y él se lo explicó. She read me the riot act: que Rolo's still in love with me, how could I fuck it up so badly, que I'd "come to South Africa to be with Rolo and I should make it work . . . no matter what." Cuando le dije que she didn't understand the whole story y que I wasn't sure Roland *was* my "destiny" anymore (al menos, no en S. Africa) she got pissed off y me dijo, "Oh well, easy come, easy go, I guess." I know she means well, Cuz. La Miss Zooloo se acuerda de cómo éramos R. y yo en San Francisco, en Houston, en New Orleans. She was right there by our side, enraptured con el Sea Lawyer. Al pensarlo, I think *that* might be at the bottom of her reaction: ella no tuvo las agallas de venir, or . . . el Steve didn't have the balls to ask her. Still, it hurts.

*(continued, 8-iv-83)*

Pardon the hiatus, the mess y el change of typewriter . . . all a perfect correlato objetivo de mi mental state. I've only slept 5 hours en las últimas 48 y el mundo se siente hazy y weird. Pero somehow me siento casi peaceful, fulfilled. Terminé la study guide on Latin American poetry and poetics for UNISA y la entregué hoy. Me involucré tanto con la reading y research,

Lee. For almost the past month I've been living, breathing—even dreaming—Vallejo, Neruda y Paz. Especially Paz, con quien tengo una curious love/hate relación (ever since Harvard, cuando I set him up casi como straw man contra Eliot—"Piedra de sol" contra *The Waste Land*, vaya concurso de belleza, jaja—en la clase del Alazraki). Me encuentro drawn again, cual imán, al surrealismo. No tanto las mechanics (tipo automatic writing, etc.) sino la actitud: toward freedom, hacia la liberación del deseo, la búsqueda del *ailleurs*, el más allá. Heartening, reconfortante reconocer esto: how much I love reading (and writing about) literature! I can immerse myself so completely que hasta pierdo la noción del tiempo, de mi cuerpo, de la realidad circundante. Peter has been staying with me, cocinando, coaxing me to eat, waking up with me when I crawl into bed a las 4 de la madrugada tiritando de frío, spent, exaltada de poesía.

*(continued again, sorry! 11-iv-83)*

Well, estuve tan molida from staying up till all hours working on that study guide la semana pasada—not to mention remnants de una terrible flu over the long Easter weekend, con fiebre, delirios y todo—I'm afraid all I've been doing estos últimos días es ir al cine con P. We saw *Tootsie*—not bad pa' commercial flick, not to mention the sublime Dustin H. y la hermosa Jessica Lange. *Gandhi* está por llegar, *finally* (censored as fuck, sin duda). También quiero ver *Frances*, ya que la JL is one of my new faves, ever since *The Postman Always Rings Twice* (which everybody except me seems to have hated).

Oh, by the way (ya que preguntaste), I made an appointment con el médico (gyno) de una colega de UNISA, Grazia Weinberg. Es italiana, amiga de Anita W. La Gra dice que her doc's good, y que "he probably won't be judgmental." Supongo que that's the best I can hope for en este dizque Christian, godforsaken country. La cita es el 21. I hope everything's . . . OK. I feel like it is, más o menos.

Desde que se fue Etienne para Cape Town (he left on the 1st), me he instalado en su flat. It's so much nicer than the dim, bare, too-large *plek* que alquilaba con Roland. Etienne's pad is small pero bright and cheerful.

Part II: Under Apartheid's Shadow

Tengo mi typewriter en la kitchen table. Peter comes over y cocinamos juntos, escuchamos música, we read. Un poquito domestic, pleasant sin ser opresivo. El tiene su propio flat and he's at work a lot. Ahora que se fue el Castells, besides P. and Etienne, mis únicas friends son Anita y Grazia. Pero Etienne's gone y ellas no viven cerca and besides they're married y tienen familia. No hay ningún . . . centro cultural. No life on these Pretoria streets. I have no car; el transporte público es weird y no le agarro la onda. When I started at UNISA, me subí a un black bus by accident, can you believe that? I just saw a bus, y subí. Todo el mundo me miró, freaked out. Cuando me escucharon el acento, they relaxed a bit, pero still. — *You must get off, missis. This bus is NOT for you.* Desde entonces I've walked to work, trudging over a mile, straight uphill, hasta en el extremo calor de enero y febrero.

I'm prepared to accept this lonely, untenable *situasie* por lo que me pueda aportar. Quizás esta extreme loneliness hasta me ampare la escritura. Pienso en Vallejo, alone in his jail cell, produciendo ese audaz milagro, *Trilce.* Or Neruda en Burma, escribiendo *Residencia en la tierra.* Hablando de loneliness: las cosas con Roland no van bien, to tell you the truth. I'd thought we might be able to see each other now and then, dejar abierta de posibilidad de volver a estar juntos. Pero se me hace que there's just no way. Tú me escribiste que for us to stay together tendríamos que dejar S. Africa, and I agree pero . . . no hay chance, primita. Not for ages, anyway. También me escribiste que R. would have to "reform his self-centered ways." Ojalá, but . . .

Según Roland, last month, mientras yo estaba en Londres, he was "hit" by the realization de que *everything* I'd been telling him was true: he hadn't been acting like he was truly committed to me; he'd put his family y las socioculturales expectations *between* us, cual barricada. Cual barrier a la intimidad, which for some reason he couldn't seem to handle here. Me dijo una cosa bien strange y poignant: while I was in England, he had a heart-to-heart talk con su dad. Aparentemente, el Gordon scolded Rolo, diciéndole que why wasn't he "opening up" to me, que what was he afraid of, now that he'd got me here, etc. Le dijo que hiciera everything in his power para no perderme. Of course, that's *exactly* what I'd been telling him, todos estos meses. Lo raro es que I really had no idea de que su dad nos hubiera observado tan closely. Ni que estuviera tan . . . on my side. Y lo más raro: Roland *had* been loving, demonstrative, apasionado—in my country. Ay, *nada* me cierra, Lee.

Anyway, he's been using various tácticas para que yo vuelva con él: insultos (que soy naturally promiscuous y weak; that I gave up on him when I should've given him "a bit more time," etc.), amorous entreaties, letters, llamadas a mi office en UNISA. Flores, regalos. Cuz, he even proposed marriage, como te he dicho. I could scarcely believe it. Pero . . . como que no me fío. Confieso que this country makes me paranoid, pero how would marriage be any better—or even *different*—bajo la mirada de esa siniestra MATRIARCA (*pace* Ibarbourou)? I admit I'm still too angry, demasiado herida too, como para tener fe en su promised "reforma." And I just can't help thinking que Rolo will be tied to his mother's apron strings pa' siempre.

Anyway darling Sloth, no puedo más con sus love-hate head trips. Cuando le vea later this week (he's bringing me las fotos de Cape Town his friend Philippe developed for me) quiero hacer de tripas corazón y decirle que I think it's better we not keep torturing each other, mejor que lo dejemos. Pero it feels dead wrong. Such a banal, sad demise para nuestra epic love story . . .

For now, I'm burying myself in my work, never forgetting dónde estoy: South Africa under apartheid. Pa' que este lugar siga trabajándome con su poison/magic y sirva de inspirational thorn in my side. Write me soon, Cuz. Cuéntame de tu James, your art, San Francisco.

P.D. I've started a little exercise routine en casa, con Peter. Quiero ir al gym down the block, pero lo frecuentan unos huge, hulking Afrikaner guys y tienen de mascota un feísimo bull terrier. Ya sabes lo que me aterran los perros. No he hecho *nada* de exercise en casi un año—since before la hepatitis. Me siento endeble y unsupple pero I shall persevere. I'm right now remembering us en tu bedroom en New Jersey, over two years ago already, ¡coño! Haciendo nuestra stretching routine to Bruce's "The River" antes de salir a las snowy New York nightclub nights. Te extraño tanto, I can't stand it.

*14-iv-83*
*Diario / Letter to Roland*

Resentment, resentment. Es jueves de noche, y tu amigo Jonathan me acaba de subir un package. He'd just seen you en Tivoli Gardens, Joburg-bound. ¿Adónde coño te ibas, for a midweek tryst con una new squeeze? Si fuera así I'd be slightly jealous, te lo confieso. Pero lo que siento más que nada es resentment. You ask me to marry you hace poco but ¿no tienes los cojones ni pa' subir a entregarme el mail tú mismo? Fuck this! Why are you avoiding me? Devuélveme mis fotos, y también mis books. My Nat Turner and Marge Piercy.

Y hablando de fotos: why did you give me that fotie of us *now*, la de Cullinan? You've had that all this time? Si eso era hace siglos. Way back in September. We look like happy newlyweds delante de ese teensy miner's cottage, yo en mi falda Norma Kamali, wearing your too-big flip flops. You're squinting into the sun, te ves happy. Tu brazo me rodea los hombros tierno, hopeful. I could go mad, Rolo, al leer la dedicatoria: — *You are beautiful. ILY, R.* ¿Me la dedicaste just now? April 1983, it says. Pero . . . eso no tiene sentido. Me das esta foto *now*, now you want me back, you want to marry me? Pero where *are* you?

Si tu complacency, tu parálisis, tu FEAR turned me into a monster. A sullen, resentful bruja en vez de la joyous, open, "cheeky" *meisie* de quien te enamoraste. Pero ese creepy, maddening stillness tuyo made me withdraw my love. Yo corté la fina seda, el hilo conductor entre nuestros corazones. Ese eternal link, as you call it. Y no puedo, I can't stitch us back together. Ahora no, anyway. Me siento resentful y frágil, Rolo. Y sad, sad, sad. Para ni mencionar: what sense does it make que yo siga aquí, living in South Africa bajo el apartheid, sin la "excusa" de mi Gran Amor? Me siento ideo-logically suspect, politically uneasy, pero weirdly . . . kind of free, too. Free at last para descubrir, yo misma, este país. Y también: free to discover who I am.

# Life during Wartime

And I must learn to live without you now
As I cannot learn to give only part somehow.

**Stephen Stills, "So Begins the Task"**

*16-v-83*
*Diario*

Lunes. Winter's really here now. Sopla un viento feroz, helado, yesterday and today. Se me han hinchado los dedos. I love this cold, pero es tan unexpected. Todo es así de inesperado aquí. Didn't have any time to adjust. Todo tan extremo.

*19-v-83*
*Diario*

It's late, pero before I forget the details, quiero transcribir mis notes de un creepy TV show que vi hace poco—en el UNICO channel (can you believe this?), English-programming, obvio. On South Africa's Arms Production. Al principio me quedé medio of rock—I couldn't believe they'd actually show this. Pero al rato vi que it was a bunch of hype, pa' convencer al viewing public (white, Engels-speaking) de la sofisticación y variedad de las weapons: missile-shooting cascos (¿queeé?), rifles similares al AK-47 soviético, etc. También se jactaban de las *arms-producing factories, manned by blacks, coloreds, Asians, and Whites*, todos juntos. Strange . . . ¿cuál sería el punto de recalcar eso? Wouldn't that be illegal?

"South Africa is self-sufficient in mortar-production." Ese es el gran tema. Self-sufficient enough para el "total onslaught. We are living in the Third World" (pero, *are* we?). Muchas de las armas son inferiores a las americanas y soviéticas, they admit, pero deemed "adequate for African bush conditions." Esto me asustó y friqueó. Sé que se refieren a la Border War.

"South Africa produces an astonishing variety of arms for a small country." Aquí enumeraron un chingo (141, creo). "Within the last 18 months, at least two Soviet planes flown by Cuban pilots in Angola have been brought down by South Africa—with no South African casualties." Pero, can this be true? Me late que no. Aquí se pusieron a hablar de Armscor, una dizque "futuristic arms-production factory near Pretoria." Me cuesta determinar si todo esto es pura propaganda, or if they really *do* have this massive arms buildup.

Ahora muestran un ATV tank, llamado "the Rattle." Debe ser *ratel*, ¿que no? Afrikaans, clearly, pero what the hell does it mean? "A wheeled, armored tank, cargo carrier, and recovery vehicle." And . . . there it is. Wow. Disconcertingly, muestran a negros y blancos, working together en la assembly line, para producir estos "monsters of South African military might." Pero, es ilegal que los negros trabajen pal army, isn't it?

Ahora hablan de la Operation Protea. Manera de ensuciar esa lovely, strangely spiky flower. Eso sí que me suena. La SADF contra SWAPO en Angola. En agosto de 1981. Exactly a year before I arrived . . .

Y cierran el show con estas ominous words: "Trends in Africa are bleak. Keeping ourselves on our toes militarily is a way to ensure our future. It is a job that needs to be done, so that you and I might sleep a little easier in our beds tonight."

¿Quién pertenece a este *we*? Do I by default, by virtue of my white-passing skin? ¿Me interpela, me incluye necesariamente, just because I'm living here? Uf . . . al contrario del reassuring efecto deseado, tengo miles de preguntas and . . . no one to ask. Quiero escribirle al Castells, or maybe le pregunto a Anita. Por mi parte: rechazo este (white supremacist) *future*. Y creo que no pegaré ojo tonight.

*19-w-83*
*Thursday, very late*

Dearest Lee,

Haven't heard from you or anyone—solo unas cuantas scattered letters de Rudi y James Z., mis padres—en casi 2 meses. Me siento tan cut off here—two months me parece una eternidad. Don't stop writing, Cuz, te lo ruego. It's late pero me siento uneasy, bien agitada después de ver un superdisturbing TV show (this fucking Nazi dizque Christian country solo tiene TV hace menos de 10 años, if you can believe that). All about las armas SA is producing—supposedly right here, al ladito mero de Pretoria. Pretty scary. Anyway, couldn't get to sleep, so aquí te transcribo lo que acabo de escribir en mi diary:

It's raining now, strangely. No hace tanto frío, not like a few nights ago. Estoy tan on edge por ese arms production TV show. It's late, pero Peter's not here, se fue a trabajar en el country. I'm grateful for his presence, su understanding. Pero what *is* it con estos boys y sus marriage proposals, hey? Le he dicho que I don't want to be pushed into getting married para fin de año, before I return to the States—*if* I return. Me siento squirrelly y restless. Sé que mucho tiene que ver con Roland pero I just can't commit myself to . . . anything or anyone (else). P. es un huge believer en el matrimonio, la monogamia, kids. Dice que no obstante lo que pase, he'll not be sorry y no me echará la culpa. Que he wants to be with me y me ama pero he won't push me. Alivio y . . . algo de guilt.

The hour y esta soledad me hacen acordar del año pasado. All the nights, tantas rainy San Francisco nights I'd stay awake so late, fumando y escribiendo. How full and rich and promising ese silencio, esa soledad. The 30-Stockton gliding past hourly en su electric rail en la calle abajo, la Trish dormidita in the next room. Mi cuarto, full of the portentous hush of creation, todos los objetos que definían mi vida: mis fotos; my Lee-painted, black-lacquered childhood dressers, el coat-of-many-colors afghan que me hizo mi Agüela Eunice; my big Georgia O'Keeffe book abierto al print de la semana. And best of all, mis libros: todos mis libros, apilados horizontalmente, in irreverent but neat stacks contra la pared.

It is still—or suddenly—so clear to me, ese cuarto. That time of waiting (mi Penelope-wait, I called it, me acuerdo, in a letter to Roland) that felt so full—ahora me doy cuenta, in hindsight. Tanto en su casi vestal expectancy como en las little day-to-day ventures: mis TA days en Berkeley, tomando café en North Beach, laaargas caminatas en la lluvia con Trish, fevered debates metafísicos con Rudi, tipsy hamburger and wine sessions en el Balboa Cafe con Helen.

Y ahora heme aquí, tan closed in upon myself . . . es alarmante, how accustomed I've grown to this solitude. Se me ocurre que I'd shatter in a million pieces si tuviera que volver a esos full-to-bursting Bay Area days ahora. Vivo demasiado a flor de piel, los eyelids perpetually peeled back, armed to the teeth contra los daily horrors del apartheid, de este boring, sexist, bureaucratic *dorp* of a capital city: Pretoria.

Me volvió la rule hoy, only two days early. Thank god for that. Me duele un poco la cabeza. It's so late, debería dormir. As I reach for some tiger balm again I see my room, mi adorable Chestnut Street apartment con su thrift store, homey, student-y clutter. And now me proyecto, deliberately, como hacía de niña con mi hermana Sarita. I time-travel, I astral-project y veo al Dan Dickison in our tiny kitchen, veo a Trish y mi prima Lee playing Dictionary. No tiene sentido (he's turned out to be such a jerk) pero ahora veo al Du Preez con su impish grin y ojos de cachorrito, veo scattered colillas and champagne corks, Spanish exams a corregir, a coca-hazed hand mirror y el tape recorder running on and on into the cold San Francisco February night, grabando nuestra conversación en esa famosa "last night." Y ahora veo a Roland. As he was then. Y es un flash tan bright y painful, I have to push it away.

Of course I had to come. No había modo de saber, de predecir que I'd never find him here: ese hombre que pasó la plate-glass window del Balboa Cafe con esa jaunty fedora y su cocked eyebrow, el que se adueñó de mi corazón a la vez gently y decisively—a pesar de que at first le dijera, —*You can get lost* (o peor), en cuanto le escuché ese notorious (a la vez hateful y seductive) colonial accent. Ese hombre—mi Montenegro—sabía gemir y llorar, he knew laughter and intimacy. And he could dance! Apenas pienso en esos días, Lee, they've been so utterly, inexplicably betrayed aquí en Sudáfrica. Pero los estoy pensando ahora y . . . it's unraveling me.

I had a brief fantasy, hace unos minutos: escribir a Roland (whom I haven't seen in a few weeks—I'm the one who told him no, no marriage, no . . . nada), decirle OK, I give up. Ya no aguanto. Please come rescue me. Pero ¿rescatarme de qué? Y más nebuloso todavía, deliver me into *what*? Y finalmente no, no quiero que me rescaten de la lonely citadel que crea mi daily existence. I need it for survival here. Here, I need my anger, mi diferencia. Aquí no puedo ser la hippie-punk feminist bohemian girl, como en mis San Francisco days. Me haría sentirme homesick. Y sobre todo, guilty.

I'm so lonely, lonely, lonely. Pero bregaré.

26-v-83

Lee, querida,

Te escribo hoy, un jueves en el southern hemisphere, in the wake of a dreadful near miss. Maybe you even read about it? A 55-kg car bomb se detonó a las 4:30 p.m., last Friday the 20th. En pleno centro de Pretoria. The target was the Nedbank Square Building (headquarters de la SAAF), y cayó en la hora pico. Full-on rush hour. Estoy viviendo right smack en medio de tremendo turmoil prerevolucionario, in apartheid S. Africa. Perhaps I asked for it, quizás a la distancia, en la relativa comodidad (y safety) de mis various student-drab Califas apartments and shared TA offices en la UC, I thought I understood it, supported it: la revolución. Ahora, after last week, me pregunto: will you *ever* understand this? Can you take the heat?

Lo describieron (in the news here) como el ataque más deadly en los 20 años de "anti-government violence" que viene desplegando el ANC since Sharpeville. Predictably, the ANC claimed credit (el MK, supongo—o sea, el Umkhonto We Sizwe, or Spear of the Nation: la rama militar del ANC fundada en el '61, creo, por Nelson Mandela). Murieron unos 19 (almost half of them black—dicen que they were air force), otros 200 severely maimed. También como era de esperar, the SAAF (las Fuerzas Aéreas) retaliated immediately: they airbombed unos ANC strongholds en Maputo (la capital de Mozambique)—where they'd assasinated Ruth First, activista del ANC, en agosto del año pasado, remember? A letter bomb, una semana antes de mi departure para Johannesburg.

As you know, Cuz, yo siempre he apoyado la meta del ANC: a free, self-determined Azania. For a long time su approach era reformista, tipo civil disobedience. Pero after Sharpeville levantaron armas, si bien contra police stations, etc. Not civilians. They're recognized by the UN, pero living here now, feeling the horror, comienzo a flaquear. Comienzo a sentirme ambivalent. Not so sure anymore about my (en todo caso theoretical, at-a-safe-remove) revolutionary ideals. En la revolución, se dice, civilian casualties come with the territory. Pero ¿y si uno de estos casualties fuera yo? Or someone I love?

Por pura casualidad, Peter was working out of town last Friday. Pero usually he drives the work van right through Church Street, camino a casa. Y el Castells (he's been back from the States for a few weeks): el vato se salvó de puro milagro. Trabaja (translating and interpreting) not two blocks from the explosion! Los viernes, he normally walks to a bottle shop (liquor store) en la Church Street, pa' fortificarse antes del weekend. A veces le acompaño, to help with his *seleksie*—since his weekends often involve inviting himself for dinner at mine! Por algún misterioso motivo, last Friday he walked the other way—y se salvó el pellejo. As did I. Our bottle shop was demolished—el coche de la bomba was parked *directly* in front of it. Como te puedes imaginar, Cuz, the atmosphere here in Pretoria desde el viernes es extremadamente sombrío, tense. And even more reactionary than usual, si cabe. Feels like a seismic shift con esta car bomb—daily reality feels suddenly more random, arriesgado, dangerous.

Cambiando (radicalmente) de tema: I'm becoming friendly with Elisabete Soares, una young Mozambique-born Portuguese lecturer. Ella es bastante traditional y hasta conservative, me parece, pero es inteligente. Y al menos she's young (25), honest y muy friendly. She often gives me lifts home after work y yo le he ayudado con algunas translations. I'm sooo bad at it, Cuz! I hate to choose! Pero el Castells has been training me y dice que we should go into business juntos. Plus, after living here desde la uni, he speaks pretty good Afrikaans, so for a laugh, I've resumed las Rock-lecciones (este es un semi-derogatory English nickname for Afrikaners que tiene que ver con la Boer war, apparently) que me impartían esos gay (oops, "bisexual") film directors en Cullinan, remember?

Anyway, entre Italy y Australia, I'd pick Italia, hands down, Lee. Pero are you really going? Hmmm. Keep me posted.

P.D. ¿Te conté que I've been going to a gym with Peter tres veces/semana? Ya sé, it's that awful, macho Rock gym, pero going with P. it feels OK. Plus, los okes (jaja, vatos) really pay no attention to me. Tienen más interés en hacer su huffing y puffing y posturing for each other. I'm getting stronger—volviendo a los días cuando era true Nautilus stud en el gym de Berkeley, remember? Jaja, hardly. Me siento puny runt, pero I persevere. I'm still not back to my prehepatitis self! I can't really drink like I used to. Y me canso al tiro. I weigh in at a stable (LOW) 55 kg (around 122 lb.).

*16-vi-1983*
*Sondag*
*Aniversario: my parents' wedding y Soweto uprising (7 years ago)*

*Liewe* Lee,

¿Te gusta mi Rock? We must be psychic (or *physic*, as you once wrote!): acuso recibo de tus poems y tu "strange book," tu carta y foto, hoy. *Baie dankie* for the goodies y la foto—I love it! Tu James is great with that Polaroid.

It's been cold and rainy. Normally, no llueve en invierno pero según todo el mundo, this has been one of the weirdest years ever. Estamos en una severe drought, y el verano pasado was—so they claim—the hottest in 30 years. Leave it to me—ya sabes que no aguanto el calor. No puedo creer que caí en Africa in the midst of this, y que on top of everything I fell pregnant, speaking of falling. Uf . . . Anyway, heme aquí in my little flat (Etienne's), enjoying this chilly rain. Me contemplo las manos—las tengo resecas y las uñas all split con el frío. Pero I compensate by piling on a mass of African bangles (brass, pewter, copper) que compré de André, un hip craftsman (blanco) que conocí hace poco en un craft fair. Cute, y creo que he was putting the move on me, not sure. Pero los tales de sus run-ins con la secret police (BOSS, le dicen) me dieron escalofríos, I'm telling you. Ahhh, the stuff of novels, esta vida mía . . .

Anyway, I'm in a race against el reloj—tengo un chingo de trabajo antes de salir pa' Madrid. Leaving in 16 days—I can't wait!

Looking forward to seeing J2, y mi hermana la Wiggue. Me encantaría ir a Feliz París—I'd *so* love to see James (Riet's ex). Maybe la Wiggue could go with, ella es la máxima francófila de la familia (well, her and Mamá).

He estado tan unsettled lately (esa fucking coche bomba *really* did a número on my nerves), I've thrown myself into work y he logrado mucho. Le estoy agarrando la onda de las homework assignments, y de cómo pre-parar y enviar las tutorial letters. It's all *so* different, Lee, to what I was used to! Mi métier es el aula, cara a cara con live bodies. And speaking of live: hace unos días ¡me usaron de guinea pig pa' checar la eficacia de video/telephone-mike, long-distance classes! It was a trip. Hice lo que se llama una "telephone conference class." O sea: mi grupo aquí en Pretoria conectó con otros grupos (by a microphone/loudspeaker/video system), in Durban and Cape Town. I was petrified—de que no saliera bien, where I should look (esa cámara was unnerving, pero luego luego I forgot about it). It was all a huge experiment, y yo era la primera en probarlo.

Well, it went over brilliantly (según UNISA). Mis estudiantes hasta me dijeron que I should get a job in TV broadcasting, que I'm a natural y bla bla. Había programado 3 horas de review y structured activities; por suerte tuve la foresight de mandar supplementary exercise packets a los estu-diantes de antemano. Guess what I used? Los exercises que inventé con la Marianne B. en el SLI de UCSC. Simón, those silly ones, donde hablá-bamos de sexo, mota, y un chingo de ridiculeces. Tuve que sostener un stationary mike the whole time (annoying y cansador) y repetir "Come in, Cape Town (o Durban)" pa' que no se confundieran los students.

You know me: by sheer force of will (y terror), within 20 or 30 minutes había memorizado los nombres de unos 20 new students que solo apare-cían onscreen. Era bien sci-fi, pero they were really chuffed y hasta pidieron un repeat, "as soon as possible." The final exercise era un dialogue entre un waiter y una pareja. Agárrate: el waiter estaba en Pretoria, la mujer en Durban y el tipo en CT. Ay, so hilarious! Al final, les leí un pretty easy Neruda poem. Cuz, some of my own students aquí en Pretoria casi lloraban, estaban tan moved. Total: I loved it, y ellos también. Al punto de que UNISA scheduled me *another* conference class para el 10 de agosto, right after I get back. Obvio, todo esto requiere all kinds of intricate scheduling, mandar los study materials, booking the room y todo el technical equipment, etc. All on me! Who the hell trained me pa' esto? Can you imagine? Todo tan high-tech here en la tierra del fucking *Ratel* tank . . .

Por si esto fuera poco, I'm right now correcting my *most* difficult assignment: linguistics. Por suerte, el Castells me ayuda . . . and all I have to do (ejém) is serve him dinner and ply him con un poco de "noooble Red," como dice él, bien poshly. Para más inri, tengo que terminar un new study guide que se usará next year, for first-year Spaans students. I'm filling it with all kinds of materia subversiva (jaja): los García (Márquez y Lorca) pasan, pero also Chicano authors, feministas latinoamericanas, even Che Guevara. Let's hope que no me hagan "disappear." And finally, tengo que preparar los October exams. I'll sit on several, incluyendo los honors orals. Simón, Cuz, así como lo ves: I've gone from 0 to 60 prácticamente overnight. De una lowly grad student TA to . . . well, una sci-fi high priestess. Too wild, ¿verdad?

Pasando a otro tema: sé que es más que ironic (and my parents will flip si se lo confieso) pero I'm increasingly uncertain about going home. Pero can I handle the terrible loneliness para ni mencionar ideological queasiness de otro año (¿o más?) bajo el apartheid? Mi amigo André (ese jeweler, the one I met at the crafts fair) me dijo que las security forces here foster precisely estos feelings de isolation y guilt en la gente con consciencia. Destabilization work (léase revolutionary) es tan dangerous here que es harto difícil contactar con gente en la struggle. Mucho más para una white-looking foreign woman. El André me dijo que si me metiera en algo fuerte, at best I'd be deported o quién sabe qué más. Me dijo que he's sure BOSS already has a file on me, por mi correspondence: Nicaragua (my sister) y la People's Republic of China (el Chino). Es todo tan creepy y top secret, Lee. I'm getting really paranoid. You have to watch what you say todo el tiempo, y con quién. Por otra parte: living here, tener que enfrentarme, every day, con las ambigüedades ideológicas (y humanas) . . . es como un crisol, ¿entiendes? Se me hace que it's making me stronger, more tenacious. Y también (often kicking and screaming, lo admito) más flexible.

Darling Cuz, hazme saber tus thoughts, *va be'* (*pace* Mauro)? I'm loving the Elvis tape que me mandaste. The "Imperial Bedroom" one. Lo escucho casi todos los días, before I leave for work. Tan emotive y lush, vaya cambio pa' ese onetime punky cynic. What am I reading, you ask? *The White Tribe of Africa*, basado en una BBC series, about the rise to power de los Afrikaners. Fascinante.

Mi daily life se ha vuelto bastante celibate. Pretty much desde que volví de England. Wow, ya van casi 3 meses. Adoro a Peter, pero it's all become quite platonic—de mi parte, anyway. Difícil explicarlo (I mean . . . rationally), pero intuyo que it's all wrapped up in Roland. Y en Lesotho. Y Londres. P. lo acepta, pero he's not happy about this. No voy a decidir nada ahora pero when I'm back from Europe, algo va a tener que cambiar. Anyway, I'll close for now. Gotta finish marking the dreaded linguistics, y cenar mi homemade curry. Mi cooking se ha vuelto tan exquisite, I promise you! Xoxo

15-vii-83
Diario
En las montañas outside Locarno
Suiza

Heme aquí, here in this small country que hace 10 años cuando visitamos en familia (don't remember the reason, pero I *know* we were here—veo a mi hermana Sarita strolling in Lucerne, tocando su recorder), bauticé de latter-day, real-life Disneyland. Paradoxically, este uptight, formal jewel box of a country me está loosening up now, trabajando como freedom balm en cuerpo y alma.

Heme aquí desnuda y spread-eagled on a huge, chalky boulder, soñolienta y comfy bajo el sol. Not a soul around except Rudi, quien me quiere sacar fotos con su trusty camera pero no me apetece. Rudi y yo pasamos por la German part of Switzerland, donde sentí a flor de piel el aire de constraint, o . . . hmmm, quizás sea solo que I can't get away from los prejuicios de Daddy. Hay que admitir que I admired the almost manicured look de las emerald, pre-Alpine mountains, los villages. Pero todo demasiado pulcro, didn't breathe any life. We climbed up into the cold, hasta había snow, ¡ahora, en pleno verano! Todo muy *Sound of Music*, subimos a los Alps pa' escaparnos de Zurich, pa' alejarnos de Riet y su pseudo-"Oriental pleasure palace" flat, su insistencia en cenar a una hora fija. I love Riet, pero he's soooo Swiss.

Este mini-país tiene partes tan hermosas, even vast. I fought hard against acknowledging the beauty, yo ya había formado mi Suiza-image y este road trip was challenging everything, messing up mis esquemas ideológicos (ay, *who* said that to me? No me acuerdo, pero tan funny . . .). También resistí la reconexión con Rudi. Tras meses de extrema soledad— and sadly, this includes hasta los que pasé con Roland—even what we've yearned for puede llegar a parecernos double-edged sword. Me está siendo difficult and awkward, abrirme con la gente. Con Riet y su hermana, sus friends, con el hermano de Rudi y su wife. They're sweet, pero me siento hosca, foreign (not in a good way). Cual si despertase after a thousand-year sleep . . . en otro planeta.

Last night nos hospedamos en la Pensione Eden on a bucolic hilltop en Locarno. It feels like northern Italy. Romantic and erotic. My hunger so overpowering though, me da miedo. If I let go, si me dejo, será demasiado el deshielo. Quiero abrirme, quiero . . .

17-viii-83
Back home in Pretoria

Hermana,

Acabo de terminar *La tregua* by Benedetti—and I'm destroyed. Lo compré, along with a few other books, en Madrid. Tan funny, terribly sad. So comforting, leer algo en español, just for myself (digo, not for UNISA). Reconocer(me en) esas tan Coño Sur words and phrases: *pibe, che, pitusa, liiindo, qué macana.*

No puedo creer que you haven't written me in all this time—ya van casi 5 meses—especially con los bombshells de mi March letter, the one I sent you via Aunt Treg (Gert, jaja): mi breakup con Roland. Lesotho.

Londres. Maybe "adapting al matrimonio" (que es lo que me contó Dad, when he told me to be patient y no enfogonarme contigo) really *is* exhausting, pero I can't help thinking que es un estado (in!)civil, like any other. Quizás simplemente no te inclines a la escritura like I do. Well, obvio. I'm busy too, dammit, y el mundo está exploding all around me (literally—¿leíste en las noticias, or did Mom & Dad tell you about the car bomb here? En mayo), pero I make time to write, siempre.

A veces, I get down on myself, precisamente por esto. Me pregunto si todo mi white-hot letter-writing es un intento (inconsciente) de esquivar mi "other" writing. Digo, Writing, con mayúscula. The novel Lee's been pushing me to write, por ejemplo, or poetry. Pero mi amiga Lydia Vélez (from UC–Irvine) wrote me something so beautiful and encouraging and insightful el otro día: "No sé por qué estás preocupada, Susanilla, por qué siempre te estás exigiendo más y más: tu generoso talento de escritora es tan evidente; tus cartas respiran un aire documental, hasta novelesco. O de película. Sigue escribiendo y no te importe el 'género'—esa es una arbitraria designación de los críticos que se masturban en dar etiquetas. Tú sigue nomás y no pidas disculpas." Isn't that right-on? She's a writer, too (poeta). Con otros pals de la UCI, ha integrado un taller literario. Uno de ellos, our good friend Miguel Muñoz (Lydia's best friend), is about to publish his first novel, en español. Anyway, my point is: *try* to find time to write me, Weeve. Tus cartas ex Managua were so vivid, informative—si bien a veces anguished.

Well, you know the saga del FIN de mi gran Love Story with Roland. Escribí a Rudi, bien tentatively, toward the end of last year. Yo seguía con R., of course, pero las cosas ya andaban mal. You remember el Rudi, right? Ese slightly older suizo que estaba madly in love with me (from 1981, after he was in my advanced Spanish class), before I met Roland. We had a fling—a bit of a Swiss "moment," jaja, ya que you know about my friend el Schweggie (aka Armin Schwegler, linguistics PhD student en Berkeley), y *su* amigo el Riet Tramèr, who became my friend, y más importante, Riet's then-beau, el James Zike. James is the one I'm closest to, entre todos ellos y—no coincidence—el único non-Swiss! James's love story con el Riet paralela la mía con Roland: James se mudó a Zurich para estar con Riet y . . . desastre. El James rajó—now he's living en París pero . . . esa es otra. Back to Rudi: he did everything in his power pa' que yo no me mudara a S. Africa, y . . . he had some powerful wiles. O weapons. Ideológicas, intelectuales (y sexuales, tee hee). Según, he was very hurt by my actually leaving, following through with my plans, aunque le había dado fair warning. Pero he'd said he always wanted to remain in contact, so cogí y le escribí.

Anyway, para acortártela, I kept writing to Rudi, y él a mí. He helped me immensely, first con la tremenda soledad, culture shock, and guilt de los meses iniciales bajo el apartheid, en el milieu de Rolo; luego con la angustia y el horror del pregnancy y aborto; finally, con la incómoda—ultimately untenable—mix of gratitude, affection y claustrofobia que era mi (waning) relación con Peter. So, con esta backstory, salí para Madrid last month.

Under pretty wary circumstances, me reuní con Rudi en Zurich. Y de allí we lanced ourselves in un epic road trip all over Suiza. ¿Te acuerdas de Luzern, Weeve? It's way more beautiful than I'd remembered! Pasamos por Geneva, Lausanne, the sublime, *Sound of Music*-y Alps, hasta Montreux (jazz!). Luego estuvimos en la Italian part of Suiza, y en el norte de Italia, then we drove all across southern France into el hermoso País Vasco pa' llegar, finally, to face los parents en Madrith with our tender new/old romance.

¿Qué te cuento, hermana? Our reunion was happy/sad (*pace* Tim Buckley!), angry (de parte de Rudi: no me dijo I told you so, pero . . . algo de eso había), cerebral, hopeful, sexy. Entre los highlights: un sublimely erotic stay en Saint-Emilion, having sex for hours, y luego tipsily wandering the ancient, gorgeous town, after drinking the most delicious "noooble Red," como dice el Castells. Y otro highlight: una visita equally tipsy (si bien cero erótica, jaja)—loving, political, impassioned—con mi adorado Alfie Sastre y su mujer, la escritora y psiquiatra Eva Forest, en el tiny fishing village de Hondarribia, donde viven.

En el curso de esta odyssey, decidimos algunas cosas (ay, Neruda poema de nuevo), si bien pretty tentatively. Le dije a Rudi lo de mi aceptación en UC Davis pal PhD (luego te cuento Mom's reaction . . . typical) y que I'd asked them to defer me by a year, hasta enero del '85. Por su parte, Rudi's earning good money en Suiza, saving pa' lograr su sueño: ir a Latinoamérica para sacar fotos (you remember, he's a construction engineer by profession, pero también fotógrafo). Pero según dice, he wants to be with me in South Africa, next year. And so . . . en una noche (de las muchas) tipsy y sex-crazed, me propuso marriage (this now being my *third* propuesta este año). No te preocupes, hermana, not for the green card. Ya la tiene (he was married to an American chick for 6 years, una judía que conoció en Israel). Y en un frenesí de faith and idealism, acepté. And we phoned June and Joe, y ya tú sabes how that went . . . (Mom: "We like you, Rudi honey, and we know you love Suzi. But do you really *know* Suzi?").

Mientras continuamos viaje hacia Madrid, I reneged. Got cold feet. Espero no friquearte ya que eres newlywed pero hermana, I just don't believe in marriage. Me aterra esa . . . fall into everydayness, como dice Walker Percy (creo). O el diario a diario, like Cortázar says. Yo quisiera poder crear y sostener una love story sin rendirme a esa institution. State- and patriarchy-sanctioned. Pero como siempre decíamos en las NARAL protests, keep your laws off my body. And heart. He dicho.

Cambiando de tema, sort of: there was *no* making Mamá happy. On anything! Of course, los dos estaban thrilled I'd "come to my senses," de- cided not to "squander my potential" y bla bla. Pero Mom was adamant que tenía que volver a Harvard. Weirdly (o . . . quizás no tanto), Daddy no estaba tan convinced. Pero según la June, the Harvard name would reign eternal, sería el factor decisivo pa' mi brilliant career, etc. Por más que lo intentara, I couldn't make her see how ludicrous this was, en un flatlining, Reaganomics job market. Caso en punto, remember my friend la Marti, Dad's ex-student? Con todo y su PhD ex Harvardis, directed by none other than "El Yerno" (aka Stephen Gilman, o sea yerno de Jorge Guillén), no ha podido conseguir even *part-time* teaching jobs en su field. Le dije a mamá que la Cacademia is such a shaky career anyway, a mí me parece que it's more a matter of doing one's best, hoping to be in the right place, right time y . . . a tirarse del acantilado. Es todo tan tenuous, tan arbitrary que en cuanto departamento o graduate program, I should at least be able to pick my poison, ¿que no? And Harvard sure as shootin' ain't mine!

Mamá y Daddy hicieron united front about this: están vehemently opposed to me staying in South Africa. Desplegaron una panoply de ar- gumentos, algunos racionales (the ideological ones, intentando guilt-trip me about apartheid) y otros más low-blow e hirientes (about my dizque "loose" character, mi dizque indecisión, time-wasting, etc.). Pero they should know better: esto solo me hizo dig in my heels. Porque lo que quiero más que nada: devenirme *skryfster* (escritora). And—aunque no lo puedo explicar más que intuitively—presiento que mi sojourn en S. Africa es y será decisive. Thoughts, feelings, observations—words—are churning inside me, Eva. Y aunque todavía no veo con claridad el final outcome—su form, digo—sé que necesito la intensidad, ese vivir on the edge que representa Sudáfrica para mí.

P.D. Speaking of: have you seen Peter Weir's *The Year of Living Dangerously*? El punto de vista, the images, I loved. One in particular, tee hee: Mel Gibson. Swoonworthy!

*27-ix-83*

Querida Weevil,

Te escribo de nuevo, although I *still* haven't heard back from you. Van 6 meses, ¡coño! Tengo algo bien urgent que plantearte: mi flatmate, Etienne, pretende abandonar el país. End of October, a más tardar. Hace siglos que quiere ir a Europe o USA, even before he met me, pero ahora le urge. He's been called up by la mili para el último día de octubre, y pretende desertar. Me parece una locura, I'm terrified pero me jura que he can't take it any more. He already served his 2 years, pero bajo esta dictadura les obligan a hacer army camps de 2–3 meses, *every* year! Ya te he dicho que he's feliz. Se ha criado en una familia Afrikaner sofocante, racista, ultra-Christian y anti-gay. De hecho, his dad's some kind of *dominee*, o sea NG preacher. Which stands for Nederduitse Gereformeerde Kerk (NGK, Dutch Reformed Church)—vaya mouthful, ¿que no? Anyway, Etienne apenas tiene contacto con su family, though they don't live far. Hasta ahora, desde luego, I haven't met them. They'd think I was the devil incarnate, me dice. I think he means it!

He's only 21—un año mayor que nuestra Wiggue pero what a difference! Etienne es muy emprendedor, superindependent. He's worked desde los 16 años. Varios oficios, mainly de restaurant manager. Le he dicho que es harto difícil—practically impossible—to get residence en nuestro país. Or even in Europe, que yo sepa. The only way, as far as I know, sería abdicar su S. African citzenship y tirarse a la merced de alguna asociación anti-A

(¿se me entiende, no?). El me jura que he's ready to do it. Que si tiene que volver de nuevo a esos fucking military camps, se suicida. Hermana, I'm really worried. Etienne no ha militado (you know what I mean). Nunca ha estado fuera de RSA, ni siquiera muy lejos de su suffocating family milieu. Pero te cuento esto: when I first met him, en enero, el café donde trabajaba (Tivoli Gardens) despidió a 6 workers (black women), y Etienne protestó. Amenazó con renunciar, unless they rehired them. Guess who won (por algo es capricornio . . .)?

Anyway, sale para London el 30 de octubre. Le he dado mis contacts en Suiza, París, Italy y España. Hopefully, puede mantener low profile, y trabajar ad hoc, como lo que hace el James in Paris (working as a dance instructor), or even Rudi, who's working construction en Suiza (bajo la mesa). Es muy hard-working, y muy pícaro (tipo Lazarillo de Tormes, our fave bedtime story by Dad, remember?). Ahora, tu misión, should you choose to accept it: ¿podrías conseguirme las addresses de algunas organizaciones anti-A? Hay una en NYC. Sigue este acróstico (ni idea si es paranoia mía, estos spy games, pero remember que ya me han intervenido el correo): Samuel Antonio Miguel Roberto Alberto. Can you get me la de Amnistía I too? I think they're based in London. Ahhh, todo esto puede ser una pavada . . . ya lo sé. I mean: Etienne es blanco, after all. Y no tiene perfil de militante. Pero for now, no lo quiero pensar demasiado. He's asked my help y quiero intentarlo. Gracias, Weeve. Love you. Write me!

P.D. Todo muy hectic lately, as you can imagine. Peter moved out (digo, se volvió a su flat) a finales de agosto, when Etienne returned from Cape Town. Desde entonces, we've really been painting the town red (jaja), me, Etienne y el Castells. A veces nos acompaña el P. —we're still friends. Fuimos al Pretoria Show—algo así como ese livestock fair en *Madame Bovary*, junto con arts and crafts, food stalls and rides, tipo el Boardwalk de Santa Cruz. An uncanny mix of scary soldados (whites) y un público overwhelmingly African (digo, black). Luego te cuento más. Fuimos a ver *Rocky Horror Picture Show* con el Castells—that was a trip. Y ahora somos asiduos regulars en un new club called After Dark. Great music for dancing y la clientela es, a veces, mixed. Strictly illegal, obvio. Oh, before I forget: me estoy mudando, ya que Etienne se va. I'm really going to miss him! Pero his place is too expensive. Encontré un estudio, bien cerca and a bit cheaper. Everything's such a huge hassle here. Impossible to get a phone, por ejemplo, it takes months and months! Igual me lo intervienen, seguro, according to my friend André, so better to keep using public ones, o llámame a mi office en UNISA. Te mando la new address soon.

6-x-83

Dear Weeve,

HAPPY VERJAARSDAG (para el 12)! Espero que esta little card te llegue a tiempo. Sorry for brevity—I've been *really* sick, con un horrendo flu, for about 5 days now. Acabo de mudarme a mi studio, which is virtually empty. Es que ¡no tengo nada en este país, Eva! Etienne gave me his bed, por suerte. Which I've been lying in, in a drugged haze, afiebrada y con mareos. By the way: le he escrito a Rudi, suggesting we take things slower. Se va a enfogonar, I reckon, pero pos ni modo. We'll see how it goes cuando regrese a Europa. I'm going for over a month, en diciembre/enero. Así me escapo del long, hot African summer. By the way (bis): did Dad tell you que la Annie Laurie (de Sam Armistead) has joined los Hare Krishna? Vaya viaje, hey?

13-x-83

Mia cara cugina Sloth,

*Hou gaan dit?* Still waiting to hear from you (hint)—cuéntame cuanto antes de tus Euro-travel plans, OK? So I can firm up los míos. Things have been algo rough estas últimas semanas. Llevo casi 2 semanas con una ghastly flu. ¿Y el remedio que me recetó un médico? Almost worse than the disease: *suppositories*. Simón, Cuz, así como lo lees. The horror! Pensaba que they'd disappeared con las Dark Ages, al menos everywhere except Spain. Ugh. On top of that, me he mudado. De hecho, on October 1st. Me ayudó un estudiante mío, and Etienne. No tengo casi nada: just a few books, mi ropa. Etienne me regaló su bed, kitchen stuff, etc. Para el día siguiente I was sick as a cane, endeble, yaciendo feverishly en esa cama cual náufraga en medio de una barren, noisy (street noice, pero *not* soothing or mysterious como el de mi beloved Chestnut Street apt. . . . last year), lonely room.

Anyway, I'm almost well now y las cosas están casi sorted. Etienne y el Castells have been helpful, y Peter too. Creo que everything looked (and felt) much worse mientras estaba tan sick. La cocina es grande y luminosa y he alquilado una fridge aceptable. Why, you wonder? Porque apartments don't come with them here, y de repente, Roland decidió que he "urgently needed" his (?) back, y vino y me la expropió. Obvio (as Etienne pointed out), eso era pura excusa. He wanted to see me, pero no tiene la creatividad de inventar algo menos . . . transactional, ni las agallas de decir, simplemente: I'd like to see you. Pero agárrate: when he came over, lo primero que me dice, after a few minutes of strangely banal chitchat, —*I don't want to talk to you right now, Chávez, I really want to fuck you*. Can you imagine? Me pareció tan clumsy y nai que ver que me enfogoné all over again. Conste: I kind of wanted to fuck him, too. Or, OK . . . I *really* did. Pero I resisted. Le mandé a volar.

Para recuperarme, I've been seeing a lot of films con Etienne, el Castells e Izelle Roux, muy amiga de Etienne. Castells le tiene crush, and they're sort of . . . dating. El otro día vimos *Diva*. Made me miss you so much, primita. Les conté de cuando lo vimos en el Nickelodeon en Santa Cruz, remember? I've now baptized Etienne Curé, after that weirdo in *Diva*, el del crewcut y las gafas de sol (remember, "je n'aime pas le parking"? Y su weird country music que finalmente we heard only after he died, pouring from those auriculares que siempre llevaba). Ay, qué risa. Pero when Etienne wears these punky sunglasses of mine se le parece un chingo, I promise you.

With his conectes to the embassies (por su familia), el Castells got us these FAKE foreign press passes, para poder ir al Italian Film Festival en Joburg. ¿Te lo crees? So we could watch these "dangerous" foreign films — sin censura. We saw *Dimenticare Venezia*, which we loved, y esta noche vamos a ver *L'innocente* (The Intruder) by Visconti, con el sublime Giancarlo Giannini. We've also seen *The Honorary Consul*, con el pouty guapetón Richard Gere y el Michael Caine. We heard it didn't get good (US) reviews, pero ni modo, nos gustó bastante. Not bad for a commercial flick. Se trataba de guerrillas and love (and sex) en Paraguay/Argentina. El Castells estaba fascinado, since he's thinking of buggering off [*sic*] to Paraguay en 1985. He's big buddies con el Paraguayan ambassador. As you can see, Castells is pretty politically bankrupt, pero . . . sigh, le quiero anyway. Buggers, oops *beggars* can't be choosers, ¿que no? Y . . . mira donde estoy.

So much for culture—oh, casi se me olvidaba. Anoche fui a Joburg con Castells, Izelle y Curé pa' ver *Apocalypse Now*. La quinta vez para mí, their first. A pesar de su descent into mysticism (al final), todavía me parece el más powerful e intriguing de los Vietnam films. The music is so amazing, y todo el jungly sweat, ese mundo verde. Not to mention el yummy Sam Bottoms (el surfer, Lance), y el sexy jailbait Laurence Fishburne as "Clean"! Me sentí . . . immersed. Y mucho del dialogue me hizo pensar en lo que vivo ahora, here in S. Africa. Cuando el Brando dice al final, "The horror, the horror. I don't want to let myself forget the horror . . ."—así me siento yo. I WANT to be marked, Lee. Emblazoned, tatuada. Este landscape, esta reality se me hace cada vez más *necessary*: no sé si será masoca o frighteningly politically "incorrect," pero quiero sentir este horror, this edge. And I want to remember it.

Y ahora, pasando a cultural events of a different order: yesterday fui con el Castells a una recepción en la Spanish Embassy, en honor al Día de la República (o sea, Columbus Day—and Sarita's birthday!). Tan chévere conocer a estos Latinos (of various ilks). I had no idea que existieran en este Anglo-Boer/African country. *Natuurlik*, el Castells was fawned over por el Spanish ambassador y muchos cronies, including—creepily—army people. His dad, como te he dicho, is really well known. Some kind of Spanish embajador or diplomat, not exactly sure what. Just laff: la gente supuso que I was Castells's *vrou* (which thrilled *him* no end), pero I rather quickly dispelled that idea, pues había una bola de Beautiful People to meet 'n' greet. Yo estaba in my sauce, pero all the while cursing myself for my ideological flaqueza, pues no me cabe duda de que most of them were far-right.

Snapshots de tu Latina Mata Hari cousin (pero OJO, for the right—es decir LEFT—side!), en una southern hemisphere diplomatic *partytjie*: the First Secretary de la Embajada Chilena took a shine to me. Kinda cute, pero I put him off. I couldn't handle los smarmy come-ons de un representante oficial del país cuyo "gobierno" (léase dictadura) desapareció y torturó a algunos de mis friends. Había otra gente fascinante allí, and I chatted them up medio lustfully, medio dutifully . . . capaz entre ellos I'll make some useful contacts. Por ejemplo, un gorgeous, totally Scando-looking español, not there in any official capacity. Piensa asistir al Harvard Business school next year, so he looved my Harvard degree. Tan raro, unsettling y comforting a la vez, escuchar ese acento castizo coming from that Nordic-looking guy. Otro era un soft-spoken, stunning South African oke. Intercambiamos una de smoldering glances, y finalmente we "bumped into each other" refilling our drinks. *Baie intrige*, pero I think he's married y salió medio early. Total, most S. Africans (los whites, anyway) son tan cold and undemonstrative y estos Latins eran tan lively, tan interactive, era como culture shock, rodeada de mi propia cultura. Much of it was likely for show, pero still . . . it felt good.

Remember that Gustav Strong guy I told you about, el fotógrafo que conocimos Etienne y yo, early last month? La cosa se puso hot 'n' heavy bien rápido. Couldn't help myself, Lee, el vato es fornido y de un guapo que te caes patrás, like they say en España. Plus, it had been *forever*. Plus, he threw himself at me con una pasión desenfrenda. He's S. African (Engels) so . . . his ardor was pretty unexpected. Anyway, se ha ido a Cape Town, to take care of family business y mientras tanto I've decided to slow things down. He's a dead sexy hunk, muy talented. Pero no quiero complications now (um . . . the little matter of la asignatura pendiente con Rudi) and Gustav's too intense, muy needy e insistente. He demands too much of me. Es muy joven y romantic pero hay algo unsettling en él. Curé and I can't quite figure out his mystery yet, ni el Castells tampoco.

Finally, speaking of (esa asignatura pendiente): I've been thinking a lot about Rudi. Unfortunately, le escribí una rather hideous letter when I was sick. Le dije que maybe he *shouldn't* come out to S. Africa, que he's 33 years old y no tiene norte and I don't want to be his norte, que it's too much pressure y bla bla. Right after I posted it me sentí como la mierda. Ese flu *really* messed me up, Cuz. Estaba paranoid y confundida, wanting to do "the right thing." Pero Curé calmed me down. Me dice que I should park *'n bietjie* (relax). Al menos, me dijo, *I* know more or less where I want to go, so let's just wait hasta que vaya a Europa en diciembre, and then we'll see . . .

*27-x-83*

Lee, cariño,

Despacho esta to Phyll and Shell's, porque I've got no clue where you are at the moment. Hope you got my last letter, te la mandé hace un par de semanas. Gustav sigue en Cape Town, pero since he's been gone, Curé and I have been breathing a sigh of alivio. Nos hemos dado cuenta de la tensión que nos trajo, con su disproportionate jealousy y sus mind games y sus tales of impending fame and fortune que no nos cerraban. Nos dejó una caja de foties, lots of amazing black and whites, cosas que ha mandado a *Staffrider* (very progressive magazine). We've been going through them y su documentary photography work no se compagina con su army brat attitude. El fucking ejército must've brainwashed him o qué sé yo . . .

Hablando del army: Etienne ha abandonado sus AWOL plans—por ahora. We hadn't thought it through lo suficiente. So, de momento ha decidido lie low aquí en el highveld y soslayar el army (muy dangerous— cross your dedos). Ha comenzado un new job en el Midnite Grill (otro restó, en Joburg) so he'll be able to save, y se apunta a un marketing course en UNISA. Sus friends pensamos que he'd be the ideal restó proprietor. Agárrate: we've given him 9 years—hasta que cumpla los 30—to open his own *plek*! Decidimos que it'll be called "Curé's" (after *Diva*). ¿Te gusta?

Y hablando de friends: la Izelle Roux (Castells's "special friend") threw a big going-away *partytjie* for Curé el día 14, y allí conocí a gente chévere. Curé and I dressed up as twins, tipo pre-Halloween. Nos pusimos estos ridiculous white karate outfits, con wide black belt. Yo dejé el jacket abierto down to *there*, y me unté ese Stagelight iridescent powder en el escote (re-member, el que nos compramos en Little Ricky's en NYC, before we went clubbing al Limelight? Ahhh . . . those were the best of times). Needless to say, mi look causó gran impacto (ejém). Huelga decir que Pretoria, South Africa's a far cry from our beloved I-Beam, mucho menos el Limelight!

El más importante new chum es Wimpy (can you believe this apodo? Real name Willem Johannes), un adorable bifeliz Afrikaner pacifist e in-telectual, who's now—brace yourself—in the police force! No te alarmes, Cuz—not by choice. De hecho, this option is vastly superior a la otra: el

ARMY. His dad pulled some strings (es un importante local doctor) pa' que le dieran basically a desk job as a CONSTABLE, en vez de mandarlo a la fucking Border War. Wim's brilliant and funny, tall and tan con un punky haircut y una sublimely sexy voice (completely bilingüe, too). I gravitated to him entre un mar de stoned y tipsy Afrikaner desconcidos porque, as I told him, — *You're the only man here who's looked me in the eyes all night!* También conocí a otro vato super sexy, WA. They all died laughing cuando les pregunté que por qué le llamaban por un Chinese name, Wa. *Nee, nee,* me explicaban, destornillándose de risa. It's his initials: WA (for Willem Adriaan). Pero por ridículo que sea (he's a Nordic-looking hunk, just picture Rutger Hauer in *Turkish Delight*), my mistake-apodo's stuck: since then, todo el mundo le dice Wa! Anyway, he came home with me postparty, aunque he's in a bit of a thing con el Wim. Who's *also* into me! Top secret porque, of course, "he's not gay" (el Wa). Y todo este fucking país is so *not*-gay. Pero anyway, nuestro *liefde*-triángulo's cool all around . . . hasta ahora.

En estos días, Etienne y yo estamos haciendo little forays around town to meet boys, mostly solo pa' admirar. Our latest recluta es un efebo llamado Robbie Peacock. How could he be Afrikaner, you ask, con ese posh, Brit-sounding name? Pos ni idea, pero he is. Very! De un pueblo en el northern Cape, Upington. Lo conocimos en un dull gay bar, Scruples. No es officially feliz, obvio, pero everybody knows. Curé y yo nos sentamos en la barra, and we noticed this adorable creature al lado nuestro, platicando— not very animatedly, hay que recalcar—con un boring-looking older oke (mid-30s). I dared Curé to just lean over y preguntarle al joven si estaba a gusto hablando con ese pelma, pero Curé insistió en que lo hiciera yo. Bueno, Cuz, ya sabes que I can't turn down a dare. Cogí y le pregunté — *Excuse me, we were wondering if you find this conversation exciting.* Y pa' nuestra gran sorpresa, sin pestañear (and he had these gorgeous, camel eyelashes), el chico nos dice que no, que —*In fact, we're just ending off an affair.* Curé y yo estábamos grossed-out to the max, pues ese older dude nos pareció tan y tan . . . *niks.* And we were surprised, además, de que el chico nos lo contara tan . . . matter-of-factly. People just aren't like that en este país.

Total, the rest of the night Etienne y yo platicamos con el Robbie. Para small-town boy, me parece bastante cultured. He studies psychology and Latin en Tukkies (la U. de Pretoria, a totally Afrikaner institution), y habla (inglés) con un odd, hypnotic accent. He sounds . . . medio Italian. O algo. Definitely *not* the choppy, heavy accent de los Afrikaners cuando hablan Engels. Anyway, we liked his vibe. He's funny, parece bright, algo debauched. I made a date with him, y el martes vino a casa con un amigo, also Afrikaner (are you sensing a recurring theme, Cuz? Well . . . esto es lo que hay, especially here in Pretoria), named Phillip Janse van Rensburg. Hermosa pouty boca y sexy-innocent Dutchboy face. Izelle cayó luego, con Wim, y tomamos vino y jugamos al Truth or Dare. Remember our famous game nights en Berkeley? Bueno, interesting resultados: el Pavorreal has never slept with a woman; el Phil has, twice, y le gustó; Izelle declined to comment y el Wim(py) can't decide which he likes best. Como yo.

As you can tell, my darling Lee, mucho ha cambiado en estas semanas. Desde que volví de Europa, especially since Etienne returned from Cape Town last month, estoy en un strange, maravilloso deshielo. A veces miro patrás, over my shoulder, esperando los guilt pangs, la voz de mi consciencia scolding me for consorting con el enemigo: the white oppressor. Por otra parte, I'm innately curious. Eso me define (*pace* Cortázar). I want to learn what makes the Afrikaner tick, por más que estos new friends representen una desviación de la norma. Son tan open, curious, and accepting, (way) beyond *verligtes*! Anyway, después de tantos meses of loneliness y desengaño con Roland y los suyos, es harto reconfortante, being part of a group of friends—mis propios amigos—sentirme aceptada.

Write me, Miss Sloth! Ya compré mi ticket—I'll arrive (in Zurich) on Dec. 8th. Xoxo

3-xi-83

Hermana,

Te juro que I'm writing to you this one last time antes de caer al TOTAL SILENCE. No puedo, for the life of me, *verstaan hoekom skryf jy my nie*? Al menos una fucking *poskaartjie* pa' darme prueba de vida. So much has happened desde que te llamé—I hardly know where to start.

Would you believe yesterday—el mere, mere Día de los Muertos—hubo una suerte de faux-vote? Era un referendum para aprobar (or not) la reforma a la constitución de este año. Una especie de enmierda (jaja), o reforma, se había propuesto, permitiendo algo de (dizque) "power-sharing" entre los whites, los coloreds, y los asiáticos (o sea, los Indians). Digo faux porque only whites voted, obvio. As you can imagine, this referendum was roundly rejected tanto por la ultra-derecha como por parte de la oposición (el PFP). Anyway, for weeks we've been going around town, sacando fotos de los campaign posters, plastered up everywhere. El racismo y el fear-mongering es increíble. Ver pa' creer. Check this: "Rhodesia Said Yes—Vote NO," "PFP—Action Committee Meeting, Brooklyn Boys High School," "Ons toekoms wil hê dat U NEE sal sê" (Nuestro futuro quiere que digas que NO, with Dick & Jane–looking little white kids smiling angelically), "Mixed Government—NEVER. Vote NO," "Kleurlinge en Indiërs nie in Parliament nie. STEM NEE" (No Coloreds and Indians in Parliament. VOTE NO). You get the idea. Predictably, it passed. Pretty much a landslide.

Pero agárrate, last night el resultado de nuestros by-now habitual games of Truth or Dare exigía que saliéramos, in the dead of night, ¡pa' robar campaign posters! Curé and I went around con Wimpy, en su auto. Nos figuramos que if the *polisie* caught us, well, we were *with die polisie*, tee hee! Era bien risky en este police state, pero we'd primed Wim to say que yo era una foreign student, fascinada con el electoral process or some such boludez. Por suerte, no one saw us. We had quite a time of it, semi-borrachos, hoisting Curé up these trees and light posts, pa' agarrar los posters. They're so beaut, Eva. I'm gonna keep them forever. Espera que los veas.

Otro creepy, strange acontecimiento político, akin to a military-might buildup show que vi en la tele hace unos meses: un Desfile Militar. Hace un par de semanas. I remember porque era el cumple de Dad: el 15 de octubre. En este peaceful, Libran day, un horrendo flexing del military muscle del apartheid. We went to Church Street en masse (no lejos del lugar de ese horrendous car bomb last May, ¿te acuerdas?): Etienne y yo, el Castells, Wimpy y Wa, even Peter y su compinche el Gary (otro Brit). Parecía que all Pretoria was out: los whites lining the balconies, the sidewalks, leaning out windows; grupos de negros standing together, por lo general bien stonefaced. Pasaban enormes tanques, y el Wa nos explicaba sus army names and principal functions: eland, ratel, hippo, mamba, rooikat. Todos estos indigenous animal names! Por si esto fuera poco, lo más desconcertante fue una all-colored brigade. Can't explain it exactly, Weeve, la impresión que me causó. Algo así como pensar en los black and brown soldados en Vietnam, quizás. Or los black soldiers en la Civil War, pero . . . they were Union and a minority. So, la analogía no es exacta—to say the least!

Anyway, cambiando—radicalmente—de tema (as Mom is prone to doing cuando las cosas se ponen heavy, "isn't that a little bird over there . . ."): este upcoming Euro-jaunt's becoming quite some venture. La Lee's decamping to Florence, pa' estudiar arte. She's gonna meet up with me en gay Paree, chez mi amigo James y su nuevo amor, el Alexis (who owns a café). I'll fly into Zurich, pa' hacer rendezvous con el Rudi (cross your dedos, hermana), luego iré sola a Paris. Then we'll all meet up in Madrid, chez los parents. Even—agárrate—Etienne! He's flying over el 20 de diciembre. By the way: he's managed to wrangle himself out of the army camp, digo, legally. So, no tuvo que ir AWOL, thank god. La lana que estaba saving up pa' su Great Escape ahora la gastó en su airline ticket. He's always dreamed of seeing Europe—ahora, vamos a festejar su 22nd birthday a todo darrr. Hasta la Trish, mi ex-roomie de San Francisco, might be in Italy, too! I'll go stay with Lee in Italy los últimos días de mi estadía. Dice Curé que we're gonna need a massive bus, tipo los Merry Pranksters! Ay, can't wait to be in the snow (con doble sentido, jaja). Va a ser el desmadre total.

5-xi-83

Darling Cuz,

*Baie dankie vir die* charming card, y la hermosa blusa! I sent you a letter la semana pasada, to your parents' house. Things *very* exciting lately—para bien y mal. Lo de Gustav turned into a huge pesadilla. Hectic, as Wim y el Robbie Pavorreal say. Para acortártela: se enamoró de mí, pero creo que es latently feliz and probably wanted to shag Curé too (who agrees with me), aunque he'd never admit it. Se volvió loco, Lee. Pathological liar, paranoico, celoso a más no poder y vindictive.

Volvió de su two-week trip a Cape Town y le dije que I didn't want him staying with me anymore, que necesitaba mi space, etc. *Groot probleem*: el Gustav had offered to do all these things for Etienne en Cape Town, tipo retrieve his expensive stereo de sus former roommates, plus his clothes, su Walkman y cassettes, libros y más. He waltzed back into town, bien Casanova—he never expected to find Curé here, ya que se suponía que he was going AWOL a fines de octubre, remember? Well, Gustav llegó empty-handed. Y solo después de mucho hemming y hawing, he admitted he'd given Curé's stereo to his sister. Can you imagine how pissed off we were? Things went de la sartén al fire as we tried to figure out how to get my suitcase back (se la había prestado pa' ir a Cape Town) y cómo coño hacerle confesar los whereabouts de las cosas de Curé.

El vato comenzó a darme miedo: coming over cuando sabía que Etienne would be at work, screaming and pounding on the door, puteándome, trying to force his way in. Meanwhile, la gente le veía gallivanting around town con diferentes *okes*, each one more feliz than the last, según nuestros friends. Como te he dicho, Pretoria feels like a really small town, everybody knows everybody y hace casi un año I stumbled onto la gente más cool in town, gracias a Curé. Now, they look out for me.

Total: el clímax fue cuando Etienne y yo fuimos al Army Headquarters (donde el Gustav trabaja para la magazine *Paratus*) to try to smoke him out. La receptionist dijo que he wasn't in, aunque I'd made an appointment with him pa' recoger mi fucking maleta. Well, Curé wasn't having any: he stormed in, dragging me by the hand y allí estaba el malvado, cool as a cuke, sentado en su desk con el famous Walkman de Curé plastered on his *kop* y mi maleta by his side. Yo estaba estupefacta, pero Curé snatched ese Walkman right off his head y agarró mi maleta y le dijo, bien dignified pero loudly, in front of all the other soldados y officers, —*Gustav Strong, you're nothing but a common thief. You'll be hearing from my lawyer.* El Gustav intentó balbucear más mentiras, pero Etienne grabbed my hand y rajamos. I've never seen him so mad—de hecho, nunca le he visto enfogonao en absoluto.

After that, cambiamos los locks en mi flat. Y el Wimpy nos consiguió una "non-molestation order" (can you believe it's called that?) against Gustav. Lo peor: nos topamos con una amiga de Etienne, de Cape Town, y nos dijo que Gustav *had* gone and taken all Curé's stuff. So, así confirmamos que he did, in fact, steal it all. Otra amiga, Mandy, trabaja en el fave restó del Gustav. Nos dijo que he'd been in, bragging about a "transfer" to Cape Town—so capaz we scared him out of town. Pero, he also threatened us (via Mandy): dijo que if Etienne took any legal *aksie* pa' intentar recuperar sus belongings, que le delataba al army. Creo que te conté que el Curé had planned to go AWOL, así que ya te puedes entender nuestro terror, el arma que ese idiota el Gustav was holding over us.

Pero nota que usé el *past* tense. Porque the gods are smiling on us. El fucking army *did* catch up to Curé—they smoked him out en lo de sus padres. So el muy *slimpraatjies* tomó el bull por las astas y fue *direk* al army con una carta del Midnite Grill, constatando que he's doing a manager-in-training cursillo y que they need him badly y que si puede postpone su army camp y bla bla. Todo eso se resuelve HOY, so we're on pins y agujas, pero all signs point to no court-martial, o como corno se llame.

We haven't made up our minds, si meterle pleitazo al Gustav o no. Pero Wimpy offered his servicios as constable (!?), y el Pavorreal (Robbie Peacock, obvio) has gone to inquire en legal aid at Tukkies (la U. of Pretoria). Whew . . .

Hay tánto que no nos cierra, Lee. How's it possible que el Gustav tenga toda esa caja de documentary foties for *Staffrider* pero a la vez trabaje en *Paratus*? There's *so* much about this country que simplemente no entiendo. For a while, barajé la teoría de que el Gustav es algún tipo de spy, o double agent. Trabajando pal army, y también en el (anti-A) struggle. Ahora, creo que la explicación ha de ser menos exotic, más . . . banal. En todo caso, we're shut of him. Pero hasta cierto punto, aren't we *all*—todos mis AlternaKaner amigos, anyone living here with a conscience—double agents? Anyway, Cuz. Te dejo con estos DEEP THOUGHTS! Meanwhile, love to Auntie Phyl and Uncle Shell and even my primo, TB.

*12-xi-83*

Querida primita,
It's a sultry afternoon in Africa . . . y heme aquí con el Castells, pleasantly tipsy tras consumir una botella de "noooble" red. It's so damn hot,

deberíamos estar tomando white. Pero *rooiwyn*'s his fave. Me lo trae siempre que le invito a cenar, which is . . . casi siempre. Hoy confeccioné una delish casserole, from memory of a hippieish dish que me encantaba en ese health restó, The Good Earth (*Die Goed Aarde*, chimed in el Castells, en Afrikaans), en Berkeley y SF. Lleva mushies, broccoli, walnuts (escasos y superexpensive here!) y cebolla en una salsa béchamel. Yummy.

Nuestro motley crew se encuentra un pelín reduced lately, porque: el sexy, Teutonic Adonis del Wa got called up to the border. Es decir, a pelear en la Namibia-Angola border. Isn't that fucked-up? Me friquea (on principle) pero I'm actually slightly relieved, pues he's a bit of an alcoholic y (especially though not exclusively when drunk) kind of a pest. A pesar de ser "straight" (ejém), he was Wim's main squeeze y se puso obsessively jealous cuando el Wim also got into me. We're still trying to figure out de quién estaba más *jaloers* el Wa, me or Wim. En todo caso, el Wimpy's really more of a compinche than amante (aunque he's really good in bed). Me cae predominantly feliz y en todo caso, he panders *'n bietjie* too much al Sir Wa . . .

En estos días it's been mainly el Castells y yo, a veces con el Pavorreal. Visitamos al Curé en el Grill, 3–4 times a week, especially lately, con el Italian film festival que te dije. He feeds us for free y le da al Castells su *medisyne*, o sea Irish coffees galore! Next on our slate: *Il Conformista* de Bertolucci. Adoro ese film. Y luego next Monday tengo movie date con Etienne y un nuevo work friend, Johnny Blow (I promise you, his real name). Curé cree que es straight and wants me to check, ¿pero how *could* he be, *ek sê*, con tal apellido?

*Goeie naand* for now, my darling. Nos vemos next month, ¡en Europa! Oh, I can't believe TB called off la boda . . . oh well. Mejor safe que sorry, digo yo.

2-xii-83
Diario

Our top discovery en estos días es André de Wet. El Italian Film Festival de Joburg led us to Mango Park, una bohemian boutique de artesanías africanas en Rockey Street. El Castells and I were going for an early supper en Mama's, antes del cine, y caímos por pura casualidad en Mango Park. As we were admiring las hermosas baskets, las trade bead necklaces y las intrincadas seedbead creations de los Zulu y Ndebele, por poco me dio un telele cuando salió el shop owner y era . . . none other than my friend André. O sea, el del crafts fair en Pretoria. We fell out laughing! — *What took you so long to find me*, skattie?, me dijo el André, mischievously. El Castells estaba atónito. I had no idea que el André tuviera esta other life. Es decir, that *this* was his life: el Kesey-like fearless leader de una banda de highveld Merry Pranksters. Craftspeople, artesanos, músicos. Ah, *vriendskap*, ah deseo, ah *liefde*, I bid you welcome.

*3-xii-83*
*Diario, written on the M1 Highway*

Dawn on the highveld. Rayos verticales, scarily low, parten el cielo plomizo. Hacia el horizonte, pale gray mist. It's raining now, la lluvia persistente, steady del verano en el highveld. Los colores atenuados, dawn-washed, pero con la presencia de Africa. A esta hora, there's nobody travelling the M1 north. We're heading back to still-sleeping (*siempre* sleepy) Pretoria, el Castells y yo en su faithful Citroën, la highway una thin, slick cinta que bifurca el altiplano que se extiende endlessly, a luxuriant lion- and emerald-colored quilt de ambos lados.

Del lado de acá it bunches up suddenly, una dense green maleza de weeping willows, del otro lado la tierra se planea, dipping and rising gently, unbroken expanse hacia el horizonte. Repentino flash of crimson bougainvillea o late-season, periwinkle jacaranda.

We've been the whole night en lo de André, communing with strangers, ahora amigos. Sam, an angular, warm African que ahora reside en Switzerland. Los Italians, Paolo y Anna. The beautiful bohemian Afrikaner actress, Michelle du Toit. Y la pregnant, early-to-bed Kathy, André *se vrou*. Sprawled out, all of us, en los enormes, plump pillows y low chairs. El Castells un little hair out of his element, pero por suerte he's cool. In fact, creo que lo está pasando pipa.

And speaking of: at André's se fuma Malawi gold—dreamy, ultrapotent *dagga*. O *chamba*, como le dicen en Malawi. Wowee! Tal estado (hadn't been this high en años) me dejó medio paralyzed, pero pleasantly, acurrucada, relaxing into the crook of André's legs with his fingers slipping ever so lightly down my spine. Hmmm . . . el vato es bright, progressive, creative y cute, pero . . . Anyway, en ese stoned haze, hablamos de todo: la política, el arte. We laughed and laughed, tomando vino (el Castells in ecstasy con *baie* copas de noooble) y luego tequila shots. Luego André *chop chop chopping* una pastilla called Obex—ni idea—pa' huifear. Ahhhh: me encantó. Superspeedy, pero sin edge gracias a la Malawi mota y los drinks. Supongo que this is as close as I'll get to my SF nightlife aquí en Apartheid-landia. We danced our nalgas off, todo el mundo, even el Castells. Cranking up los Talking Heads, "Speaking in Tongues," full blast. "Burning Down the House"—what a righteous jam, *ek sê.* Ay, si yo iba a Joburg casi todos los weekends, last year. How did it take me so long to find these people? Pues obvio, *meisie*: you were with Roland. *Ag*, no sé si llorar o reírme. Los amigos de Rolo tan uptight y boring compared to la clica de Casa de Wet. Total, what a heavenly night.

*3-i-84*
*Postcard. Gauguin self-portrait*
*Madrid*

Dear Weeve,

¡Feliz Año Nuevo! What a difference from last year, festejando el cumple de Rolo in the blazing heat—our tense/hopeful tregua, soon to be blown to smithereens (by me) . . . Pero pos ni modo. *Sterkte!* Lee and I saw in the New Year en una extraña, slightly juvenile, coca-laced fest en lo de un amigo que Wiggue y yo conocimos last July. Todo muy hectic here, to say the least. Rudi volvió a Suiza, thank god (more on him luego); Etienne en París con el James y su "amigo" (new Madrid term for ligue/amante), Alexis. I'm sort of looking forward to getting home. Oddly enough, me estoy dando cuenta de que por más que no quiera (por más que no quepa allí), South Africa's becoming home. A slightly irritating, unproductive haze settling over me here en el Viejo Mundo, entre tanta coca y *partytjie* y familia. Anyway, soon enough I'll be back en el Sur. But first: Italia, pa' ver a la Lee en sus Florentine digs. Xoxo

P.D. Casi se me olvidaba: can hardly believe que el Nick Vidnovic haya pasado por casa, looking for me. Wow—no le habré visto en . . . 3 años. I think I'll write him. Should I?

6-i-84
Reyes
Madrid
Diario

Estoy desconsolada. No, not exactly. Más bien una fofería resignada. Las cosas de la familia *never* change. Las sensaciones de bienestar son ilusorias. Hoy es Reyes. Curé *se verjaardag* in four days, y ni sé dónde coño está. Me imagino que he'll pitch en estos días. We made a pact: festejar su cumple juntos, in Madrid. Letters mean nothing. La tenue y frágil "amistad" que parecía se forjaba en las cartas between me and Mom is an absolute farce. A mirage that I allowed myself to see, *needed* to see, en estos inconsolables meses de soledad. Pero now I'm reading *Cry the Beloved Country* y es raro. No me lo explico pero while I'm reading Paton, confirmo algo que vengo sintiendo, ever since I arrived in Europe last month. Al leer este libro, es como si se desatara un nudo de hielo en la garganta: I long to return to Africa. Y esto me reconforta y me aterra.

Como dice Alan Paton, siento que para mí esta visita a Europa ha esclarecido algo, something definitive: "la tribu está deshecha." Y es triste (I'm trying *not* to be melodramatic), pero I have to face it: Mamá es una embittered martyr, una víbora que quiere echarme todo el veneno de su propia desilusión en la cara. Being with her, our old roles are re-created, las mismas tired polemics de la adolescencia. For her, apparently, hasta que no me case, I'll *never* really be a certified adult. Scarcely a person, even. He allí el asunto. Por eso she had such high hopes for me con el Rolo. Well sorry, Mom. De esa agua ya no beberé más . . .

15-i-84
Madrid

Dear Eva,
Heme aquí, stricken down con un caso de bronquitis, can you believe

that? Vaya holiday, hey? Me lo pegó el Lex, James's beau, en París. Me puse fatal en el train trip a Madrid, con Lee, pero then we beat it into submission a base de gin tonics y coca en los bars y fiestas de la Movida madrileña, tee hee. Todo el mundo ha estado engripao. Agárrate: Dad blamed his (tiny) bout on "Lee's kleenexes." Hace unos días, I admitted it'd come back with a vengeance. Habíamos festejado el cumple de Curé (el 10) en un fancy-ish crepe bistro. Los parents invited him, Mamá habló French con el camarero y estaba in her sauce—it was great. Al día siguiente, Curé buggered off to S. Africa. Al tiro, caí en cama desplomada—and I couldn't get up. Couldn't breathe, hear, nada. Llamaron al trusty Dr. Muñoz (remember him?) y vino y luego me recetó 1,000 remedios (including supositorios, ugh). Estoy mejor, pero still not 100 percent. Te juro que I'm actually almost looking forward to the warmth—OK, el calor—de Africa. Pero first: the *massive* trek en 2nd class train, through Italy, luego a Zurich para coger el avión de regreso. Uf . . .

*Major Topic: Rudi*

Oh, how I wish he hadn't come to Madrid. Yo tengo la culpa: le hubiera dicho en Zurich que no, y punto. I hoped he'd get it, pero no. Todo se crispó definitivamente una noche que we all got dressed up superpunk y lúgubre—me, Etienne, Lee, Wiggue y su oke, José María, y Rudi—para ir a Rock-Ola, this fab, dark antro Wiggue loves. It was fantastic, rodeados de "punkis" en toda clase de high, bailando. The music was superb, they were playing this weird, sexy macarra oke, Ramoncín (su grupo se llama WC, pa' que te des una idea, jaja), bien loud, plus "Billie Jean," Big Country, los Cabezas Hablantes, etc. Wiggue y el Joe Mary left after a bit, y yo me quedé bailando con Lee y Curé. De hecho, that night we barely drank— agarramos puro contact high, te lo juro.

En una, we spied Rudi bailando cual hippie, swirling around sin ritmo, tipo latter-day flower child. Which, al pensarlo, he sort of *is*. I reckon I'd never really noticed it, pero en ese club, de repente, desentonaba. Nos dio vergüenza ajena. Al rato vimos que he'd sunk into this big lounge chair y parecía estar dormido. Weird, porque la música estaba a toda pastilla, *really* loud. Cuando decidimos irnos, we went to wake him up y . . . nada. Curé le dio un shake, bastante rough, y para nuestro horror, he slumped down en el dirty floor! Pensamos que estaba passed out so we tried to pick him up, pero he was a dead weight. En eso, nos abordó un vato enorme, —*Oye, ¿necesitáis ayuda?* Le dije que sí pero he couldn't drag him too far. El Rudi flopped back down on the floor, esta vez boca abajo. By this time todo el mundo nos miraba, it was a total scene. Yo estaba bien mortified, y también worried that he was OD'ed, aunque none of us had had much to drink. Finally, vino corriendo un bouncer—even huger than the other oke—who slung Rudi over his shoulder y le llevó a la recepción, donde le aflojaron la ropa y le echaron ice water.

Hermana, can you picture all this? What a scene! Naturally, Lee y Curé no entendían un carajo and were scared out of their wits. El bouncer me aseguró, —*Es un pedo, un pedo fuerte lo que tiene. Vamos, digo yo que no ha tomado nada o casi nada porque respondió un poquito al agua.* I was getting pissed off, porque sospechaba que he'd staged the whole thing pa' llamar la atención or, if he really *had* OD'ed, que era pa' "get back at me."

All of a sudden así sin más he sits up, como si nada, perfectamente sober. —*Did you like my little show?* Estuvimos DE PIEDRA. Lee, Curé, and I were LIVID. We stormed out—a estas alturas eran pasadas las 4 de la madrugada (Rudi's "little show" had been going on over 2 hours)— cogimos un taxi y no le dirigí la palabra the whole way home. Mientras tanto he hounded me the whole way, tipo, —*Did you like my game? I thought you liked games. I did it just for you.* Huelga decir: we sent him packing to Zurich al día siguiente. Hermana, espero que no me juzgues demasiado "belle dame sans merci," pero ese "show" terminó por darme asco. Me di cuenta de lo unbalanced que es el Rudi. Y también, aunque dicen que la nalgavista es 20/20, I should've trusted my instincts and called the whole thing off earlier. Remember la crisis que tuve, back in October? When I was so sick with that awful flu y le escribí pretty much una Dear John letter al Rudi? Luego I second-guessed myself. Or he talked me out of it. Pero en todo caso, it's over now.

*Major Topic #2: Mom*

Hace unos días, cenábamos con Lee y se trajo el tema de "living together." Lee mentioned que her parents had been horrified, at first, cuando ella se mudó con el James N. I jokingly said que los míos también, back when I'd lived with el Paul Nyland, o el Nick Vidnovic. Al pensarlo: I was only 17 con aquél, 19 con éste (no wonder, me decía pa' mis adentros). En eso, Mom chimes in, —*And I still AM* (horrified). Me levanté de la mesa y me fui. Estaba completely pissed off, pero no quería que se armara una huge fight delante de Lee. Me sentí como si me hubiesen mandado por un time tunnel, patrás a la high school. Remember how much we used to hate her, pero nos sentíamos tan powerless against her? Tú sabes que more recently, finge ser toda palsy-walsy pa' que le contemos nuestras cosas. And then *smack*, cuando menos te lo esperas, just when you're beginning to think que capaz *finally* puedas tener una more adult relationship con Mamá, the knife twists.

Bueno, she wouldn't let it go. She raged on and on, totalmente fuera de control—just like the good ol' days. A todo esto Daddy (para variar) sat medio cowering at the table, tras unos feeble attempts to rein her in. —*June, June, honey, come on* . . . Pero she slammed herself in and out of her bedroom, chillando que si no creía en el matrimonio, how did I think I could be part of a family (¿queeeeeé?) y—this is rich—did I "expect" my family to "take care of me forever"? Le dije, —*Don't bother being "horrified" with my life; eres una miserable, frustrada y resentida porque yo vivo de una manera que tú nunca pudiste.* Le dije que I felt sorry for her por no poder vivir a su manera y dejarme en paz, let me live my own life. En eso, she yells that *she* feels sorry for me. Le digo, — *Why? No sabes nada de mi vida.* —*Oh yes I do*, she crows, triunfante, *from all those SORDID letters you write me from Africa.* Eva, eso fue la gota que colmó al camello . . . She's been sucking up to me, que "let's keep the lines of communication open," que how much she "enjoys hearing about my life" y bla bla. And now, this.

Anyway, las cosas se pusieron hasta *más* weird. Esa noche, Lee and I went out to la Vía Láctea (to drown our sorrows con ese sexy bartender Manolo, el del pierced pezón y cabellos hasta la cintura, who lines up la coca right en la mere mere barra) y no volvimos hasta el día siguiente. I was determined to leave, take off pa' Italia early con la Lee, pero Lee talked me out of it. Cuando volvimos a la tarde, in deep trepidation, we found Mom en la cocina, *singing*, y preparando "all Suzi's favorites": ternera a la milanesa, judías verdes, etc. Era surrealista, Weeve, I swear. No se dijo nada más del "incident," pero talk about gaslighting! Ahora que he vivido lejos de los parents for so many years, especially being this far away, en Africa, veo las cosas bien clearly. This is a pattern, Eva: she blows up, proyecta to' el veneno acumulao cual víbora venenosa y luego, once she's had her catharsis (doing her damnedest to make us feel an *utter* fracaso en todo—love, work, ethics), pos como si nada. Ella tan contenta. Mommie dearest . . .

Anyway, BASTA. For me, el tema de este Año Orwelliano—en lo que a los parents y Wiggue se refiere—es la DISTANCIA. I'll keep writing to Dad, supongo. Me saca de onda que él no tenga los you-know-whats como pa' stand up to Mamá, pero . . . what else is new? Al menos he and I have a lot in common y somos compinches. Y hablando de marriage (yours, obvio, NOT mine, jaja): todo el mundo, from la Granny Eunice a la Aunt Betty y la Aunt Treg (tu suegra), lleva raving how "radiant" you look, como la vida de casada "must be doing you good," etc., ad nauseum. So let me know how you're feeling on that score ¿vale? Espero que mejor que en tu latest letter—*finally*, after 8 months of SILENCIO!

5-ii-84
Back in Pretoria

Mia carissima cugina Lee,

Come stai? Speriamo che tutto bene. Es domingo a la tarde. I've been back home a week. El Castells se ha ido a Joburg, pa' visitar al André & Co. No aguanta los weekends en Pretoria. Pero somehow I wanted to relish the solitude. Didn't feel like drowning my culture shocky sorrow en lo de André. Didn't feel like seeing people, doing drugs, *jolling* . . .

Oh, how could I forget: el domingo pasado, the day after I got back, le robaron el brand-new auto al Curé. Estaba trabajando el late shift en el Midnite Grill (which he hates) y cuando salió, at 4 a.m., el auto no estaba. Of course it was locked—ni me lo preguntes. Esto ocurre con shocking regularity aquí en S. Africa, especially Joburg. Hasta lo tenía en un covered apartment parking lot, con night watchman y todo. El fucking ladrón made a nice haul: el tape deck, un chingo de cassettes (some of mine in-cluded). Y el wallet de Curé. Why he left it in there, y con la bola de lana (R700), ni puta idea. Anyway, como te puedes imaginar, el Curé está de-stroyed. He'd only just gotten the car from his dad y se lo estaba pagando.

Considerando que we were barely recovering from el robo de ese sociópata el Gustav Strong (Curé's stereo, un chingo de ropa, etc.), esto del auto has been a real setback.

Total: se ha comprado un cheap secondhand Mini to get around in, pero esa lana was meant to be our enganche on a flat for the two of us. The Zen haven of tranquility (y un pelín de debauchery, obvio) que soñamos. Sigh . . . Anyway, Etienne's gonna stick it out en el Grill hasta fin de mes, y yo aquí en el studio con el Castells (who'll stay on here after I move).

En el Swissair return flight, yo estaba en la ventanilla y al hacer la transición al continente africano, which we began to cross just as day was breaking, me sorprendió una extraña sensación. It was *so* beautiful, Lee, tan arid, con esos pale, dusty greens, la tierra roja. Digo strange porque in a way, I really felt like I was coming home. Like part of my heart belongs here, aunque es difícil explicar por qué, in any but the most bizarre, inchoate, uncomfortable way, ahora que estoy aquí de nuevo en este governmental capital of South Africa, Pretoria, con el calor y la altura y las blank, suspicious, xenophobic faces de estos Afrikaner citizens . . . sigh. Life stops at 5 p.m. here. ¿Y los domingos like today? Ni hablar, *niks*. Life never began, jaja. El día del Señor. Anyway, it's late, Cuz. And still *so* hot. Me voy a dar un refreshing bath. Nite-nite!

16-ii-84

*Liewe* Miss Weevil,

Howzit, my china? Well, supongo que you've recently aced el court interpreter exam, ¿que no? Let me know *asseblief*—antes de que pasen otros 7 meses . . . Anyway, I was yearning to be back here tras semanas de second-class train travel, schlepping esa maleta pesadísima (se nota que I do *not* have your packing skills). Pero se me había olvidado lo debilitating de este atroz calor. Plus, creo que supiste (did Dad tell you?) que le robaron el brand-new auto a Etienne. Doesn't that suck huevos? He'd been planning to quit el Midnite Grill, ya que tiene new chamba lined up as manager en—agárrate—Kentucky Fried Pollo. ¡No te rías! It actually pays pretty well, plus it's a day job (las late shifts en el Grill le estaba matando), plus it's in Pretoria. A él no le va Joburg. He prefers Pretoria, que es, en todo caso, su hometown. And in a weird way, I do too. No te creas: I know it's the seat of apartheid and dull as doornails and all the rest of it. Pero a diferencia de Joburg, I can actually get around a pie. My preferred mode of transport y menos mal, ya que I've successfully managed to evade getting a driver's license hasta ahora. Anyway, we go to Joburg to *jol* all the time—me, el Castells y Wimpy—para cenar o ver cine o teatro, o visitar al André & co.

El pobre Curé's had to stay another month en el odioso Grull (Rock pronunciation), y yo con el Castells en este cramped studio. Pero por milagro, la *polisie* found Curé's car, would you believe it? En una ritzy northern suburb, con la back window all smashed y los alambres all over the show. Pero other than that, it's OK y el seguro le paga los arreglos. And we've found a *lekker* two-bedroom flat a solo 2 cuadras del studio, en Barclay Square. En la ground floor hay un shopping complex con grocery store, launderette (*so* handy no tener que caminar cargando la ropa en este calor) y *apteek* (farmacia), que es donde usamos el teléfono anyway. La pharmacist is sweet and she lets us talk a long time sin joder. Plus, even our fave restaurant, Sir Loin, is here! No quisiera parecer una *completely* unrepentant burguesa, pero hermana, I wish you could taste the meat here. ¡Para morir por! Whatever they do, es la más rica del mundo, I promise you.

*18-ii-84*
*Diario*

Pensar que hace dos años—this very day—Rolo y yo concebimos nuestro little zygote. Ahora no me parece ni remotamente posible. Houston a distant planet. Sad, sad, sad. And on this same day, ¿hace un año? Pregnant again. Sick, aterrada. Also *hartseer*. Running around to all those asshole, machista médicos. Luego Lesotho. London. Hace tanto que no lo había pensado . . .

To clear my head of these painful telaraña-recuerdos, salgo a caminar. Out for a late-morning paseo. Hay un olor pungent, industrial en el aire pero the sky's mercifully overcast. Y aunque tras las nubes amenaza el blinding summer heat, it's a bit cooler this morning. I turn left into Celliers Street, mi hermosa calle, overhung with frilly green jacaranda fronds que en la primavera—para octubre—florecerán en ese glorious haze of periwinkle.

De repente, I feel a man invading my space, le veo por el rabillo del ojo, walking a bit too close and quick on my heels. I pick up the pace. Intento despedir confident, hasta jaunty vibes, humming a Silvio Rodríguez tune ("Nadie se va a morir, menos ahora . . ."). As usual, I'm hoping everyone will realize que no soy de aquí, por la canción que canturreo, by the gentle sway of my (*definitely* non-Pretorian) unfettered breasts, my long, loping, high school distance-runner's stride en mis alpargatas de Casa Lobo en Madrid.

The man is right on my heels y me detengo, quite abruptly, en la esquina de Jorissen y Celliers, to gaze longingly at my favorite block of flats. Modest in scale, blanco, vaguely mediterráneo, named after me: "Susanna." The man passes me y sigue caminando y siento un alivio posiblemente irracional. He's light-skinned, 40-ish, quizás younger, con cabellos algo largos, enmarañados. Slight build, bastante alto. Bouncy step. As I draw side by side to him me saluda, —*Dumela, sisi. Why you soeh-frrraid?* Ay, coño, pienso, how can he know? Balbuceo unas weak rationalizations (mientras pa' mis adentros me digo: I wasn't *really* afraid; siempre pauso pa' admirar los "Susanna" flats; siempre camino jauntily): —*I'm not afraid,* le digo, *I just don't really like this place and I'm wishing I were somewhere else.*

Right away me doy cuenta de lo lela que debo parecerle pero ahora tengo verborragia and I blunder on: —*Where I'm from, a woman alone can't be too careful on the street,* y bla bla. ¿Cómo hacerle saber que even after a year and a half en este país, ese wariness hasn't vanished altogether aunque this is South Africa—this is apartheid—donde ningún hombre de color se atrevería a abordar a una white-looking woman en Celliers Street, mucho menos a las 10:30 a.m.?

Somehow this knowledge, lejos de reconfortarme, me hace sentir queasy and helpless. A pesar de mis ridiculous stammerings, el hombre me mira, bemused. Camina sprightly, by my side. —*Where you from, sisi?* Le cuento de California y él, a su vez, elige contarme de un very good white *baas* que tuvo, for seven years. Engels, not Afrikaner, he takes great pains to tell me. —*Blacks have their place here,* me dice, *and whites their place but we are now walking side by side because there's only one god. For blacks and whites. No difference. I know you know.* And my throat knots porque me doy cuenta de que this is the first time I've walked side by side — paseando, platicando — con un hombre negro en Sudáfrica.

How brave he is, me digo. ¿Por qué me habrá hablado? We're in Pretoria! Perhaps we're protected porque la gente se imagina que he's the "garden boy" y yo la "madam," towing him off pa' comprar fencing, or some such. Ah, if they only knew . . .

*25-ii-84*

*Liewe* Hermana,

Thrrrulled (Afrikaans pronuciation) to receive your carta, y package! Mil gracias por los libros, especially the Carolyn Forché: sencillamente, a revelation. Lamento confirmar que you're right about Rock Dalton. Sigh . . . and here I'd been hoping que quizás he'd be a good dissertation topic. Pero ni bien ojeé las primeras páginas y ¡vaya balde de ice water! Dogmatic, maniqueísta y tan . . . well, ¿qué se podría escribir de esta poesía en una *literature* dissertation? I wonder why JC y tantos otros rave about him? There must be something there I'm just not getting. O capaz es por su compromiso, pero they're too afraid to admit it ya que le mataron y es monstruo sagrado.

Me gustó ese libro de Benedetti, *Los poetas comunicantes*, and in it Rock's idea about "la poesía exteriorista." Pero la teoría vuelta praxis (en su propia poesía) boils down to un producto demasiado ideológico pa' mis gustos, which wouldn't be bad si fuera compelling poetry (ouch, harsh, lo sé). Piensa en Miguel Hernández, por ejemplo, about my fave en esta línea (superior al Neruda en su fase "política," creo). O en la misma Forché. Oh, I wish I could write about her! Pero ¿eso sería un PhD en . . . what? American lit (en términos continentales)? ¡No existe!

Ahora, pasando a los temas de tu FAB letter: hemos llegado a un punto de extreme mutual understanding, lo cual celebro ya que our lives have taken us in *very* different directions. Digo, en cuanto al estado civil — o INcivil, in my case, tee hee. I get what you're saying, que a pesar de estar en un marriage que (from the outside, al menos) parece "practically perfect," you still entertain fantasies of escape, que tengas vague sensations of dissatisfaction.

Creo que you held on longer than I did a la *idea* del matrimonio, what it would—or should—mean. En cuanto a mí, I doubt I'll ever marry. Es más, I've always felt this way, desde niña. Don't you remember how I freaked out Mom (me lo ha tirado en cara repeatedly, I'm sure you remember) cuando aparentemente le dije, when I was about four, —*How can you wake up every day looking at the same face en la almohada de al lado?* Ella estaba tan upset que lo anotó en mi baby book. Anyway, I've thought it out (more recently, jaja) y estoy convencida de que, como dice la Germaine Greer, hasta que caiga el patriarcado, women must never marry. Y quizás not even then. Sé que esto representa una "on the edge" choice, decidir no casarse. Pero me mola esta marginality. De hecho, setting myself *against* an institution like marriage—como acto de voluntad—I find rather thrilling. No sé si me sigues.

Y te digo más: hasta cuestiono el ideal de "la pareja," I mean for *me*. I've gotten sort of used to my own company—aparte varios interludios (Jeff F., Paul N., Nick, Mauro, and of course, Roland). Y si bien I used to question myself, angustiada—isn't one "supposed" to be in love, want to be in love, qué coño me pasa—lately I'm asking other questions: who says que los humanos tenemos que estar mated for life? Who says I can't have a child aunque no esté con su padre? Of course a veces extraño, even achingly, having someone to rely on, y me pregunto si no estaré missing out on something fundamental to human happiness. Pero las más de las veces acepto que the way it looks like I'm heading es el mejor de los mundos posibles (viva Candide!) *for me.*

Anyway, Eva, he dicho. Me vienen a recoger Peter y Castells—we're going to see a play en el Market Theatre, uno de los pocos (legally) mixed venues en el país. No sé cómo lo hacen, pues los interracial públicos defy el Group Areas Act y además los shows que hemos visto en el Market son radicales: *Woza Albert* (brillante sátira política—propone la 2nd coming of Christ en apartheid S. Africa), de Percy Mtwa y Mbongeni Ngema, directed by Barney Simon, *Master Harold y los Boys* de Athol Fugard, y muchos otros. Lots of music, too.

Mañana a la tarde, Curé's taking a day off and we're starting to move. No tenemos mucho and our new flat's only two blocks away, pero in this heat todo es epic empresa. I'm gonna press el Castells into service too. He owes me one (*of twee*), ya que I'm pretty much his fave full-service gourmet rest-RON, as he poshly pronounces it!

*25-iii-84*

Mi querida Sloth,

It's Sunday afternoon y heme aquí sentada en mi teensy study, *peck, peck, pecking* away en mi trusty Olivetti. Tengo una olla de veggie curry simmering on the stove para después, cuando regrese Curé. It's raining! A real late-summer storm, con truenos y relámpagos, like in Guadalajara. Y no es flash in the pan, pues it's been raining since last Wednesday (mi cumple—maybe it's a sign: I'll regenerate this *verkrampte* wasteland yet). Tutto bene, Cuz? Haven't heard anything in a couple of months, desde que volví de Europa.

Our new *plek* is great. Etienne trabaja crazy, long hours en su new job, so I have the place to myself a lot. Me encanta. I've been reading a ton. Dio la casualidad (or . . . not) de que ha llegado a UNISA un Italian scholar (de la U. de Firenze, your cuello del bosque), experto en English lit. His thing is Shakespeare, pero he's been giving a brilliant series of lectures. Un po di tutto: Shakespeare, *natuurlik*, pero también Pirandello y Beckett y en mi cumple he gave a sublime seminar on Eliot. Esto mi inspiró a releer *The Waste Land*—and most of Eliot's poetry. Uf, no había entendido ni papa when I read it en la "Modern American Poetry" class de mi UCI mentor, el John Carlos Rowe, en 1975. The hubris: ¿cómo coño intenté escribir term paper on *The Waste Land*? I cringe!

Also, Sarita sent me *The Country Between Us* de Carolyn Forché y me ha hechizado. El libro trata, mostly, de su lengthy stay in El Salvador aunque también poetiza otros temas más cotidianos (pero equally close to my heart): chance encuentros con erotic strangers on European trains, life in another country, lo que hay que elegir—y rechazar—para honrar la artistic vocation que hemos elegido o que, quizás, has chosen us (ese "us" is aspirational). Para mí, la Forché balances brilliantly en ese edge: entre el compromiso ideológico—witnessing—and soaring, intimate lyricism; entre lo intelectual y lo erótico. La leo con despair—y también hope.

Qualcosa d'altro: I'm having an affair. Se llama Neil Strickland. Es senior lecturer in French en UNISA. South African (Engels). Estuvo on long leave en Francia el año pasado, that's why I only met him now. De hecho, we bonded at the T. S. Eliot seminar. Comenzó como lite flirteo, meeting of the minds. Es brillante y bookish, very different from the average *soutie*, jaja. Habla español e italiano, and he loves poetry. He's really funny.

He's 41 pero se ve younger. Tall, pale, ginger hair and beard (no soy beard fan, as you know, pero it looks cute on him). Se ve rakish, pues perdió un ojo (teenage gun accident) y lleva dashing pirata eye patch. Pretty sexy. Lleva casado 15 años con una francesa (she teaches en la U. de Pretoria). Tienen 3 hijas que él adora. ¿Te creerás que I've even met them? A mí me parece perverse, pero al Golpe (así le apodamos) le fascina que vaya a su casa. Tiene un set-up bien bougie: *lekker* big house en un sleepy Pretoria suburb, la de rigeur piscina, criados, etc.

I've been over there to dinner a few times. Me da como un semicreepy thrill, estar allí in the belly of the beast. Ver lo que podría ser mine, but . . . La wife o no se da cuenta de na' or she turns a blind eye. Can't be sure. Usually I go over there con el Castells, who's known Golpe for a few years, de UNISA. Pero I've even been over with Curé, who's hit it off famously con Golpe y hasta con la wife. El Curé es bien charming, as you know. La middle daughter, Simone, has taken quite a shine to me. She's coltish and freckly and adorable. Muy inteligente y sensitive. La adoro. In fact, creo I'll miss her more than Golpe, cuando llegue la hora de dejarlo. El siempre me dice, —*You must do what's best for you*, pero creo que he's falling in love with me. Hmmm. *Ons sal sien* . . . For now, la pasamos bien en la cama. And we often go out for long, languorous, white wine–fueled almuerzos en el Sir Loin, a veces con el Castells, or with Curé or Wimpy, mis bodyguards.

Have I shocked you, Cuz? No creo. Ya me conoces. Anyway, las cosas están bajo control . . . more or less. Sex is *really* good with el Golpe. Y es tan tender and funny and lewd and brilliant. Stay tuned.

*28-iii-84*

Querida Hermana,

Pa' cuando recibas esta, J2 will probably be visiting. Hope you haven't had to detonate a pulga bomb, ni echar dead plants over the back fence como esa vez cuando nos dejaron house-sitting en la Provost House, remember? Anyway, te escribo con un pedido puntual. Pero first: I've been even more psychic than usual en estos días. Llevo dos meses rereading, rather obsessively, casi toda la obra completa de Cortázar. Compré los complete short stories (en Madrid), y también *Historias de cronopios y de famas* (*HCF*), ese teensy book que según yo, es mise en abyme de su obra como totalidad. Por alguna razón me dio por leerlo, ever since I got back from Europe.

Well, te dije lo de mis psychic powers porque supe, belatedly, de mi amiga Carmen Ivette Pérez (from Harvard), que Julio murió el 12 de febrero. Broke my heart, enterarme de eso. Aquí las noticias nos llegan tarde, slant or . . . not at all. Anyway, that's *exactly* when I began to reread him! ¿Te acordáh de esa Halloween party que le hicimos en nuestro Oakland apartment, yo y la Marianne Breidenthal? Hace casi 4 años. I'm picturing it now. Tenía que reunirme con JC, pa' recibir su blessing en el paper topic. Can you imagine my terror? ¿Tener que balbucear unas pavadas racionales a mi longtime ídolo—about his own work?

We'd formed an imitation Club de las Serpientes, entre algunos grad students en Berkeley: la Marianne y yo, plus Galo, this groovy ecuatoriano I was having an affair with, plus Oscar Góngora, Armin Schwegler, Dan Dickison y algunos otros, plus dos jóvenes profesores we loved, la Em Bergmann y el sexy feliz medievalista, Jack Walsh. We drew straws y a mí me tocó la corta: I was charged with inviting JC to the fiesta. Anyway, entré a su despacho, y por poco me desmayo when he fixes me with those gorgeous, wide-set, green axolotl eyes. Abrí la boca pa' comenzar mi spiel—que en vez de otro ripiado y masturbatorio ensayo on "the meaning of la Maga" en *Rayuela*, o algo más ostensibly "meaty" e ideológicamente "correcto," like on *Libro de Manuel*, pretendía estudiar la función de lo lúdico en *Historias de* . . . Y en eso me semi-interrumpe así sin más, —*Vos, Susana, también sos cronopio. ¿Fumás?* En eso he offers me a Gitanes (negro), y le invito a la fiesta. —*Ehh, ¿irán también profesores?* he asks. — *Noooo*, I tell him. *Solo estudiantes.* —*Entonces*, he looks at me teasingly, *contá conmigo.*

Ah, Julio. Me acuerdo de la presión de sus enormes manos on mine, su voz ronca, afrancesada y un poco sardónica. I remember him arriving at the stroke of midnight vestido de Dracula (well, in a dark-brown robe, con las uñas pintadas de negro y unos fake colmillos), acompañado de Carol, dressed as la Bride of Dracula. Me acuerdo de tánto . . .

Pero anyway, a lo que iba: for whatever insane reason, me ofrecí a dar un seminar on Cortázar to the entire Romance Languages department en UNISA. No es hasta agosto, pero I *really* need my essay on *HCF*. Ya te he dicho lo *kak* que son los resources aquí. La head de la Spaans section, esa nefasta American, Cathy McDermott (Castells's and my archi-enemiga), es una anti-intelectual mediocre. And besides, peninsularista.

I'm pretty sure that paper is in a box labeled "Research Papers" (jaja, obvio) en el garaje de J2. I'll be eternally grateful si me lo puedes encontrar. Do you think you can? También existe a *faint* possibility de que haya una copia among Dad's things. Solía mandarle mis papers. Could you ask him, ya que están allí de visita? Mil gracias de antemano, Weeve. *Skryf, hoor.* And let me know about the lay of the land (énfasis: lay). Es decir: did you decide to try to get knocked, ¿o no?

*2-iv-84*

Hi Eva,

¡Mil gracias por el cassette y la carta! The timing was *perfeksie*, actually. Castells y yo teníamos que ir a Joburg and were lamenting no tener nada que escuchar cuando lo and behold here comes a notice from the Sentraal Poskantoor that there's a parcel for me that "might require the payment of duty." Yo estaba aterrada, as packages always come *direk* to me en UNISA. Plus, el Castells freaked me out al decirme que they (o sea, el dizque gobierno) have the tendency to call you in si te llega algo "suspicious" (which could be *anything*) pa' que lo abras en el acto, in front of them.

La notice ponía que it was from the US, and I was wracking my cerebros pues I'd just gotten your Carolyn & Rock poetry parcel, y no esperaba nada de ti. Castells y yo rocked up to Correos, this daunting official building, y tras una espera interminable, surrounded by all these official-looking or polyester-frocked, secretarial Afrikaners, finalmente nos llaman. En el counter, me presentan con tu parcel. Al verlo, I sang out jovially, — *Oh, it's from my sister.* — *Your suster, eh? Then it must be a guft?* Me aferré a las palabras de ese midlevel burócrata cual a crucifijo, all the while doubting wildly that it *was*, in fact, a gift. — *Yes, yes! It was just my birthday*, respondí entusiasta. — *See? Here's my passport.* — *Ag, well then, s'allright. You can take it.*

No te imaginas mi alivio, al no tener que abrirlo delante de esos prying apartheid ojos. Al salir al blinding sunlight, legs atremble, pensando que what if it was some revolutionary book que even those thick-as-a-plank gansos oficiales could make out was subversive, we ripped it open and found . . . to our delight, ¡tu cassette! Ay, hermana, we're mad about it! Castells's Citroën fairly shimmied its way down the M1 to Joburg as we salsa-ed and sang along con el Willie Colón y el Rubén Blades. "En la unión está la fuerza y nuestra salvacioooón." Lots of love from el Castells and me. ¡Mil gracias!

*8-v-84*

*Hou gaan dit*, hermana,

I should be marking 3rd-year tareas on Lorca's *Yerma*, pero aprovecho pa' hacer algo de catch-up en mi correspondence, ya que la McDermott's mercifully out toda la semana for minor surgery. Been keeping company con una nueva amiga de Canadá, Heather. El Castells me la presentó, pero now we often spend time together sin él. Ella es biochemist, y ya lleva casi 4 años aquí. Piensa que "if she puts my social life right," I'll be much happier y que she might even convince me to stay on here. Uf, ¡ni en pedo! You can guess that politically we don't really see ojo a ojo, pero it's a sweet thought. Lately la Heather's been introducing me to una sarta de eligible bachelors, pero no capta que por más que un vato me haga wine 'n' dine, if he's a full-on, unredeemable racista, it's a no-go. She just laughs. Me cree too picky. She's sporty and tall and adorable, and somehow tenemos bastante en común. Parece haber un . . . algo, common to North Americans. I can't

put my fingie on it, exactly—a certain openness, friendliness, espontanei-
dad. En todo caso: it *definitely* doesn't exist here.

En estos días, la Heather and I've been seeing un chingo de films.
Recently vimos *Een Vrouw Als Eva* (jaja, tu apodo)—maybe you've seen it?
No es nuevo. Se me hace que la Heather maybe me tiene un little crush: el
film se trata de una relación feliz between two women. Starring my fave
Dutch actriz, la sublime Monique van de Ven (of *Turkish Delight* fame, o
digamos infamy, jaja) y la pouty, sullen Maria Schneider (of *Last Tango in
Paris* fame). Well, a pesar de esas dos thespian Euro-delicias, y un director
supposedly feminista, el film was a bit of a flop. Pero . . . sexy, nevertheless.
También vimos *Angel*, the directorial debut de Neil Jordan, con el brooding
Stephen Rea. Se trataba de la turbulencia en N. Ireland, one of my obses-
sions, como sabes. Nos gustó. Y anoche la Heather me invitó a ver *Coup de
foudre* (or *Entre Nous*), espectacular. Very evocative and moving. La dirigió
Diane Kurys y se trata de una intense, years-long friendship entre dos casa-
das (one a Jewish refugee) en la Francia de WWII. La judía la representó
Isabelle Huppert, mi sine qua non. Again, I'm sensing a pattern here . . .
hmm: la amistad entre las mujeres es tan sensual y apasionada, it bordered
on la felicité, o tal nos pareció. Total, after almost two years here sin girl-
friends, la Heather's a breath of fresh air. Es *uitlander* como yo, y es mi
primera amiga (aparte de Anita Wurfl, who's on long leave this whole year
y con quien, anyway, realmente no me junté mucho tras el breakup con
Roland).

I've been rereading Cortázar's *Rayuela*, aunque me pongo muy exasperated con todo ese hypercerebral (hasta un grado masturbatorio) posturing.
Por otra parte: a veces me identifico totalmente con el Oliveira, y otras
veces con la Maga. Pero me irrita que Julio haya dividido sus qualities tan
diametrically y según el gender. Me encantaría preguntarle what the *hell*?
Pero sigh . . . he's not here anymore. También leí *The Color Purple*, by
Alice Walker. Brilliant. It's the kind of thing que capaz les guste read
aloud, you and Gary. ¿Te conté que la Wiggue made me read O'Connor's
*Wise Blood* to her, en Madrid? Con todo y mi Tennessee-Arkansas acento
(picked up from Nick Vidnovic's imitations of people from his Little Rock
infancia)—which she insisted I maintain throughout. ¡Menos mal que it
was a pretty short book! You should also read Marge Piercy's novel,

*Braided Lives.* La he leído dos veces. I was just remembering . . . it got me through the worst agony de las dos semanas que estuve en England last year, ¿te acuerdas?

Oh, casi se me olvidaba: Curé's been seeing this colored oke, Ian. Léase sleeping with, porque obvio, they can't be seen around town (digo going out, en una romantic *situasie*), por las byzantine, completely racist apartheid laws: Group Areas Act, la Immorality Act, etc. En este caso, they're *doubly* marked, pos además de interracial couple, son felices. El Ian is sweet and very funny. He's obsessed con mis perfumes. Siempre que viene a casa, he makes a beeline pal baño and douses himself with Kouros, Antaeus y demás elixirs que le compré a Curé en el Corte Inglés. Desde luego, the oke has good taste! Stay tuned . . .

22-v-84

Querida Lee,

I was thrilled to receive your letter. You really have a way with words, Cuz. Lucky you, tener talento en dos artes: writing and painting. Por mi parte, I'm hopeless artistically. Well, salvo la fotografía, or designing and making clothes. Guess what? Ahora tengo *naaimasjien* (muy funny: "naai" significa to fuck, en Afrikaans), lent to me by none other than la M., Golpe's wife! Don't think I'm mad, pero I'm actually preferring her to him lately. She's warmer, más amena, easier than he is, strangely enough. Capaz sea porque we're both foreigners, both from dizque warmer, Mediterranean cultures (ella es French, remember).

Al principio, pensé que sería potentially destructive, or painful, to keep going over there. Pero él insistía, and I love seeing la Simone. Plus, I really wanted to pick up esa fuck-machine! So la otra noche Etienne and I went over for dinner y lo pasamos bomba, a pesar del Golpe, who acted like an aloof, moody child. Me daban ganas de gritarle, en una, you smug bastard: con una adoring (y aparentemente clueless) wife, three beautiful hijas, y una passionate—and discreet—mistress. After that night estaba tan disgusted (como dice mi Granny Chávez) I felt like ending it. El Golpe tiene sus moments, pero a la larga I don't think he's enough for me. And he knows it, creo. Y está comenzando a irritarme con su Scorpio sulking y sus moods.

Speaking of women: esa quote que me mandaste de la Doris Lessing, about los orgasmos vaginales. What *kak, ek sê*! Que the ultimate, que the only "true," que esa dark pool of sensation and emotion. ¡Vaya telenovela masculinista! What slavery a la verga, por dios. What a sellout. Fuck her!

Speaking about women (bis): ¿te platiqué de mi new Canadian friend, Heather, right? En cuanto a la política, we don't mesh at all. She's accepting of the status quo here, bastante laissez-faire. Pero she's intelligent, sporty-sexy y muy divertida. Resulta que el otro día she told Wimpy que sus hormonas están "very confused around me." Wim me dijo que la Heather was semitipsy when she said that to him, pero he has the definite impression she'd "go for it." Hmmm. A mí me ha dicho que she's not really feliz— pero *only* because she's been too chicken to try anything hasta ahora. *Ons sal sien . . .*

16-vi-84
*Doble aniversario: my parents' boda y Soweto uprising*

Carissima cugina Lee,

El Wa has returned from the Border War, héroe conquistador. Actually, más bien todo lo contrario, aunque who could blame him? Potential cannon fodder en esta bullshit apartheid guerra colonialista. He's more mercurial y fire-crackery than ever. Hicimos un *braai* a few weeks ago, more or less en su honor y . . . para variar el guest of honor got wasted, sloppy drunk. El Wimpy tan embelesado con su tipsy Adonis que le estuvo making googly eyes toda la noche. He's way more tolerant—or lovestruck—con el Wa than I! Pero pos ni modo. I've got la Heather, si bien she's gone off for a month-long holiday en el UK.

In her absence, I've been spending every weekend en Joburg. Etienne está trabajando en un *lekker* new restó, managed by some friends of his, called Prohibition. It's only 4 blocks from Mango Park (André's Rockey Street shop), so Curé me deja allí pa' pasar el weekend con André y la Kathy. André had been asking me for months to spend weekends with them y la verdad, hay una vibe tan chévere entre los Merry Pranksters del highveld I don't know why I waited so long. Lately ha estado un vato de New York que hace import-export de artesanías. Fue con André up to the

Ndebele y volvieron con collares, wall hangings y otros gorgeous beaded things. We've started selling en un flea market que recién abrieron los sábados, next to the Market Theatre en Newtown. Es algo así como el Rastro de Madrid, remember? Much smaller scale, pero como el Rastro, multiracial. Muy unusual (for here)—bordering on illegal. Hmmm, me pregunto cuánto durará.

Anyway, I was helping André hawk his wares en el Market market (he draped me, de pies a cabeza, in baubles, bangles y beads, tee hee, una maniquí viviente), y con ese look—between Maasai y punky—conocí a un nuevo galán, amigo de André: Charalambos (Harry) Kentrotas. —*And who are you?* me abordó. Ahhh, Cuz, el Harry es bohemian dreamboat deluxe! Greek South African. Slim pero bien fit, tall, dark, cabellos largos. Beautiful eyes. Just . . . *mooi* all over. Plus, he smells soooo good! Tiene tu edad y es Aries, like us. Inteligente, voraz lector, very funny. Y con un espíritu tan childlike, playful. Lee, es tan sensual y místico en la cama. Pasamos horas y horas, licking each other! Desde que nos conocimos, he's come through to Pretoria todos los días pa' quedarse conmigo. While Curé's at work, el Harry y yo nos damos masajes, *rook* it up, y tomamos long, luxurious, sexy baths, contándonos cuentos hasta que se enfría el agua del todo . . .

Harry's a painter like you, y artesano. He makes these ethereal, beautiful metal mobiles, y los vende en el flea market. André lo adora, pero me ha dicho, "Harry's not of this world," o sea: toma un chingo de drogas. Se me hace que if you can get 'em, y tienes la inclinación, this is one way to rebel against the relentless repression de esta sociedad—without getting yourself killed or thrown in jail. Aunque, on that score: acaban de hacer aun más draconian las leyes anti-moteriles. Y unfortuNATEly (como lo pronuncia mi amigo el Pius Nkoe, de UNISA), our friend Glen just got busted: intentaba traer 3 kg de Swazi gold y *wham*. Straight to *die tronk*. Tiene excelente lawyer, y no parece estar muy flipado, pero I would be, en su lugar. The penalty's 25 years, R50,000—o las dos cosas. Can you believe that?

Pero anyway, while Rome (or Joburg) burns . . . he reincidido en una vida moteril the likes of which I hadn't seen in years. Pero this Malawi y Swazi mota's about a *zillion* times more potent que la "sin semilla" que fumábamos, Cuz, I'm telling you. Last Friday was the grand opening en

Prohibition, y el Curé nos invitó a todo el André crowd. It was a real scene, packed, great music. Y después, dropeé ácido con el Chari-mou (my nickname for Harry), which I hadn't done in maybe . . . a verrr ¿10 años? Incredible viaje: sensual, visionary. And out-of-cuerpo sex, for hours and hours, en el spare bedroom de André y la Kathy.

El Harry's a bit of a drifter (per André). He's just taken off en una especie de month-long walkabout (mixed metáfora, I know it's Australian) o safari, digamos, through Botswana, Zimbabwe y Malawi. André's warned me—in a tío-like way—que el Harry got burned in a relationship y está gun-shy, pero creo que el aviso is more about André's ego (o semi-celos) que otra cosa. Me tiene un little crush, y . . . Por mi parte, the way Harry is suits me; ya sabes lo que me sofoca when someone comes on too heavy.

Hablando de eso: the Golpe scene's on its last patas, se me hace. It would've been anyway, probably, aun si no hubiese conocido al Harry. Pero check Golpe's *reaksie* when he found out: he's thrown so may rabietas infantiles, se ha puesto jealous y petulant, y para colmo, bellowing que yo debería sentirme grateful por su reacción because "it proves how much he loves me." Rich, *nê*?

Y ahora, cierro con una lista de hiLEHrius Afrikaans hippie-surfer (druggie)-*taal* I've picked up from el Harry. Oh, I *wish* you could hear this! Keep this forevah, Cuz, pal historical record:

Crave=dig, enjoy; blade=papel de liar; *dagga*=mota; bra/bru=bro; *ek sê*=digo yo (common crutch); check=check out, look at; how's=how about/what about; I scheme=creo; I tune you, bra=I'm telling you, dude; *nooit*=no ways, never; *lank*=lots, big, many; my china=mate, pal, dude; *pomp, fok, naai*=to fuck; *Jirre, Jussus*=Jesus; jweb=mota.

3-*vii*-84

*Liewe Suster,*

Según los records históricos (ejém), I've heard nothing from you desde que te llamé (en abril) and you promised to send me "detailed updates" immediately. Well? Sigo esperando, too, lo que te pedí hace siglos: my Cortázar paraphernalia. I *really* need it, Eva. It's now down to el alambre: tengo ese seminar en cosa de 3 semanas. Also: did you ever get my parcel?

Te mandé un hermoso vintage Zulu necklace (from André's stash) hace siglos. Let me know, please! Y una cosita más: did you ever manage to track down el Bob Durling (UCB)? If so, ¿me mandas su address, plis? Quiero pedirle una letter of rec (for UC–Davis), and I want to give him ample time.

¿Te conté del Market Theatre rastro? Llevo dos meses going there every Saturday, ya que paso los weekends en Joburg en lo de André y Kathy de Wet, where there's always an interesting vibra. Last Saturday fui con mi amiga la Heather, then we stayed at André's. On the Sunday we were invited to luncheon donde la Mary Menell, Wiggue's Harvard chum. She's home con la familia, working on her senior thesis. What wealth—wow! Esa mansión made el Bedfordview spread de los Fraser look like a favela. Chihte, pero you get the idea. Los Menell son muy liberales—conocen a mucha gente en el struggle: el Bishop Desmond Tutu, por ejemplo, y la Helen Suzman es tía de Mary—pero of course tenían the usual trappings of white S. African (extreme) privilege: enormous, beautiful house, full complement of servants, etc. Daddy habría estado *muy* uncomfy—you know him. Pero Mamá habría estado en su sauce.

I could see que la Heather se sentía out of her element, pero I found them fascinating, y muy warm. There was Mary, muy animatedly (Wiggue me había dicho que la Mary reminds her of me—she *does* talk rather a lot, tee hee, and was waving her Mantis-like appendages around quite a bit!), informing me and Heather que sería trotskista "if the situation were viable." I had to suppress a laugh: her next stop is Europe, tras las 9 semanas en el regazo del lujo en Joburg. Ah, well . . . Living in S. Africa under apartheid requiere lanzarse a la tightrope de la ambivalencia. Si no, you'll go mad.

5-vii-84

Darlingest Cugina,

So chuffed to get your latest, greatest lettera, my China! I'm a bit dozey, sufriendo los aftereffects de una surprise 4th of July fest que me brindaron la adorable de la Heather, con Wimpy y otros amigos. It was planned down to the (mandatory) costumes y el decorado. So hilarious! La Heather vino pa' recogerme; she insisted on borrowing this totally weird, punk, vintage Popeye blouse que compré en el Market flea market, y me obligó a vestime de red angora sweater, white pants y una vincha azul de seda. Fuimos a una commune (what they call it cuando mucha gente comparte casa), semi out en los sticks, y de repente out pops Wimpy, también vestido bien patriotic, waving this teensy American flag. I about died. Estaba otra chica americana, eccéntrica, Joanie. Es geóloga, studying los no sé qué habits of some South African vulture. Y estaba una alemana, su novio británico y otros. Wait till you see las fotos, really choice. Lo pasamos bomba. Era todo muy ironic (we all hate Ronnie y la política norteamericana, obvio), pero it was sweet too. We blasted Bruce Springsteen y bailamos, luego fumamos *lank* Swazi *dagga* and had a *lekker braai*. You know me— lloré.

Cambiando de rumbo, o *rubro*: on T. S. Eliot, give him a chance, Cuz. *The Waste Land* is hermetic as hell, es verdad. Maybe try *Four Quartets*? Si te sientes adventurous, ¿por qué no buscas al Prof. Alessandro Serpieri en la U. di Firenze? Tell him you're my cousin! Es el que vino a UNISA y dio esa lecture series—on Eliot. Es brillante, pero muy accessible y nice. Y habla perfecto inglés.

Otro rubro: el Harry's been writing me desde su odyssey. Acaba de mandarme una beautiful letter de Botswana. Es tan juguetón y smart y apasionado. Me caliento just thinking about him: our stoned, hours-long, candlelight baths. Hacer el amor tripping on acid. Mirarle mientras se quita la ropa, watching me watch him. Escucharle gemir. Ahhhh . . .

Y te dejo con esa sexy imagen. Oh, almost forgot: Harry me regaló el tuxedo de su Greek grandpa. What do you make of that? Raro y maravilloso, *nê*? Creo que es un romántico . . . in spite of himself. Me dijo, —*So you'll always remember me.*

Oh, y *otro* almost forgot: Curé me invitó a otro Italian film festival! Right here in Pretoria. Remember the one I went to el año pasado en Joburg, con el Castells? That's when we stumbled down la conejería, jaja— discovered Mango Park, y nos metimos a full con André & co. Feels like light-years ago! Anyway, Curé y yo vimos *La notte di San Lorenzo*, very beautiful y de hecho; it was filmed around Pistoia, where you're staying! We also saw *Dimenticare Venezia* (por *2a* vez) and *Tre Fratelli* (mi *3a* vez). I love, love, LOVE this film. It's so slow and sun-dappled. Y ese Michele

Placido—¡para morir por! Have you heard of this oke (músico), Pino Daniele? Búscalo, you'll enJOY him. Usan su canción "Je So' Pazzo" en el film. Canta en napolitano y . . . te arranca il cuore, I promise you. We *must* find his cassettes cuando esté en Italia. ¡Faltan solo 2 meses!

*27-vii-84*

Carissima Lee,

Where've you been lately, Cuz? Miss you! Tengo *lank* tales to tell. I'm feeling very alive lately. Heme trabaje y trabaje, muy busy preparing el Cortázar seminar para el 16 de agosto. He leído tantísimo, estoy saturated de JC. Weevil finally came through: me mandó los articles que le pedí, and my research paper. Ahora es cuestión de reducir. Elegir. How to do JC justice in an hour-long seminar, y para gente que no sabe nada de él. Pero besides work, my social life's really been taking off.

Pero oh, before I lance myself into that tale, agárrate: Etienne's been called up to the BORDER! Translation: sent to try to shoot "kaffirs" (término racista y despectivo para los africanos negros) en la frontera con Angola. Estoy angustiada, pero también algo irritated. Because he could've gotten out of it si hubiese estado un poco más organized. Sigh. A pesar de ser Capricorn, y super hardworking, siempre anda de crisis en crisis. He's totally scattered. El padre de Wimpy could've maybe helped, o quizás Curé's own dad. Pero no. Es muy stubborn. Y como te digo, disorganized. Anyway, he's gone, y estamos todos muy worried. El Wa es mucho más butch que Curé, y mira cómo volvió de la border: absolutely *finished*, like they say here.

Cambiando de rubro: Heather and I've been going out a lot en Pretoria y casi siempre a Joburg los weekends. We help André sell en el Market Theatre flea market los sábados, luego a la noche we hang out con los De Wet, *rooking* it up, escuchando música, charlando, etc. Me he hecho fast friends con la Beth Miller, una joven arquitecta de Virginia. Su situación tiene uncanny overlaps con la mía: she moved here para estar con un sudafricano. She met him in Europe, donde estaba road-tripping after graduating del architecture program en la Virginia Tech. Like what happened to me with Roland, la Beth's scene con su oke se tronchó here in S. Africa. Pero she began to get these unreal job offers, fresh out of school! De la noche a la mañana she found herself a full-fledged arquitecta. En eso también la Beth tiene overlaps conmigo: catapulted from being parte del rebaño de underpaid grad students desperately buscando jale en las humanities in Ronnie's America to being one of only *three* full-time lecturers in Spaans en todo el país. What a trip, nê. Y por ende, expected to teach—and know— about . . . well, *todo*. Believe me, la ironía's not lost on us: sabemos que esto es otro toxic efecto secundario del apartheid. Beth y yo lo hablamos, pero creo que I feel more conflicted about it than she does.

Anyway, es muy inteligente y talented. Excelente fotógrafa, too. Me ha presentado a otros jóvenes bien creative, including some hot young local architects. And so, our circle's expanding from the André de Wet artisan scene para abarcar otras órbitas. Tras año y medio de intense alienation, heartbreak y un proceso de adaptación, both Beth and I have stumbled— or tumbled—al inner circle de uno de los grupos más "in," más muy muy, en el Witwatersrand. We laugh about it, pues for both of us ha sido sin querer, just that Cortázar kind of azar objetivo que me lleva por la vida.

Entre los architect friends de la Beth se encuentra un tal Ian Hosak. He's 26 y parece Slavic movie star: rubio, rock-star haircut, labios carnosos y pouty, una penetrante mirada azul and this amazing, large, buff cuerpazo que te caes patrás. El vato es stuck-up a más no poder, even calls himself "dangerous" (translation: his career's skyrocketing pero emotionally, es medio troglodita). Word en la calle es que he goes through women cual si fueran changes of *broekies* (bragas) and can't handle "weakness" (léase commitment or emotional depth). I'm sure you can see what's coming, Cuz: los vatos así son mi catnip; perversamente, I'd like to bring him to his knees. Todo el mundo le dice Hos, and I quickly baptized him Hoss, y luego la Beth y yo comenzamos a llamarle Bonanza. Lo más hilarious: he (Hos) *looooves* el apodo, aunque of course, el Highveld Hoss no tiene nada que ver con el big ol' lunk del TV show.

Something else hilarious (aunque sort of unsettling too, la verdad): el Bonanza's connected to Roland, porque eran classmates en Wits. Esto lo supe anoche, in a completely surreal scene. Estuve en una festichola con la Beth y con Wimpy, in some architect or other's gorgeous northern suburbs mansión, y de repente el Rolo's making a beeline for me. No le había visto en siglos, maybe desde comienzos del año. I was a bit high pero por suerte not too far gone. Still, menos mal que I had my bodyguards, *ek sê*. Rolo tuned me his usual Mr. Cool, cocky *kak*. Por suerte, el Wim, Beth y yo estábamos dressed to kill. Yo vestía slinky black knit trousers que diseñó la Linda Weech, y una skimpy T (sin sostén, tee hee). Ahora llevo siempre un chingo de André bracelets, all up and down my mantis-brazos, y la Beth wears even more. —*Lookin' good, Shug*, me dijo Rolo. I think he was really surprised to see me y hasta taken aback, cual si yo fuera interloper in "his" highveld social scene.

Anyway, after exchanging a few banal pleasantries and bragging about las *partytjies* he attends and his regular tennis circuit (gag me), las cosas se pusieron bien heavy all of a sudden cuando la Beth, out of the blue, mencionó al Hoss, and let slip que he finds me "intriguing." You should've seen Rolo, Cuz! —*What? How do* you *know Hos, Shug?* bufó cual Cape *buffel*. Me agarró del brazo and steered me to a corner pa' darme "consejos." Que he knows Hos well y que me cuide, que el vato intenta ser cryptic y tough y es "arrogant prick," y bla bla. ¡Estaba furioso! Wimpy y la Beth estaban medio cowering, mirando este trainwreck. I was unnerved y medio me dio pena, pero te confieso que me sentí un little hair triunfante, too. Let's not forget Rolo's "rough, rugged, and independent" act, y lo que siempre me decía, que he "never gets jealous," etc. Well, here he was en un frenesí de celos—over a year after our breakup, *nogal*. When I'd had my fill of his bellowing, le dije, in my best Southern-belle accent, —*Why Rolo, darlin', he sounds a lot like you!* y le dejé allí plantao, fuming.

Minor *probleem*: como te dije, I myself *could* be "intrigued" con el Bonanza, pero la Beth's hot for him, le tiene *lank* crush desde hace un año. Según, she lusts after his architectural ability (más bien su su architectural *build*), pero apparently él no le da bolilla. Pero no quiero problemas. El Harry K. vuelve pronto, plus I'm taking off in a month (la bella Italia, here I come!) and besides, desde que se fue el Harry, *another* oke's been sending me smoke signals. Se llama Rich D'Uberville. In a weird, "strangers in a strange land" way, tenemos bastante en común. He's American, de hecho Russian Jewish, de New York. He's really into music, nos fascinan los mismos bands pero he's also turned me on to some more arcane artists. My latest obsession es un tal Tonio K. Check him out! Y hablando de turning on: el Rich tiene gorgeous accent (y gorgeous thighs). He's funny, droll, algo shy. Dark, ojos oscuros, jet black, curly hair. Picture . . . a ver, un sexy Frank Zappa. Pero he's married (con una South African judía), y tienen dos hijitas. Para variar, we met at André and Kathy's. Richie's a printer, y nos está haciendo las invites pa' una surprise party que le vamos a hacer al André en su muy Leo cumple, el 18 de agosto. Por suerte, just after my Cortázar seminar, so I'll be able to really cut loose. Can't wait!

*17-viii-84*

My dearest Sloth,

Ciao bellissima, come stai (bet you're getting sick of *that* line)? He estado tan busy, on so many levels, que casi ni sé which nalga's up! My Cortázar seminar was yesterday, y me fue bien. So that's an immense relief. Comencé citando a Neruda, quien dijo que whoever doesn't read JC is "doomed"; seguí con la anécdota de nuestra Halloween *partytjie* y luego estructuré el seminar around JC's major dialectic: la tensión entre *Homo ludens* y *Homo sapiens*. Or, como dice Horacio Oliveira (en *Rayuela*): "the effort to get beyond the Greek criterion of truth and error, to get beyond Aristotelian logic and Kantian categories, to get beyond the great, rotten mask of the West." Mis colegas estaban on the edge of their seats, Cuz. Y ahora, that's done y ¡a festejar! Mañana es la birthday fest pal (über-Leo) Pied Piper, André de Wet.

A verrrr . . . ¿qué te cuento? Oh, el Harry K. volvió de su odyssey, brown as a berry (and as juicy) y caímos en la cama al tiro. We can't resist each other, pero aunque es brillante y está fascinado con mi work (y mi cuerpo), he's a bit too will o' the wisp pa' mis gustos. Algo tiene de Peter Pan (si ese green-clad creature fumara *lank dagga* and trekked around Africa). En fin, when we get together lo pasamos bomba. Effortless, fun, supersexy y sin expectativas. Pero meanwhile, while the cat was away . . . I've been keeping company con el Rich. Hasta ahora, we mainly see each other en lo de André y Kathy. Stay tuned.

La otra noche fui con Beth y Wim a Joburg pa' ver *The Basileus Quartet*, a new Italian film. It was fantastic! Pero la highveld intelligentsia is *such* a small mundo: en el lobby, we ran smack into Bonanza, con su (official/latest) jailbait guhlfriend. We all said howzit, bien *vriendelike*, pero el vato se puso como un tomate when he saw me. La Beth afirma que he's more into me than she's *ever* seen him into anyone; she and Wim theorize que he's likely feeling intensely uncomfortable ya que me reveló tanto de sus inner demons (una noche que salimos y terminamos en la cama) y, según todo el mundo—including himself—las emociones no son su fuerte. Frankly, Cuz, if I intrigue him, él a mí también, in a Slavic rock star kind of way. Pero I'm not going out of my way to get with him. De hecho, al contrario. I've got (more than) enough en mi plato. Y la Beth carries a torch, por más que me haya dado la green light.

Have I told you about our latest Saturday night *jols*? Después del Market Theatre rastro en la mañana we (o sea yo, André, Beth, Glen, Linda W. y otros assorteds del Club De Wet, plus Wimpy y a veces la Heather) head to the Park Five Saloon. Es un black club, medio dive-y, en Bree Street en el mero centro de Joburg. Completely illegal for us to be there, pero tocan allí unos bitchen bands y hasta ahora, we haven't been hassled. Es decir: by the police. Porque la clientela es bastante rowdy. No van muchas mujeres and we're the only nonblack women. Muchas de las mujeres negras son working girls—they've even tried to hit on me and Beth! We've been resorting to a new dance form, que la Beth y yo bautizamos "defensive aerobics": consiste en flailing elbows and knees with great vigor. Easy to do, pues la música es dy-no-MITE, my china. Tocan allí los Dynamics, a mixed-race band who play this wild, raw, super-bailable township fusion, una mezcla de jazz, soul, funk y hasta punk con dos choppy, funky guitarras, dos wailing tenor saxos, bajo y keyboards, plus the hottest (white) drummer en el southern hemisphere, I promise you!

A veces toca en el Park Five otro grupo, los Mapanzulah. Similar vibe, a bit more polished. El sábado pasado los Mapanzulah had a huge, all-night fiesta en su commune y nos invitaron a todos porque el bass player y el drummer son amigos del Harry K. y de André. It was amazing, Lee. Six bands, jamming toda la noche. *Lank dagga*, mucho baile. *Ag*, it was only *lekker* my bra, como dicen mis AlternaKaner pals.

Y ahora, one of the most chévere adventures of my life: el fin de semana anterior, todos los highveld Merry Pranksters fuimos a un massive music festival en Soweto. Nos enteramos en el Park Five Saloon—they sponsored the concert en el Jabulani Stadium. Fuimos un chingo de amigos, all the usual suspects en el Club André, plus la actriz Michelle du Toit y algunos que yo no conocía. Entre miles de festival-goers, había solo un puñadito de nonblacks. Check how we got there, Cuz: we caravaned en varios autos; Wimpy and I rode with la Beth, en su beat-up old station wagon. Lo que no sabíamos Wim y yo (hasta llegar al concert): Beth traía un mogollón de *dagga*, hidden en el auto. Enough to get the whole stadium high, I promise you (or us clapped *in die tronk*)! We actually breezed through several checkpoints porque el Wimpy, cool as a pepino, flashed his *polisie* credentials, pero can you fucking imagine? La Beth is *mal*.

The hands-down highlight was Juluka. Son Johnny Clegg, un (ex) antropólogo blanco y Jewish, grew up en los northern suburbs de Joburg y aprendió Zulu de joven y también la guitarra y el baile tradicional de los Zulu migrant workers. As a teen, se juntó con Sipho Mchunu y formaron Juluka. Lee, they took my breath away. Of course, just like our Saturday nights en el Park Five, el concierto fue ilegal, pero no one hassled us. Los townships have been heating up lately, tras la General Election (de agosto). Total *kak*, condemned internationally, según escuchamos. As it should be. As per usual: excluye a los blacks y brinda token power-sharing a los Indians y coloreds.

Anyway, no (white) police in sight, por suerte. We danced and danced. El Johnny y su banda cantan en Zulu e inglés, en una hermosa, wild, jive-y mezcla de ritmos africanos y western. Picture unos gorgeous vatos descamisados, all sweaty y apasionados, thrashing about, kicking up their legs, chanting i-YUM bo hum, *i-YUM bo* . . . y en el downbeat del *HUM* stamping their leather y feather-clad legs, todos a uno. Un poco como esa wedding, o el soccer game Rolo took me to, fue una out-of-body experience. Rodeada de miles de personas, a sea of black humanity dancing ecstatically, con unos few little bits of pale entre la muchedumbre. Ay, Cuz, I *wish* you could've been there.

I'll close with otra nota cultural, of a *very* different order: me he metido en otro affair, con André Hartmann, un German scholar. Abogado e intelectual. Le conocí en UNISA, en un centro para Latin American Studies. O sea: Institute for Friendship with Dictators, as I cheekily told him cuando nos conocimos (I think that turned him on). Don't even say it, Cuz. Ya sé que es una locura—for sooo many reasons: casado, German y hay algo . . . slightly suspicious—officious—about him. Pero: es brillante y icily attractive in a Teutonic way. He mainly comes to my flat, pero el otro día me invitó a una reception en su casa ¡y fui! Ya sabes lo perverse que soy. I took my bodyguard, Wimpy. Habla perfecto alemán, and he distracted la Katja, el Hartmann's wife, mientras el AH and I made out behind the sofa en el lounge. Vaya vidita de international intrigue, ¿que no? Anyway, te dejo con esa—admittedly bizarre (even for me)—imagen. No te preocupes— it's not serious. Anyway, I'll see you soonest!

*8-x-84*

Mi querida Lydia,

Me puse tan happy al recibir tu letter y cassette a few days ago, cuando volví de Europa. Just the ticket (como dice mi dad) to keep me going en estos últimos meses en Africa. Me siento al borde de un abismo, aunque sé que that sounds ironic. Las cosas aquí están cada vez más tense (politically) pero por weird que te parezca, living here me ha forjado, cual crisol. Te juro que mi partida va a ser wrenching, como la de Dorothy al final del *Wizard of Oz.* Tengo gente muy, muy querida aquí. Los que te he dicho: Etienne and Wim, my AlternaKaner bodyguard best friends. La Izelle y el Wa. El Castells. Peter and Gary. André, Beth, y la Heather. El Neppe. Y mis boys, my loves: el Golpe, Harry K., Richie.

And speaking about that (gente querida): mi hermana Sarita's leaving soon. Returning to Managua, y nadie sabe un carajo de sus plans. Es *pésima* corresponsal. I haven't heard from her desde hace meses. INTERRUP-TION: Lidita, how psychic is this? Te estoy escribiendo desde el *kantoor* en UNISA y me acaban de entregar un huge manila envelope, ¡precisa-mente de Sarita! Incluye mi official acceptance to UC–Davis, con graduate fellowship. So that's set then. No puedo rajarme. Ay, espero me den TA-ship too. Otro poco de weirdness: I'm actually looking forward to el aula, después de casi tres años de disembodied "distance-tuition," occasionally buttressed por esas extrañas video conferences.

Well, el update on my family: Sarita's leaving for Nicaragua next month. Va por México (y quizás Honduras), pa' visitar los Salvadoran refugee camps. Se queda dos meses. Así que she won't be there (en casa) cuando yo regrese pa' mediados de diciembre. My parents either! Seguirán en España con mi little sis Laura (la Wiggue), who took another of her famous hiatos de Harvard, dizque pa' terminar la senior thesis. We'll see . . . hizo lo mismo last year y na' de na' . . . So I'll probably spend las Navidades con mis abuelos Chávez, en San Diego. ¿Vuelves a Puerto Rico, o estarás behind la Orange Cortina? Me muero por verte.

The longer I'm away from Califas, más desarraigada me siento, Lidita. It's strange, pero no (del todo) desagradable. If my body were a tree, un brazo/rama is reaching toward California, hacia mi pasado, mi hogar, hacia los recuerdos y con (algo de) esperanza: being able to have a drink o ir al cine los domingos, for fuck's sake. Y con quien yo quiera, LEGALLY. El otro brazo/rama se extiende hacia Europe. Especially España, especially ahora, en su hermoso, complicado post-Franco flowering. Pero los pies/el tronco me tiran hacia el Sur, toward Africa. Con el resultado de que no me siento entirely a mi aire in *any* of them.

Regresar a la Amerika de Ronnie gives me pause, Lydia. Los gringos, in general, son tan fofos e ignorantes. Especially about la política internacional. En Europa, everybody has an opinion. No sabes lo que me han impactado mis stays en Europa, these last few years. Los 6 meses en Madrid after I graduated UCI, viviendo la Movida madrileña a full antes de enterrarme viva entre ladrillos y snobs en Harvard. Y ahora mis Euro-sojourns, mis flights de la oppressive, guilt-inducing daily reality del apartheid: London me salvó la vida, last year; winter in a cold climate—París, Spain, Italia, even uptight Suiza—me restauró, me fortificó pa' encararme con otro long, hot highveld summer.

Y ahora un septiembre sublime. Me quedé con mi prima Lee. She's caretaking a villa entre hermosos Tuscan vineyards en las hills above Firenze. Pasamos los días catching up, yo escribía, la Lee dibujaba. We cooked, went for long walks en esas rolling, soft green hills, platicamos con tutti quanti en los little rustic bars y cafés y en las hermosas, golden streets y puentes de Firenze.

Pero speaking of bitter (were we?): descubrimos un trago chévere, llamado, ironically, Amaro MONTENEGRO. La Lee dice que sabe a Coca-Cola with spices, pero yo discrepo. Rico y mysterious. En otra versión de mi vida, Roland (mi Montenegro) would've mustered the courage pa' mandar a volar al apartheid—*and* his overbearing, hateful mother—y habríamos estado sipping our namesake elixir juntos. Sigh. Pero anyway, gracias a mi ex, el Mauro Ritucci, al menos my Italian worked like a charm. Lee y yo fuimos a un chingo de free concerts al aire libre, organizados por la Gioventù del PCI. Ahora soy rabid fan de Gianna Nannini, Pino Daniele, Fabrizio d'Andrè, y Francesco Guccini. We also traveled. Fuimos en tren a Pisa, Bologna, Génova, Pádova y mysterious, foggy Venezia. Beautiful city, pero overrun de turisti americani, con el fucking almighty dollar.

Pasamos una semana en San Sebastián, with my family. Los UC study abroad students (los charges de mi papá) tenían su orientation allí. Yo no conocía bien el País Vasco, pero Lydia, it's *so* beautiful. Con la Lee, asistimos al San Sebastián Film Festival. We even met Robin Williams, en la calle. Can you believe that? Muy gracious y, por supuesto, hilarious. Y adivina con quién pasamos mucho tiempo: none other than mi adorado Alfie (Sastre). Te manda muchos saludos, by the way. Estuvimos mucho en familia: mis padres, my little sister Wiggue, my prima Lee, plus Alfie y su wife, Eva Forest, y los three kids. Mi papá es bien mensch: contrató al middle son, Pablo, pa' enseñar un cursillo a los UC students, de lengua y cultura vasca. Alfie estaba chuffed, porque el Pablo needed la lana pero also porque (as Alfie solemnly told me, en una) esto demostraba que mi papá tenía fe en su postura política: pro-ETA. Esto es *muuuy* controvertido (and freaks my mom out), y te lo platico en más detalle later.

Alfie y co. viven en Hondarribia, un hermoso fishing village (pero que tiene su Parador, ojo). El piso Sastre es small y tipo cambalache, overflowing with books, fotos, dibujos, delicious food smells, vitalidad. Just how you'd picture it! Hablamos mucho de la lucha de ETA, entre otros miles de temas. You know how Alfie is, re parlanchín. My mom adores Alfie, pero no le perdona el que apoye a ETA. Lo cierto es que desde que Alfie y Eva rajaron de Madrith y se hicieron honorary Basques, han adoptado Euskadi—y su lucha. Lo triste, Lydia, es que el Alfie claims he's "marginado," hasta en la "nueva" España (I mean, post-Franco). And I can see it. Escribió una carta (algo patética) a *El País*, complaining. Yo le dije que he shouldn't have, and he knows it. Pero igual, está amargado. Dice que "ya no le presentan, o casi." And it's true.

Lo mejor de esta Alfie reunion: their oldest son, Juan. I'd fallen in lust with him el año pasado, cuando visité al Alfie y Eva con mi amiguete suizo, Rudi, remember? I mean me enamoré de su foto, jaja. I'd seen it en el study de Alfie y WOW. Juan estudió para médico 7 años en Cuba (se partía de risa con mis Cuban imitations). He's friends with our ídolo, el Silvio Rodríguez, y vivió experiencias intensas. Pero cuando asesinaron a su best friend (etarra), decidió que su destiny was here. Digo, *there*, en Euskadi. Ha renunciado la medicina (his passion desde la infancia) y está un poco . . . desanclao. O mucho. We bonded over that . . . inter alia. Creo que la Eva's as freaked out about Juan as la June is about me. Total, Lydia, el vato es de un guapo que te caes patrás. Te mando fotos luego. Or, I'll just show you—ya falta poco, amiga, for our reunion.

His sister, Evita (quien es, de hecho, feliz y hasta tuvo un little fling con mi hermana la Wiggue), me dijo que el Juan es "algo mujeriego." En eso my cousin Lee laughed y le dijo, en pocas palabras, don't worry, la Susi can hold her own. Tras una noche chévere, wandering in and out of little tapa bars and clubs—Hondarribia, by the way, tiene más marcha en su pinky que all of South Africa or even Italia—con Lee, Evita y Juan, dancing, drinking, strolling en el malecón smelling the sea air, me quedé en lo de Alfie y pasé la noche con Juan. With Alfie and Eva's bendición, *natuurlik*!

La primera noche, Lidita, we talked about everything. Compartimos las mismas dudas y yearnings (horror a la domesticidad, why don't los flechazos last, querer algo "más allá," pero y . . .) y fue fantástico en la cama. Tender, experto, cariñoso y muy pícaro. Can you imagine, ¿hacer el amor con el hijo de mi gran amigo, el dramaturgo Alfonso Sastre? What a trip. Tuvimos que taparnos la boca, so our gemidos wouldn't wake Alfie y Eva. Me quedé una segunda noche (the whole family insisted), y cuando me llevaron para coger el bus back to Sanse, el Alfie estaba tearful y el Juan y yo también, or almost.

Coño, amiga, why does it have to be this way? Conozco a un vato firme, politically committed, guapo y sexy, de buena familia (jaja) y . . . resulta que he's a lost mujeriego former médico ahora fisherman living in Euskadi? Y te dejo pondering esta incógnita ontológica.

*12-x-84*

Dear Miss Weevil,

We're psychically connected as usual: justo le escribía a mi amiga la Lydia Vélez hace unos días que I hadn't heard from you in months y wham, viene corriendo Phyllis, la secre, pa' entregarme ese bulging express envelope. Mil gracias, hermana. So grateful to you. First all the Cortázar stuff y ahora todo esto para UC–Davis. Mis transcripts, beca forms, etc. Pero con todo el 11th-hour express mail te vas a la bancarrota, jaja.

Estoy super disappointeada (as Dad would say) you won't be there pa' mi return, especially porque me siento bien anxious about my reentry al US of A. Pero pos ni modo. Hoy te escribo para desearte happy 27th birthday. Y para decirte cuánto te admiro. I'm so proud of you, Eva. You're really living your compromiso con la lucha.

En cuanto a mí, me siento cada vez más desubicada, like I've been telling you. After almost 3 years here, me atrae mucho quedarme en Sudáfrica. I know it sounds crazy, considerando mi abhorrence for apartheid (y recordando la extrema enajenación de los initial months). Pero creo que precisamente por esto—vivir en esta weird, tense twilight zone—me siento constantly on edge, fired up. Me hace sentirme viva. And it makes me write. Y quizás esto mismo—this in-betweenness—sea el punto. The point of *me*. La comodidad es anonadante. Plus—otra ironía—I have incredible friends here.

Uno de ellos es Mmome Neppe Selabe. Aries, like me. Nos conocimos en UNISA, trabaja en photocopying. Nuestra *vriendskap* es algo . . . sui generis, for sure: he's Sotho y vive en Mamelodi, uno de los townships satélite de Pretoria. Para mi sorpresa (initially), his Afrikaans is much stronger than his Engels—así que ya te puedes imaginar nuestras convos. Of course, it makes sense, con la preponderancia de Afrikaners aquí en Pretoria (most of them *deeply* English-challenged Rocks, burócratas or *boers*, *verkrampte* y racistas y suspicious of . . . everything). Pero anyway, we battle a bit (as they say here) linguistically, pero we've developed a friendship, especialmente este año.

Neppe me contó que el día que salí para Italia, Mamelodi exploded with violence. Todos los townships, all over the country. He took my two hands in his, when I ran down to photocopying el otro día, pa' saludarle al volver de Italy. Vi que he was dying to tell me something pero los blacks suelen ser unfailingly polite y primero me pregunta, —*And how is your family, your parents, Suzi, are they well?* Le digo que todo bien y le doy una leather tie que le compré en el flea market de Firenze. It's a ridiculous gift y lo sé, we *both* know it y comenzamos a reírnos y en eso I blurt out, —*I just wanted you to have something to remember me by, and maybe you can wear it for formal occasions—you know, like dodging petrol bombs and bullets in Mamelodi.* Obvio, es obscene gallows humor y cómo se me ha ocurrido soltarle eso pero conozco a Neppe y él a mí so I risk it, supongo, porque all of a sudden the notion of friendship, of breaking through—layer upon layer of arbitrary, dehumanizing dizque "petty" apartheid *kak*—me parece tan tenue, frágil y precious.

I can sense he's weighing whether he can tell me (someone not black), and I press him a bit, —*Come on Neppe, what's going on? Aren't we friends?* —*Yes, we're friends, Suzi. But you need to learn my language. Then we'll be real bosom friends.* El Neppe fue el que me instó a aprender Afrikaans, remember? —*To understand the boer, Suzi. To understand all of . . . this.* Pero he finally relents and he begins to tell me, de forma bastante críptica, his voice low, in case some facha Rock professor comes in y le pide fotocopias. They're all around us here! Me dice que tras las elecciones, el ANC (no los nombra, pero I know what he means) quiere que los townships se vuelvan "ungovernable." —*It's becoming terrible, Suzi. Our children are staying away from school now, many deaths in the townships, much more than you will read about. And it's going to get worse, much worse. You are doing a good thing, going away. Go home and be safe. And remember us, and write about us.*

Y sé que tiene razón, pero me siento guilty, conflicted y sobre todo, sad, sad, sad to be leaving. Oh, on that score: I'm giving up my flat pa' fin de mes. Me mudo con una amiga, Melanie Sacks. Agárrate: Wim and I met her a few weeks ago, "al azar" (muy Cortázar). Like how I met Curé, André de Wet y a tantos otros. We were having a coffee en un little gelato *plek* en Barclay Square, y la Mellie nos aborda, asking where I'm from. She's managing the gelateria for her dad, quien también es dueño de Sir Loin, our fave steakhouse. El mundo=hankie, ¿que no? Anyway, she's been living in Joburg con un boyfriend, pero se dejaron. Sus *ouers* viven aquí en Pretoria y decidió volver. She's rented a flat aquí mero en Barclay Square y me invitó a quedarme con ella, until I leave.

Wim y yo la llevamos a un chévere concierto la otra noche, featuring some of the groups que te he comentado. The Dynamics were sendin' it,

my China. Y estuvo otro group, los Jazz Pioneers. All black, con smokin'
sax players, trompetas, bass, batería y una fabulous singer. Cantaba skat,
pero en Xhosa. You would've loved it. Get this: we're (el Club De Wet)
organizing a Halloween fest! Van a tocar los Dynamics y los Mapanzulah.
Y ese weekend vamos al opening del art show de otro amigo mío, Ranko
Pudi. He's showing en el mere, mere Market Theatre! I'm bringing some
of his woodcuts home, ya verás. Basados en su libro, *The Illustrated Life of
Makhanda*. De joven, el Ranko trabajó de goatherd y se volvió muy troubled
y violento, semi-*tsotsi*, from what I can piece together. Pero luego se volvió
Christian. Vive en Ga-Rankua, otro township outside Pretoria. Super in-
tense, quiet, fascinating oke.

OK hermana, I'd say write me antes de que salgas para Nicaragua,
pero . . . ya te conozco. So I guess this is good-bye for now. Cuídate mucho
and remember I love you.

*20-xi-84*

My dearest Sloth,

It's *soooo* hot y estoy tan y tan busy. I think this'll be my last letter "out
of Africa." La Dinesen, by the way, is one of Wim's fave writers. Me ha
hecho leer sus cartas—he says my epistolary reminds him a bit of her
writing. ¡Ojalá! La adoro. Comparte tu birthday, by the way. Anyway: my
departure looms. En 3 semanas I'll be gone from here, quién sabe for how
long. With the way things are going here, quizás para siempre.

On that score: no more going to Soweto, según mi amigo Neppe Selabe
(de UNISA). He seemed surprised, de hecho, we'd made it in and out in
one piece cuando le platiqué de ese Juluka concert en Jabulani. Contemplé
contarle que we'd had a *polisie* escort (Wimpy) pero decidí rather *not*,
como dicen aquí. —*Don't go back to Soweto, Suzi. Very dangerous! Promise
me, no more townships. I'm trying to keep you alive!* El Neppe también estaba
bien uneasy about our Saturday night *jols* en el Park Five, aunque he didn't
make me promise not to return . . . yet.

A verrr, ¿qué más te cuento, Cuz? I did tell you about la Melanie Sacks,
¿verdad? Wim y yo la hemos bautizado Miss Mellie, como la de *Gone with
the Wind*. Me mudé con ella last month. Es muy sweet and funny y el

Wim y yo la estamos inducting a nuestro club. I think she thinks we're *'n bietjie* wild y . . . ¿sabes qué? Es verdad, jaja. No way will we take her to our fave antro, el Park Five, por ejemplo. Pero we've gone to movies, out to dinner, y nos fascina hanguear en el condo de sus padres, Sollie y Babie (her mom's really called Girlie, pero ese nombre me pareció tan weird, plus I could never remember it, así que mi accidental apodo stuck, ¡como tantos!). It's funny, Lee, pero la Mellie's practically the *only* non-Afrikaner friend I've made here (aparte los otros foreigners), besides Ian and Neppe. Pero she's not Engels (like Roland) either, or not exactly: es judía.

Y hablando de eso (los Jews): Etienne regresó in one piece de la fucking border, thank god, y tiene un new—gorgeous—Jewish modelo beau, Craig. El Craig se va de modeling trip to Israel next month, y Curé jura que he wants to come join me en Califas. Ditto el Richie. Hmmm . . . a ver cuál de ellos me cae primero.

Oh, and get this. Irony of ironies: ahora que ha comenzado el countdown para mi departure, I finally went on safari! Just this past weekend. Digo irony porque I'm sure it's the *last* thing Roland would ever expect me to do. Ya que no tengo ni pizca de sporty (don't play tennis, por ejemplo) and he met me in a city, se supone que I'm not keen on nature. Y después de todo el lead-up—training me to recognize animal calls, jactándose de los wilderness trails he was gonna take me on, etc.—he only took me once or twice to the bush. Eso nunca dejó de irritarme. Especially ese hideous weekend en el farm, rodeados de toda su boisterous family y yo todavía tan weak and faded por lo de la hepatitis.

Anyway, el Rolo se equivoca. He just didn't give me the chance to acclimate; ni yo le di el chance, I reckon, de verme en mi salsa (jaja) en su país. Bueno, *natuurlik*, I did it my way! Wim y yo fuimos al Mabula Game Lodge con Manja (friend of Wimpy and Etienne) y su novio, Tienie. We pretended to be two honeymooning couples, ¿te lo imaginas? ¡Qué risa! Lee, fue espectacular. Just like you'd imagine it. Less than 3 hours from Pretoria nos metimos en el mere mere bushveld: red earth, scrubby savannah, thorn trees y acacia por doquier. Ese hermoso dry, dusty scent of Africa. ¡Y los animales! Caminamos y vimos giraffes y *lank* impalas (way too many para enumerarte: besides the springbok, creo que el que más adoro es el teensy klipspringer), zebras, warthogs y baboons. Los littlies son cute, pero de mayor asustan. Tienen un horrendo bark, *haw haw*, con todo y los colmillos bared.

Fuimos en varios game drives, a la mañana, bien early, y luego de tardenoche. Por la mañana, vimos los lions. Cuz, estaba entre terrified y thrilled. I was convinced que en una, se trepaban al vehicle pa' devorarnos. Pero el guide nos dijo que no way, que these are wild lions y tienen miedo. Estábamos en open-sided vehicle, así que . . . ya te me puedes imaginar. Otro scary moment fue cuando nos aproximamos a un full-grown bull elephant. En cosa de segundos he could be upon us, nos contó el guide, if the wind changed and he caught our scent. Así que el vato kept the jeep in gear, "just in case." Y otra vez we were out walking, no lejos del camp, cuando aparecieron un flock (o herd o pride o como corno se les diga) de ostriches, *right* behind Wimpy. —*Shhh*, le dije, *don't move an inch.* Y les saqué foties. When he turned around and saw how close they were, por poco le da un telele.

Ay, Lee. To think: eran los tales of Africa que me contaba Rolo (en la cama en San Francisco), lo que me hizo soñar con venir a ver todo esto. Y heme aquí, about to leave this beautiful, troubled place y estoy viendo los animales, crushing the marula berries underfoot, aprendiendo a identificar las plantas, el spoor, los olores. Drinking sundowners at dusk, charlando con amigos en el *braai* . . . todo lo suyo y sin embargo, all this without him. Digamos que I found my own South Africa, mis propios native guides.

Y hablando de eso, por poco nos morimos (de risa) on the return drive. It was late at night y estábamos molidos tras el strenuous (jaja) safari. El Tienie was driving y de repente he shouts, —*Look werrrr'e comes!* Yo no entendía ni papa, plus we were all half-asleep. Pero en eso, we all look up y vemos los headlights heading straight at us. El Tienie leans on the horn and swerves y el tipo swerves too and we're all OK, solo muy shaken up. Pero yo sigo bien puzzled con lo que chilló el Tienie. Miro al Wimpy, sentado en el back seat conmigo, y veo que he's convulsed with laughter. He leans over y me susurra que el Tienie será lawyer y además de un guapo y buff que te caes patrás (le bauticé el Transvaal Tarzan, de hecho), pero he's *verrry* Afrikaner and a bit of a paleto, ¿entiendes? En otras palabras: English is *not* his punto fuerte. To say the least.

Anyway, Cuz, I've begun saying my good-byes, y ya sabes lo que detesto los good-byes. Curé, Craig y el Wim me llevan al Jan Smuts airport el 15. Agárrate, I even called Roland el otro día, from UNISA. I'd been feeling kind of bad desde nuestro apocalyptic showdown (over Bonanza) en esa *partytjie* hace unos meses, remember? Le dije que I was headed back to Califas, pa' terminar el PhD. He had heard I was leaving, "through the grapevine." —*I still love you, Shug,* me dijo. —*I love you too, Montenegro,* le dije. And you know what? Aunque parezca una locura, it's true.

## PART III

# Sleeping Beauty y Rip van Winkle Despiertan

# En Montalvo

Under the wishing tree, everything's fine
Nothing can touch us here, nothing, not even time
Halfway around the world, someone is listening

**Charlie Sexton**

6-*w*-08

Querido Roland,

Do you remember?

Me gané una three-month artist-in-residency fellowship and . . . and, here I am! Estoy, once again, in our beloved northern California, en el Montalvo Arts Center (Google it—it's a beyond *lekker plek*). I'm staying (as from last Saturday) en un teensy pero architect-designed live-work studio. Hay un upstairs nook, a little loft, accessible por spiral staircase. Here I sit for hours, como en un treehouse, writing and dreaming, rodeada de esta trembling green aliveness. My own private *Green Mansions*.

I'm working on a second volume of *crónicas*. Trabajo con la memoria, I paint with words. Bueno, you know this. Like I always have. All this green, este silencio (except for bird sounds I'd love to hear you imitate, hear you teaching me to imitate!) is generating a strange flood of memories. I brought my old diary here (you know the one, yes?), sin entender exactamente por qué. I hadn't read it in a long, long time, quizás desde que dejé S. Africa. Ahora que lo pienso, definitely. Not since I was in Pretoria. Wow. Casi 24 años . . .

Hoy empecé a leer 1982. *Early* 1982. You know, el "transcript," as we solemnly baptized that record I kept of our first weeks together: nuestro apocalyptic meeting en el Balboa Cafe el 28 de enero, y los varios US sojourns—Houston, New Orleans, Chicago. I kept reading, into the spring of '82, esa epistolary chronicle o como quieras llamarle. Lo que yo escribía durante mi Penelope espera, after you returned to S. Africa en marzo. Todas esas diary entries de mi bohemian (if poor as a churchmouse!) grad student San Francisco vida, that I later copied y te las mandaba como cartas. Well, they *were* letters, ¿que no? Letters to you. And letters to me, a la girl que yo era, back then.

Ahora me siento bien pendeja, digo, for having assiduously avoided reading it all these years. No sé qué es lo que tanto temía. Porque it isn't all *that* cringe-inducing. Not at all, en realidad. There *are* some over-the-top bits (it's "me," after all, hey?), pero overall, it holds up well: como love story, como una historia—*our* story—de palpable intensidad y pasión.

Rolo, do you still have all my letters? Creo recordar que I destroyed yours en una especie de funeral pyre, con Wim, en Pretoria. I can't believe (digo the "I" here, writing this to you, today) I would actually do that, pero . . . te confieso que I'm pretty sure I did. You know when I mean. En el . . . después.

Pero anygüey, leerlo hoy (el transcript, digo), reading (about) me, about us, was a kind of . . . reunion, una suerte de recognition. Es mejor en español: *reconocer*. To remeet, (get to) know de nuevo.

That's what happened to me, todo el día. Mi escritura, I have to tell you, tan vívida even all these years later, I could almost literally feel myself *reentering* those spaces. Esos lugares nuestros lugares. My own mind and 25-year-old cuerpo. Los olores, ah the scents: de San Francisco y de New Orleans. Especially NoLa, nuestro Mardi Gras pleasure palace. Y de ti, Roland: your scent, the feel of your body, tu cabello.

I reckon you could say que hoy, de alguna manera, comencé a perdonarme. For something I've always chastized myself about. I mean, cuando me he permitido pensarlo siquiera (which is to say, casi nunca): enamorarme de ti. No, no enamorarme de ti sino for falling in love with you and then having it turn out so fucked up en tu país, tan *utterly* unlike what I'd envisioned, lo que habíamos soñado, together.

Today while I was reading I wept, y te juro, Rolo, que no había *nada* de remorse. *Niks*. Creo que más bien it was a pure, wide-open llanto of . . . gratitude, weird and oxymoronic as that sounds. Por la intensidad de mi vida, my life as I've lived it. For meeting you on 28-I-82 en el Club, as we called it, my every-Thursday-night club, el Balboa Cafe. That event— conocerte—would *completely* alter the course of my life. Meeting you that night me hizo dar ese tremendo leap, traveling to you, moving to live in apartheid South Africa (it was one and the same, ¿que no?): it blew my life as I knew it to pieces. Pero ese vivir—staying there, *living* there, with and then without you—transformed me.

Me siento bien dizzy, Rolo. Hasta weirded out. Ay, preferiría mil veces no tener que bajar ahora, put on my *publiek* face, ir a cenar con los otros resident artists. Now that I live such a HEALTHY vida, no tengo las distractions of smoking any more (ni cigs ni *dagga*, tee hee), ni mucho menos la coca (remember us?), to get a little distance from all this remembering, *ja maar dis* OK. I'll be OK.

I am *sommer* high on my own journey into the self. High on la memoria y sus frutos extraños. Esta letter es para decirte gracias. *Baie dankie*, for coming into my life.

*10-v-08*

Dearest Wimmie,

You must be *baie* busy *vandag*. Te mandé *dos* astral charts ayer, plus a merge chart. I'm dying to know your opinion. Me siento muy sola aquí en Montalvo, pero very close to you.

Get this: me traje la novela *David's Story* de Zoe Wicomb. I'd read it years ago and remembered que me había hechizado. I remembered it was *baie* strange en cuanto a structure, "plot," *alles*. Todo muy vague, indefinite, unfinished. Circling back on itself. Deshaciéndose. I just read the after-word by una tal Dorothy Driver, an English S. Effrican academic. Totalmente brill. It was erudite and scholarly pero helpful (jaja), 'cause the novel's structure, las alusiones históricas, culturales, etc., son *bien* complicated. Publicada en el 2000, pero its *aksie* takes place in 1991 (aunque vuelve patrás in history, también). Just three years before Mandela's election, shortly after he was released from jail. Se trata de este Colo *oke*, David Dirkse, who was an ANC member, pero que luego se pone a cuestionar ciertos ANC . . . excesses. Que yo recuerde, his own machismo remains essentially unexamined. I *think*. No me acuerdo claramente. He's also doing some kind of investigación de la herencia Griqua. Anyweg, it is an incredible *boek*. Todo el issue de la identidad colored me atrae. Interpellates me, de alguna manera. You *must* read it ASAP, if you haven't already, para que lo podamos analizar.

Abrupt cambio de tema (just oso with me, *asseblief*):

Wimmie, *is ek fokken MAL*? ¿Qué coño me pasa? I am not "unhappy" in my present, dizque vida real. Te lo juro. Or "I promise you," as Roland would say. Pero debo admitir que vengo detectando, these last few days, algo de . . . no sé, a sense of growing un/ease, o hasta . . . regret, creeping over me. A veces me siento almost paralyzed by it. Swallowed by it. Or *in* it. En este feeling. Where *am* I? *Who* am I?

I'm reading about "me," hace 25 años. HALF my life ago. Te pregunto, what is *wrong* with me? ¿Por qué esta repentina obsession with "the road not taken"? And not only that sino también con "encontrar" a Roland? ¿Qué coño haría—what would I *want* to do—si realmente estuviera, de nuevo, face to face with him? I have no fucking idea.

And yet, algo en mí oscuramente intuye que this is exactly what was *meant* to happen now. It had been a long, long time—*too* long—desde que estuve realmente sola. Since before el Juvenil (mi hijo) was born, si lo pensamos: my god, 21 years! *Alleen*, independiente, fierce. Like I was in S. Africa después de dejar a Roland. Like I was when you and I met. Y se me hace que it's fundamentally *this*, digo todo este tiempo sola, in my own mind (esta little glass jewel box, esta *treehuis* among all this green a perfect correlato objetivo), establishing my own daily rutinas, apenas interacting con otros humanos ni haciendo "normal" things (haven't gone to the shops, por ejemplo, since Pierre left—hace una semana, can you believe it?), a radical disruption of my *everydayness*, todo esto es lo que me está provocando esta intense internal recalibration.

I'm going to wager que "it's all good," como quien dice, even though it feels *really* weird. Simón, me siento "strange" to myself. Pero me doy cuenta de que it's not anxiety I'm feeling (gracias a Dios). Just . . . a kind of self-strangeness que es a la vez una especie de self-recognition. *Verstaan jy?* A rejoining of parts that had separated, un reconocimiento de partes de mí que había olvidado. That I buried, supongo. Well, I mean yebo. Buried, *definitely*.

Sorry for the melodrama, *maar dis baie* disconcerting, todo esto. Write me, *asseblief.*

P.D. Please save these *briewe* for *altyd.*

*13-v-08*

Wimmie,

Esto que me escribiste, yesterday, made my day:

*Thinking of the incredible impact you have had on my life. You brought glamour into my apartheid Pretoria life: Fiorucci, Yves Saint Laurent fuchsia mascara, leopard print cigarette papers and all your fabulous fragrances. I have such a vivid image of you doing your toenails on the balcony at Barclay Square, wearing only your red Sausalito T-shirt. It all feels so long ago and yet so real.*

Made me cry. Porque that's what I've been feeling, *presies*, this past week. Digo: about S. Africa. So long ago, yet so *real*. Es como si . . . opening that transcript has made it all come suddenly blasting forth, 25 years later, con una huge, unsettling sense of immediacy. Scary and exhilirating, en igual medida.

OMG: make me laugh, about our Mabula Game Lodge faux luna de miel, con la Manja y su swain, el "Transvaal Tarzan," aka Tienie. Ella una Prrretorian hypochondriac drama queen *deluxe* y él un bronzed, sporty Afrikaner Adonis abogado. Oh, I am making myself shake with laughter, all *alleen*, right now!

P.S. (to *your* P.S.) About el Cabo das Tormentas y la Colo-*identiteit*. Qué raro, pero appropriate: Cabo das Tormentas literally just means

"Cape of Storms," in Portuguese. But of course, la idea de "torment," vis-à-vis your own life, cannot be underestimated either. Living all the way down there en *Kaapstad*, en la mere mere punta del Africa. Missing (y)our beloved Pretoria, tu familia, tus amigos. Not to mention your challenging ministry con los Colos. Coño, I had no idea about these hid stats: *the Colos have the highest murder, imprisonment, crystal meth, and teenage pregnancy rates of all population groups in SA (they make up about 9 percent of the total population, but 30 percent of the prison populasie).*

Everything you're writing me about los Colos is truly moving. Me identifico—more, me parece, than with any other (ethno-racial) group (certainly in S. Africa)—con ellos. One of my *huge frustrasies*, mientras vivía allí, en S. Africa, was the way I was consistently misread as white. I mean, I get it, now. Intelectualmente, I get it. Digo, there simply *was* no category for me en ese país tan obsesado con las categorías (other than *foreign*, which I'm pretty sure is the way most people—blanco, Colo, negro—read me).

Casually observed (if you can say *anyone* looks at anyone else "casually" en Sudáfrica in terms of race, hey), supongo que I came off foreign-but-white. Cierto uncategorizable exotismo, especially with my easy Mexitanning skills, my Spaans y mi "interesting heh," as Roland's then-thirteen-year-old twin hermanitas put it, remember? Pero comfortingly white *enough*—y con mi flawless if American Engels—to not provoke *too* many questions. Pensándolo ahora (en términos de las ethno-racial identity categories disponibles en tu país), creo que estaría closest to Colo. Pero mos def NOT with the cultural identity they seem to have developed.

¿Te parece que su high jail, murder, alc y crack use, etc. tiene que ver con su in-betweenness? I mean, en un sentido identitario. *Is* it really in-betweenness though, o más bien otra categoría—a discrete identity—just not one that overlaps con la identidad negra? ¿Tú crees que la Colo-*identiteit* sea una abject identity? Ni fu, ni fa. You know: neither fish nor fowl. Not white enough durante el apartheid, when white was the hegemonic, privileged category, not black (*genoeg*) now, cuando la dinámica se representa, largely, como una black–white struggle. Am I right? Or is it as much—o más—about class? Uf, tántas preguntas. Qué pesada.

Insisto: you *must* get your hands on *David's Story*. The protagonist, el tal David Dirkse, is Colo, y la parte que estoy leyendo ahora se trata del development de la Colo identity. Quiero decir, within the struggle, y a lo largo de la historia. It's *sommer* fascinating! I'm obsessed. La Wicomb es una escritora bold, original.

*14-v-08*

· Dearest Wimmie,

*Vandag*, debo confesar que I haven't done much—due to hideous HEAT! —except send emails y friquearme por los internido connectivity problems. Thank you for these amaze comentarios about los Colos! El tema seems to have struck a nerve, ¿que no? With *both* of us:

*The Colos are trag, in a way, but also have such incredible vibrancy and a sort of defiance that I find fascinating and inspiring. I think that their basic problem is one of identity, especially from the apartheid times. The blacks have their tribal and clan identity that anchors them, the whites their European heritage and superiority complex, leaving the Colos floating in the middle. By and large they identify with the whites and reject their black identity completely, always using "white" surnames or slave names rather than indigenous ones. Now, like you say, they are not black enough (nor do they want to be) and share, for the most part, the fears and discontent of the whites. They are not seen as black enough, especially when it comes to affirmative action, and are despised by many blacks for having been privileged over them in the old days. Another layer is that many of them were slaves and labourers on the wine farms and they often received alc as part of their payment, which has led to generations of alcoholism and fetal alc syndrome, etc. It is painful to see their suffering and to realise that my ancestors contributed to it. In a way it makes sense that I am now living here in Manenberg, one of the worst Colo poverty areas, trying to bring some hope and new insights.*

Yo también tengo una *obsessie*, as you know, with la identidad. And I know (bueno, lo intuyo) a lot of this is wrapped up in being mestiza, una hybrid, ni fu ni fa yo misma, pero passing white.

In *David's Story* la Wicomb delves into so much Colo history. She goes on and on about this Le Fleur *oke* (*die groot* leader?!), lo cual me sugiere que los Colos *did* have, historically, a kind of tribal *identiteit*, albeit bien different to la de los blacks. However, from what you say parece que they've . . . subsumed it, or it's been fragmented. ¿Me equivoco?

*Interessant*: me dices que los Colos are often despised by blacks, por haber tenido más privilege under apartheid. Pero *did* they, really? Supongo que what interests me es la naturaleza del privilege. The definition of it. I suppose while I was there there *were* a modicum of Colo-*concessies*, digamos. *Onthou jy*, how we went round Sunnyside at night, stealing and collecting esos referendum posters, del voto constitucional, en noviembre del '83? OMG, I still have those ancient posters! Los Colos y dizque "Asiers" (los Indians, *nê?*) could finally vote on this or that. Pero no, it wasn't that. Not exactly that. Se trataba de que they'd now have parliamentary *representasie*, ¿que no? Pero NEVER los negros. Anygüey, no me convence que esto (*any* of these concessions) ever was the same thing as advantages, or privilege. Was it? *Seker* que todo esto es muy controversial. Or vexed, como dicen los culti studies cacadémicos. (Used to be me, hey? Enfasis *used* to, jaja.)

OK Wimmie. I simply must go back down the spiral staircase; it's way *te baie fokken warm*, and I must turn off this little molten silver *masjien*, no vaya a ser que it has a meltdown. I did have a dizque health walk earlier, pero volví a mi crystal box toda covered in sweat y casi DIZZ, and I failed even to do my feeb little yoga routine, por estas extreme weather *condisies*. Night night. *Lekker slaap*.

*15-v-08*

OomBie,

Anticipo tus *briewe* more than anything. Tus Coloradito insights son mega-helpful (don't laugh: this is actually a type of Oaxacan mole. Remember, cuando te mandé esa review de Guelaguetza, ese Oaxacan restó in LA, and you freeked, pensando que era un disgusting y mos def nonvegetarian *rodent* dish?). I'm carrying on reading la Wicomb. Hay tanto allí, Wimmie, en esa novela, de la separate Colo identity (digo separate from black). I really didn't understand this clearly. Digo, before. When I was living there. Y esa (to me) bizarre política de los Colos—supporting the NP. WTF? Menos mal que you gave me this background, y de paso replied to my (zillions, *ek weet*) quessies from last letter:

> *Colos did receive better housing and other small privileges under apartheid.*
> *A major issue is that here in the Cape, all domestic and other menial jobs were*

*reserved for them. One had to get special permission to have a black maid in-
stead of a Colo! Some blacks even adopted Colo surnames to be able to work
here as waiters or domestics. The Colos also received a sort of vote in 1983, as
you mentioned, while blacks were still excluded. But there is no doubt that
Colos see themselves as superior to blacks, more civilised and westernised. In the
1994 elections, the Western cape was the only province where the National
Party remained in power (the other eight were all won by the ANC) and this
was entirely due to Colos voting for the NP (now defunct). Since then, more
Colos have gone over to the ANC but the resentment about this history is still
there.*

Thanks for *this* too, BTW. Made me laugh—and cry:

*As you've been saying, you (like Dale's first novio, René, the Puerto Rican)
read as white here, and thus you were immediately treated differently. I can see
how this misreading must have been very frustrating and even alienating. The
Colos are super aware of race and can tell at 50 yards when someone is pretending
to be white (one of their fave pastimes is laughing at those who try), and I always
ask how they can tell. The answer: Father, a coloured knows a coloured! Of
course, ironically, they would insist that you are white or maybe Jewish, which
they see as a special category.*

Al leer esto ahora, I feel my hackles rising. The very idea of them, los
Colos, telling me what I am. Insisting I'm white! Naming me, categorizing
me, themselves, everybody forever *naming* everyone else, all over the show
(as Curé used to say, QEPD). What an obsessively, persistently taxonomic
society you live in. ¡Hasta ahora! Pero how could it be any other way, *nê*.
Hasn't even been 20 years desde el fin del apartheid.

Pero además: it reminds me. De lo que me dijo una well-known old-
school Chicana faculty member, shortly after I arrived at Pomona College.
Algunos estudiantes me dijeron que she was going around saying que yo
no era una "real Mexican"! Can you fucking *believe* that? Bueno, me la
enfrenté en el weight room (she was chubbily huffing and puffing, en el
treadmill) y le dije, listen: the *next* time you want to know what I am, you
can ask *me*. Oh, me dijo later, solemnly, magnanimously, tú eres una REAL
MESTIZA.

Anygüey, it's blazing hot here, aparentemente near record-breaking heat.
Ya no tan green mansiony here at the mo, con este ATROH heatwave.

Según, it'll reach 100 today (39-ish?). Horror! Excepto el heatwave, which (se supone) will start to wane by the weekend (Sarita will be here visiting, menos mal), this retrete is pretty chévere so far. I'm actually semibonding w/several of the other artists. Ese triple-PhD arquitecto is sort of strange, pero . . . hay algo. We both feel like we've known each other "from before."

*22-w-08*

Dearest Wimmie,

Heme aquí, reeling in shock. Me fui en un health walk, earlier. Hay un harsh, howling wind. Las hojas y ramas de los eucalyptus and oak trees producen un terrifying roar! It sounds like the ocean. O como un badgered, precharge león. En el walk, unnerved by the wind y por el freaky *frrrote frrrote* de los trees, agarré un downed eucalyptus branch to drag back to my glass slipper, oops, digo glass *cube*. I'm assembling a collection of found objects. O de totems. Talismanes contra el friggin' cougar, que estoy cada vez más convinced is lurking in the underbrush, esperando su chance pa' devorarme.

Patrás en el studio, subí al treehouse. You'll *never* guess what was awaiting me: un e-macho de Roland. Tú sabes que por irónico que sea (given the violent way we broke apart, en Sudáfrica, digo), R. and I have never really *completely* lost contact with each other, en todos estos años. O bueno, hardly ever. Pos sí hubo ese period (late '80s–early '90s) cuando su first wife "intercepted" (his word) mis cartas, and he thought it best to "go underground" for a while.

Por mi parte, confieso que I eventually got a bit bored (OK—exasperated) con sus "news 'n' views." I'd just started teaching at Pomona; I was busting my nalga trying to get la ternura; tenía al Juvenil. Nuestros respectivos mundos parecían, qué sé sho . . . two remote, discretely orbiting planetas. So I really didn't pay all that much attention cuando el Rolo would surface occasionally. Sus "hail fellow well met" misivas were the perfect mise en abyme, me parecía, del emo-*verkrampte* (*double* Capricorn), falsely jovial (pero OJO: closet melancólico) northern suburbs mining engineer I'd always suspected he'd become.

I would write him, de vez en cuando, a Bedfordview. Al ancestral homestead. Por más que she hated me, la bruja de la Ma F. would pass my letters to him. Estábamos up to date: our work, matrimonios, kids, divorcios. Nuestros siblings. Mi escritura (he was proud of me, me escribió, I remember; he "always knew" I'd become a writer). Su segundo marriage, in the late '90s, creo, or no, a little later than that, a una "old friend from varsity." No me contó *nada* de esta current wife, *niks, nooit*, my bra. Sólo eso: an old friend.

Anygüey, I hadn't heard patrás from him yet, in reply to my "onthou jy?" e-macho, y me estaba irritando, pero *bigtime*, I'm telling you. It had been almost 2 weeks! You know me and my Aries ways. Debo admitir straight up . . . uf, que I hadn't written *him*, for a few years before that. Maybe since my mom died. Hace cinco años, ¡coño! Can it really have been that long? Pero ni modo: once I'd opened that . . . Pandora's box (mi diario de 1982, aka el transcript), sentí un repentino, overpowering urge, la necesidad de estar en contacto de nuevo.

So hace unos días le mandé algo totally silly (or something I was sure que le parecería *a él* silly e irracional): un astral warning on los efectos nefastos de Mercurio retrógrado. And *this* ostensibly frivolous topic is what prompted my Bok Boytjie to loosen his tongue? Check his opening line: *Shug, Mercury in retrograde is even known by me to be bad karma—esp wrt electronic devices!!!*

Al menos he retains his trademark (wryly self-aware) sense of humor, pensé. Pero after that amusing apertura, he quickly segues into one of his (infamous) tratados políticos. Uf. Disappointingly generic, I groused pa' mis adentros as I read, si bien debo reconocer que I myself had emailed him (like I did you), hace unos días, paniqueada por la xenophobic violence all over the news. *In RSA*, he writes, *the recent xenophobic attacks bring back memories of the bad times of the '80s and early '90s. I do perceive the politicos here are starting to grasp the fact that Africa can't have a set of rules that is out of sync with global best practice. My deep cynicism of politicos of all hues continues . . . . The electorate here have worked out that you can get screwed just as well by black brothers as by honkeys (never mind the Chinese). So what do they do? Well they pick on the nearest most vulnerable group, which in this case are mostly Zimbabweans fleeing Mad Bob Mugabe.*

So that was his (stealth-emo) way of *reassuring* me, explicando el rationale behind los ataques xenofóbicos, and their main target: los Zimbabwean refugees. Hmmm.

Pero entonces I reached his last paragraph. Más bien, the last two sentences: *I will respond to your "Onthou" email—you raise feelings and thoughts that roll around inside me. Makes me smile—good smiles. L, RF xxx*

Hence my shock. *Verstaan jy?* Out of the blue, *that*. Ese emo-zinger. Totalmente out of character for Roland, el ingeniero. Pero totalmente *in* character for my Montenegro. So surely you won't scold me for sending him—out of the blue, también—the letter I just sent. Al menos, I hope you won't!

I just haul off y le pregunto, with no warning, cero preámbulo, si se acuerda de . . . lo que nos pasó en New Orleans. Something terrifying and tragic, totalmente life-altering. You remember what I'm talking about, *nê*? Check this: *I* myself had no memory of it, Wimmie, te lo juro. Lo tenía buried, I reckon. Digo, I *absolutely* did, until just a few days ago. True's God.

*Wat sê jy?* I shall await your comentarios.

22-v-08

R., darling,

Thanks for *skryfing* patrás. The contents of your carta (tu voz: political, droll, *'n bietjie* sarcastic) me recuerda esas epic discussions—heated, impassioned, ideological, intellectual—entre tú y yo en 1982. OK, OK: más bien debates, in actual fact. Or sparring matches entre dos leones, as you used to say. Two mating lions, *hoor*. Así éramos, right from the *moment* we first locked eyes, esa primera noche en el Balboa Cafe.

I need to tell you, Roland, acabo de releer la novela *David's Story*, by Zoe Wicomb. I don't remember clearly cuando la leí por primera vez. Pero me encuentro intrigued (*obsessed*, my students would probably tell you), de nuevo, with the subject of mixed-race identity. En el caso de esta novela, the so-called colored identity. It touches something primal in me: una biracial, bicultural US-born Mexi-judía whose identity was kind of . . . in flux, digamos, while I was growing up. Too Latina and judía para los surfers I so badly wanted to fit in with en la Harbor High School, pero too Nor-Cal hippie-cool pa' los Mexican high school cholo wannabes en Santa Cruz. Too güera and not nearly Mexican *enough* en Guadalajara as a girl, aun con mi flawless español. Y too American (o peor, sudaca) en Madrid. Always something else. Something *other*. Uf.

Y ni modo in your country. I was never read or recognized as mixed, only as a white girl (if *exotiese*, foreign, fo' sho). Sentí esa lack, acutely, ese misfitness. Pero I had no idea how to articulate it, entonces. Or even *identify* it, se me hace. Did you ever think about that? me pregunto. We sure as hell never talked about it.

¿Te conté que mi amigo Wim (remember him, from our Pretoria days? I met him through Etienne, QEPD) is now an ordained Catholic priest (although he was raised NGK)? Hace 3 años que vive en Manenberg, a very turbulent (um, eufemismo) colored township in Cape Town, en los Cape Flats. Do you know the *plek*? He and I have been exchanging lengthy epistles for years pero especially lately, desde que trabaja con la colored comunidad.

R., bebé, just *hold* on (as you always used to say), 'cause this'll probably blow your mind. And I *want* to, pero sólo un poco—for now. It certainly has blown mine:

*Do you remember we conceived and lost a baby together, in February 1982?*

Confieso que I myself had totally, 100 percent suppressed this memory (me with my famous *olifant*-memory hey?). Pero last Sunday, my sister Weevil (Sarita) was here visiting y le estaba contando que I'd brought my diaries from 1982 with me, de San Francisco, from before South Africa, pero without knowing exactly *why* I'd brought them. Después de tanto tiempo, after all. Pero anygüey, le contaba del . . . impacto de conocerte. No, that's not the right word. Fuck. Lame. A verrr, how the epic force of that encuentro (in the most Breton via Cortázar sentido de la palabra)— and the weeks and months of its aftershocks—had propelled me, *compelled* me to move to Africa. OJO: también le dije que I'd come to realize (given my political militancy and the everyday realidad del apartheid) that there was just no way it—we—could have survived, como pareja, in your country.

En eso, de repente my sister gets a funny look on her face y me pregunta, —*Didn't you go to the Mardi Gras with Roland? You had a miscarriage too, right?* Así nomás, right out of the azul. Me puse a temblar, uncontrollably. It was like I was falling into a huge black hole, pero ese hole . . . era yo. I felt a great *whooshing* inside my *kop*. —*¿Qué te pasa? If you* *don't believe me*, me dijo Sarita, *just open your diary*. So I did (the transcript le decíamos, remember?). Y allí estaba la evidencia, in black and white. (Or red).

I need you to remember. And to tell me.

*23-v-08*

OomBie,

I hadn't realized que las xenophobic *aksies* were so extreme. Estoy preocupada. Moving on, or, a otro RUBRO, like they say in Argentina: don't the bits I sent you from R.'s letter give you a glimpse of him, de lo inteligente, lo thoughtful que es? As well, his deeply sensual potential, si bien (mostly) suppressed . . . uf.

Last night, antes de quedarme dormida, I was allowing myself to savor the way I'd felt cuando me estaba enamorando de R. I've just realized this: ya que nuestra relationship had failed so spectacularly in South Africa, once he got me *all* the bloody way there, I've always obsessed on its *failure*. All these 25 years, stoking esa narrativa del fracaso. Digo, rather than acknowledging (or even allowing myself to *remember*) la fuerza y pasión de . . . nosotros. Nuestro amor, pre-apartheid.

Me doy cuenta de que all those years ago, I buried it. Lo enterré en Pretoria. I buried *us*. Habría sido demasiado painful to have kept the memory alive, I reckon: of how good it was, how good *we* were, juntos, al principio. En San Francisco, Houston, New Orleans, Chicago.

Sólo aquí, ahora, en Montalvo, have I finally been allowing myself to do *precisely* this, por primera vez en la vida. Remembering. It's scary, dizzying. Me siento como si estuviera . . . unlocking something. The pain is still in there, aparentemente. Suddenly, puedo acceder ese mismo sense of betrayal of late 1982: ¿Cómo pudo haberme amado tan passionately (and the fact that he *did* se ve claramente en mi diario, in the transcript) and yet behave in such an insensitive o bueno—to be fair—al menos recontra *conventional* manner in S. Africa? How could he, my Montenegro, not understand que yo necesitaba más—more of *him*—than just to be his arm candy en los fucking *braais* todos los domingos en Joburg, o en su family "farm" in the bushveld? Por otra parte (again: *trying* to be fair, ahora), how could I have expected him to *not* fall back into all that? Porque eso también, el peso de la tradición, *familie*, *werk*, hasta sus yuppie amigos, is *also* who he is, ¿no?

## 23-v-08 (continued)

OomBie,

Creo que it's about 9 p.m., your time. Get this: hay un huge incendio, un forest fire raging in the Santa Cruz mountains. I feel like my past is burning . . .

I've just now finished fishing thru my diary—el transcript—anotando ciertos key passages. I'm going to type it out now, y te lo mando later. Me parece un crucial document. Semillas for my *ars combinatoria*. Possibly a movie (jaja). Just take your time reading. I'm very curious to see what you find on those pages. And *who* you find. Luego se lo mando a R. Pero EYE: *only* after I hear your comentarios. It feels . . . no sé. Dangerous.

## 23-v-08 (hours later!)

Wimmie,

Both you AND Roland *must've* gone to bed already (ya que no recibí nada—*geen antwoord nie*—in reply to my plaintive quessie: are you OK?), so I'm going to *assume* neither of you is in immediate need of evacuation (due to xenophobic attacks). I don't seem to be, either (por los incendios), de Montalvo. Uncanny, all this burning. Now, brace yourself: *kyk* at what crossed en el cyber-ether, *just* as I was sending R. a worried e-macho sobre los xenophobic mobs!

*Shug,*

*I remember the miscarriage clearly—I remember lots of things. I'm not so sure we couldn't have survived, even flourished, as a couple. Dysfunctional, you might say—but wonderfully so, I think.*

And then, me pone unos medio-random comments, about "an old BBC documentary on the life and times of mollusks" (WTF?). Para mitigar la emo-intensity, I reckon. I mean, OB-vio. But then, this: *I am very curious about the "coloured" identity issue you're exploring—even as an* "umlungu" *(white man in Zulu).*

Y finalmente, as if realizing how wack, how utterly *remote* his mini-lecture on las ciencias naturales would strike me, escribe esto:

*I can hear you formulating your rebuttals—but I've always had great respect (love) for that part of you. L RF*

Wimmie, doesn't this absolutely blow your mind? Who, in a zillion years, would've said that Rolo Babee (as my old SF roomate, la Trish, used to call him) would remember, digo would hold onto—alive—todos estos años, this über-memory? And I didn't! I think I'll *never* get over the shock, de cuando Sarita me dijo eso del miscarriage, as if it were the nost natural thing, digo, you know, readily available knowledge. Bueno anygüey, y no sólo eso: that Roland would still think we belonged together. Digo: from way back then.

*23-v-08*

R.,

I'm stunned at the mo, *my liefie*. Not quite as much as last weekend, cuando mi hermana me hizo recordar nuestro (entirely buried, al menos by *me*) "little zygote" (remember, that's what we called it?), pero still. Your country is burning again, ¡coño! Wim wrote me this, hace una hora:

*The xenophobic attacks have come as a huge shock to the whole country. There's been unbearable expectations on the poor, since 1994. The thinking being that now they have the vote, they should be dancing in the streets. Health services, schools, even ELECTRICITY have become worse than even under apartheid, and the government's allowed an unchecked stream of refugees from other African countries to come here. Now, the locals are lashing out at the* amakwerekwere *(onomatopoeia imitation of their languages, which the locals can't understand). Black politicians keep appearing on TV saying these attacks are "barbaric," the exact word the old (blanke) politicians use to use to describe the current politicians when they were rioting! Things are very ugly in the townships at the moment. Feels like a flashback to the eighties. In the back of our blanke minds: "what if we are next?"*

This replicates (bueno, he *expands* on your version, Mr. Lacónico) what you wrote me, ayer.

Mientras tanto, on my end, los desastres son naturales. Hay un horrible forest fire in the Santa Cruz mountains. Humo, ceniza, flying singed leaves. I feel, somehow, like my past is burning up. Simultáneamente en S. Africa y Califas. And on *that* score (el pasado, *our* past, digo), check what Wim wrote me today:

*Your Roland-memory (and Roland's memory!) blew me away. It makes the perfect core for a movie, or a book, don't you think? It's wonderful that you have time now (and are in the right place) to begin to examine that primal wound. And don't be too harsh on yourself, darling. It makes perfect sense that you had to go straight into survival mode after you broke away from R. So you never mourned for what you and he had, or what might have been (would have been, anywhere else but apartheid RSA). I am maybe too soft on him, but thinking back now, R. was probably just too naïve and inexperienced to think of ways to try to make you more comfortable, happy here.*

Hmmm, Wim *is* softer on you than what I was back then, *nê*. Much.

### 23-v-08 (later)

Rolo Babee,

Fuck me sideways: este tu teensy, tongue-in-cheek reply (as was—is?— your wont) just crossed en el cyber-ether the one I was about to send you! Ah, ah, ah, you make me laugh, con eso de que you can hear me formulating my rebuttals y tu gran respeto (LOVE, you write, don't think I didn't notice) por esa part of me. Hmmm, *which* part of me, me pregunto. Ni modo, la nalga *and* my rebuttals are both in pretty fine working order, me parece.

P.D. Your memory not so good after all, Montenegro: ¡se te olvidó que I *already* know what *umlungu* means!

### 24-v-08

Querido Wimmie,

Yesterday was otherworldly, charged, magical. I've just fished up this chev quote, de la novela *Song of Solomon* de Toni Morrison. I brought it up here with me y la estoy releyendo. Irony of ironies: la compré en Cape Town, en diciembre 1982, when I was there with Augusto Castells (aka Agustín, as I nicknamed him, remember?), en ese road trip. Según, Roland couldn't get away from work, en la diamond mine, pa' mostrarme su país. *Otra* gran irony: he spent *so* much time telling me que eso era exactamente lo que quería hacer. En San Francisco. In New Orleans. He talked and talked, de todo lo que me iba a mostrar. Pero I ended up going to see it for myself. Crossing the entire country—el southern tip of Africa, *nogal*— alone. O bueno, con el Castells. Pero I mean, without R. And I bought this book, por una black American novelist, en una used bookstore in Cape Town, in apartheid South Africa! Anygüey, check this: "Funny how things get away from you. For years you can't remember nothing. Then just like that, it all comes back to you." Uncanny, *nê*?

Me HORRORIZA lo que me escribes, about the continued violence there. Tengo miedo. In fact, no puedo creer que me escribas esto, in the same sentence, o casi: *Our white skins are still safe for the momento! But one can't help wondering if we (blankes) are the next target. Pretoria is having a major crime wave. Yesterday our cousin's father-in-law was beaten to death in front of his wife by intruders.* Do you have *any* idea how this sounds? Como si describieras . . . otro planeta.

Me alegro que hayas encontrado tan moving esa letter de Roland. Y que puedas vislumbrar . . . el underneath, as it were. O, como dices, what attracted me through his jocular (jock-ular!) façade. *Great depths there, rarely plumbed or revealed.* Beautifully put. About his "dysfunctional" comment, hmmm. I hadn't though about that in reference to his own marriage. Porque ¿sabes qué? He's *never* mentioned it. Digo, her. Them. Nunca.

### 24-v-08 (continued. later)

Can't believe you're taking off to Durban tomorrow. I didn't like it there. Remember, me fui con el Castells en ese mismo road trip, in December 1982. Visitamos al Steve du Preez, Roland's pal. Me acuerdo que he tried to cheer me up, intentaba asegurarme que he'd *never* seen two people more in love, que surely Rolo couldn't be "all that bad," things couldn't have changed *that* much between us.

And yet, I *know* what I felt (or don't I?). Esa slide into convention: I felt it as coldness, back then. Distancia. Pero come *on*: tener que sneak down to his CHILDHOOD bedroom para hacer el amor, in the dead of night, como si fuéramos niños. I was so far past that—¡no había vivido con mi padres en años, coño!—so much more independent than he was. Irónico: when I met him, los Boys, sus amigos Ken and Steve, me dijeron que el nickname de Rolo era "Mr. Rough, Rugged, and Independent." And he reveled in it, OB-vio. And I loved that about him in the States, me acuerdo. Su ruggedness, precisamente. I wanted him to "take a stand" of some kind, in Joburg, y él parecía . . . incapaz de hacerlo. Pero to me, it felt like he was unwilling.

Anyway, let's turn the lente on me (for a change, jaja). No puedo creer mi HUBRIS: how *could* I have descended from the plane, cuando me recogiste esa vez que volvía de España, and exclaimed, "How ugly your country is"? Uf, I cringe! ¡Qué vergüenza! I can't believe you remember that—y que lo encuentres hilarious. Menos mal. Strange: me doy cuenta de que I began the work of resemanticizing Suid-Afrika, digo, my *relasie* to it, viviendo en Buenos Aires. Eight years ago.

Think of my "Anniversary Crónica." La que me ganó esa obscure literary prize (because Weevil FORCED me to enter ese Raza literary contest, remember?) y que me comenzó la carrera de cronista. OB-vio, allí se ve la evidencia de que somehow I'd erased the fact—puf, right out of my brain and body—that South Africa had ever looked ugly to me. Even as I did the exact *opposite* with Roland, fíjate. De él, había borrado—buried—lo bello.

Agárrate: hace un frío de la hueva here. The smoke is gone, gracias a Dios. Hubo un savage wind, howling all night. Pero I drifted off to sleep pensando en Roland, allowing myself just to *be* in that place, de nuevo. En mi San Francisco apartment, en la Marina, esperando sus letters, sus phone calls (simón, hasta *telegrams* me mandaba, back then). En esos momentos antes de caerme profoundly asleep, it was like one of those movies, o un libro, donde el yo es como . . . un seeing eye. O un ave, soaring over the landscape, miles and miles. You know what I mean.

Pienso en una escena de *Sin rumbo* de Cambaceres, donde el main character, Andrés, se duerme en una carreta and has a dream just like this. Pero dammit, you won't have read that 19th-century 'Tine novela. A verrr, oh, I dunno. Pero you get the picture. Anygüey, it was like that. Te juro que I teleported myself back to Chestnut Street, y no sólo eso: patrás en el tiempo, too (don't think me daft!). Ohhhh, I'd like to see him, be with him. Part of me como que apenitas puede creer que I just said that. Pero otra parte (much stronger) is allowing myself to admit, finalmente, que R. was (is?) "el amor de mi vida."

I was down in the commons just now, lavando ropa and for whatever reason (you know me . . .) I picked up this beautiful, semi New Age-y revista, *The Sun*. Una entrevista sobre PTSD caught my attention. El escritor era un therapist con el unfortunate surname of Tick, pero te juro que the gist of the essay stopped me en mis tracks. El tal Tick ha trabajado con returning veterans de un chingo de wars, from WWII to Vietnam, y ahora, to fucking Afghanistan and Iraq. Según el Mr. Garrapata, PTSD is pathologized in our culture, pero it's not a disease sino una especie de moral and ethical, psychological trauma, que exige *healing*.

And get this (this is the bit that really got to me): dice que the *only* way to truly heal is to go back and *reexperience* the pain, por medio de rituals, etc. He uses Eastern and Western therapeutic techniques, as you might expect, y mencionó una cantidad de more or less Sarita-like Shamanic this 'n' that. Al principio, me sentí entre irritated y aterrada. Pero también, I admit, intrigued. Sobre todo, I think, me sentí . . . interpelada. As if the oke had written ese ensayo just for me. En un flash, me tenía perfecto sentido, overriding my skepticism toward overly New Age-y prácticas y actitudes.

DRUM ROLL:

Llevo 25 años *avoiding* the pain. A verrrr, el dolor de *qué*, exactly? De mi Gran Desilusión. My disappointment in R. Digo, in the R. that he became, o el que se me manifestó en Sudáfrica. The pain of the *relasie*'s failure. El fracaso de mi Gran Amor. No. The pain (guilt?) of my having left him. There, I've said it.

I sealed it off, supongo. Undergrounded it. Locked it away. Allí en Pretoria, en el '83. You know when I mean, *nê*. Unos meses antes de conocerte. It must've scarred over, pero never healed. Por alguna razón, this time (my complete aloneness?) and place (this sublime Green Mansion/ Emerald Bosque) holds the key. Es curioso (ahora me parece, suddenly, *harto* curioso), pero this is the *first* time I've ever faced it, Wimmie. It's as if I've *reentered* it, la totalidad de la experiencia. Y es por eso, creo, que tengo la sensación de que it's "all coming back to me," like Toni Morrison wrote.

I'm going to finish the transcript now, pa' mandártelo antes de tu departure for Durban. You are the *only* person seeing this, digo, besides me and Roland. And I'm bloody well *not* sending him this—este palimpsesto or whatever—until you've commented on it and approved it. Necesito tu perspective. Algo en mí intuye que es medio . . . radioactive. No letter from him hoy—¿quizás la wife o familia occupies him los weekends, what do you think? Probably. I mean, duh. OB-vio.

I'm so curious to hear what—whom—you'll find en estas páginas. Is it the "me" you knew? ¿Me reconoces? Can you understand now—al menos un little hair better, anygüey—mi pasión por él? Me doy cuenta: we never really discussed this! Cuando te conocí, en Pretoria, the wound was fresh. I'd only just left him. Based on my tale of woe—and outrage—you helped me stoke the bonfire (we really *did* burn his letters, remember?), cavar el hoyo, enterrarnos.

27-ᴠ-08

Wimmie,
    Thank you for this. I'm including it here in our palimpsesto fashion, so we can keep track of . . . *us*. De nuestros thoughts, palabras, *reaksies*, feelings:
    *I suddenly realised how uncanny it is that you are making this journey into your past, this journey of healing, at exactly the moment when South Africa is suddenly back with burning people and the army in the townships. It ripped me back to the way it was in those days, when you lived here. Then of course your beautiful words about Roland. I can't help feeling sympathy for him (back then), remembering my own naïveté, your sophistication, amazing focus, your self-knowledge. Like no one I'd ever encountered before. You were like someone from a film or novel to me. A clash of cultures, unacknowledged maybe because*

*we all spoke Engels and looked more or less alike. This so much speaks about our denial of your racial identity, something which I'm only now beginning to realise. I don't think it was hubris, by the way, your telling me how ugly my country was. Just your usual honesty, and also fear. Because you were already falling deeply in love with South Africa by then, but struggling to accept this contradiction.*

LITTLE EYE: Wimmie, lo he estado pensando un chingo, what you wrote me earlier today:

*DO send the transcript to Roland, perhaps rethinking some of the deeply sexual bits, for the time being . . . I say this only because I have no idea how this may destabilise him and his life. Because they are so powerful, even after all this time. Am I being overly cautious?*

Creo que I'm just going to to send the transcript to R. tal cual. Me parece que sería una mutilación—de su impacto, de su scope—if I were to fish through and excise those parts you mentioned. Porque the whole *thing* is so *baie erotiese* anyweg, ¿que no? So, quizás sea, precisely, algún tipo de "destabilizing" that I'm (not so secretly) hoping for? Is this EVIL? ¿Estoy loca? Escribí en mi diary, earlier: OK, well, you've already *got* la confirmación de Montenegro (albeit in his laconic Capricornian way) de que simón, he *does* remember, "everything." De que simón, he did (even *does*, his word) love you. So ¿qué (más) queréh, muñeca? *Wat soek jy?*

## 27-v-08 (later)

Dearest OomBie,

Esta carta tuya (two in one day, ¡órale!) was . . . *te veel*. I was *so* looking forward to reading lo que me habías comentado en el transcript, and then . . . uf, enterarme de todos esos cyber-glitches, how you'd put your comments on in orange, y luego ¡puf! They'd all been erased—crushing! Menos mal que you've at last been able to read, and scrawl your comentarios longhand. Esto es hilarious (hiLEriuhs, *pace* R.), si no fuera que te conozco, you and your *extreme* airplane phobia:

*I read the transcript on the plane to Durban, hideous turbulence. I thought it was going to fall at any moment! Scrawled my comments all over it (see attached!), imagining that maybe it woudn't burn if the plane crashed, and you could read it still. It was time travel, extreme eroticism, overwhelming rush of memory. I only cautioned you to make you fully aware of what a powerful punch this packs. But as you say, it would mutilate it to leave anything out. It is all so imbued with erotic energy it would be pointless. I can't wait to hear how R. reacts. I think maybe you just hope to elicit a response, to make this all real again, because of the way you made it unreal long ago, during apartheid, in order to be able to carry on living.*

27-v-08

Querido R.,

I'm writing pa' mandarte esto: he aquí el transcript, especie de palimpsest I've created, as promised. I hope you can print it, espero que puedas estar en alguna parte . . . somewhere *streng privaat, alleen*, para leerlo.

29-v-08

Rolo Babee,

*Baie* relieved to hear from you. Tú sabes que no creo en las coincidencias: Wim was just in Durban, too. Tengo que admitirlo, the idea of you visiting your daughters in Durban . . . hafta put that one en mi pipa and *rook* it. It fills me with tenderness. Anygüey, cuando puedas, read what I sent you (el transcript, OB-vio). And then write me. Time has *always* been "few," darling, *nê*? So *gebruik* it well.

P.D. Is your handwriting any better (digo faster?) que tus (non)typing skills? It used to be. If so, ¿por qué no me mandas una real letter? Digo, por caracol. Erase una vez . . . you were *very* good (OK, swoonworthy) at that.

2-vi-08

Wimmie,

*Baie dankie*, por tus words of encouragement (in re el—brief—silencio de R.). Reconozco que soy (medio) ridiculous. Or ridícula y medio, como dice mi gran pana, el Tinker Salas. I have NO patience. I want things when I want them, on my timetable. Uf, infantil much? Still and all, me ayuda que me recuerdes que he "may be pondering a response (for himself and for me). Or he may simply be caught up in his own life"—como la gente dizque normal. I'm relieved que te des cuenta de que "few people are as into writing and correspondence as we are." Amen to that, my china!

Quizás, reflexiono ahora, esa . . . blandness, the neglect I felt from Rolo (back then) sólo era su habitual modus vivendi: la familia 24/7, los boring northern suburbs amigos todos los weekends. El quería, he tried to include me, pero . . . me encontraba cada vez más horrified, enajenada. I wanted something . . . more, algo diferente. Algo intenso y apasionado. I remember que lo que me había parecido tan *Martian Chronicles*, entonces, was that he *had* been that way with me in San Francisco, en New Orleans (you've seen la evidencia: the transcript, todas sus cartas). I didn't want to be (only) "included," incorporada en esa realidad.

And so, I bolted. In December, antes de Chrismy y del New Year's eve cumple de R. (Christmas en verano, chale to that! No me cerraba entonces— and it still doesn't), rajé en ese two-week *groot trek*, ese road trip across the entire country, con el Castells, remember? I'd yearned to see the country with R. The veld he'd seduced me with. Pero by the time I pitched up in S. Africa, él estaba trabajando. All the time en la Premier fucking diamond mine y yo sola, sola, sola. Scribbling into my giraffe-print diary, hours on end, ese pen scratching y los highveld birdcalls la banda sonora que me acompañaba in our tiny miner's cottage en ese dweedly *dorp*, Cullinan. Pero the alternative to that forced solitude was no better: las obligatory hen parties en Joburg con sus chatty hermanas y la cotilla, supercilious de su sanctimonious madre.

Agárrate: I'm now reading *When She Was White*, por Judith Stone (2007), a kind of hybrid history/memoir, sobre esa Colo chick, la Sandra Laing, nacida en una familia Rock, near Piet Retief. *Seker*, conoces el caso. Well, just tell me WHY am I becoming so FIXATED en todo este tema de los Colo, NOW? I didn't have a clue about the Colo *situasie* back then! And: their *situasie* was, for me, deeply overshadowed por ese discurso binario que enmarcaba todo como black–white, en los '80s. Or . . . did it? Así lo recuerdo yo, anygüey. And besides: there weren't that many Colos in the Transvaal, ¿que no? O al menos . . . reconocibles, visible to me, en Pretoria. Por eso ese Ian stood out so much, *onthou jy*? Ese vato con quien el

Curé was having an affair. Y me lo traía a casa, pa' spend the night. I just remembered that! Ian used to douse himself con el Kouros que le había regalado al Curé, from Madrid. I can see his face clearly, can you? Tan guapetón, con todo y su sexy Afro . . .

*3-vi-08*

Wimmie,

Verás por el time stamp que it's after midnight, Califas time. I've worked and worked on this. Esta *bloed* crónica es, creo, one of the most challenging pieces I've ever written. I needed to finish it. It was an animal hunger. Once that ur-memory (el miscarriage en New Orleans) was un-buried, ansiaba escribir de todo eso. The memory had unsteadied me (to say the least!), y tenía que encontrar el sense of balance en el texto. Didn't want to sensationalize or trivialize it. No quería que se aflojara la intense emotion pero tampoco—the horror!—rendirme a lo sentimentaloide (as my dad would say). Uf!

Pero LITTLE EYE: también me sentí constrained en otro sentido. I really struggled with this, pero no quería meterle any (or . . . much?) explicit eroticism y sin embargo, OB-vio que I had to al menos *hint* at it, ¿no? Porque what else (if not that) had been the CAUSE of our little zygote's presencia in the first place? Pero while I was writing me sentí shadowed por el temor—terror, really—de friquearle al Pierre. Me aterra su posible *reaksie*.

*7-vi-08*

Dear Wimmie,

Leí tu letter right when I woke up—PERFEKSIE. Creo que you're right: algo un little hair más "lite" (jaja, who me?) is in order! For some reason, casí perdí el plot ayer. Digo, *again*. You're right: clearly I *had* under-estimated the extreme intensity de lo que vengo haciendo. Por algo los culti studies teóricos y los psychoanalysts le dicen memory-*work*, nê? Anygüey, la Cronopia Raz (la mamá de mi just-hatched faux advisee, el J-Raz) got tickets, and tomorrow afternoon vamos a SF de nuevo, a Fort Mason (en la marina, right on the water). Vamos a un yup-scale wine tasting! It's a benefit for—agárrate—the SLOW Food Movement of San Francisco. I'm dying laughing! Casa casi me había convencido de que *I'd* invented that term. Porque a cada rato le digo a la gente (apropos di mi writing y su dizque "difficulty"), ¿conocen el Slow Food Movement? OK, so vincúlense al Sloooow *Reading* Movement!

Pero, all this lite, fun stuff no obstante, me pregunto what is up with Rolo. Supongo que it's possible he *is* overwhelmed (as you suspect), quizás hasta (partially?) by his *own* response to all this. Encuentro, frustratingly, que mi writing (¿yo misma?) often does that to people. Digo: a veces (muchas veces, la verdad) están simply stunned into silencio . . .

8-vi-08

Dearest OomBie,

Llegué a casa (oh, I wish it *were* my home here) to find two letters from you, con la latest versión del Palimpsesto (digo el transcript), *en ook* una carta de R. Super long, *nogal*—I mean, for him. *Baie dankie* for this:

*Your note to R. is perfeksie. You give him all the space in the world to maneuver and respond. I don't know how I would react in his place, quite a tough one. But like you say, stunning people into silence is one of your strong suits . . .*

Mil gracias, too, por esto:

*It makes total sense that Roland personified your shock, alienation, and horror at what you found here. How else could you deal with it but by rejecting him? I think Roland became the personification of white South Africa to you once you realised how deeply implicated he was in it all. All of us were, of course, but it was worse for you in his case because you'd met him far from apartheid. You two fell in love outside of it, then suddenly you had to deal with the fact that he was one of the* blankes, *part of the ruling class here in SA.*

*If the two of you had stayed in America, you would likely still have been together today, but South Africa and its realities were too much for you (who could blame you) to reconcile with the love and joy you found in him. It wasn't a place then where one could be truly happy without being very adept at blotting out most of what is happening around you. We who had lived with it, grown around and over it, could do this somehow, but for you it was impossible.*

*Ag*, Wimmie, I'm so angry at myself! The pain of having let R. go—no, de haberle desterrado—is simply too great. *Ek's hartseer*. That's the word for it, *presies*. Y es ahora, sólo ahora que I'm feeling it. OB-vio (ahora caigo, oh, qué boluda) *esto*—its magnitude—es la razón por la cual lo había reprimido. Buried it. Enterré el fin de mi Gran Amor así como el memory of our miscarriage.

It never made sense to me before: how could I truly feel *nothing*—o casi nada—about the end of that love affair? Y más weird todavía: how could I have forgotten? Yo y mi dizque *olifant* memory? Pero tus insights me brindan un modo de entender esto. You help me contextualize, al menos, my horrible (and to me now, casi imperdonable) behavior: it was a survival strategy allá, en RSA.

And later, una vez patrás en USA (feeling completely desarraigada, en todo sentido . . . pero esa es otra), supongo que I was simply unable to go back there, volver a esos radioactive memories. And a few years after my bumpy reentry, patrás en Califas . . . pues Pierre nunca mostró ni siquiera un tiny bit of interest in my exotic vida en S. Africa. Al contrario: era como si fuera un Forbidden Subject. Estrictamente off-limits. Anygüey, aquí te comparto unos snippets from R.'s latest letter:

*Shug,*

*I have printed transcript, but have not read it yet—mea culpa! Mercury in retrogrado notwithstanding, I have had a very busy weekend. This is not conducive to replying sensitively to a magna cum laude co-correspondent!! As you well know—you have previously stunned me into silence (qui silencio consentire) with your fine rebuttals. And what fine rebuttals you have, n'est ce pas?*

*I did think that my quickie response would likely not be well received and that I could expect some abuse by return. He! He! As an African I must protest that I find your 'New World' insistence on instant communications gratification to be evidence of neoliberal tendencies that do not sit well with my African worldview. You see—even honkies can learn new tricks.*

*Here I am on Sunday evening typing like Cyclops (one finger, one eye) trying desperately to compete with your touch-typing and superior database. Los my uit tot ek jou 'transcript' gelees het en dan sal ek voledig (en skriftelik) jou beantwoord. Love, RF*

True to (Capricornian) form, he's scolding me for my need for speed! El Afrikaans siempre era sexy and playful entre R. y yo. Irónicamente, by the time I'd begun to pick some up (encouraged by Neppe Selabe en UNISA, *nogal!*), we were no longer together . . .

P.D. El olor de mis nardos—three bought this a.m., for an outrageous price, cinco de la semana pasada (the oil of which [spikenard!] la Magdalena anointed en los pies de Cristo)—is now wafting up, arriba a este little loft-*treehuis* desde abajo, hechizándome con su intoxicating waxy, wet greenness. Wish you were here. Or, no. Rather ojalá estuviéramos en Oaxaca, and I could take you to the huge market, el Mercado de Abastos (donde estaba, buying nardos—I promise you—cuando murió Mamá, hace cinco años). Allí te venden un chingo de nardos—like two dozen—for around $5.

*9-vi-08*

Dear Wimmie,

It's a relief to me que me confieses que you never used to understand what I saw in Roland (back in Pretoria, digo) pero que ahora, when you read some of his writing, you're beginning to get why I fell in love with him. Wimmie, ¿tú crees que sea posible que (part of me) still loves him?

*18-vi-08*

*Liewe* Wimmie,

Me encanta este palimpsestic mode. Ahhh, the wonders of e-macho, jaja. Roland me escribió patrás, pero uf! Check this:

*Have just read your pre-RSA boekie! You're right—it awakens many more memories and details than I could remember off the top of my head. I'll have to read it again to get myself back into California/New Orleans/Chicago memory mode. I know you read fast & write & respond fast! I may be slow to respond but remember 'non ti scordare.'*

He's reminding me, *yebo* he may be slow, pero he *doesn't* forget: esta frase la leímos juntos, on a vintage Italian postcard en una long-defunct, weird little shop en North Beach. It means "don't forget." Pero then, como que he jacks up the evocative mood, con esto:

*Just got up from underground and must get onto analysis of fractional gold content results. Mooi ne? If I don't get the report updated you'll make me forget and I won't be paid come month end! L RF*

Speechless! I reckon I am (a *teensy* bit) more patient than I was 25 yrs ago. Pero ¡coño! Does this not *prove* que tengo razón (and I was right back then)? Roland and I *never* could've lasted as a couple! *Nooit*. Y no entiendo cómo él cree (he *fantasizes*) que we could have. As *if* I would've put up with this superfish *kak*.

*18-vi-08*
Header: *eGoli Standard, or fractious gold . . .*

R.,

. . . or whatever the HELL it is you're doing underground these days, bebé. Menos mal que I've a sight more patience ahora que back then, hey, mi querido Capricornio? Translation: termina ese damn analysis para hacer safeguard tu paycheck, and then read me *again, asseblief*. Las veces que te haga falta para jog your memory back, back to a *dieper plek* than underground. I'm actually laughing (well, almost). No puedo creer que hayas podido leer nuestro transcript—and write me about "fractional gold content."

*30-vi-08*

Wimmie,

Menos mal que I have you. You just . . . *sommer* get me, *heeltemal*. Tan frustrating, intercambiar estos teasing, semisexy, FUN, nostalgic emales con mi antiguo compinche de Berkeley, el Rápido Dickison (with whom I hadn't been in contact en siglos) y contrastarlos con los "halting efforts" de R., as you put it. Eres generoso: "clearly he has been deeply affected by what you've written, but doesn't know quite what to do with it. Not yet." Quizás sea tu priestly training . . . sigh. Pero con esto, "how horrid to be scratching around under the earth for fragments of gold, quite a primeval image," veo que you haven't lost your impish, evil Gemini wit! Ay, you've made me laugh!

Only four more days here, and then you arrive. Yippee! Can't wait. Entre el calor y todos los hetero-macho artistas que han invadido el Montalvo lately, creo que I'm ready to get outta here. Aunque I can't say the same about the prospect of returning to my dizque vida normal. Me dieron esta artist residency to be an artist, coño, and so I have done. Estos dos meses han sido una especie de *extreme* detox: aquí en el vortex me liberé del flow constante de news, words, words, words about "el mundo": la política, la moda, el jodido stock market. Toda mi obsessive "keeping up"— *pant pant*—con la cultura popular. Obligación cívica. Obligación de mi chamba. Obligación ideológica. STOP! Todo ese infernal constante buzzing en la cabeza.

Me parece que only by radically stopping all the random noise of my life (que sólo la distancia me hizo *ver*, starkly, como tal) was I able to . . . clear a space inside me. Y allí en ese secret garden fue donde mi escritura hizo BOOM: todo este silencio y verdor y distancia y strangeness me abrió el wormhole de la memoria. Sólo aquí, ahora (far, far from home and its dangerous lulling), en estas cocooning yet risk-inducing green mansions, pude encontrar mi jouissance.

# En casa

Pero yo ya no soy yo,
ni mi casa es ya mi casa.

**Federico García Lorca,**
**"Romance Sonámbulo"**

*9-ix-08*

R.,

    *Wat maak jy?* Espero no haber hecho nada como para . . . friquearte (unduly, I mean): por más que digas que no, sé que I've *always* unsettled you. Once upon a time, al menos, this was a good thing.

*9-ix-08*

Dearest Wimmie,

    Cuando camino en el health trail, me pregunto, *What did (do) you really want?* I mean: con el reconecte. OK, me obligué a rebobinar, forced myself to go back, back into myself, patrás al pasado (at Montalvo), *nê*? *Maar*, como me dijiste entonces, ese nivel de peeling back, that searching, la spotlight intensity cannot *possibly* be kept up: nos volveríamos locos. Y sin embargo . . . I've always prided myself on being an intensity junkie, una edge dweller. Pero ese EDGE is precisely what's faded, cada vez más en años recientes. Or . . . not even tan recientes. For a while now, hay que admitirlo. Supongo que eso—that edge—was what I wanted to touch again, find in myself, reclaim, en el retrete.

En Montalvo I figured out que la "verdad" que había abrigado, all those years, era sólo una versión. Una distorsión. Digo, que Roland was "the bad guy," completely. Y: not only did I "figure it out," R. me hizo saber, in no uncertain terms, que había tenido high hopes for our relationship. That he loved—loves—me. Que simón, he remembers. No, la verdad es slippery, malleable, elusive. Es . . . otra. Está en otra parte. In-between.

I still doubt he could've sustained ese passionate, guantes-off self que me reveló en San Francisco, en New Orleans. Just not in his nature. Pero OJO: tampoco es—or not entirely—el stolid, icy oke my disappointment and frustration turned him into in South Africa. *Alla fine*, las vastas diferencias entre nosotros wouldn't have allowed us to "flourish" (his word) over the long haul, *ek dink*. Por otra parte (as R. himself asked me), how do I really *know*? Ya que, as he reminded me, I never really gave us a chance. Ay, ouch.

18-ix-08

Querido R.,

*Baie* unsettled myself en estos días, por el suicide de mi colega, el escritor David Foster Wallace. Había sufrido de la *depressie*—over 20 years. Como sabes (I think you know), mental illness runs in mi familia. So, el tema me toca bien close to home. Además, recalca la urgencia—the cruciality (not a word, *ek weet, maar*, you know what I mean)—of connection. Making, keeping, renewing.

Leading me to this *kak*: —*Ek's nie uit-gefreek nie! I don't think you unsettle me.* No one believes that ni en pedo, Rolo! Not even you. Oh, I unsettled Ma F. all right: she about had a fit of apoplejia when she first laid ojos on me (not so tu pa, QEPD). Y supongo que even now (how old *is* your ma, anyweg?), sería lo mismo. Pero I've *always* unsettled you too, Rolo Babee. Y érase una vez, you weren't so . . . in denial.

What's *happened* to you todos estos años, my darling, that aside from the few tantalizing vislumbres que me has mostrado (your keen memory—visceral, immediate—of our miscarriage, your instant conjuring del Club Zanzibar de nuestro film, *Montenegro*), tus cartas sean tan "hail fellow well met"? Al parecer, as protective an armor as ever (¿tal vez más? Aunque can't say I blame you, not entirely. Once mordido, twice tímido, como quien dice) te resguarda ese "rough, rugged, and independent" corazón capricorniano.

Y en cuanto a esto —*Must admit I've been a little tardy in response, but remember you're the wordsmith—I'm just a miner who has to get his thoughts in order before committing them to writing!* Dame un break. Recuerdo otro skill set (y no hablo de tus forays underground, pick-axing away). Y OJO, you were a damn fine wordsmith también, once upon a time. Resuscitate him, *asseblief*!

P.D. Some foties of you con las hijas sería *lekker*, *natuurlik*. Pero bebé, what *really* intrigues me is some of you alone—ropa opcional.

*24-ix-08*

Querido R.,

*Totaal uit-gefreek* con el imbécil, *skouerkop* del Zuma! What a riDIC presidente! What the fuck is up with that oke? Is everything OK? Let me know, y escríbeme patrás soonest.

P.D. A brilliant flash: mándame tu cell *nommer*. It won't work qua phone, me parece (aunque confieso que I'm dying to hear your voz), *maar* I can send you some teensy poetic SMSs. En el down LOW. I do it with Wim todo el tiempo.

*29-ix-08*
Header: *He wakes*

R., darling,

Huelga decir: mi header remite a tu Rip van Winkle allusion. I loved, loved, loved your latest *briefie*. Si eres el Tin Man, I'm anointing you with oil (preferably nardo-scented). Y si eres el mere mere Rip VW, pos entonces I'm waking you up. Your hijas are lovely. Ditto tú. Muy sexy (I can't believe you still smirk).

*Met baie liefde en soentjies,*

Tu Shug

P.D. ¿Te acuerdas cuando no tenía ni clue how to say that kind of thing (algo tan sencillo como love and kisses) and I'd ask you—command you—to teach me? I'm proud of myself for holding onto this obscure, vexed, evocative *taal* (even just . . . little bits 'n' pieces), que érase una vez despreciaba, deep down in my too-ideological (lo reconozco) heart. Aunque me doy cuenta, post-facto, I called Zuma a fucking SHOULDER-head en mi última carta. ¡Uf, qué risa!

P.P.D. Here's a cyber-fotie, pa' que me tengas en la compu, too. I took it near Abiquiu, New Mexico, en julio. ¿Ves? I've finally become the "nature girl" (I think) you always wanted me to be. Estoy cerca de la casa de Georgia O'Keeffe. It's my mother's "clan territory."

*30-ix-08*

R. darling,

Humor me (aun si te parece totally silly): can you send me your exact birth info (digo, con la hora—ask *jou* ma, *hoor*) so I can compare our natal charts?

And about your header: *people of heaven (los amaZulu)* . . . Se me ocurre algo, en este unseasonably blazing the fuck hot (105F, no sé *presies* in centigrade, creo que around 40, *miskien*?) dizque autumnal day, when the US economy is plummeting. Rereading your words, de ayer, I wanted to tell you:

One of the most compelling things about you, cuando nos conocimos, was the way you'd learned to speak Zulu. Saber eso de ti, escucharte hablar . . . that gave me *such* hope, nudging up against and unsettling, a bit, la rabia y desesperanza por el apartheid. Esa esperanza: oh, *why* couldn't I sustain it, en tu país? Those Zulu sounds que me enseñaste. I can still hear your voice, making those sounds. Sexy. Urgente. I loved and admired that. Eso, y tus animal sounds.

*30-ix-08*

Wimmie,

Mercury messing wit' me, coño. Pero must send you este intriguing palimpsesto con R. Agárrate:

> *Dearest S.,*
>
> *I've changed my mind (or merely reverted to original truth)—yes you do unsettle me. I have read your transcript a couple of times and I must admit that with each reading another aspect of our relationship reveals itself. Perhaps that's just my memory kicking back into gear. And as for my allegedly "hail fellow well met" style—I can only speculate that I've got out of correspondence practice and that you are watching me limber up (so to speak) after playing Rip van Winkle for a couple of years.*
>
> *I'm not too concerned about Zuma's imminent ascent to the presidency. The amaXhosa (Madiba & Mbeki) had their chance, now it's the turn of the amaZulu (the people of heaven). The amaZulu, the Brits and the Boers know each other well—each have fought with the other and won and lost on different occasions. Google the 'Battle of Isandlwana' as one example that lives on to this day in the Zulu and British national psyches. Must rush! Love, RF PS: You got sexy eyes.*

Stunning, *nê! Wat sê jy?*

*2-x-08*

Rolo Babee,

No te friquees por mi prolixity (wd?): U know me, la Marquesa de Sade of words. *Maar*, por si acaso—y para head off at the pass you crawling back into *another* Rip Van Winkle–like eternidad—te mando aquí some show 'n' tell. La primera foto está algo blurry, pero te la mando anyway. It's of us en el umbral de ese mega-magic *plek* (without which, *niks . . .*): le Club (aka the Balboa Cafe). Las otras están un pelín vintage too, pero bien evocative, hey? Tú y yo en un doorway en San Francisco (la habrá tomado mi mom o mi prima la Sloth, aka Lee W.). And you in front of 2370 Chestnut Street by the Vasbyt Dodge van. La otra es legendary. *Miskien* U retain your own copy? Possibly my fave fotie of all time:

los Montenegro, New Orleans, circa 1982. Milagro que esa ciudad did not ignite mientras tú y yo flaneábamos por sus recovecos. Or maybe it did . . .

*7-x-08*

OomBie,

He aquí some visual aids. How do you like the recent one, la que me mandó R. el otro día? He took it of himself—con su cell, I reckon. The others are from 1982. R., in front of 2370 Chestnut Street, #212. Our beautiful old apartment block! Al ladito mero del formerly porn Presidio Theatre. I made a peregrinaje there myself con la Cronopia Raz, just this past spring cuando estuve en Montalvo. R. posa al lado de Vasbyt, ese Dodge van he drove all over the US con el Ken y el "Sea Lawyer," aka Du Preez. Checa mis safari shorts in the French Quarter one! ¡Coño! Remember I used to wear them to that club After Dark in Pretoria, y al Park Five Saloon in Joburg? Milagro I wasn't arrested! And check Roland's teensy gray athletic shorts. Ay, tan glam, tan louche. So '80s.

BTW: I unearthed some letters que R. había escrito a la Trish, mi roommate en San Francisco, remember? Ella me las había mandado years ago, pero I'd never even read them, creo. OB-vio, estas cartas—digo finding, rereading them—only became important to me *ahora*. Post-Montalvo. How is it, Wimmie, that things "all came back to me" this year, sólo ahora? The need to probe esta . . . herida primordial, to wonder and puzzle *HOEKOM, ek en* R.?

What does it mean, el AMOR, si nuestro arreglo doméstico, por así decirlo, me pareció almost from the get-go (tactically, ideologically) imposible? Intuyo que we'd *never* have agreed on domesticalia. Por ejemplo, ¿el "temita" de los domestic servants? Para R., no biggie. Al contrario. They're just part of the furniture, sine qua non; para mí, an annoyance *and* an ethical no-mosca zone. Where to make our (permanent) home? Para Roland, Joburg, sin lugar a dudas. Y para mí, Califas. Children? OK, *this* is maybe the one *plek* we would've *heeltemal* overlapped. Ay, sad, sad, sad. Oh, y el sexo. Yebo. Lots. Siempre. No matter what.

*21-x-08*
Header: *Slaap jy?*

My dearest (*former?*) Rip van Winkle,
   Hey, bebé, pensaba que era una *ex*-nap you were bragging about. Three
weeks ago. Coño, even SNAIL mail en los '80, bajo Reaganomics y el
apartheid, never used to take so long (sabes que patience is *not* my fuerte).
*Wat die fok maak jy?* What about those promised calisthenix? Yawn and
stretch, my *liefie.*

*25-x-08*

Wimmie,
   I *myself* am now extremely unsettled (ja ja, R.'s fave word)—by his
letter from yesterday. The more I reread it, cuanto más strange, erotic and
*diep* (ja ja) it seems. El vato fetichiza mi handwriting. Such tenderness,
digo, hasta en las partes más ostensibly . . . offhand. Pero then whoa
(hablando de deep), what more intimate thing could he say? Blown away,
te confieso, por eso de *come deep inside you for a long time.* Esta carta es
una especie de . . . quantum leap, ¿que no? It signals, graphically, that he
remembers. Pero también: he desires, ahora. It's getting late, *skattie. Maar*
check Heilige Liefde's insights:
   *Well, it sounds as if there's now more than "little ripples, recurrences of*
*electric erotic spark." How did you put it? That R. was the one you were*
*waiting for? I've been trying to imagine what it's like for him to read your*
*work—both your diary entries and your recent crónicas detailing your return,*
*via memory, to the time you spent with him, the child you conceived and lost. I*
*can only think he has undergone an awakening—Rip Van Winkle indeed!—*
*of some part that was fast asleep. How alien, how marvelous it would be to*
*have some slumbering part of your core start to warm again thanks to reacquaint-*
*ance with a lover through her writing. Called forth, called back, unsure whether*
*the recent encounter has been about checking to ensure that you are mutual*
*repositories of a shared past or about something new that's simply (simply!) en-*
*kindled by that past.*

*28-x-08*

Wimmie,

Concuerdo contigo (I *think*). It's probably for the best que R. y yo vivamos tan far apart: we already "destabilized" each other una vez. OJO: I'm not sorry for what happened, lo que elegimos (estar juntos, en S. Africa). Occasional remordimiento. OK . . . amend that script: deep regret actually. Tan sharp, since I began to let it in, en Montalvo. De que esa choice could not *somehow* have . . . lasted, worked out. De alguna manera. Somewhere.

I mailed R. a copy of that letter he'd written to my ex-roomie la Trish, junto con hard copy del transcript. La versión que saldrá en *Scenes*. His phlegmatic, Saturnine naturaleza (tan vividly represented in his *glacial* correspondence skills) me conduce nueces. Even now! O, digamos, now more than ever. And yet, and yet . . . puede que esto sea the very thing that drives me into heights of rapture. Controlled rapture (oxymoron), ya que I'm powerless to "act" upon it (in any immediate—unmediated—way), y debo, por ende, canalizarlo. Into my dizque real life (?), o (mejor), en la escritura.

*4-xi-08*

Dearest Wimmie,

I love your analysis of R.'s latest. At first, cuando leí "glacier," pensé que you meant cold. Pero luego vi que you were exploiting la polisemia de lo glacial: his millennially *stadig* relationship with movement. Tienes razón. Esa sensación de slooow y caution permea su astral chart, según he podido calcular (so much has been happening to me este año que la Joanna and I are having a "refresher" astral reading el jueves; va a mirar la chart de R. as well). This is the polar opposite (jaja) of me. And yet, it's like we were fatally (digo por el hado, not lethally, aunque . . .) drawn to each other.

*11-xi-08*

Rolo Babee,

I got caught up in the anodyne diario a diario (*pace* Cortázar), about which me parece que you know a little something (hey, Mnr. Invoice?). Di mis dos clases, back-to-back. La una invigorating, inspiring pero la otra (the more advanced one) has been going pretty *kak*. Flatlining students. Aburridas discussion quessies. Like pulling teeth. Pero check this: cuando entré al aula vi un *huge* bouquet of tuberose (mi flor favorita) on the table. I looked at them, incrédula. —*From all of us*, me dijeron. —¿Por qué? —*Just, Happy Autumn*, they replied.

Ay, adorables. We'd read a story by Silvina Ocampo donde los nardos (tuberose o spikenard) figuran prominentemente. Predictably, los students no conocían esta unusual, over-the-top southern flower. So I doused myself con el sublime Carnal Flower de Frédéric Malle, un nardo-heavy perfume (¡carísimo!) que compré en SF in June (mientras flaneaba por Union Square, day-dreaming of you). ¿Te creerías que I walked around el aula, letting each one sniff me? I promise you! Can you picture this?

Anygüey, this has been such a *lekker* day. Primero esas flowers, tan late in the season, totally unexpected. Y ahora not one sino dos emails de ti.

*14-xi-08*

R.,
   Fair Pilgrim, about this —*You know me*—*I would have responded promptly to any missive received through whatever medium you had chosen.* Orale, then. I take thee at thy word. My medium of choice? Skin (what are you gonna do about *that*?).

*14-xi-08 (later)*

R.,
   *Ek's jammer* for the *vloed*, pero I reckon you're used to it (to me) a estas alturas. With just a teensy 25-year hiato, ¿que no? It's now late afternoon chez moi; you must be fast asleep in Africa y heme aquí, fervently hoping my little SMS (second try, correct *nommer* esta vez) vuele straight as a shot a tu cell y que lo puedas leer in some (*streng privaat*) momento del weekend.

   Agárrate: I just found a whole bunch of our foties, like 20 or 30! *Ons twee* en SF, en Houston y New Orleans. Encontré la del famous kiss en el Quarter, *onthou jy?* De la cual me escribiste—on the fotie-back—"not necessarily Rodin, but *what* a kiss"! Hasta encontré foties que me mandaste later, much later. After I'd returned to CA. The *inskripsies* que me dedicaste al dorso are a whole *other* (lapidary, incendiary) epistolario: very you. You burn with animal longing, tenderness, humor. *Baie, baie erotiese.* Y tanto amor. I'll copy or scan them somehow y te las mando.

*14-xi-08*

Querido *OomBie*,

You'll *nooit dit glo*: I'd been obssessing about one particular fotie, me and R. besándonos en plena calle (I think it was actually Bourbon Street, ¿trillado, no?) en New Orleans, oblivious al Mardi Gras chaos que nos rodeaba. Bueno, guided by quién sabe cuáles unseen forces, I went and fished en aquel large plastic bin en el closet de "tu" *slaapkamer*, and sho 'nuff, bingo. Encontré una bola de esas sexy (nude) foties of me, que me sacó ese guapetón fotógrafo suizo that was in love with me, el Rudi. Wow. Pero lo más importante: hallé todo un cache of foties of R. and me.

And GET THIS: además de este tesoro-trove (which I'll *immediately* spirit to my office for safekeeping), encontré todas mis famous carpetas. Our magazine cutouts de S. Africa (y Europe—remember how precious *those* were to us?)!! Circa 1982–84. Incluyen nuestro ídolo el sublime Marcus Abel, todos los models que nos obsesionaban back then. La ehpectacular Patti Hansen, Jerry Hall, Rosemary McGrotha, Janice Dickinson (OMG, *what* has that girl done to herself), la Renee Simonsen, Iman, la Kim Alexis, y ese sexy Jeff Aquilon. Just wait till U see it! We can fish through and analyze juntos, cuando vengas next summer.

*Natuurlik*, everyone was at least 20 lb. "fatter," en esas revistas. The eyebrows were thicker, *everything* was thicker! La gente se miraba más robust y mucho más sexy, altogether a more colorful time than now. Ay Wimmie, vivimos tiempos pálidos, anoréxicos.

*20-xi-08*

R., mi amor,

Hope you've had time to read lo que te mandé al *kantoor*, pero I'm apprehensive! *Water* damage? Sounds biblical! Glad (*ek hoop*) it was only around the edges. OB-vio, I *never* got any text mensaje (SMS) back from you. Tan upset, coño. Creo que ya te dije: my messages *can* get through (aunque solo intermittently, parece) to Wim in Manenberg, pero his *never* get back to me. He surmised that you (oh, Sr. ingeniero de minas) would have a more ritzy cell plan que el que tiene un humble township priest. Y que por ende tus mensajes *uit* Afrika *would* be able to reach me. Can U investigate *probleem, asseblief*?

My "mountain santuario," hey? In your sueños, bebé! Eso era green mansions, el Montalvo Art Center. Pero in my "real" life, alas, I reside at the *base* of a *groot* montaña (Mount Baldy), not thereupon. Y ahora, to reward your paciencia (I can scarcely believe I held out this long!), read these pieces—los llamo *droom*-diarios—ever so *stadig*, voluptuously.

*19-x-08*
*Diary*

*Sueño*: Estaba patrás en S. Africa. I didn't fit exactly (jaja . . . understatement del siglo). Pero el sueño clearly allegorized el acto de recordar. Retrieval. Revival. Estaba en Pretoria: esa golden light, las dusty, wide streets. La última parte del dream, especially, felt very emotional. Peligroso. *Erotiese*. Me había escapado de una casa (my parents'? La de tus padres, en Bedfordview?). Era de noche. Estaba con R. Creo que estábamos desnudos. We were running, juntos. Gazelle-like, easy. Partíamos hacia alguna parte, together. De repente, we had to run, escaparnos, flee. We were running naked, de noche, together, cogidos de las manos. It was beautiful and terrifying. No sabía, at first, what we were running *from*. It felt like a wildfire, quizás. Pero luego, it became clear it was a thundering herd of wild beasts (*wildebeests*, ¿quizás?). Esta manada was being pursued, por su parte, by a predator. I remember I thought (en el sueño), ¿tigre? Pero al tiro (also inside the dream) descarté esa idea por *ridícula*: era Africa, after all. Estábamos en Africa. So, tenía que ser lion.

We outran them, R. and I, juntos (este tumultuous, hermoso dream: rewriting the history of our renuncia, torn asunder by history, geography, por el apartheid; nuestra historia de haber tenido la experience, *pace* T. S. Eliot, without—en ese entonces—being able to access or understand the meaning). Outran that herd (esa horda).

En casa 211

Pero later (the next day?), yo tenía una hoof-shaped scar, a cut, cual del zarpazo de un animal, on my left shin. Se lo explicaba a mi mom. Ella estaba incrédula—R. and I had outrun a herd of wild beasts? I'd been "marked" (mauled!?) por un aparente lion (pero not . . . caught, ni desfigurada ni devorada). Me había escapado—we'd escaped, together—sanos y salvos. WTF? En el sueño, I mean, in the recounting (a Mamá), nada de esto me tenía sentido. Pero *now* it does: writing it out here, leyendo lo que escribo. Lo único que quería, I remember, era ver a R. Estar (de nuevo) con él.

Ah, pero ese zarpazo. Se veía clean, healthy. Not angry, suppurating. Limpio. Just . . . a reminder.

5-xi-08
Diario
Election Day

Barack Obama es presidente. I didn't want to let myself believe (in) it. Y ahora ganó. Es la ascendencia del mestizo. De los mixties. Of *us*. Now is our time. We got the hybrid vigor, baby! Mixed *is mooi*. Anoche (night of Election Day), *otro* incredible dream. One of those that's so real you just can't believe it (al despertarte). Que it wasn't happening, que I wasn't *there*, back there. Estaba patrás en S. Africa, with R. La imagen más nítida que recuerdo is us, sentados en el suelo, facing each other. It was you, ahora. Digo, looking like esa recent fotie que me mandaste. El pelo más corto, cropped. I was holding your bare feet, te los acariciaba. It was a feeling of overwhelming tenderness, como esa vez cuando te agachaste para meter ese little slip of paper, to shield my strap-abraded ankle, mientras paseábamos por el Quarter, en Mardi Gras. Remember?

You'd been out, trabajando. Traías los pies vendados, al menos the one I was rubbing, and every so often me tenías que prevenir, —Passop *baby*, me decías, *don't press too hard there. It feels so good*, me decías encouragingly, *but it's a bit sore*. En uno de los dedos del pie tenías una herida, a cut; me dijiste que you'd stepped on a nail. Se me ocurre (now, awake) que esto es (OB-vio) highly symbolic (y también, análogo al zarpazo from my other Africa dream, last month). The slightly penitent, attentive act of foot-washing (worshipping?), ¿no es como la Magdalena, con Cristo? Reverential? *En ook erotiese*, somehow. And you, con esas *nail wounds* en los pies. What's that about, me pregunto. Loving, restorative, reparative gestos: me performing them, you accepting, *welcoming* them. Inviting them, tus pies in my lap, in my hands. Estabas sentado allí, facing me, allí mero, mirándome con tanto amor, deep into my eyes. Pero (this time): asking me to be gentle. —Passop, *my babe.* Not to bear down too hard en las (antiguas?) heridas.

Hablábamos (in the dream) about work projects, strange, arcane proshectos telúricos, juntos. I was telling you about taking some underground system (tipo el Metrolink) de LA to Joburg. I can hear myself saying to you, —*Joburg would be the perfect city for it. No earthquakes.* ¡Qué absurdo! *How* did I develop this "mining" expertise, en el sueño? Especie de extraña . . . rapprochement, supongo. Some radical, creative compromise (lo que no supimos encontrar, back then). You were convinced by my plan though. Proud of me, entusiasmado. This dream . . . tenía la solidez, la naturalidad, the comfort we never got to, never *allowed* ourselves (OK: *I* never allowed us) to get to, la primera vez.

*9-xi-08*
*Diario*

I exist floating cual medusa entre dreams, fantasías, memories. Apenitas "en el mundo." Lo de Barack es mega-chévere. Lo de la fucking Prop. 8 y la anti-Felicidad sucks, bigtime. Y lo del stock market (el nauseating plunge, ay, ay, ay, mis jubilation investments . . .) ditto. Pero de alguna manera vivo *aparte* de todo esto. Remembering, writing out todo lo de R., desde la primera, smoldering mirada we exchanged, the plate-glass window of the Balboa Cafe between us. R. putting his hand over mine (so strange and bold ese gesto, al pensarlo ahora, within minutes quizás solo *seconds*—of our meeting). Imploring or commanding me—*wait* (when I, in turn, commanded him to get lost, al aprender que era South African). Ese "wait," ese gesto tan emblemático de él: his deliberate, stubborn, solid capricornismo y a la vez (oh, la eléctrica corriente between us at that first touch) su explosive, impulsive Mars in Aries. Una rara—fated—fusión, porque he aquí que mi Mars is in Capricorn, y mi Sun is in Aries. Según Joanna

Woolfolk, esta symmetry produce una powerful attraction. O como decía mi pana la Trish, it was slated.

Pero oh, tras ese promisingly passionate beginning, why oh why couldn't I "read" your love in Joburg? *Why* couldn't I adapt to you, a tu lugar, your (way of) life? Why couldn't I smooth out *any* of my rough edges, tan desafiantemente independent, tan intransigent. Was my self-hatred and scorn such—por haber aceptado tu invitación, por haber ido a tu country, pisoteando mis ideological and ethical convictions—that I had to implement a scorched-earth policy para no morirme de guilt? Al parecer, yes. It was.

Reliving that trauma. Y el de antes, primordial: the loss of our little zygote (which I'd repressed, pero tú no). Y después: lo que hice, how I left you, how I shattered us. Todo esto, Roland, I'd managed to avoid examining all these years. Hasta este año. Lejos de casa (this must be significant), magically—ábrete Sésamo—it all opened up. Darme permiso, obligarme a decir todo esto. Writing my way back, hacia la integridad. Memory (y los sueños) a way (back) to you.

*23-xi-08*

*Liefste* Wimmie,

Heilige Liefde me mandó *otra* spectacularly insightful carta. Intuyo que he's half-apprehensive, half-fascinated by this whole . . . thing. Mi Montalvo-spawned reconecte con el amor de mi vida. I'll just leave you to ponder this, por el momento:

*Of your recent emails to Roland I observe the co-presence of acid and balm, wound and healing, regret and recovery. The phrase that comes to mind is 'truth and reconciliation.' Is it too obvious to observe that you're doing a personal version of that reparative (your word) work in your writings to and about R., and that the way you both conflate him with and disentangle him from the RSA, from his 'beautiful . . . and tortured land,' signals that you understand the writing in this manner. Full in the recognition that to remember is not the same as reconciliation or reparation but is, at least, their sine qua non. Necessary if not sufficient. No less necessary for being insufficient. Now, the question of what would suffice is (as it always is) more difficult. Because the things for which we seek reparation are just the ones that lie outside the bounds of equivalence, sufficiency. But then again you live amid excess; that hinterland is your home, you for whom only too much is ever enough.*

*30-xi-08*

Montenegro, my love,

*Ek kannie dit glo*: parece que estamos ante un general international gadget meltdown. Pero mientras tanto, muerta de risa con la imagen de ti que me das: getting grouchy, or ¿qué dijiste?, "grumpy" (ay, mi crochety Capricorn) at *all* matters that don't respond to your perfectly clear instruksies. Well, yes SIR! At your command!

Te mandé este email, last week: *Imperialistic US airwaves—or whatever you called it—mos def fucking with our comms, I'm afraid. No SMS from you!* Didn't you get that? Luego I called Verizon (phone company) pero they tuned me *kak* about how "they can't guarantee receipt of intn'l text messages." About which luego te mandé un pissed-off text. No te llegó, I'm assuming. It seems *dis* a one-*weg straat*, bebé, as far as what our cell phones can do juntos (or . . . not, más bien). Telephonic apartheid!

*8-xii-08*

R.,

Drove Saturday para asistir al Memorial Service en la First Presbyterian church downtown San Diego para mi adorada (Great) Aunt Priscilla Rodríguez. Bien chévere, seeing so many rellies de la familia de mi mom: Chávez, Rodríguez, Salgado, López, and Van Wagner (mi bisabuelo era Samuel Van Wagner, un Dutch Mexican Presbyterian minister de New Mexico, remember?).

Anygüey, it's cold now (bueno, for SoCal), sombrío y dreary. Mi primo Chuck me escribió esto, just last night: *Sad news again, prima: Joe Jr. called us a few hours ago to say that Uncle Joe passed away at home under hospice care at 11:45 this morning—two weeks to the day after Aunt Pri's passing.*

En casa　　　　　　　　　　　　　　　　　　　　　　　　　　215

So ahora, it's the end of a generation. I've decided to use, como contratapa del new book, una hermosa old family photo: mi bisabuelo tall and august and Dutch pero tambien dark-skinned and Mex, mi bisabuela Rebecca chubby and dignified y bien indigenous-looking, rodeados de sus six children. Mi beloved Agüela Eunice la mayor, y la Aunt Pri the youngest. They called each other Alpha and Omega! Now, all have passed on.

*9-xii-08*

*Liewe* OomBie,

It *is* strange, como dijiste, that we both go back to the Dutch. Otro invisible link! Capaz eso—my maternal heritage—explique mi entirely out of left field (e incómoda) atracción a los Rocks. Maybe it was my landing up in Pretoria, of all places? Digo, it's *so* Afrikaner dominant. Pero aunque of course I came across many virulently racist Rocks, me acuerdo que los Engels seemed . . . no sé, more . . . hypocritical, and priggish. I've just thought about this for the first time, pero . . . bueno, it makes *some* kind of sense, me parece (however essentialist). Mi papá adoraba a los Dutch, por su pro-judío role in WWII. Y supongo que I've inherited his fixation. I'm obsessed, desde que vi *Turkish Delight* a los 18 años en Santa Cruz, *onthou jy?* Ay, Rutger Hauer for evah!

What do you reckon is up with R.? I mean: con sus lax (or intermittent, para ser algo más charitable) comms. After all, *he* was the one who upped the ante, por así decirlo, al mandarme ese shocking, casi throwaway yet también scorchingly *erotiese* remark (about coming inside me . . . for a long time, ¿te acuerdas, lo *uitgefreek* que estuve, when I read that?). Es más, *he* sent me his cell number (como 5 veces); *he* badgered his ma for his birth time. So ¿por qué corno no responde a *direct* quessies about his household setup y quién carajo le contesta el teléfono?

Esto lo encuentro tan frustrating, puzzling. Straight-up bizarre. I'd say it *almost* . . . puts me off. Pero no del todo. I'd written a kind of "up to here," pissed-off letter to R. y se la leí a mi amigo José last week. He was kind of freaked out. Porque para él esto—R. and me—is a Great Love Story. José me dijo, —*OMG, is this a good-bye from you to him?* Y le dije, —*No. Not really, solo una especie de pausa.*

Lo que se me ocurre: when R. *does* open up, reveal himself (como si fuera por primera vez—which it isn't!), luego luego se friquea y es como si tuviera que dar un giant step—patrás. Make sense?

*19-xii-08*

R., my darling,

Do you mean you SMS'd me just *vandag*, tipo noon *your* time? You really *are* Mr. Magoo, bebé: Califas is 10 hours behind S. Africa, *onthou jy* (or maybe it's 9 now). That would've been the middle of the bloody night! Por suerte, my phone was off. Pero *natuurlik*, para variar, *niks, niks y niks*. Wim's convinced the CIA is jacking our attempts at cell-cell comms. Hmmm. En 1984 I might've been convinced, pero . . . *now*?

Make me laff: tú, quien a pesar de ser ENGINEER parece tener major techno-difficulties with gadgetry, on Gesigkak? My son, Etienne, has been badgering me too, pero resisto. La gente que usa Facebook se pone "ADD"— and MIA, let me add! Despite being known for (self-)revealing—y, según, emo-truth telling—escritura autobiográfica (esa es la standard-issue expectativa of life-writing anyweg), en realidad I'm very private. Ironic, *nê*. Pero ni en pedo would I send out messages all over the show, a un enorme grupo amorfo, en el internido. Uf. Besides, me parece superfish to the nth. And narcissistic.

CaraBobo and the like promotes speed. Me parece que it actually encourages impersonal comms, homogeneity and conformity . . . por más que sermonee ese vato el Sugarmountain de crear "community" y bla bla. OB-vio, *all* my students are on it, y cada vez más friends (real-life ones, jaja). Pero no way sucumbiré a la presión, ¡jamás! You'll see. Uf . . . estar constantly sending out little sound bites to all and sundry, para ni mencionar todos los dizque "updates." Dizzying! My ANX would soar off los charts. Se me hace que los que se vuelven avid Caraboberos (and it seems . . . addictive to me, ¿no crees?) lose their mojo for a more intimate, considered, patient form of comms. Anyweg (says little Miss High Caballo), my advice to you, bebé? Resist! Hell, si apenitas puedes keep up with your (formerly long-lost) true love en el (relatively) old-fashioned medium of email.

7-i-09

Rolo Babee,

Are you still crazy busy, down en ese *groot gat*? Y hablando de social NEEDia (have you succumbed to the lure of CaraBobo yet?), follow our little hilito, here:

—*I don't know what bedevils our SMS attempts, but I did get through to your voicemail once.*

Yo te mandé un reply text al tiro, and a couple of others from SF. ¿No te llegaron? Damn, I thought we *might* start out 2009 con mejores techno-comms.

—*Did you try to call me late last night? I got a 'withheld' number, but I couldn't hear anyone speaking. I shot out of bed with a 'groot skrik' when the phone went off. I checked with the mine but they said they hadn't called, so I thought maybe you had managed to get through?*

From this, veo que tampoco recibes—or not consistently—mis texts. I'd been lulled into thinking it was a one-way *probleem*. OB-vio que fui yo. Pero jamás me imaginaba que you'd actually pick up, bebé.

—*Has SF changed much over the years?*

*Yebo*, unfortunately. Mucho. Chestnut Street está del todo yuppie: un enjambre de trendy, overpriced restós, wannabe hip, social climbing young profesionales y muchas eco-aware, techno-riche families con sus designer strollers. You get the idea . . .

—*Or is its essence still there?*

Miraculously, this is also a (qualified) yes. Mis visitas last year (del Montalvo), con la Cronopia Raz, me confirmaron ese feeling elegíaco—change and loss—que siempre me ha asediado tan pronto pongo pie en SF, over the years. You were my ur-loss, *natuurlik*. Pero also, los friends lost to AIDS, los barrios todo warped y vendidos, lost to relentless gentrification. Our old haunts gone, gone, gone. The revamped Cliff House, por ejemplo—pale sombra de su former self. Un horror. Y sin embargo, some things do remain. Remember esa vintage card shop, la de Grant Avenue in North Beach, donde compramos el "non ti scordar" *poskaartjie*? It's long gone, pero ese funky dive across the street, el Savoy Tivoli, sigue allí.

—*Hope I've made up somewhat for my lax comms over recent days!! L RF*

Well, un little hair (concede la Marquesa de Más).

*19-i-09*

OomBie,

Tomorrow is Obama's *inaugurasie*. Un momento histórico for all, especially for us COLORADIT@S! Kind of mind-boggles, que yo estuviera deeply pondering este temita (jaja) del mixedness in my early 20s. En esas transcript entries que escribí para Roland, remember? Digo, porque realmente there was no reference to this en la cultura popular (que yo recuerde), ni siquiera en grad school, ni mucho menos in college. Remember los MECHA leaders en UCI challenged my membership porque "I had green eyes"? Uf. ¡Qué barbaridad! Las categorías me parece que eran . . . más defined, discrete, back then.

Anygüey, a pesar del market meltdown (and my own hard-won *jubilasie* ahorros being down more than $300,000), against all odds tengo la sensación de que 2008 was one of the best years EVER. Para mí, *vir ons*, y quizás para el mundo, especially este país. Today el último día del egger del CHIMP, hooray!

*22-i-09*

Montenegro, mi amor,

Relieved to hear from you! Menos mal que mi (*baie* well-wrapped) parcel finally reached you. Pero, you must be the most techno-*uitgespaced* engineer en el mundo. Wim was taking an MA course up in Joburg la semana pasada. He belled your cell several times, pa' darte mi amor *in die vleis* (o casi). Me dijo que it rang off the hook, pero you never picked up. Ni siquiera la answering *masjien*. What gives, bebé? Is that phone actually in your possession? Now on this tema (of comms), —*I will attempt to match your prodigious writing talent upon return.* Orale, I'll hold you to your word!

*27-i-09*

Montenegro, darling,

My son, Etienne (named after Etienne Kapp, my dearly departed onetime flatmate en Pretoria), turns 22 on Friday. I've been thinking: if our little zygote had lived, Joey (el middle name de Etienne, after my dad)

En casa                                                              219

tendría un older *boetie of sussie*. Y tú y yo un hijo. Tomorrow, hace 27 años, we caught each other's eye por la vitrina del Balboa Cafe. And the rest, como quien dice, is (t)history.

*2-ii-09*
*Header:* Tectonix/exposure

R. darling,

Only limited "exposure time" a mis emails? ¿Qué soy yo, una especie de jungle fever, o qué? Como te puedes imaginar, I'm champing at the bit pa' que consigas e instales ese chismecito, what did you call it, a portable modem? Pa' usar cuando estés *in die veld*, bajo tierra, in situ, or wherever, anywhere *away* from la casa (de Bernarda Alba, jaja). Capaz entonces puedas leerme (and more to the point, escribirme *terug*). Properly (as you say), instead of "skimming" en la mosca in your cozy, "wrestling over the remote" mode.

Me encuentro sorrowful hoy. El sábado murió mi colega y mentor, Howard T. Young, un conocido scholar-teacher, y gran role model y amigo. Aunque initially he was skeptical (recuerdo que me dijo, —*Suzi, eventually you're going to have to choose—English or Spanish*), cuando salió *Killer Crónicas* he wrote a rhapsodic article en el *London Times*, calling me the first Latina code-switching flâneur! Anygüey, he pasado la mañana platicando con su widow, Edra.

I can't *not* write, Montenegro; *ek kannie anders doen nie*. And you've said this desde siempre. So I'm at a disadvantage! Pero, recuerda esto: *geen kompetisie* entre nosotros. So *hou jou bek* about this: —*You know and I know that I don't have a realistic chance of competing with la prodigiosa!* Modest Mouse, much? Ay, ya sabes que tu laconism drives me crazy! Your tectonic slooowness. Were you *always* like this, solo que antaño I just didn't notice? Por otra parte, I can't help reflecting: *miskien* this is a reason for my abiding attraction toward you. This telluric quality—tu cautela, simón, hasta ese emo-laconismo—spurs my yearning. Which is, me parece, el recurring leitmotif de mi vida. Al menos, of my writing (la même chose). Don't get me wrong though: *'n meisie* needs *affirmasie*, también. So don't take *too* long setting up ese modem, *hoor*?

Header: *Deep inside*

Montenegro,
El header remite a algo que me escribiste hace unos meses: dijiste que you'd *become very peevish* si no pudieras correrte dentro de mí, *deep, often* y por mucho tiempo. Remember? Once in a blue moon (and there *was* a lunar eclipse *vandag*) you blow me away, Rolo. La dazzling, lapidary belleza de tus palabras shoots right to the heart: cual tu teensy e-macho de hoy. So, deja te mande off to slumberland con esto. On second thought, creo que más bien it's rise 'n' shine time, *nê*? Pero ni modo. Try this on: Ojalá estuviera allí, stretched out encima tuyo, nuestras matching looong legs entrelazadas, my hair brushing your face, mirándote a los dark, dark eyes, sintiéndote deep inside me.

18-ii-09

R., my darling,
Wish I could say que me sorprende tu atroz mountain bike smash-up: los huesos rotos, y punctured lung *nogal*. Pero it really doesn't. ¡Coño! You've *always* been into dangerous, macho activities con esos boy toys, ¿que no? (Remember your windsurfing *fixasie*, el año que llegué RSA?) Anyway, *jammer*, my darling. Perdona el teasing. Y espero que te pongas bien quick quick.
Now check this: descubrí ayer, in my bedroom closet (cupboard, dirías), una carta que había mandado a mi amiga Lydia Vélez. Ex Chestnut Street en marzo de 1982. She'd sent it back to me hace años, diciéndome que la usara one day, "in a book." En esa letter, I confirmed con un uncanny frisson que hoy fue—according to our "calcs"—el mero día que concebimos (in an act—o dos o tres—of bestial mating, in a suburban house in Houston, *nogal*) a nuestro little zygote. La inundación, later, esa unstaunchable bloodjet, in New Orleans. Funny the way things come back to us, hey, como dice la Toni Morrison. Or Faulkner. Anygüey my rule came, just now. La sangre such a key memory medium for me. OB-vio, como quien dice, the body remembers.

En casa                                                                                              221

*25-ii-09*

Hey bebé,

¿Todavía te duele? O como dirías, is it still *very soh*? Solo un quickie, este Ash Wednesday. Agárrate: what's the likelihood? In one of the zillion university press catálogos que me mandan al college, hoy vi que ha salido un new study on . . . none other than Dušan Makavejev. Remember, el director de *Montenegro*? Well, it *only* took los culti studies scholars 27 years to get hip to him. Pero tú y yo podemos jactarnos de ser early Makavejev canonizers!

*9-iii-09*

Montenegro, my *liefling*,

*Extremely erotiese droom* anoche. Pero so your screen won't melt, te voy a dosificar (*vertaling*: I'll only send it later). Oye, it's beyond hiLErius que *siempre* me llames around midnight (hora Califas). Y que when I call you (even if it's 3 a.m.) siempre contestes, pero either you can't hear me, o tenemos ese bizarre NASDAQ/*groot swart hond* soundtrack.

P.D. *Miskien* debo ir a visitarte (don't have a heart attack . . . I'm just dreaming out loud), so we could go watch soccer again (pienso en el up-coming World Cup, OB-vio). Didn't we watch los Kaizer Chiefs contra los Orlando Pirates en un enorme stadium en Soweto, gracias a tu pa? Was it Jabulani?

*18-iii-09*

Wimmie,

You (*en* S. Africa) are on my mind. Trabajo horas y horas on my book. Me alivia (sort of) que you also got that auto-response del email address de R. *Daardie oke* must've gone *totaal* flake, durante su recuperación. Su inbox debe estar *oorlooping* to hell. Sigh. Supongo que hay que recordar que he *was* majorly injured: broken collarbone, punctured lung, varias costillas rotas. ¿Te importaría textualizarle, ask him to freshen his inbox? Le voy a pedir al Mike Chip que lo haga, too. Now, changing rubro to fi-LUMs, our fave *obsessie*. I can't believe this:

*Matt Damon is here and Roger spotted him in Fishhoek! They're making a film about the world cup rugby in 1995, when we won and which created a moment of true national unity and rejoicing. Matt plays François Pienaar, the captain of the team (about double his size!). Will be amuse to hear how he does a Rock accent. Morgan Freeman is Mandela and Clint Eastwood is directing.*

No puedo creer que el Matty D. has to "go Rock," to play Pienaar en *Invictus*. Ya sabes que I don't much enJOY his thespian skills (aunque dicen que he's a really good person). Pero let's give the *oke* a chance, *nê*. Pero ¿Morgan F. as Mandela? Puh-leez! No me convence. Y hablando de trout Rocks: remember Leo DiCaprio in *Blood Diamond*? El filum itself era maomeno, *maar* Leo's Rock-in-Engels (or was he meant to be Rhodesian? No me acuerdo) kicked some major nalga! He was actually, for the first time desde su adolescencia, GOOD—as a Rock! Y hablando de good (actually smokin'): I've just seen Russell Cuervo y la inimitable Charlotte Rampling en el ('91) film *Hammers over the Anvil*—run don't walk to get it ASAP. Moving, odd, *baie erotiese* and tragic. Muy us.

## 28-iii-09

Mi *gunsteling* ingeniero,

Exactly two weeks ago tu inbox comenzó a mandar patrás mis emails, marked "undeliverable." I've had quite a time con el Denis Recéndez, el ITS honcho del college, asking me about "trigger words" en los emails! *Natuurlik*, le dije que if that were the case, my entire vida—all my writing, fo' sho—is a *groot* trigger . . . and people's inboxes habrían estado exploding all over the show, long before this.

## 31-iii-09

Wimmie,

Eso es tan weird, our disembodied voices connecting en el ciberespacio de tu cell vozmail. Mañana presento mi Howard Young tribute en el faculty meeting, y estoy algo nervous. Como sabes, soy un poco Boo Radley para el public speaking. Hoy por hoy, though, a pesar de estos slight nerves, estoy contenta. As he always does if I scold him for any "extended" silencio (or "hail fellow well met"-ism), R. respondió de inmediato y muy contrite.

It seems he has a touch of the *masoquista*, *dink jy nie?* Dime qué te parece esto. I find it lovely. Algo . . . Capri-crochety (driving himself around, *nogal*), sensual (en esas alegóricas palabras de las flood waters en New Orleans), melancholy y muy tender. Pero *how* can an engineer be so techno-clueless? And yet, al parecer, he *werklik* is!

*Dearest Susana,*

*I don't know why my inbox should have started acting up like you say?? All my usual mails have been coming through and no one has mentioned that they're being bounced—except you, my faithful co-respon-dent!! I thought droll reply was in order for your ITS man!*

*I have had a good look through your last package and I must say that just a few reminders and a map makes me remember the sea air smell of SF and the smell of the brakes on the cable cars. I did have to look very carefully at what I concluded was your 'grainy groin pic' He! He! I looked at it from every possible angle (as oft-times before) just to make sure. Looks yummy.*

*My thorax is still sore (ask Lance Armstrong), but I have started driving myself around, albeit rather gingerly.*

*I have also received your SMSs, but I use it so infrequently that I forget to check and/or reply. Mea culpa. Sometimes a reply would be so late as to verge on bad SMS protocol!! So I just hope you will forgive me.*

*The article on NO just shows how hard the residents got hit by Katrina. Water damage is so messy, worse even than hurricanes—it leaves no nook or cranny untouched.*

*Hope this little epistle pleases you more than my very short epistles!! L RF*

31-iii-09

My darling Montenegro,

Now *that's* more like it, *ek sê*. Ni puta idea, why all the bouncing (ay, ojalá). Pero con esta new g-male adress, we shouldn't have problems. *Onthou jy*, when I was at Montalvo last year nos pasó lo mismo. Creo que tiene algo que ver con el Pomona server, from an off-campus location. Pero I could be wrong. *Ek weet nie.*

Funny, leí tu evocative descripción de los aftereffects de Katrina como alegoría. Of us. I mean: de cómo esa water-edged, sensual, mysterious ciudad nos impactó. Rushing fluids (tidal surge, escribiste) leaving no nook or cranny untouched, inDEED.

Anygüey, keep on getting better, Mr. Gingerly Driver, you (confieso que I can't picture you gingerly . . . *anything*).

*9-iv-09*

Montenegro,

*Yebo*, I do indeed remember us at the farm. Nítidamente. I shouldn't have gone though, al pensarlo. Me sentí tan out of place. Perdida, sola. I remember when that *uitstappie* was, *presies*: sólo tres semanas después de mi arrival en Sudáfrica. It was September, primavera. Pero so hot already! And I'd been *so* sick, de hepatitis (remember?). Milagro que el médico let me travel. Nothing could've kept me from you! Pero I was so skinny, tan endeble. Ay . . .

Recently unearthed a *poskaartjie* que mandaste a la "Sloth" (my cousin Lee) just before we went to the farm. Creo que te conté que la Lee sent me back a bunch of letters I'd written her from RSA, telling me to "use" them in my writing. Just like Lydia! Ay, me siento una retroactive pendeja, ahora, that I couldn't really share that place (ese lugar *tan* tu lugar) with you. Es medio ironic también, ya que I'm now widely known as—inter alia—a "nature writer"!

And about this: —*Hey Shug, maybe I'm out of practice??* OB-vio. Big-time! We already established that, el año pasado. Pero we *also* established que yo te estoy limbering up, te estoy despertando, oh mi (ex?!) Rip Van Winkle.

*14-iv-09*

Montenegro,

Well, Mercurio doesn't lie. InDEED (pronounced en la voz de mi fave character en la serie *The Wire*, Omar Little), it seems we *have* been much on each other's minds en estos días, como dices. Nevertheless: nuestros comms están un little hair *gefok* (Mercury is a tease). Rolo Babee, no way do your SMSs reach me. Te lo he dicho mil veces. OJO, I blame Zuma! En serio, it is *so* awful, porque amo los texts. Lo encuentro *baie* sexy, in a compressed, haiku-like way, escribirte texts. I'm glad you receive mine, al menos.

Your kids are cute. The farm looks . . . *as ooit*. Dry and African and beautiful, con esa belleza austera a la que hay que acostumbrar el ojo (and the body). Even that daunting-sounding *groot swart hond* is kinda cute, para cane (not a dog fan). Pero my fave is *die olifant*. Just standing there en toda su . . . hugeness. I can almost almost smell him!

*17-iv-09*

Rolo darling,

*Moenie* worry *nie*: the irony of empire's atavistic failure (como tan elegantly dijiste) to receive your SMSs is not lost on me. *Maar*, I had no clue you were *already* using ATMs en el '82. ¿De veras? Was I? Te confieso: I don't remember much about *geld*—or anything else—from back then, excepto la sensación de tus voraces ojos, your hands on me, your mouth.

A ver si este attachment te satisface el penchant for ever-higher *resolusie*—por ahora. Prometo mandarte el original (higher *resolusie*) de la blurry one (of my "groin," tee hee) ya que te me has quejado tanto de la falta de nitidez. *Maar* paciencia, Bok Boytjie. Is *your sterk* suit, not mine, no?

P.D. Can't believe you asked me to text nude foties a tu cell. Las tecnodestrezas pa' hacer eso currently elude me. Pero besides, *is jy mal? Gevaar*, much? Con tu desconcertante tendency to leave that cell lying around wherever, turning it on sin querer (nalga-dialing!), o que te lo "conteste" un big dog (not to mention un hasta ahora unnamed manservant . . . pero esa es otra), no me parece buena idea. Muy *un*-engineerlike, tus (non)skills (si irresistible). So, paciencia, bebé. Y caracoles.

*29-iv-09*

Mnr. M.,

Sé que estás en divorced-dad visit con tus girls down in Durban, or on your way to them, pero just wanted to tell you: mi pana el Austra just sent through my formatted book from Sydney (ah, the wonders of email!). He's made it look *so* beautiful! Lo he leído todo, *vandag*. Como si fuera otra persona. *Not*-I. Digo: cual si yo fuera just . . . another reader. Una experiencia *harto* through the looking glass.

Rolo: if my sister Sarita hadn't shaken loose that long-buried recuerdo de nuestro *kleintjie* perdido—last year en Montalvo—*none* of this would've come about. Ni libro, ni . . . nosotros. *Sommer* heavy, *nê*. Como de película. Enamorándonos de nuevo . . . 26 years later. Pero not just the fact of it. *Ook*, el impulso de tantear, en la escritura, los edges. De explorar todo este maravilloso, strange acontecer, como si fuera *nuwe wêreld*.

7-ʋ-09

Wimmie,

I swoon. R.'s devotion to las hijas me enternece. And then, lo del fossil. The oke's getting all cocky, "rough, rugged, 'n' independent" nature guide de nuevo (como cuando nos conocimos), and I love it. Me pone bien *jags*. Y check su sign-off! Así firmaba las cartas y sus fotie backs to me, often. ILY. Digo, our first time. *Lees dit*:

> *Hey Shug,*
>
> *I am back in the saddle! Took me a while to find out what had changed in my absence etc., etc. Nonetheless, long weekend in Durbs with the girls was great and—as always—was far too short.*
>
> *Steve contacted me a few weeks back (out of the blue) and I said I'd call him but haven't had a gap to follow up. Wouldn't mind contacting Chiappetta again though.*
>
> *Today I went to a preview of a most amazing hominid fossil discovered near Jhb. Watch your news in about 8-12 wks. When you see a truly amazing skull and other skeletal details you can say (boast?) that your Mnr. Montenegro saw it in the flesh so to speak.*
>
> *Will be at the office tomorrow (Friday) for the first time in two weeks and hope to find new pics of the 'Emerald Forest'—magical place. ILY RF*

11-ʋ-09

Montenegro,

Did U get my SMS from last Thursday? ¿Y hoy? I had this incredible *droom* anoche:

A year ago, exactly, me despertaba en Montalvo. Emerald Forest, like R. says. Sola, en aquel glass cube. La cajita blanca en la pared (ay, what's its name? No me acueeeerdo, in any language) registered the damp morning chill. 52 degrees, ponía, many mornings. I'd open the front door and bird-song (si bien apenitas brisa . . . damn arquitecto) would pour in cual miel. OB-vio, sólo dos semanas después y esa caja de cristal sería más bien tinderbox. Terrarium en vez de jewel box. Pero, oh, what that long, hot mid-May weekend would ignite (gracias a la visita de mi hermana, her sudden, como si nada memory flash of our embarazo, el subsecuente miscarriage): a tectonic shift. So, tiene sentido que mis sueños, since then, sigan sorting out, working through . . . all this. Anoche soñé que I was back in RSA, con R.

Ay, tan fraught for my Bok Boytjie—emo-openness, self-expression. Pero can I blame him? After what became of us? For which I lay the blame, ahora—180 degrees, lo sé—pretty much squarely at my *own* feet. Pero he *is* passionate. And his heart is true. Hasta ahora. Esto yo lo sé.

En el dream, vivía con R. The house was large y era Joburg, creo, pero nada que ver con la casa de sus padres. Multistory, de madera. Old. Victorian (esto no tiene sentido para Joburg, pero what can I say? Era un sueño). En una, comenzaba a llegar un chingo de gente, tipo party guests. R.'s sisters were there, y la Ma F. Esta parecía . . . algo wary of me (para variar), pero no del todo unpleasant (now *that* shows it was a dream, jaja).

Era de noche. I was waiting for R. to return from work, y mientras, me tenía que vestir, fancy, para la cena. Abrí un old-fashioned wardrobe (era como si la casa fuera a la vez mía y . . . no, like I was in some slightly off-limits, enchanted *plek*) y allí vi un dazzling array. Todo era sexy and tempting, y todo me quedaba perfecto. Tipo Goldilocks y la camita. Elegí unos soft, fawn-colored gamuza (tipo Ultrasuede, ay yummy) trousers. I was wrapping the buttery leather ties de unas gorgeous Grecian sandals (gladiator, avant la lettre!) around los tobillos. Luego me puse un close-fitting sweatery knit top. Clingy, sexy. *Rooi* (evidentemente, era invierno).

Al llegar R. a casa, fui a saludarle. Bajaba la escalera y le vi entrar. Eras tú. I mean, you *now*. Como en las (recent) foties you've sent me. Ahhh, you were happy, happy, happy to see me. Como si no me hubieras visto en un siglo (which is true, OB-vio, pero no en el sueño). I touched your hair (cropped, canoso); I stroked your chest. Acariciándote allí, right over your heart, me sentí welcome, safe. En casa.

Te mencioné el vello (uncharacteristic, digo, en la vida real), laughing. Y me dijiste que era "a winter thing" (I *promise* you, eso dijiste). A bit like an animal in winter, me explicaste. In summer (and you, trabajando under-ground, en las minas), one doesn't need it. Esto suena bien weird, I know, pero en el dream, tenía sentido.

Suddenly, me fijé que estabas bien sleepy, hasta algo dozey. Like you were . . . coming up from deep underground, o cual si emergieras de una cueva después de haber hibernado años y años. I touched your face, con ternura y repentina lujuria. My body felt hot, debajo de ese jersey rojo y los strange, sexy fairy-tale gamuza pants. Me abrazaste, con urgencia. I could feel the entire length of our bodies pressed together, entrelazados. I felt your hard-on through los heavy work pants, through mis trousers de gamuza. Todo se sentía charged, feverish. *Maar ook*, como un recono-cimiento, a homecoming. Entonces me besaste, your hands in my hair, on my breasts, my butt. Como ese iconic kiss of ours en el French Quarter, el de la fotie, oblivious al frenzied Mardi Gras whirl que nos rodeaba. *Onthou jy?* Entonces, me agarraste de las nalgas, you pulled me up, onto you. I wrapped my legs around you, como hicimos en New Orleans, en plena calle, *nogal*. Y nos besamos, *baie honger*. Long, wet. You holding me like that, apoyados en la pared.

—*I've brought you so much, muchos regalos, all kinds of stuff from home, from California*, te dije. —*What stuff, my love?* I can hear your voice now, como si fuera ahora, como si estuvieras aquí, right now. Your low, beauti-ful voice. Quería que te espabilaras, creo recordar. Shake off esa strange *winterslaap*-modorra. Either that, o que sucumbieras del todo. Que su-cumbiéramos los dos. Subir las escaleras para dormir contigo. I wanted you to fuck me y entonces, long luxuriant together winter sleep.

—*It's* muti—*plenty* muti, te dije. —*Oh Shug*, te reíste. *You still believe in that? Come up and show me, then.*

En casa                                                                     229

Montenegro,

El Mike Chip just wrote me this: — *Girl, you sure started something. But you knew that!* To think: el Mike es nuestro "ground zero," ¿que no? The place we all started from, de alguna manera. Aunque sabes que soy una *baie* resourceful *meisie*, seguro que you're just the *teensiest* bit surprised que conozca este mining term, *nê?* "Deflagration." Well, fishing about en el internido di con una nota intrigante. Explica un new rock-breaking system invented by ¿adivina quién? Según la nota, este new system se llama Regalo (jaja) — for "gas-induced fracture technology." La ventaja de tu Regalo, as far as I can make out, tiene que ver con *soft* blasts (relativamente hablando), versus conventional explosive blasting, que involucra un violent release of energy.

Hmmm, *miskien* esto nos alegorice. To a T, hey? I mean: us, *ahora*. Y te confieso que reading that article about you me dio un inexplicable thrill. Well, no inexplicable, supongo. Al imaginarte allí, working with the earth, todo ese sexy blasting pero *gently* (casi pero not quite an oxymoron), te juro que me puse algo breathless, hasta aroused. Si bien not *nearly* the way I got al leer tu latest missive (after you read my dream). En la cual me concedes que *kissing is the best starting point*, pero luego you explain, con lujo de detalle, all the things you want to do with me para que me corra.

And about this: — *I thought that you were about to describe in detail how you came upstairs and seduced me while the guests were gathered downstairs.* Hmmm, well I *was. Maar* hold your horses, *jong!* ¿No ves? I've learned to be (*'n bietjie*) more patient últimamente. ¿Qué, no te gusta? Aha . . . now *die skoen* is on the other foot, bebé. I'm gonna make you wait pal próximo installment.

14-v-09

R.,

I worked on two texts for you today. Pero quiero hacerte rogarme, so voy a dosificarte. Just sending one for now. Here you go. OJO: *streng privaat.* You'd better be *alleen*, coño!

*9-iii-09*
*Diario-Sueño*

Loathe to get up, incorporarme, alcanzar este diary sitting there al lado de la cama, waiting for me to transcribe it for you, anotarte estas palabras, estos dreams. If I sit up, si me incorporo it'll mean I'm awake, que estoy aquí, here in my so-called real life, en vez del dreamtime al cual intento aferrarme con este jacaranda-ink pen.

Montenegro, sé que I conjured this dream by watching *Hammers Over the Anvil*, ese film con el Russell Crowe y Charlotte Rampling. I'd seen it years ago por primera vez y me hechizó, I remember. Se ve que it's adapted from a collection of stories. Loose, algo disjointed, moody, atmospheric. Con ese quirky preteen polio-survivor protagonista, *crutch, crutch, crutching* along, espiando, watching everything.

The rural Oz landscape golden and sensual, amenazante y prometedor a la vez. And oh: la escena donde el Cuervo (playing a solitary, hypermacho horse-whisperer llamado East) y la Charlotte (a British aristocrat, eccéntrica, mayor, casada con un complete fop, childless) hacen el amor en el barn—I've *never* forgotten it. Imprinted in my memory, electrifying en su sensual, natural intimidad. Se miran tan unflinchingly (esto es, quizás, lo que más recuerdo de ti). Es todo tan lento y deliberado: ese gradual, *unbearably* gradual, sweat-sheened buildup, her foot slowly caressing his leg. Solo ese detalle.

What I most remember is sitting astride you, naked. Los dos desnudos. I'd returned to RSA. Había vuelto por ti, to be with you. OB-vio my mind, mi subconsciente trabaja esto, working, working. In the TRC of my memory I need, I *need* your forgiveness, tu absolución, tu amor. Ah, pero no nos hace falta *tu* apology, también? For not having been able to shelter me, por no saber guiarme por las landmines del apartheid? El peso del white privilege and black oppression me cayó cual lápida when I pitched up in Joburg. And your indifference to my plight (capaz haya sido helplessness e ingenuidad, like Wim says, pero I *felt* it as indifference, then) sealed the tomb. My awkward, guilty extranjería! Pero how could I, a northern Califas-raised, politically active mestiza (oops, colored) *ever* have imagined que iba a poder sobrevivir allí? Ay, Rolo, perdóname. Ask my forgiveness, *my bokkie*.

En el sueño, I see your body clearly. You are moaning with pleasure, pero al borde del llanto, too (como en nuestra "last night," en San Francisco). I see your dark eyes, tu boca. Te cubre un light sheen of sweat, hasta algo de grime, I think, cual si te hubieses vuelto de la mina. Up from underground, home from work. *Baie* sexy. Me inclino para besarte, rozarte la cara, lightly, teasingly, with my eyelashes. You reach for my breasts, los coges y me frotas los pezones, hard. I'm right there with you, en esa cama, pero a la vez I'm watching us. El placer es intenso pero hay también un . . . deje achicopalado.

Creo que en una, te pregunto por tu ma (I'd always unsettled *her*—not you—me dijiste el año pasado). Me dices que she's worried, apprehensive about my return. Se me ocurre que she's worried I'll hurt you again.

I'm licking your skin. Decididamente, pero slowly, like a lioness. Quiero llevarte al edge, just with my rough, rough tongue y . . . pero no te dejes caer. Not yet, not yet. Te estoy lamiendo el cuello, los hombros, the hollow of your collarbone, te trazo una raya desde el pecho, down your belly, to your cock. Remnants of the outside cling to you (tu siempre-connection a la tierra): gritty sand, soil, tierra. Me parece que hasta some kind of insect (this por esa weirdly sexy scene, de las ants in the sugar bowl, en el film, next to where Charlotte y el Cuervo are fucking), pero we scarcely take notice.

I wanted to taste you, me acuerdo. Sentir tu verga en mi boca. Es un impulso intensely focused, specific. I can taste you. How is this even possible? Una especie de sinestesia onírica, I promise you. I'm tasting your skin y a la vez nos veo, como . . . desde arriba. Tu cuerpo boca arriba, me astride you, shifting down to take your cock in my mouth. Te escucho gemir, al borde de, —*I'm gonna come, Shug*, you murmur. Todo el placer se me concentra en la boca. Allí me despierto, Montenegro, wet, wet, con la certeza de haber estado follando contigo.

15-w-09

Hi Wimmie,

Checa este palimpsesto. Primero de Mike Chip (as we called him). El es como nuestro "ground zero," the one that links all of us (me, R., Helen, el Du Preez, Ken, Tina—even you) from San Francisco in 1982.

*WOW S.—that was really incredible! The way it seems to have affected Tina is making me anxious to read your stories and experience your writing too. R. has been very responsive in my requests for emails as he just sent his sister's email . . . I had lost track of Martha twice over the past 28 years, but I met Roland thru his sister, who was my best South African friend while I lived down there . . . Their family turned me on to so many things and lent me all the gear I needed to hike the tip of Africa . . . Thanks for pulling everyone back together!*

Y esto, de Tina:

*Ahhh, S.!! I have to spend more time feeling this but I am so excited I had to write immediately. So much has happened to you since you last wrote. Your "memory vortex," in which your "past returns with almost no loss of resolution or intensity," is such an incredible, fantastic gift to us all. Since the unconscious knows no time, everything that happens is frozen in there, mostly to never be seen in a form that we would recognize. You've let yourself just ride out or write out what was there. How cool is that, since typically people are so inhibited and terrified, the need to control the present (and the PAST) totally cuts us off from so much of ourselves. You have let me embrace my love and fear and hope and loss and youth and friends and sadness and happiness and run with it all smack into myself.*

Deduzco, de lo que estoy piecing together only now (from being back in comms with Mike himself, y de la Tina): Mike had gone to live in S. Africa in 1981, y allí conoció a Martha, R.'s sister. *All* these bonds are now coming back to me, to us all. ¿No es mágico?

*16-v-09*

R.,

WTF? Todo el mundo me escribe, *except* the person I most long for. Wouldst thou leave me so unsatisfied? Agárrate: Squirrel hit a power line esta mañana (ni me preguntes . . . *flying* squirrel? Solo en *Rocky & Bullwinkle*, one would think). Power out todo el día. Blazing hot outside pero pitch dark en casa. Re weird. Calificando los final exams in primitive conditions, pensando en ti.

En casa                                                                                           233

18-v-09

OomBie,
   Perceive this charm emale de R. Tan hiLAR (or hiLEHreeus, per R.).
   *Shug,*
   *I am here! I would not leave thee unsatisfied. . . . you know that. I have*
*two new opportunities on my plate at the mo . . . so I have a lot of thinking*
*and calcs to do. My writing skills (?) and time are currently getting some stiff*
*competition from my analytical requirements. Terribly sorry about power*
*outage! Flying squirrels nogal!? We suffer the same, it's just not attributable*
*to squirrels. Whilst you're 'graduating' on Monday, I'll be mining as usual.*
*ILY RF*

18-v-09
Header: ~~stiff~~

Montenegro, my love,
   Ese subject header was *just* to make you laff (*en droom*), allí deep down
en la mina, busy, busy, busy con tus calcs y tus opportunities (no te estoy
retando, I *promise* I'm not). My *skryfing* has been lately inspiring nuestra
motley tripulación. Mike Chip y Miss Tina están mega in comms. Look
what Wim's just written:
   *I am absolutely amazed at the DNA strands of memory that your remem-*
*bering has activated, spiraling out of your heart and mind to all these people! It*
*is truly incredible that you've even reconnected with Mike Chiappetta, "friend-*
*ancestor" to us all. Amazing how his trip to SA in '81 (why did he go?) and his*
*connection with Roland has changed all our lives. It is truly an extraordinary*
*love story, yours.*
   *How impoverished my life would be if Mike hadn't met Roland's sister, if*
*Roland hadn't gone to San Francisco, if the two of you hadn't tumbled madly*
*in love, if he hadn't convinced you to come to SA, if you hadn't hated everything*
*about it and run away from him, if Curé hadn't recognized your foreignness*
*and spoken to you on the street, if Izelle hadn't thrown that fiesta for Curé . . .*
*The matrix of relationships flowing from Mike's visit to SA and now being*

*reconnected by you is fascinating. I even dream of some visual representation of it. It's all so vivid to me!*

So go ahead, Sr. Capricornio: persigue esas *werk* oportunidades, haz tus calcs. Ya sabes que I admire—and love—that "defibrillating" part of you (¿cómo corno se llamaba ese device? That soft blaster *masjien* you invented?).

*22-w-09*

Wimmie,

Hace un año (today *presies*) R. wrote me that extraordinary email: que se acordaba del miscarriage, and everything else too. Re —*Your Roland palimpsest left me without words . . . it is truly one of the most beautiful, romantic, and erotic things I have ever read. A wonderful yin and yang contrast between your rich and elaborate writing and his lean and more direct style.*

I knew you'd totally get the cruciality of that palimpsest, el que te mandé ayer. Pero poor R., *ag*, shame, man, in S'th EFFri-speech. El vato está bien grouchy (cross, *sic*). Pissed off porque la mining industry aparentemente no aprecia ese conflagrasie gadget, that device que él inventó. *Maar werk*-grouchy or not, read this, de la semana pasada:

*Shug,*

*Baie eroties!! I read through your sexy dream carefully and also your geographical astrology. Both read together are most compelling! I see your dream insists on a double-storey Victorian. Well, that places us squarely on the Parktown Ridge (very upper crust) although we're not that big on wooden houses here in Jozi. It'll have to be brick with woodwork. You would like (surely) filigree metal balconies (a la New Orleans) and a view since you've become a mountain girl.*

*I thought that you were about to describe in detail how you came upstairs and seduced me while the guests were gathered downstairs. I would have ignored any phone calls from the mine of course. Kissing is the best starting point, but I had more detailed thoughts of first kissing your lips and neck . . . . . . After that I thought I would continue to explore . . .*

You can fill in los blanks. Contenido bajo presión, *hoor*. Gobsmacked— y ponderando este quantum salto—o *bokkie-spring*!

*26-v-09*

Montenegro, amor,

Casi keeling over in shock con tus *tres* emails de hoy. Long ones, *nogal*! Me hizo acordar . . . esos days, patrás en 2370 Chestnut, #212, when I'd get a letter from you y ese black (mostly inert) *plastiek* object llamado teléfono would ring. Casi siempre late at night. I'd scurry out into the little hall, pa' no despertar a la Trish, y arrastraba ese Slimline phone en su long, long *extensie* cord, hacia la cama. Then, acurrucada en mi island bed (as you called it), the wires would crackle and hiss and hum y eras tú, llamando desde Joburg. Parecía tan far, far away, back then. Didn't it? Your soft, sexy, low voice. And everything would settle into place. Caía en una endorphin haze, me acuerdo (aun cuando me quedaban apenitas $60 en mi checking account).

Pero about what you wrote me, de que you understood my feelings about apartheid pero que you always knew it wouldn't last . . . hmmm. No sé. Justo hoy llevo escribiendo, working on a crónica for you llamada "Explosión Suave/GIFT Crónica." I'm playing with the name of that dispositivo que inventaste. Ay, Rolo. How ironic, que hayamos llegado a una especie de . . . acuerdo. A meeting of the minds (and hearts) ahora, across so many miles and years. A site of passionate compromise. Esta idea me habría sido oxymoron, back then. Pero ya no . . .

Anygüey, my faith in the postapartheid RSA postal system is renewed! Menos mal que hayas recibido mi parcel. Y la fotie. And in re —*Is there more, I wonder in my hotter dreams?* Well *natuurlik* there's more! *Baie*. Pero I'll leave you to remember and imagine for a while, I think. So, aquí tienes algo más, to fuel your dreams:

*6-iii-09*
*Diario*

Ay, how stupid, stupid, *stupid* it seems to me now. Discutiendo con R., about the importance of nature—can you *imagine*? Oh, bebé, *miskien* we should've talked less, and just . . . fucked more (aunque, how *could* we have, en la casa de tus padres?). Ahora recuerdo esa vez que me dijiste . . . we were broken up, debe haber sido en el '83, maybe even '84. Me habías venido a visitar a mi flat, en Pretoria, *onthou jy?* Se me hace que maybe you were already seeing Anne, con quien te casarías, a few years later (when you were the last man standing, como me escribiste: after all your amiguitos en tu northern suburbs social circle se habían casado y también—vaya casualidad—the same year I got married, creo): —*I don't want to talk with you anymore right now, Chávez; I want to fuck you.* Ay, estaba tan offended then, me acuerdo. Spitting mad. Yo tan Bolshevik entonces, tan feminista (even though I *really* wanted to fuck you, too). Pero ahora, I see an odd, moving belleza en ese remark (y todavía quiero follarte).

## 26-*v*-09

Wimmie,

LITTLE EYE: Supe que there's a Francis Bacon exhibit at the Met— and it will still be there when we go to NYC! Anygüey, after a few days of *frustrasie*, de no saber nada de R. (pero he'd warned me que estaba badgered at *werk*, con un new project y que se sentía grouchy and unrelaxed), today I received THREE emails.

First, he sweetly (and in *groot* detail) explains que ha estado fuera del email (*myn besoeke*). Plus, some mine director's breathing down his cuello y cuando llega a casa, the *only* thing he feels like doing, *om te* relax, es jugar con ese cane. Más o menos lo que dedujimos, *nê*. And then, la segunda (responding to a semigrouchy *admonisie* from me):

*Bebe,*

*Your letters didn't slip far down my inbox. I've read and absorbed everything. I understand your feelings for apartheid SA, but remember I had been raised in SA and I always knew that the social engineering that was apartheid could not survive in the long run. Maybe I was in a way reconciled to the outcome and knew that I would continue to work for a better country. ILY RF*

So, he does (really) read and "get" me.

## 31-*v*-09

Montenegro, bebé,

Hechizada por esta (no) coincidencia or invisible link entre tu northern suburbs, 21st-century living room (I know, I know "lounge"), the former

Yugoslavia, and our Makavejev-obsessed, 1982 San Francisco beginning. Hablo de lo que me escribiste: —*It's surreal that [these* Montenegro *TV adverts] are aired just when we remember our own wild and beautiful Montenegran experience. Your words bring a powerful immediacy to our meeting.*

It's *not* just us, my darling, patrás en el memory vortex activado en el Emerald Forest. In equally surreal fashion, Mike Chip and even el "Sea Lawyer" Du Preez are very much patrás en la montura, so to speak. And Tina too. So poignant, her remembrances, ya que no estoy in touch with Helen (o al revés).

Llevo pensando un chingo, these days (jaja, to vary). De lo que me escribiste, about me and you and apartheid. Lo he venido platicando con Wim. Le había contado, ever since last year, that I was in a lot of pain (digo, *reactivated* by my remembering). About the way you and I ended. O sea, como rajé. I'd been *so* angry with you, tan self-righteous. Pero ahora, 26 years later, I'd done an almost 180 degree turn, y estaba queriendo asumir toda la culpa. And Wim said, well, it's neither-nor. He wrote:

*Roland could not have "understood your feelings about apartheid SA," much as he would like to think he did. Having been raised in SA, he was just not equipped. Not equipped to deal with you—the woman you were and are—nor to deal with and help you navigate your reactions to apartheid. Yes, he'd traveled to the US and abroad, but he was just a tourist. It's very different. Not his fault, but none of us, raised under apartheid, could possibly fully understand your horror. If we'd allowed ourselves to really understand, it would've made us feel too guilty, too complicit. And so we looked away, and carried on with our privileged lives. (Even as we also looked away or could not read your mixed-race identity!)*

*In Roland's case, I know he loved you, passionately! But the best thing—the only thing—he could do was to try to incorporate you into his life here. And you could not let yourself be incorporated—that would've made you guilty and complicit. Your love, in South Africa under apartheid, was a no-win situasie, for you both. Your love was nothing more nothing less than a casualty of apartheid.*

Yo no era una typical American girl (*pace* Tom Petty). Raised on promises, pero las de una intellectual, politically progressive family. Y yo había ido más allá de mis (left-of-center) parents, in terms of beliefs, activism. Hasta Wikipedia pone esto: — *The vestiges of apartheid still shape South African politics and society.* How could they not? And this is from Tina, del otro día. She was, *natuurlik*, aware of my ideological inclinasies in the '80s:

*Apartheid. You did not have any options. You would have eventually been jailed or institutionalized if you had stayed in SA at that time. Open (much less revolutionary) consciousness was not allowed. And you going into the townships, taking pictures. Having "suspicious people" over at your place all the time. Oh, my darling.*

Rolo, no way, man! Es solo con la nalgavista que puedes afirmar (now) that you "knew it [apartheid] could not survive." That's *sommer kak*, bebé. As history has shown, I would've had to wait 12 years para vivir en un South Africa libre. Para vivir contigo, tener hijos under apartheid. Untenable for me. For the 26-year-old radical that I was, no obstante mi total enamoramiento, mi arrojada entrega. Imposible. Pero me era *equally* imposible visualizar, crear una vida sin ti, fully conscious of the pain I had caused (a los dos) cuando rompimos. So I buried it. All these years, hasta el año pasado.

P.D. El otro día you asked me, — *Do you remember what you said when I told you that I hailed from the racist Republic of South Africa?* I remember que medio me levanté de la mesa, intending to grab la Trish and leave. Or, no . . . no fue así. Más bien al revés: I told *you* to fuck off, ¿no? Pero either way, this much I know for sure: you put your hand over mine, me imploraste, — *Wait. Listen to me.* Esa tu rara, totally inappropriate urgencia (we'd met only moments before) y la corriente entre nuestros dedos, our welded gaze—desafiante, pleading, deseante—nos selló el destino. Algo así. Isn't that how it went?

*7-vi-09*

Dearest OomBie,

Me encanta tu header, "Apartheid, mon amour"! InDEED, los efectos secundarios de nuestra reignited love story keep rippling out, wider and wider. Aunque *die man* himself hasn't written since Sunday night. Este vato is an emo-*verkrampte* trabajólico. Le amo, le deseo. Pero—uf—jamás podría vivir con él. Not in in a million years! Pero checa lo que le escribí a Rolo esta mañana (*confessie*: to make him *jaloers* . . . solo un pelín). How chev is Mike Chiappetta? Now *this* oke (passionate *Italiaans*, jaja) roquea fuerte:

*R.,*

*I can't believe that after asking me for that explicit sex story, me dejes . . . así.* HONGER. *OK, OK. As you point out, writing is* my métier. Y *bla bla. Pero coño. How 'bout a quickie? Try, just: I'm here. I read you. Thank god for us "passionate Latins," con un acceso más directo, menos mediated a las emotions. Y su expresión.* Vertaling: *I'd sent Mike C. little bits of this 'n' that, partes del original transcript, partes del new* boekie-in-progress. *Here's what Mike wrote me:*

*S.—I read your chapters 2 weeks ago while flying home from Chicago and I loved them. WOW, the story . . . I barely remembered many of the parts because I came in at the tail end, before you split for RSA. I knew bits and pieces from Helen and Tina but because they were 3rd hand I had forgotten them until your stories . . .*

*I really dig your style; fluid, like speaking to friends, direct, yet your use of your own vocab and your Spanglish really give it an intimate voice. I felt as if you were personally telling me the story rather than me reading one. Pretty intense feelings are oozing from your pen when you are writing this. Your head must be rocking with thoughts about this man, about this place on the other side of the world. Hard not to be aroused by the feelings you emanate, it is almost like being a voyeur . . . I want to read more.*

*I also solved the Spanglish with a program on my Mac that does instant translation so I can quickly follow along yet stay with you in your style and cadence. It's also interesting as I believe our languages, cultures, races continue to melt into one another and reading your Spanglish is like looking into the future of the written word.*

El Mike Chip's totally chev, *nê?* Anyweg, Wimmie, te estoy escribiendo algo lengthy: mis musings en ese hermoso ensayo de Jaime Alazraki que te mencioné, "Reading 'The Night Face Up,' Julio Whispers a Key Beneath the Text" (on Cortázar, el pasado, memory, time—todos mis greatest hits!).

*3-vi-09*

Dearest W.,

You were *completely* psychic in re: *— How amuse that R. reacted so fast to your news about Mike Chip's reaksie to your writing. I'm sure he is JEA.* Porque me mandó *dos* emails. Here's one:

*Bebe,*

*Don't get so baie kwaad vir my! I penned a quickie to you yesterday. I have received shmesses and emails. Maybe my phone isn't strong enough to get my shmesses all the way round the world to you?? I'll get some more powerful batteries I think. I see you've got Mike C. reading (and loving) your wonderful prose.* What sex dripping from your words?? *RF Montenegro.*

You're right! He *is* JEA, que el Mike responda tan enthusiastically (and suggestively!). Pa' mosquearle aun más (ay, so high school, lo sé, pero en las inmortales palabras del Malkovich in *Dange Liaisons: —It's beyond my control*), I wrote him a semiflip reply (about Mike's dizque "sex-dripping" comment). Le dije, *—¿Y qué?* And then I commanded him to read my emails and write me back in kind. Y: le dije que I'd deprive him of sex until he did so. Well, you'd be so *uitgefreek* con su reply . . . ni te lo puedo poner. Your pantalla would fucking melt, trust me. Quedé completely OF ROCK.

Anyweg, hope all this sex talk hasn't thrown you off your game con tu St. Augustine essay! Y hablando de Augustine . . . Remember how we used to make phone sex calls al "Agustín" Castells, and pretend he was my husband, un horny southern "preacher man"? We'd drive him crazy, con nuestra performance art avant la lettre! ¿Cómo podríamos haber hecho eso? In Pretoria en los '80, *nogal.* Whose phone did we use? Were we at my *kantoor* en UNISA? Digo: yo estaba tan aterrada de los Special Branch spies, *onthou jy?* Fuck, ni siquiera tenía phone en casa. Wow. Tan weird, recordar eso ahora . . .

*8-vi-09*

Wimmie,

*Baie dankie,* por esta gorgeous letter. Estoy (to vary) llorando.

*Roland's heart must have been trembling in those days in SF, but true to his reputation (and stars!) of course he played it cool. You are a seismic force in all our lives, wonderfully moving what seemed solid and sure, challenging comfortable and lazy attitudes and ideas. Hard to accept that he takes his time to reply even to the most explosive and penetrating (haha) missives.*

*Rocks are a mysterious bunch, seemingly so superficial and conformist, then suddenly very accepting and open. Zuma claims that Rocks are the only true white Africans, which of course has deeply irritated the English whites. It is another symptom of the familiarity debate, like in your south. Blacks here are always saying that they prefer dealing with Rocks, even if they are racist, because what you see is what you get, whereas they feel other whites are equally racist but less honest. It is an area of extreme complexity, as you say. Last year I sat next to an American botany prof on the plane who also said that whites who grow up around blacks may be more racist on one level, but also more accepting on another (he was talking about the American South, not SA). Afrikaners are deemed by most blacks as another tribe, like Zulus or Sothos, but other whites are harder for them to place and understand.*

*Liefde uit die suide,*

*W.*

*P.S. Roland really does love this place, it radiates from his writing. Our relationship to Africa is easily written off as colonial or paternalistic, but it's no less real for it. I love how he is informing you about his schedule and even inviting you to look at the place he is staying, more and more intimate in a different way. It must be very stressful for him to be under pressure to find new business, but thank heavens the gold price is more or less steady. Back to St. Augustine!!*

Por suerte, I just heard from Roland:

*Hey Bebe,*

*Got your latest package. I haven't read through it as I am leaving for a mine called Mototolo Borwa (meaning 'steep valley in the south') in the Sekhukhune district. You may vaguely remember driving down the Steepoort valley road to the farm? Mebbe? Bebe? Will be there until Wed., then off to a dolomite mine until Thurs. Bit rushed (and all that) as Central Rand Gold has embarked on a major cost-cutting exercise (including my consultancy) so I have to secure new business PDQ if I want to have any whiskey during July! Coño! I will catch up when I get back. L RF*

Estos problemas con sus consultancies . . . hmm. Me preocupa. *Ek verstaan nie.* Parece que es más o menos freelance. O algo. Pero freelance

*¿qué?* Something doesn't quite add up. Anyweg, he's SO proud! And from that *familie* of his, tan muy muy. So snob and upper crust. *Maar* sweet *briefie, nê.* Lately he's taken to "warning" me cuando va a estar de viaje.

Funny, Wimmie. About what you wrote me. Porque mis feelings (on R., on S. Africa, on "the" truth) are a moving target. I can't pin them down. Me acuerdo que once I was living in S. Africa with Roland, his attachment to the (African) land comenzó a parecerme casi casi stereotype. In my impatient, revolutionary, feminist apogeo, su actitud me irritaba. A diferencia de cuando estábamos en SF, when it had seemed . . . hopeful, romantic. Bajo la deforming lens del apartheid it seemed an extension of a colonial, macho mind-set. Pero ahora, aquí, de nuevo me parece poignant.

12-vi-09
Header: *Amor vincit omnia*

Well, Montenegro,

It sure as shootin' *didn't* back then! Pero por otra parte, not many get (or *take?*) a second chance, aided by documentary evidence (the transcript, las cartas, las fotos) *and* the softening, Leth(e)-al elixir of memory's merciful selectividad. To wit, I've only just now remembered—or uncovered— this episode:

Para mediados de 1983, about 8 months after I arrived in your country— y tras regresar de ese terrifying, life-saving sojourn en Londres, where I'd gone to have that aborto (about which más luego, *miskien*)—me dijiste que you'd had a "change of heart." Mientras yo estaba en la Rosslyn Clinic en Twickenham, y luego, joining an anti-apartheid protest en la embajada sudafricana en Londres, and later still, walking through the crocus-lined campos de ese incongruously bucolic Essex village, Sible Hedingham, bleeding, healing, you'd been talking to your pa and doing a lot of thinking, me dijiste. Te habías dado cuenta de que todo, *everything* I'd been telling you all those months, casi desde que puse pie en Joburg, was true. You *had* put your family, tu "northern suburbs lifestyle" entre nosotros, as a kind of . . . buffer. Para protegerte. From the strength and certainty of my love, y de la destabilizing fuerza de tu amor por mí. Esto—el estar . . . arrebatado—me dijiste que era algo completely new to you. ¿No ves, Rolo? I *didn't* only "unsettle" your mother. My love for you—what I was willing to *do* for you—y también la desconocida ferocidad de tu amor por mí had knocked you sideways.

Total: después de esa *openbaring*, you did everything in your power to "win me back" (tus palabras). Me admitiste que up to then, desde mi llegada a RSA, you hadn't really been there for me. Y me juraste parriba y pabajo que la verdad, the "real you"—tus convictions, tu amor, what you wanted for us—could be found in what we'd experienced in the US. Y en las love letters que me habías escrito. And you asked me to marry you. Do you remember any—or (con tu *olifant* memory) likely *all*—of this?

*12-vi-09*

*Liefste* OomBata,

Pasé todo el día de ayer, after we spoke, skimming through some of those letters *uit* S. Afrika que la Lee W. me había devuelto. Like the letter to Lydia Vélez I unearthed hace unas semanas, these were disturbing, illuminating, a la vez confirming and *tragies*. Esto es solo un quickie for now, so you'll *asseblief skryf my terug*. I'll come back on here in a few hours, pero I MUST get to a Pilates class. Me siento emo-drenada, fuzzy, exaltada, triste. About S. Africa, unos facts:

Did you know that in early-ish 1983 Roland suddenly, *uit die blou* (and *after* I'd broken up with him) admitted everything I'd been saying to him was true? O sea: que se había escudado (del amor: mine for him, and his for me) tras la *familie*. I mean right away, ni bien llegué a Joburg. Did you know that even as he called me "terminally promiscuous"—está todo esto allí en las cartas a Lee, ouch!—después de mi aborto in England (con ese mystery *baba*, Roland's rather than Peter's casi seguro, aunque I'd told them just the reverse), Roland begged me to forgive him? Can you believe he sent flowers, letters? He kept calling me at work, intentando verme. All the . . . intensity he hadn't managed to muster cuando estábamos (officially) en pareja, spending every fucking *naweek* en el seno de su *familie* in Bedfordview, ahora BOOM. Se detonó. He even—agárrate—asked me to marry him. Did I ever tell you that, digo back then? OB-vio, I myself had totally buried that fact.

Pero para entonces mi dolor, mi rabia (not to mention my *own* "rough, rugged, and independent" streak, my fucking orgullo) se había adueñado de mí. I couldn't see anything else. I couldn't see *him* anymore.

*Ag*, Wimmie. Esas letters to Lee confirman que I was justified, for want of a better word, al sentirme traicionada. Y (pero . . .) estaba devastada, after my own scorched-*aarde* policy, in 1983. And yet, and yet: after "blocking" Roland, after I met Curé, y después de conocerte a ti, a la Izelle, al Wa *en almal*, esas Lee letters also show that I began to feel increasingly fulfilled, hasta, de a ratos, *gelukkig* (aunque también guilty and uneasy, por lo que esto significaba: to feel happiness in South Africa bajo el apartheid). My last two years in S. Africa, viví una especie de convivencia conflictiva. Like they said about los católicos, los árabes y los judíos en España, from 711 to 1492. Oxymoronic pero fruitful. *Exactly* ese edge donde me siento en casa.

P.D. More highveld factoids de las Lee letters: ¿Te acuerdas de un vato egresado de Wits, a big star de la Witwatersrand jolling scene, llamado Ian Hos . . . algo? A hot architect, perhaps. Le decíamos Hoss, remember? Y luego yo y la Beth Miller, esa *dagga*-loving American architect, rechristened him Bonanza! Ay, todo esto es *te veel*. Did I ever get with him? I have a dim inkling de que *yebo*, I might have. Aunque creo que it was la Beth la que le tenía mad crush, ¿no? Roland lo detestaba, that I do remember.

29-vi-09

Montenegro,

Siguen los intense *verbindings*. Or invisible links, o como quieras llamarlo. Wim arrives in just a few days. Good thing he's a Gemini, pues he's on another *groot trek* even as we speak! Un amigo (otro S. African priest), Father Roger, le llevó de Baltic cruise through Scandinavia y hasta parts of Russia (my ancestral clan territory, on Dad's side). Me acaba de escribir esto:

*I am, amazingly, in a bizarrely steamy London (it feels like Pretoria in summer!) tonight after an unforgettable time on the Baltic. St. Petersburg was more than I have dreamed, a magical place, and I hope that one day we can go there together. Copenhagen was the highlight for me. I took a train up the coast and visited Karen Blixen's house where she was born, where she lived when she* returned from Africa, and where she is buried in the woods, her own green mansions. It was a touching and beautiful experience, the woods filled with birds, the garden full of peonies, and the house full of memories of Africa, of love, and of art.

Wim y otra gente me han dicho que mi writing reminds them, en algunos aspectos, of la Dinesen's.

Even el Du Preez has now joined the chorus! And I know that you too, my taciturn *delwer*, are touched por todo este warp 'n' weave de testimonio: to the continuing "afterlife"—esta rara resurgencia, as from last year, cual tentáculos que (se) buscan, hermosos y otherwoldly as strands of seaweed o medusas preservadas en ámbar, fossilized más de dos décadas y ahora reconstituted, so wet, wet and vital de nuevo—of our historia de amor.

Gracias, bebé, for letting me know que leíste esa letter to Lydia. Y que te ha impactado. Me terremoteó, that's for sure. As did my other old letters, las de Pretoria, que me devolvió nuestra querida "Sloth" (Lee W.). Uncanny too, encontrar esa fotie of us in Cullinan. Taken (by whom? no tengo idea) in front of our little miner's cottage. Aun más shocking que la foto misma was what you'd written al dorso. —*I love you. You're beautiful.* Even "as late in the game" as April 1983.

I'm going to scan some foties for you. *En ook*, I'll xerox las *inskripsies* you wrote me al dorso. I'm doing my *own ondergrond* heart-*werk*, Rolo. Tú mismo eres como la faz de la tierra. Ostensibly hard, solid, impervious, and yet, and yet . . . I am probing every crevass, buscando el lugar donde la tierra se licua, in an unexpected flash. Ese lugar que cede, finally, after painstaking excavation.

## 30-vi-09

Wimmie,

Los astros must be propitious. Prendí la compu, hoping there'd be something from you, y voilá. *En ook*, quite unexpectedly, algo del "Sea Lawyer" (Du Preez) y de Mike Chiappetta! Hasta de tu Xavier, *kan jy dit glo*? And best of all: una hermosa carta de R. It's really *so* other-league, te la tengo que mostrar. Le había dicho que I'd found a fotie of us taken in Cullinan, cuando vivíamos en la Premier Diamond Mine, remember? That hideous *dorp*—all Rock, all the time—donde por poco causé un traffic accident, just walking to the shops (in shorts). Uf. Pero anygüey, on the fotie-back, él me había escrito una conmovedora *dedikasie*. In April 1983, *nogal*—*after* I'd left him (and taken up with el Peter—pero esa es otra). Esto es lo que me mandó R., ayer:

*Shug,*

*Mea culpa*—*especially on the reading and reply front. "Sommer kak" is about as accurate and descriptive as any language can describe my recent responses*—*or lack thereof. I have received your SMS and emails, so no worries on that front. I am engaged in some fairly abrasive negotiations with the mine manager of Lyttelton Sodomite Mine. As a result my mood is mostly grumpy at the moment because I had ramped up production to supply him and he is now ducking and diving.*

*So while the sodomitic manager dithers I have to go out on the hustings to source other business*—*and that is not easy in the current economic climate. I am therefore somewhat distracted and rather uncommunicative. I know that you demand a much higher level of attentiveness!! I have read your Lydia letter and I marvel at your ability to write with so much insight not only of the emotions of the moment but how you weave into your words the way places "felt" to us and how everything around us impacted on our feelings.*

*You found a pic from Cullinan? Amazing, esp. since I work with some of the guys from those days and they all ask me what that 'wild American girlfriend' of mine is doing. One of the guys caused much mirth when he told me, 'Daardie vroumens was wilder as die wildtuin!' Not that I ever doubted it, but your sojourn in Cullinan left memories with people that you never even met.*

*I write to you from a very chilly Jhb under the clear pale blue sky of a high-veld winter's day. My emo-laconicism is not a terminal condition and I agree with my 1983 inscription*—*you are beautiful. ILY, RF*

Este es el Montenegro que recuerdo. The one I love.

*9-vii-09*

Mr. M., my darling,

Por fin, Wim and I have it figured out—we think. We're pretty sure *dit sal werk*: how to foil the evil international *sangomas* who've been preventing proper intercourse entre nuestros celulares. T-Mobile is a slightly rasquache phone company, pero como tú y yo comprobamos hoy (through our dear alcahueto Wim's US cell), it *does* allow reception of texts *uit* Suid-Afrika, mientras que hegemonic Verizon does not. So, Wim will leave me that little sim card cuando se vaya, and I can just switch it in & out of my Verizon-(non!) powered cell.

Y hablando de in 'n' out: so *baie* sexy to be able—por fin—to exchange texts with you, in real-time hoy, en el cell gringo de Wim. Antaño we used to have *such* scorching—si carísimo—phone sex, *onthou jy?* (ATT was the only phone company in the US en los 80.) Remember how I used to make you come, desde mi black Slimline San Francisco phone, all the way down to apartheid Joburg, solo con mi voz?

*11-vii-09*
Header: *Green Mansions / Witwatersrand Merge*

Montenegro, my love,

*Baie dankie vir die foties!* Y salúdame a tu best pal, el Ken. Wim me dijo que el Rand Club is for la crème de la crème de la white (Engels) S. African "aristocracy." OMG, no way podría estar con un marido who belonged to that sort of club. *Aikona*, my china! Por otra parte, ¿un amante? *Geen probleem nie* (haven't I evolved?). Y ya que me mandaste esas foties, I'm attaching one for you. Sacada en un supermarket en New Orleans. Perdona el no muy body-revealing atuendo (pero you *do* now have in your possession otras *baie* revealing shots, ¿que no?). Pero just check the brand of bread: "Bunny Plantation," *nogal*?

Las fotie-backs que me inscribiste constituyen un lapidary epistolary—nuestra historia de amor, condensed, as is your wont. Pero your letter yesterday was anything but emo-laconic! *Exactly* like you used to write me. Y a propósito, you must be mad, Rolo. ¿Que mis readers will "throw you to the literary wolves"? My nalga! Take it from me: cualquiera daría su eye teeth pa' poder confeccionar siquiera *one* of your swoonworthy frases.

En mi diario, I wrote this earlier today:

*Diario*

Montenegro, tu carta me ha hecho pensar y recordar. Tanto. OJITO, eh: I must *still* spar with you (for old times' sake). Besides, I know it turns you on. Me escribes que el apartheid es just *one* explanation for our split.

Luego dices, just sticking to the As, that Africa *itself* was a reason. Dices que Africa es un continente de contrastes, y luego que these contrasts are difficult to reconcile, especially for someone "sensitive and American." Whoa, cowboy! Back that shit up *'n bietjie.*

No tengo quarrel (en particular) con tu description of Africa. A modo de shorthand, it'll do. I know only S. Africa and Lesotho. Algeria and Morocco (de niña). For practical purposes, para mí, Africa was *South Africa.* And South Africa in the '80s *was* apartheid. And I would mos def call *that* particular political system—y ambiente—algo muy diferente de solo . . . "contrasts." Por ejemplo: sinister, overwhelming, authoritarian, deeply racist, lo que quieras.

Podríamos esbozar múltipes reasons pa' explicar por qué nos separamos: class differences, nuestra crianza, our respective—vastly different—life experiences a los 26 años. Lack of love was *not* one of them. Pero todos estos factores, for me, are inextricably bound up in apartheid. South Africa to you, en cambio, was something else. Un lugar más complejo, a vast potential waiting to happen, lo que sea. Es decir, not just the "evils of apartheid." Y entre otras cosas, it was home.

Irónico (digo, considering I hated Africa's bleached dryness cuando llegué), now I live on the edge of the desert. Yebo, I'm a Californian, pero de NorCal, which, as you know, is green(er), más sylvan. LA *looks* lush, pero that's the Hollywood version. En el interior, como dicen en Argentina (about the whole rest of the country, excepto Buenos Aires, jaja), only a few miles from the coast, es desierto. En estos 20 años (wow, hard to believe), I've learned a different way of looking. First to tolerate, luego aceptar, and finally to appreciate SoCal's subtle, harsh topografía. A similar dryness, al pensarlo, to the highveld. The same pale, bleached sky, dry *aarde,* the same aloes and red-hot poker, plumbago and tecomaria and canna and coral tree y hasta jacaranda. Pero con nuestro autóctono evil (digo *inland*) empire, southwesty flora: yucca, agave y salvia. And our fauna, los coyotes y circling hawks y hasta (ay, Dios no quiera) bears and mountain lions. Somewhere out there, no tan lejos.

I adore your lyrical *beskrywing* of South Africa and of Mozambique. Y de ti, my *bokkie*, en tu tierra. Y esa extraña, allusively apt imagen de mí: a black springbok, a la vez indigenous and aberrant. How'd you decide on that, me pregunto, as my avatar . . . You say the highveld is not *my* Africa, pero esto no es (del todo) cierto. La tragedia es que after a while, I *did* grow to love it. *Tragies, omdat* you weren't around to see that.

Las cartas que escribí a mi amiga Lydia Vélez (*uit* Pretoria) show this complicated love, clearly. Para 1984, me había hecho amiga de un grupo de artists, architects, músicos y otros creatives. We used to *jol* casi todos los weekends in Rockey Street, en Yeoville. Descubrimos esa vibe, yo y el Castells (and later Wim, Etienne, mi Canadian friend la Heather y otros), al hookearnos con un bohemian Afrikaner, André de Wet. Tenía un curio shop, Mango Park, on Rockey Street, donde congregaba su motley crew: South Africans, Americans, europeos. I'd met André in 1983 y para mid-1984 hangueábamos todos los weekends en el Market Theatre's Saturday flea market. Through André, I became friendly with those okes en ese multiracial music group, Mapanzulah. Y los Dynamics. Hasta me acuerdo que hicimos una Halloween *partytjie* where they played, *kan jy dit glo?* Ay, they were smokin'! Para ni mencionar las almost weekly (strictly illegal, OB-vio) township jive gigs en el more than slightly sleazy Park Five Saloon en Joburg.

Hacia fines de 1984, when I was about to return to CA (para terminar el PhD), me hice amiga del artista Ranko Pudi. No me acuerdo ahora dónde le conocí. Pero he actually persuaded me to take clandestine foties—en los townships *nogal*—después de ver algunas de mis fotos (y artefactos) en casa. Y agárrate: my mail was routinely intervened (hay que reconocer que I was *regularly* receiving mail from the People's Republic of China—de un amigo, former student—and from my sister Sarita, in Nicaragua and El Salvador). I'd open my mail (mi lifeline al mundo), y encontraba obvious signs of state censorship: the letters folded wrong, random pedacitos de papel sealed in there, con numeritos, alguna especie de code, I reckon. Fucking creepy. Scary. Por eso, I had no phone at home. Etienne y yo usábamos el pay phone en el *apteek* de Barclay Square. Or we'd made calls from my *werk*, I remember, en UNISA. No cell phones entonces, bebé! Y . . . así.

Did you know *any* of this about me, digo, back then? No me acuerdo. El Du Preez lo sospechaba. Maybe that's why I never heard from him again, después de esa disheartening *besoek* in December '82, where he trashed you to me, *onthou jy?* Some friend . . . Pero back to me, yo y el highveld. El 8 de octubre 1984, escribí una carta a Lydia. Estos bits 'n' pieces'll give you an idea (or remind you?) of . . . me:

*Me siento uprooted. No del todo uncomfortable, or it is, pero I'm not sure I mind, exactly. Si me cuerpo fuera un árbol, las branches are reaching toward California, toward the US, donde ya ni sé si quepo. Me atrae, no lo niego, cierto tipo de . . . freedom: relations between the sexes (ay, the stifling machismo of S. Africa!), la posibilidad de publicar (oh, the crushing censura here—it's everywhere, en la tele, los diarios, las magazines, all around me, siempre), of being able to have a drink and see a film on Sundays, coño (illegal in South Africa, ¿lo sabías?—it's the Lord's day, te lo juro). Más que nada, being able to have friends, hasta lovers, de cualquier raza (OK, not perfect at home, pero al menos not illegal). Viviendo en Sudáfrica, I try to hold myself apart, most of the time, de (casi todos) los blancos. I feel myself definitely an* uitlander.

*Y sin embargo (sé que me contradigo), otra parte de mí—the tree trunk— pulls me irremediably toward Africa, Lydia. Aunque desprecio todo de Sudáfrica que lo hace South Africa (beginning, of course, con el apartheid y todo lo que esto implica—the current* kak *of these false elections, for example). No obstante los blockades, the disinformation, the brainwashing que fomenta un inconsciente colonialista, this other (South) Africa exists. Y lo amo. Mi amigo Neppe Selabe (he works at UNISA) me dice,* —Suzi, you are doing a good thing, leaving. It is getting very bad. The children in Mamelodi won't even go to school. I think it's going to get very big. Very much danger. Maybe even for you. There is a file on you; count on it. Go home, Suzi. Go home and remember *everything.* And write about this.

*Después de estas fucking fake elections, debo atenuar mi hope, my love for this country. I must store up my anger. Tengo que convencerme de que as an American, as a Latina, como mujer, como escritora (not necessarily in that order), puedo hacer más—digo, for the Azania that must come, para el futuro— al volver a California. Where I can speak. And remember. Y, como me dice Neppe, write. Quedarme aquí (which I yearn to do), ay, everything is so fraught with contradictions.*

Montenegro, this was one of the last letters que escribí de Sudáfrica, before I went home. "Home." Ya no había nada para mí en Califas: my parents were in Spain con mi hermana Laura, my sister Sarita había vuelto a Central America. Many of my friends had moved o se habían muerto (AIDS). Me sentía lost, tironeada, fragmentada . . . for years after I returned. Y pues, you know the rest: got pregnant (adrede) cuando diagnosticaron a mi dad de stomach cancer, en 1986. Una boludez, *totally* crazy (al pensarlo ahora). Pero como te dije, I was lost. De milagro, Etienne (mi hijo) me ancló al mundo. Or he returned me to the land of the living . . . qué sé sho. En gran medida, I finished my PhD, y tomé esta chamba en el college, for him. To make a life for him, para nosotros.

And as for us (*ek en jy*)? Contra viento y marea I still loved you then; I still love you now.

*17-vii-09*

Wimmie,

Sigo en shock por nuestros sudden mutual memory flashes sobre el André Hartmann. No puedo creer que yo haya hecho eso que tú dices: traerle de regalo esa silk tie from Italy, tied it sexily around his neck y enfurecerme porque he wouldn't keep it on, por temor a que la *vrou* would find out about us. *Is jy seker*, did I really kick him out of my apartment por eso? OMG, I really was an evil Mata Hari (albeit marxista)! Hay que admitir que el vato *was* hot, in that buttoned-up, Teutonic manner. Hmmm. Remember those *partytjies* en su casa? While he and I smooched (inter alia) there in the lounge, cerca de ese huge brown leather sofa (how come I remember this detail?), tú me hacías de wingman, on high alert for any sudden approaches de la *vrou*.

Y pensar que el André was a spy, o una especie de double agent (ditto esa wife), working for los Mozambican rebels *and* the ANC? Huh? How could we *possibly* not have known that? What did we think he was? ¿Solo un profesor de leyes? No, recuerdo vagamente que we thought he was some kind of diplomat, *nê*? What was his cover, ¿te acuerdas? I know we met him en UNISA, pero más allá de eso I'm drawing a blank. Oh, Roland habría estado livid, Wimmie, si hubiera sabido que yo estaba enrollada con el Hartmann. *Seker* he'd have accused me of ideological hypocrisy (o peor) . . . y en este caso, he'd have been dead right. Pero I plead ignorance.

¡No teníamos ni puta idea! And: el Hartmann era brilliant y charming. And dead sexy, a su manera.

Anyweg, hablando de exciting, dangerous vidas . . . I'm reading Gillian Slovo's memoir, *Every Secret Thing*. Acuérdate de que her mother, Ruth First, had been killed by a letter bomb in Maputo. Solo una semana antes de mi arrival in South Africa, el 26 de agosto de 1982.

*18-vii-09*

Querido OomBie-in-America,

Estuve hojeando mis S. Africa fotie albums and I just noticed this: en las fotos de mi *slaapkamer*, you can see foties of me and R. in New Orleans en la pared. Even in late '83 y después, long after I'd left Roland y ya estaba metida en mis cosas, in my own highveld vida. Allí seguían esas fotos. Even then, Wimmie (lo veo claro ahora), some part of me refused to resign myself to the loss. No me cerraba. I just couldn't reconcile our tragic (y de alguna forma casi sordid, anticlimactic) end in RSA con la outsized passion, the endless hope que nos caracterizó en USA.

P.D. How *could* I forget to tell you about this? Debe ser porque you're here, with me, bueno, no conmigo todavía, pero al menos in my country and yet (weirdly) traveling to all those *eksotiese* Midwestern pueblos. Anyway, R. continues to astound. Check this, de hace unos días:

*Shug!!*

*You're throwing me to the literary wolves!! They'll tear my 'delvish English' and my lacklustre emo responses to pieces before your flood of artistry. Hau! Madam!*

*What Wim experienced at Karen Blixen's house is a pointer to the way I feel about southern and eastern Africa. (I am not at all familiar with central, western and northern Africa.) It is such a continent of contrasts—both in its people and in its landscapes. Hope and opportunity contrast with poverty and corruption. Kindness and dignity contrast with brutality and buffoonery.*

*As for the effect that apartheid had on you and me and our togetherness, I have always seen it as one of many influences. Sticking with the As, I believe that Africa itself had an influence—those contrasts are difficult to reconcile, especially when you see them through the prism of educated and sensitive America. Never mind that apartheid cast its shadow over everything and everyone. It all contributed to creating a 'Dry White Season.'*

*In Africa dry means dusty. The all-pervading grit gets into your eyes and nose and mouth—you can taste and feel life being evaporated, dusted dry. Dusty is the opposite of you. You are moist and passionate. Latin, flashing eyes, passion and beauty. Your Africa is not the highveld—you stood out like a black springbok on the pale tawny grasslands. You stood out in the land where the Zulu impis had put all before them to the sword, who were themselves then chased into Zimbabwe by the Voortrekker Commandos, who in turn were defeated by soldiers of the British Empire. And then the English and American and Australian gold diggers arrived to claim the highveld as their own—and I (one of their descendants) am still here. L RF*

*23-vii-09*

*Liefste* Wimmie,

R. wrote me this a las 4 de la mañana, hoy. Where is he? *Hoekom* despierto a esa hora? I just cannot believe all this. Study on this . . . *vloed*, por favor.

*Bebe,*

*I knew and used to work with Jonathan First—if I remember correctly he was Ruth First's nephew. Yes those apartheid days saw some remarkable people come to the fore—Ruth was one of those.*

*You know that the story of 'domestics' in SA is more a commentary on the state of those economies than on the laziness of those who employ them. In Africa the more labour-intensive work there is the better. No doubt, the net result is that the wealthier portion of society (b&w) can hardly boil water without burning it!*

*You knew who and what I was from the moment I sat down with you at the Balboa Cafe—and I quickly found out who you were. We loved what we shared, including our differences—that made our relationship much deeper. And we never feared saying what we thought about things to each other. I knew or rather felt that your coming to SA would be fraught with emotion and that you would be fighting (emotionally and otherwise) a regime and a system that was itself fighting for survival, but which was always doomed to fail.*

*Love you, RF*

23-vii-09

Montenegro, mi amor,

*Another* fucking "glorious" day here aquí en la cuenca de LA (highs over 100 toda la semana), como dijera un personaje (la Sarah Miles, *miskien*) del film *White Mischief,* as she arose from her Happy Valley bed, yawning and stretching en su luxurious Kenyan boudoir, y vio que de nuevo, *soos elke dag,* the sun was already ablaze, cual despiadado ojo de Dios, high en el cielo africano.

You continue (or, de nuevo) to surprise, challenge, and thrill me. Ahhh, invierno en el highveld. Pienso en Karen Blixen y su Africa. I long for it now. In re — *You knew who and what I was from the moment I sat down with you at the Balboa Cafe—and I quickly found out who you were. We loved what we shared, including our differences.* Touché, *liefie.* Fingie en llaga.

Te escribo más *'n bietjie* later. Don't laff, pero heme aquí, thinking about los black holes. Digo, as a metaphor, para hablar de la memoria. El olvido versus le recuperación. Ponderando la memoria (and forgetting), sus operaciones nefastas o balsámicas. Leí un ensayo fascinante, the other day. Something my former mentor at Harvard, Jaime Alazraki, wrote, inspirado en una carta que Cortázar le había escrito. Alazraki's essay fue lo que me mandó por esta *swart gat* rabbit hole! Forgetting, remembering. Por una parte, it feels like we've been thinking about this a long time, *ek en jy.* Pero en realidad it was (tú y yo) *all* a "black hole," for so long! Al menos para mí: over 25 years. No sabes cuánto tu recuerdo me friquió, bebé, when you wrote me patrás right away y me dijiste que *yebo,* you remembered our miscarriage. Caught me *completely* off guard, porque I hadn't. Remembered that. Todo esto comenzó apenitas last year, en el Montalvo memory vortex, or Emerald Forest (as you call it). Ah, Rolo: I long for Africa. I long for you.

P.D. Memory-prompt fotie attached. It's the one of us in Cullinan, *sien jy?* La que me dedicaste después de esa huge heart-to-heart you'd had con tu pa mientras yo estaba en Inglaterra. A bit of a last-ditch *geskenkie*, me parece, shortly after you'd asked me to marry you. *Onthou jy?*

*24-vii-09*

Wimmie,

Ni sé dónde comenzar. This is all *veel te diep*: first Roland, y ahora our idol, el Marcus Abel! You MUST immediately *skryf* back to that CaraBobo "friend" thingie, and confirm our "amistad" (?) con el Marcus. Luego le mandas un *persoonlike* message from us, *hoor*. Ay, I can't believe this is all real (*is* it?)!

Cuanto más pienso en R.—then and now—más siento una ambiguous, irresoluble mix of emotions. Me he dado cuenta de cuán painstaking, how *stadig*, how much Roland has to *labor* to get his thoughts out on paper (as it were). Nunca había caído en cuenta de esto antes. I mean, the first time. What he's been writing lately me hace acordar how much of our *relasie* was always about testing . . . todo. Intercambiábamos constantemente thoughts, impressions, feelings. Sparring. Arguing. Era frustrante, pero electric. Sexy. Era—es—tan well read, tan intelligent.

Es conmoving que R. recuerde eso, the way our love encompassed (y no buscaba eliminar) nuestras diferencias. Y como nunca nos daba miedo discutir, airing our differences, probing them. This is true, Wimmie. Ay, pero I used to get furious with him! Yo era tan little Miss Marxista, and his "evolution, not revolution" slogans used to piss me off. Y sin embargo, we were able to . . . qué sé sho, negotiate through that. Bridge that. Con el amor—*en baie seks. Ag*, but then why did it go to shit, en RSA?

El sigue insistiendo que he understood how apartheid would feel (for me). Ese understanding emanaba de su amor por mí, I reckon. And yet, he also claims he "knew" apartheid was always doomed to fail. ¿Cómo coño puede haber sabido eso? That is *sommer kak, nê*. Eso es pura nalgavista, *ek sê*. Digo, even the ANC didn't "know that," hasta años después. Tu emailcito acaba de entrar. Uplifting little *ping, ping*:

*R. seems to have a strong optimistic streak. I, and most other South Africans, were convinced that apartheid would only end after a civil war or violent revolution. I will never forget standing on my balcony atop Barclay Square a week before the 1994 elections, crying and watching red emergency vehicle lights streak across the city to where the AWB had detonated a bomb. It was all, as you say, very fragile and complex until the last minute, and continues to be that even now.*

25-vii-09

Montenegro,

About your stunning *briefie* de hace dos días: vaya invisible link, you used to work with el sobrino de la Ruth First. Wow, what a strange mundo: the South Africa I arrived in en el '82 (yo era hiper-consciente, OB-vio, que hacía solo una semana she'd been blown to bits by a letter bomb en Maputo), the country where you live, ahora, postapartheid. The US I lived in then (los "excessive '80s," Reaganomics—I was hardly loathe to get away from that part of it), y el país de ahora—donde a un conocido crítico African American, el "Skip" Gates (Harvard prof) le arrestan por "public disturbance," entering his own home in Cambridge, *nogal.*

And about "domestics" (tu palabra): I'm afraid we'll never agree. Pero ¿sabes qué? Ni modo. Esta friction (jaja) ha sido fuente de puzzlement y frustración (más para mí, creo, ya que I was the one who went to live in your mundo) *maar ook*, de gran poder erótico e intelectual. En cuanto a mi repugnance hacia los criados: this isn't a "Latin" thing, like you asked me. Porque mi mom—raised tan poor que tenía que elegir entre gastar su dime en el school bus or save it up pa' comprar una caja de crayons— enthusiastically embraced la costumbre de las domestic servants when we lived in Mexico and Spain, cuando yo era niña.

And no way is it a US thing tampoco! Hay plenty Americans que adoran las maids, nannies, etc.—you just picked the wrong one, Rolo! *Nee*, it's personal. I've felt this way desde muy joven. They thought I was nuts cuando vivía en Buenos Aires, by the way, ya que no quise tener mucama, aunque es sine qua non de todo hogar de clase even *semi*-media, en Argentina. Y todos mis friends, BTW, me daban la misma clase de "economic reasoning," just like you do.

OB-vio, I take after the New Mexican–Presbyterian–Dutch strain, tipo mi Granny Chávez. Soy independent, do it myself. No soporto a los strangers en mi casa, doing things for me! Sudden memory: la idea de que tu family maid me lavara los *broekies*? *Nooit*. And waiting on me, en la mesa. Y ese "garden boy" (Shadrack, wasn't he called?) bustling around 24/7. Nel. Not for me. I don't know how to give orders at home, Rolo! Excepto en la cama. So, I reckon we'll have to have *twee huise*, como Diego Rivera y Frida Kahlo. Linked por un drawbridge . . .

*25-vii-09*

Querido W.,

*Jy's reg.* R. must resort to that lite/jocose tone como mecanismo de defensa, contra el onslaught of deeper feelings: los recuerdos y el amor. He *does* have them, OB-vio. Pero le cuesta revelarlas. Soltarlas. Frustrating to people like us, *nê*. Pero por otra parte, we wouldn't want to get *too* used to it, hey? We'd probably run for the colinas. Y deja no me olvide de esto:

*I am totally overwhelmed by Roland's letter, especially that last paragraph! It actually made me emotional to read it. How hard it must be for him, even now, to put those thoughts and worries into words. I imagine that as a young man he just pushed them aside and tried to carry on. It is truly amazing that he feels safe enough to say these things to you and that he is able to formulate them. You have really transformed his life (again), more and more in these last months, I believe.*

I will treasure those words, *vir altyd*, Wimmie. I am right now laughing at the sublime invisi-linksy hilariousness de nuestra vida. Anoche musitaba: how *utterly* bizarre, que el Marcus Abel sea a real person, viviendo en Florida, and he's communicated with us. There he was en los early '80s: inalcanzable, Teutonic magazine god. Y ahora, our Fwiend (en CaraBobo). Brave new mundo, inDEED!

*27-vii-09*

Ah, my darling,

Te me quejas, —*So don't label me as emotionally challenged.* I bloody well didn't, pero si el chancla fits . . . Y luego you claim, —*I've just perfected the art of encapsulating emotion in a very concise manner.* Weeeell, this *may* be so. Pero is it an art, or something else? ¿No será laziness, o miedo? I remember a time when you were more (consistently) expressive. I brought that out in you, Montenegro. Me lo has dicho mil veces. *— It doesn't mean it's not there.* I know this! Pero for you, feeling and expressing it are not one and the same (digo, versión 2.0). Y ¿cómo coño quieres que yo lo sepa, if you're so damn self-immuring? Do you think I'm a mind-reader (OK, *don't* answer that)? *— I'll teach you to be concise in matters of the heart.* Jamás. ¡En tu vida!

   P.D. And would you love me as much si lo fuera?
*— You know I wouldn't.*

### 28-vii-09

Rolo babee,
   Continuando nuestro mini-palimpsesto, our hilito on domestic neo-colonialism (jaja):
   *— I agree that the situation [servants] is less than desirable. However, you are going to have to concede to me that you are opposed to the practice in principle — but that you understand why the practice exists!* Yebo, absolutely. *Geen probleem nie.* Concuerdo. Or, I concede (jaja). So, in re *— We're going to have to have a rule that if I win the argument you come to my house and be very nice to me. Vice-versa holds too. When I say very nice I mean all of you must be very nice to me!* Orale. You got it (either way) . . . pero, ¿quién coño ganó this time?

### 28-vii-09 (later)

Montenegro,
   Well, we can't say que el 28 no haya sido siempre our day, *nê?* Your phone call this morning me sobrecogió. Completely! I didn't recognize the *nommer* — pensé que era Wim *miskien*, de su Philly hotel. So I picked up, aunque eran apenas las 6:30 (de la mañana, OJO). And already hot as fuck!

Bebé, ¿cómo describirte el feeling? Exciting, *baie erotiese* y a la vez tan weird to hear your voice. *En ook*, uncannily familiar. Porque you sound the same, *exactly* the same as ever. ¿Y yo? Difícil creer que hasta hoy, we hadn't spoken in more than two decades. How is it possible que se sienta tan . . . lo mismo?

NEWSBRIEFIE:

La Somali-born modelo Iman (casada con David Bowie), when asked when she knew he was "the man for her," respondió así: "We were walking down the street, and I noticed my shoelace was untied. Without a word, he got down on his knees and tied it for me." Doesn't that remind you of a certain man (bastante más macho que el Bowie, hay que reconocerlo) who, also without a word, knelt down en los cobblestones del French Quarter e improvisó un bandaid con un trocito de papel, to soothe his lover's abraded ankle?

15-viii-09

OomBie,

"Now that we are cool," para citar a mi fave Anglo-'Tine (W. H. Hudson en *Green Mansions*). O más bien, now that you're *terug*, patrás en tu continente, having been here and gone, me siento melancólica. So alone. About this: —*Did you get the SMS from Roland that I forwarded just before I flew?* No. No fucking SMS de R. Pero here's his latest:

*Ms. Montenegro,*

*I still clearly remember that day in SF with your mum and dad. My feelings remain immured, cemented in my memory. I am here, in contact—albeit trying to make up ground after having been dumped from my previous contract on account of being too white. Nice turnaround from the days you experienced in SA? Anyway, faint heart never won fair maiden. Am working to keep hearth and home together—but otherwise am alive. L, M*

So *pragtig, nê*? Wimmie: I totally get you, lo que me sugieres de vivir *in-between*. RSA/USA. Or back 'n' forth, de alguna manera. I wish I could actually live like that (*twee-land* living). *Maar* creo que sería way too DANGE! Digo: what to do about Pierre? Ay, where is this all leading? I'm frightened Auntie Em, I'm frightened . . .

*15-viii-09*

Montenegro,

I felt a pang, te confieso, cuando te leí estas palabras, —*Am working to keep hearth and home together.* Jealousy, remordimiento? That I'm not the one there, compartiendo ese hearth and home contigo? Oh, *ek weet*, ya sé lo que me vas a decir: —*You could've been, Shug, you forfeited that.* Or *miskien, I don't see why we couldn't, still . . .*

And yet: what I yearn for with you no es la domesticidad—unless we could do lo de Frida y Diego. Ya sabes que we'd never get past the domestic servant *probleem* (just for starters). And we'd lion-wrestle ourselves to death antes de que ni tú ni yo dijera uncle, ¿no? Ni que eso fuera, necessarily, del todo unpleasant! *Ja nee*, more our scene, a fin de cuentas, es esa Zanzibarian "wild beauty" you've incongruously reported en la tele of late. *That was*—and is—our love, bebé. Don't you agree?

My darling: *ek's so baie jammer* you were sacked for being demasiado blanco—OMG, is that for real? O ¿tu paranoia poscolonial, más bien?

Anygüey, I'll happily lion-fight you about politics till we're on our last breath. Pero ojalá y estuviéramos breathless from another venture. To wit: soñé anoche que estábamos de beach camping trip. Era un lugar rugged y outdoorsy, achingly familiar—esa NorCal coastal topography that is my heart-home. Era de noche, I could hear the sea lapping, lapping. Tú estabas desnudo. I peeled back your sleeping bag (our green one) y te lamía el pecho, down your belly, las piernas, demorándote. Todo era slo-mo y sinestésico. I could taste that briny Califas sea salt on your skin, sentía el calor de tu cuerpo al lado del mío, al ladito mero, just before waking up. Ahhhh.

And in re —*Anyway, faint heart never won fair maiden.* Tru dat, my Bok Boytjie. So show me.

*16-viii-09*

Dearest OomBata,

Did you enjoy what R. wrote me (hablando de los white males losing ground)? Me cayó tan poignant, especially about my parents. Porque I didn't remember that Chinatown almuerzo myself. Su "immuring memory"! Y esa sexy amor cortés phrase, "faint heart never won fair maiden"! It pierced me, somehow. Wimmie, yo no soy la mujer de su hearth and home, OB-vio. Pero ¿de su heart? *Yebo*: esa soy yo.

*17-viii-09*

R.,

Wim *se boetie*, Mauritz (a diplomat currently stationed con su familia en Oz—if somewhat testily: they were hoping for somewhere else . . . *meer eksotiese*) le mandó este article. Wim sent it to me, y ahora I'm passing it on to you. Tu dosis diaria, jaja.

*DELICATE, YET RACE ISSUES MUST BE FACED (PRETORIA NEWS ONLINE, 13-08-2009)*

*Lindiwe Sisulu's call for the ANC to engage in a discussion about race and what is meant by transformation is as welcome as it is long overdue . . . It is a topic most shy away from—at least, in mixed company. But South Africans have nothing to lose and everything to gain by confronting, once and for all, what is meant when we say we want to build a democratic, non-racial, non-sexist society. Does it mean passing over people from "minority groups" in favour of Africans for important economic cabinet positions, as ANC Youth League leader Julius Malema has suggested? It does not, for this is the path of racism and division exploited so well by successive apartheid governments. Does it mean tackling the racism and sexism that still underpin society? Yes it does. South Africans have nothing to be ashamed of in admitting that, 15 years after democracy dawned, we are not yet gathered as one nation around the "simunye" table. Perhaps we were in so much of a hurry after 1994 to draw a veil over the evils of our past and embrace a new, democratic future in which everyone would be equal that we failed to deal with the rhinoceros in the dining room. It would be crazy to imagine that the damage done by centuries of oppression could be healed or erased in such a short time. Those who are uncertain about this need only to cast an eye across to the world's oldest democracy, the United States, where voters have elected a black president, but still grapple with issues around race. We must grapple with them too. Racism is no longer a system imposed on us, but it lives on in the way we live our lives and the way we think.*

Bebé: Not sure if after discussing this we'll spar and claw more—or less. And dare I ask: have you managed yet to "sodomite" *somebody*, digo, encontrar otra chamba instead of the one donde esos eggers let you go for being dizque too blanco?

Por el momento, to soothe the savage beast: imagina que estamos en esa forest bed, doing what we do best: talking, fighting, fucking—ferozmente. Or, as you say, — *We don't have to stay on the bed of course* . . . The (Emerald Forest) floor's fine by me, *liefie*.

*31-viii-09*

My darling *delwer*,

Wim me mandó estas evocative words ayer:

*Got your SMSs and Roland's while I'm doing the dishes, one of my fave things in the world on a Sunday night after having friends over, somehow makes me feel complete and full. So wonderful that through the textuals I can know that you are there, in the SD zoo where we were together last year, and that Roland is OK in Joburg and somehow all's well. Now there's Ladysmith Black Mambazo on the radio, melancholy, very African and beautiful.*

I'd texted him (ya te dije de los magical powers de su US-irradiated cell) when I hadn't heard from you en unos días. Y más tarde (as he recounts, arriba), while I was attempting to escape the local heat and flames en lo que irónicamente resultó ser una visita bien muggy and tropically unpleas al SD Zoo, a text from me in San Diego y otro de ti en Joburg pinged into Wim's phone simultaneously. Rara, *mooi*, esta brave new world cybergeografía que habitamos juntos.

*7-ix-09*

Wimmie,

Gracias a Dios que mi best friend's a priest (who would've thought?). Y hablando de Dios *and* moving on to true love, here's what R. just wrote me:

*Inshallah! If God wills, so be it. (Ref to your email titled 'como Dios manda.')*

*I have been watching Cali get scorched on CNN International. Keep hoping to see you jump in front of the camera shouting, "Hey Mister M., can't you see I'm burning!" I know you're a cool SF fog girl—not (as we've discussed before) a dry heat girl.*

*Caster Semenya got a raw deal from our 'progressive' athletics authorities. The coach (not that I think he bears responsibility) resigned today. However, the incompetents that screwed the situation up will not resign.*

*But back to your burning sensations . . . . . I am (as you well know) a keen supporter of your hotter tendencies. You can withhold pics but I know how you look and how you feel (literally) so I can do without pics and rely on my memory and on my imagination. Nevertheless, pics are always welcome—he said pleadingly. ILY RF*

Stunning, *nê*, como este gender-*skandaal* con la Caster Semenya has caused him to wax so prolix. Oh, quisiera estar face to face with him again! Inclinándome hacia él (sounds like a Delmira Agustini poem) across the table en tantos bars. Or beds. Sparring.

*10-ix-09*

Montenegro, amor,

Your last *brief* was sublime. *Maar* demasiada política! Ya sé, ya sé, demanding mistress. Y con mixed messages además.

*Ek's moeg, liefie.* Second week of the semester's almost over. The fire's out, por fin. The chaparral's scorched y el cielo luce unos tonos insólitos, a bizarre periwinkle and rust, en momentos inapropiados. Capaz te escriba en el weekend. Pero for now, I'll cut to the chase:

Why don't you meet me in New Orleans? Tengo dos invites, with a possible third one, all in Baton Rouge. Red Stick no es chévere, pero ni modo: it's only an hour away from NoLa. Un former student, Luis David, me ha invitado al Delta Mouth Literary Festival. Y ese congreso CHISPA (on Highspanic literatures) will also be going on. Pensé que estas dates might intrigue you: 11–14 February 2010.

Según recuerdo, you had a rather *kak* Valentine's Day this year. Anygüey, *baie* invisible linksy, que el Delta Mouth Festival *and* la CHISPA coincidan exactly with Mardi Gras, ¿que no? You can read entrelíneas, yes?

*21-ix-09*

Oopa,

Tal y como sospechamos: R. *had* been grouchy. Pero there's something down 'n' dirty y a la vez courtly en esta carta, ¿no te parece?

*Shug,*

*Week was v. busy and yet slow. I was not in communicative mood—I was, in fact, rather grumpy all in all.*

*However, I loved the pics and did have a good giggle at your 'meid' pic at your sister's house—I knew you were intending me to get the message i.r.o. our 'domestics' discussion. Point taken and I must say it rather changed my mind about 'meidnaai'!! Very racist and sexist comment, I know, but I am referring to you in particular. I rather fancy the idea of you in what they call here a 'huis rok': getting fucked in the kitchen, sitting room, bedroom etc., etc. By me of course.*

*Your voicemail I have on my phone—it keeps you very close to me. ILY RF*

*2-x-09*

Wimmie,

Mi astral reading *vandag*, con la Joanna Woolfolk, ha sido genial. *Miskien*, the best one I've ever had with her. Inter alia, dijo que my life (and work) work now is all about S. Africa! How's that! También dijo que people from that time (you, and especially R.) will be instrumental en mi próximo libro. Pero ella intuye que cambiará el title. Según, debe ser más "soulful and evocative." More about my life, emotions. Menos sociological-sounding. No le gusta *What Apartheid Did to Us* (as subtitle). So en el health walk, musité el temita en mi ponder-heart (como dice Joanna), and this idea came to me en un flash: *Montenegro y yo: Del Balboa Cafe al Apartheid and Back.* Something like that. *Hou jy daarvan?* Porque al pensarlo, it hasn't really been "adiós" a Montenegro, after all. Just a (25-year) pausa, like Joanna says!

*9-x-09*

Dearest Wimmie,

Brace yourself: Roland is trying to get a "mine concept" job (¿qué coño será eso?) in the US. Right now! I'm struck dumb. Te dejo que ponderes esto. *Lees*:

*Bebe,*

*As you were unwittingly involved in a three-way conversation arranging whether Ma F. could make a Saturday lunch or a Sunday lunch, I understand your skepticism as to whether or not I could multitask on that scale!!*

*One of the projects that I am hoping to land includes work for a gold mine in Nevada. It's early days, but if I get the work, then maybe, just maybe I will have some 'delwer werk' in the US of A??? The mine is called Hollister Mine and lies north of Elko and west of Salt Lake City. Managed to Google Earth it eventually. Real outback America. It looks like a small version of Cullinan—in fact a very small version.*

*Will keep you posted on progress. Work is still hard to come by here, but I am pushing hard to get new projects lined up. It is time consuming and energy sapping, but there isn't an option. As always, I am confident that once our technology becomes more extensively used, there will be a little more time to sit back and smell the roses as it were! LLLLL M*

*9-x-09*
Header: *diamant/goud/nieve*

Mnr. M.,

Mi header (in case it's not obvious) remite no solo a nuestras incursiones into montañas of fluffy snow in our Chestnut Street love-in days sino también a tu "maybe just maybe" *voortrek* to the neighboring estado de . . . Nevada (jaja). Bebé: I'll *glo that* one cuando lo vea . . . says she, bahtante skeptical.

Pero darlin', even if such a *droom* were to come true, why'd you pick *that* fucking state? Nevada me parece más . . . barren desierto que Wild West, kind of a right-wing, retiree-laden, homophobic badlands, if you ask me. Elko? ¿Un pequeño Cullinan *nogal*? Can such a *plek* even exist?

*Dorp*-deluxe! Tienes que admitir que much, much more our latitudes (tal y como lo confirman esos astro-geografía reports que te mandé) are the streets of San Francisco. Ditto New Orleans. Por ende mi Louisiana invitación, for next February.

*12-x-09*

Montenegro, amor,

Touching thumbs para esa "mine concept" conference call el viernes, *hoor*. After I slagged on that revolting *dorp* (Elko, NV), lo busqué en ese astro-geografía website, remember? Y agárrate: it has mind-blowingly *good* energy. Para cada uno, and for us, juntos. So "maybe just maybe" I spoke too soon (para variar), about not wanting to meet you in Nevada? *Ag, jammer*, my *bokkie*. Pero that's an Aries for you. Perdona. Pero still, OJO: no fucking way podría hacer un repentino, unexplained trek to the badlands. Alone. *Maar* to the Bay Area? Esa es otra historia. And . . . SF is *only* a hop, skip y salto de Nevada. Hint: what would you do for love?

P.D. *Sneeu*, desierto, fog, pantano. Bring it. Tú sabes que (if push comes to shove) I'd meet you in a fucking mine dump . . . or anywhere.

*15-x-09*

My darling,

Algo haunting, *erotiese* . . . and melancholy in your voice el otro día. The connection was ridiculously bad, pero somehow just hearing you say, yes, yes, I *can* (hear you) era, de alguna manera, *genoeg*. Wim wrote me this:

*I still cannot get over the maturity and profound love in Roland's latest words. It is really as if the relationship were never broken off, as if it continued to grow and live in each of you, even when you weren't consciously aware of it. Truly extraordinary!!*

*25-x-09*

Dearest Wimmie,

Funny que digas que yo represente, for you, an alterna, "less fragmented" realidad. Porque me parece que mi *werklikheid* is quite fractured, entre aquí y allá. Ni modo el here. Y allá, with my love, Montenegro, pero . . . And speaking of him, no e-machos de R. en un par de días. Pero ever since last month, cuando misteriosa y repentinamente they started getting through to me, el vato me textualiza all the time! About this:

*The Roland chronicles continue to astound me and touch me deeply. It is amazing to see how love, true affection, affinity, can be excavated and re-discovered in this strange, beautiful way. If he does come to the US (!), it opens a whole new area of complication, so I sort of hope that it doesn't happen, or happen yet. At the right time I think it could be magical and good.*

Bueno . . . hmm. *Ons sal sien* . . .

Those ladrones breaking into your ma's neighbor's home, robando y demandando guns, is fucking chilling. And yet, too, how poignant it is to me, tu reconocimiento de esa uneasy voluptuousness and slightly queasy comfort al sucumbir a la nostalgia in *die nuwe* Suid-Afrika. Recordar la almost-bucolic tranquility de tu infancia en Pretoria (similar a la mía, en muchos aspectos, in Sepulveda—ahora North Hills—en el entonces-sleepy San Fernando Valley). Sentir el inevitable guilt pang when you re-flect on the why, en el cómo de esa tranquil domestic tableau.

Me lleva a mi propia guilt, about having gone to live in S. Africa at a time when that world—el que tú describes—was still going strong. The surface shimmering (para los blancos) like all the pristine *swembaddens* in every suburban backyard. Si bien bajo la superficie, ya se sentía los ripples. Bueno . . . ripples, she says. What an egger. Chale al eufemismo. Para cuando yo llegué, en agosto de 1982, it really wasn't tranquil anymore. Not the way you remember your childhood. Not for anyone, ni siquiera los blancos. Remember? Bombs and border wars, tanques en los townships, and the quiet, lurking violence del dizque "petty apartheid." Eramos jóvenes, pero no longer children. And we saw.

6-xi-09

Liewe OomBie,

Quiero que veas este croosh hilito con Heilige Liefde from a couple of weeks ago. Here's him to me:

*What I do need to know more about is this prospect—fantasy?—reverie?—plan —for your Montenegro to move to Cali. Which would be insane, incredible, impermissible, fulfilling, endangering. What would be gained, and what lost, and what created if the generative distance between you and R. were suddenly to collapse? You seem to take it in stride, to communicate all this with a kind of easy casualness. What, I want to know (always), does Wim think? Things are quiet in my inner life. No sturm, no drang. Not like the apocalyptic scenario you mentioned so offhandedly. But you always did have a stronger stomach for upheaval—or, maybe more accurately, for returning to places where you were ecstatic and endangered.*

And me to him:

*Me voy tanteando hacia la idea de que it might be too great a risk for me to get together with R. Porque you nail it, truly and startlingly, con tu pregunta, arriba. LITTLE EYE: no hubo "easy casualness" in me, BTW, mientras contemplaba—o contemplo—todo esto. This strange, dizzying panoplia de posibilidades raised by Roland's out-of-the-blue invitation to meet him in Nevada. Tan raro, escribir eso. Pero it's true. Creo que quizás what you sensed was that I don't really feel white-rabbity. Capaz I'm coming to accept my unusual capacity to "live with the question" (una de mis fave quotes, from a vastly underrated film,* The New Age, *con Peter Weller y Judy Davis). Abrazar la ambigüedad, in other words, sin el apremio de decidir, adjudicar, tie things up, choose. Hmmm, se me acaba de ocurrir: this also bleeds (jaja) into mis musings on mixedness en estos últimos . . . meses.*

*R. wasn't proposing coming to LIVE in CA, o al menos, not directly. Sin embargo, hasta la idea de renovar nuestra relasie, I mean, in the flesh . . . I'm not certain it would be such a good thing (para mí, digo). Justo por lo que señalas, arriba, in the word "generative." Quiero decir (and it kills me to say this out loud): is it unspeakably selfish of me, el querer honrar lo que me posibilita la escritura? Me refiero a algo en mí que me duele (por weird) pero igual, me constituye: the need for nondomestic ardor, for distance. Even absence.*

*He estado leyendo mi S. African diary again, el de 1983, después de romper con R., beginning my life alone. Get this: yo ya sentía que love and eroticism no se compaginan—at least not comfortably—en mí. I realized even then (solo tenía 26 años) that for most people, esto remite a un "masculine approach" al mundo. Y por ende: there was something unaceptable about it, hasta monstruoso (punishable), en una mujer. Fast forward: por más que (todavía) me cueste articularlo con certeza, I still feel this. Even more strongly, quizás. This is how I'm "wired," al parecer.*

*Mi mayor miedo: going through the looking glass—realizar un conecte in the flesh—me acercaría peligrosamente a la necesidad de elegir. ¿Cuánto amo a Roland? Do I want to "take a chance on love" again? ¿Dónde quiero—o puedo—vivir? Uf, sorry for this telenovela plotline, pero . . . this is my vida. Not sure I want to go there. Demasiado risky. El mayor riesgo para mí es el silencio. I do like—crave—to be in a place where, como dices, me siento "both ecstatic and endangered." Así me siento now; this drives my living, and my writing. Pero the finding out, the confirming. Temo que me destruya. I love danger, simón. Pero no mayhem and destruction. Intento vivir allí mero, right on the edge of that difference.*

*11-xi-09*

*Liefste* OomBata,

Por suerte, R. sent me two emails *gister*. Tiran hacia lo analítico, *maar* I can't blame him. Tal es su naturaleza (analytical, thoughtful, practical), and I *had* been sending him a ton of stuff on race. Uf, pero el vato tarda siiiiglos pa' leer, amid all his *myn besoeke, groot swart hond* petting, su red wine drinking, todas las family *partytjies*, etc. Aunque as you've observed: *never* a mention of any sort of "coupledom." Jamás dice "we" ni alude a la *vrou*. Curious, *nê*. He especially emphazised to me que iba a tomar ese *rooi wyn ALLEEN*. Hmmm . . .

Some *mooi seleksies* from R.'s brief:

*MS. M.!*

*Taken together with the 'colour of skin' excerpt you sent and my Capricorn-ness and my 'whiteness' on an African soil, I conclude that the colour of a person's skin is also 'coloured' by our life experiences and each person's desire to tell their story and to reaffirm their worth in the eyes of humanity. Some call it 'ubuntu,' others call it 'menslikheid.' There must be some common human values that we can all use as the starting point in this quest? Maybe there aren't! Scary thought. Please advise . . . L Msr. M.*

*20-xi-09*

Querido Wimmie,

Este update es adorable. Heartening pero scary as fuck. He sounds so . . . casual about it! ¿Tú crees que realmente venga? What if he does?

*Shug,*

*I can tell you that I'm sparrin' wit that damn mine plan for Hollister, Nevada!! From friggin 06h00—till 22h00 (most nights). It's drivin' me crazy 'cos there are millions of assumptions, numbers, graphs & figures to check before the proposal can be issued. Professional liability, etc., etc. Yawn . . . . . . . . . . . . I know you're bored and pissed off with this pitiful excuse, but I am afraid it's true. Do think of you though (in between working out "stripping ratios," etc., etc.) Know what a stripping ratio is?? I'll show you. ILY RF*

*8-xii-09*

Wimmie,

Loved this:

*I just watched a wonderful song on YouTube called "Staan My By" by the Radio Kalahari Orkes, written by Rian Malan. It is a poetic and musical art-work, an anthem for all of us "bittereinders" (used in the Anglo-Boer war for those who refused to capitulate and acknowledge the English victory) who have decided to stay on in SA to the bitter end. It encapsulates so much of Rock bitterness, loss, and passion for this country that I just wept and wept. PLEASE watch it ASAP and tell me what you think. Rian is also in the video, looking quite groovy if a bit dilapidated. I think you will get most of the lyrics, especially "staan my by, my bra."*

Fished it *op* en BoobTube, y lloré un chingo while watching it. *Baie* difficult, captar toda la letra. My written Rock mucho más fuerte, OB-vio. *Natuurlik*, I got the refrain, y otras key bits (about the *bittereinders*). The *feeling* of it . . . . ese feeling me llevó por un time tunnel, patrás a la gente who most embraced me in S. Africa. Vaya ironía: those I'd most come armed to the *tande* to despise (los Rocks) acabaron constituyendo mi propia tribe, en Pretoria (y hasta en Joburg, if you think about it, con el André de Wet y su crowd).

Wimmie: if it hadn't been for Curé (aka our darling Etienne Kapp, QEPD), quien me rescató en la calle de Pretoria when I was so desperately unhappy, on the verge of breaking up with R., ¿qué habría sido de mí? We'll never know. Pero I *do* know one thing for sure: if not for you y nuestra motley tripulación de Alterna-Rocks, yo no sería quien soy, my life wouldn't be the same. Es la mere mere verdad. Not to go all drama queen en tu nalga, pero *dis die waarheid*.

*15-xii-09*

Montenegro,

Un quickie to say I love you and *yebo* vivo cerca, within shouting distance, prácticamente, and mos def within sight of Mt. Baldy. A pesar de los hideous problems que he tenido en el college (more in the early years pero still: I'm an outlier, me consideran una renegade, and this place has tried and tried to wear me down), overall he llegado a la perhaps somewhat startling conclusion de que este dozey provincial college *dorp* en el eastern-most edge of LA county is an OK *plek* for me. *A good disguise, profa*, como dicen mis students.

He aquí tu b-day and Nuwe Jaar *geskenk* all in one. So, sit down (*alleen*, OB-vio), con una copa de tu fave *rooi* and read me.

*24-xii-09*

Montenegro, my *bokkie*,

Last *brief* from me here, for 2009. Tu última carta es hermosa. So *roman-ties*. Glad you read (and loved) your birthday crónica. Pero no, it wouldn't have been the Ventura highway (that's a '70s song!). Esa es la 101 al norte, *uit die* San Fernando Valley. You must've driven out here to Mt. Baldy desde downtown LA por la 10E. Hace 25 años it was much wilder, menos poblado out here. Already beginning to be a suburban sprawl, supongo, pero nothing like Orange County (the horror, the horror). Y ni siquiera ahora es así. Todo dense y beige y cookie-cutter. Out here es diferente. Especially Claremont. Y simón, it is pretty out here. Ya sabes de la flora y fauna, por lo que te cuento en mis carta-crónicas and in my texts: coyotes, hawks, rabbits, the occasional tecolote, my adored colibríes y los muy dreaded mountain lions. Aloes and yucca, salvia, acacia, y hasta jacaranda.

Anygüey, Feliz Navidad. Y feliz cumple, my darling. Text me from Durban, *hoor*.

*1-i-10*

Querido R.,

Estoy sin palabras. What the fuck happened? So relieved que me texteaste ayer, en tu birthday. Pero te tengo mil y una preguntas. Volví del MLA en Philly anoche, tarde. Un día bien spooky: full moon y lunar eclipse. Pero no entiendo, how could your hija be . . . so placid-looking en esa fotie que me mandaste, of her standing in the burnt ruins de su casa, holding los hockey sticks? No me cierra. Por el amor de Dios, how the hell did your ex-wife's house burn DOWN? Suena como cuento de hadas . . . o más bien nightmare. Durban isn't wildfire territory, que yo sepa. Pero wildfire o algún tipo de weird electrical malfunction is the only reason (besides arson?!) que se me ocurre para explicar tal hideous occurrence. Muy *uitgefreek*. Thinking of you.

*5-i-10*

Dearest OomBata,

Se me acaba de ocurrir: do you think R.'s ex-*vrou*'s house was thatch-roofed? I haven't heard from him in a few days. Supongo que estará back home in Joburg, intentando volver a su *delwer-werk*. Pero vaya chingazo de "sorting out" (as he rather vaguely put it en un SMS), *nê*. I still find myself waking up a la mitad de la noche with disquieting images floating around in my brain, de llamas y escombros. El vato es tan y tan emo-*verkrampte*—digo, that matter-of-fact way of presenting it. To me and to you. No es normal, ¿no? How could he not be utterly *uitgefreek*? Por otra parte . . . sigh, ese veneer of capability is very *him*. Y hablando de (veneers) . . . this really rang true:

*I was blown away by the picture of R.'s daughter with her hockey sticks, in the burnt-out ruin of their house. She resembles him, and does look quite calm and serene. Maybe that is due to her parents making her feel safe although this nightmare has happened. Or perhaps, like her papa, she is just very good at masking her feelings to the world. It seems so bizarre and unlikely a thing to happen, almost supernatural!*

Today as I was driving to the health walk escuchaba ese old English Beat CD. Escuchábamos el cassette que la Lee Weiss had sent me, pogo dancing about, wildly, in my almost-furnitureless Pretoria flat, *onthou jy?* The song "I Confess," donde el vato canta: "always searching for paradise / I confess I've ruined three lives / didn't care till I found out that one of them was mine." Stabbed me *in die hart*, my china.

Sospecho que it would *not* end up being a very good idea que acepte esa invite de Roland Meeting him in Nevada, digo. Porque una de dos: either I'll immediately know we should be together o al revés. Y me aterra, either way! Way too risky. Not to mention (*pace* The English Beat): the potential to jack up my current (dizque) vida. Y la de R. con esa never-mentioned *vrou.*

*12-i-10*

Wimmie,

I do take your punto about getting together with Roland (*in die vleis*). Sin embargo, José me escribió esta extremely intrigue and astute *obervasie*. ¿Qué te parece?

*Sobre R., la respuesta de Wim es muy directa (lo cual debes apreciar) y sensata. Los separa todo un océano y un continente, así que la idea de un re-encuentro en vivo y a todo color requiere más que un acto impulsivo. Sería, por así decirlo, un acto muy premeditado y planeado y eso es precisamente lo que mantiene vivo el deseo. Si tuviera que adivinar creo que R. se enamoraría aun más al verte en persona y tú todo lo contrario. Es solo una corazonada . . .*

Perhaps *this* is my deepest fear, after all. No que él se quede disap-pointed in me, sino al revés. Creo que no me atrevo a correr ese riesgo, the loss of my Muso máximo (so imbricated is R. with what drives me, mi escritura: distance, memory, yearning). *Is ek mal,* o te hace (algún) sentido? Has Roland replied to your SMS, BTW? Estoy preocupada. Todo esto del incendio, occurring right before the lunar eclipse en su mero cumpleaños . . . all *te baie* weird. I have a bad feeling.

*13-i-10*

Wimmie,

Mil gracias por esto:

*R. never responded to my SMS, what can be happening in his life? I think José's analysis is perfection, beautifully put. It would be very difficult (considering your present circumstances, and R.'s) if you were to meet and instantly confirm that you had to spend the rest of your life with him, but even more terrible if you were bored or put off by him. Better, I think, to keep him as a muse, a (semi) unobtainable love.*

Estoy cada vez más freeked out. I texted R. myself esta mañana—and *niks.* Le dije, did you drop your fucking cell down a *myn* shaft, ¿o qué? Como me dijiste, how hard could it be, que mande tres palabras, either to you or me? Este extended silencio feels . . . strange. Off. Algo no anda (como dicen en 'Tinolandia). Total air silence desde el 31—his own *verjaarsdag,* coño—when he emailed me so lovingly con esa fotie de la hija, standing there so . . . placidly entre los escombros de su burnt-down house. He sent a loving, sexy text, too! Y el email que me mandó Chrismy Eve was one his most *romantiese.* Me parece aun más poignant now—ahora que ocurrió este desastre en el *plek* que describe tan beautifully, tan bucolically. *Lees:*

*Darling Suzi,*

*I remember driving out of LA a long way—could it have been along Ventura Highway?—and as the countryside got drier and drier, rather like the Karoo, the mountains grew before us. I remember lots of new housing developments that were growing on the flat lands. The town Claremont? I don't remember exactly except that as we got into the canyon leading up to Mt. Baldy everything got a lot prettier than the scrubland.*

*On Saturday I drove down to Durban to spend Xmas with the girls. I am writing to you on a misty day in Crestview with Guineafowls chattering in the background. Crestview is to Durban rather like I imagine Claremont is to LA—higher, cooler and away from the crowds.*

*I have read your birthday crónica and I am sure that each memory sparks off more and more, other memories. It's not that they're forgotten—it's just that we've forgotten to remember them. The crónica is a lovely geskenk and as always it gets better with every reread. Safe travels to Philly, Shug. ILY Msr. M.*

# After the Lightning
I

*14-i-10*

Dearest Wimmie,

It's so invisible linksy (de un modo oscuro, horrible) that I should receive this email de R. esta mañana. I was rereading my giraffe diary anoche (you know the one, el de 1983, de S. Africa, en el . . . después). Me sentía bien unsettled, twilight sleep, all night. I couldn't even tell where I was exactly, si aquí o allá, now or . . . back then. Difícil explicarlo. Pero you know I've had an awful feeling of foreboding estas dos semanas: what did that New Year's Eve eclipse trigger, ¿qué es lo que alegorizó—y detonó— ese house fire?

*Shug,*

*I have received your SMS & emails. In one email you mentioned lightning— well, I have had a personal lightning strike. For whatever reason N. saw your SMS sent via Wim and the results were not pretty. We can't (I can't) communicate with you any longer. Only option is snail mail—back to where we began! RF*

OomBie, tú sabes que in *all* his letters, Roland never mentioned his wife. Ni una puta vez. He was *so* ardent, de hecho, que me acuerdo que en una you even asked me whether he was actually married. What did you say, BTW, en ese text que le mandaste? Was it *that* . . . intense? No puedo creer que le hayas mandado algo dange. Pero then again, what does that even mean—peligroso—a estas alturas? Casi todos mis texts (y OJO, his to me)—right from the get-go, desde 2008—han sido over-the-top. Declaraciones de amor, swooningly erotic, raunchy, and hot. So, why *now*? *Ag,* nada de esto tiene sentido. He *never* told me to *passop.* Al contrario. Look. Exactly three months ago, R. me mandó esto:

*Shug, mi bebe,*

*I take it you're not that enamoured of Nevada for various reasons. You will be even less enamoured when I tell you that not only does my next project come from there—the deadlines are sooo tight that I have been working on it 24/7.*

*I was complaining about too little work—now I've almost got too much. Anyway, my correspondencia will be a little too short and, I guess, a little too terse for your liking until I get this stuff finished. I am not purposefully stretching your patience and I do read all that you send me with joy and sadness and happiness. Please don't take a vow of silencio or of celebicio! Because you know that I would like to do all the things to you and with you that your heart desires. If not in Nevada, then where? Salt Lake City?? ILY RF*

OJO: Sin lugar a dudas, he's been channeling himself—y todos sus recursos—into this Nevada job. You tell me, pero me parece que the *only* reason he'd suddenly seek work in the US sería por mí. He implored me (repeatedly) to be patient, me pidió que no dejara de escribirle, de amarle. Se me ocurre que his daughters' house burning down served as some kind of allegorical "warning" to him. De la noche a la mañana le sobrevino un guilt attack. About his Nevada "*werk*" plans. Y sobre todo: about the unruly passion que motivaba esos planes. Don't you think?

Yo sospecho, Wimmie, que he even *let* la Nora see your (harmless, as you said) text. And her seeing it, su outrage "did the dirty work." No entiendo su outrage (me parece disproportionate), pero . . . it's clear she hit el techo. Y: su reacción le habrá obligado a R. . . . pues a esto. A poner un límite. Completely *uit die blou*, tajante, repentino. Ironically, lo que Roland no sabe es que I *myself* would've contained his freefall. I'm sure he assumed I'd be ready to jump, cuando me propuso lo del rendezvous en Nevada. Pero, tú sabes que I've had my doubts, right from the get-go. Lo platiqué con José, too. Y el mismo R. lo entendía (and was *not* happy about it): mira su—frustrated—mention of Salt Lake City.

*Ag nee*, man, Wimmie, the lightning strike was *me*. The oke spooked *himself* con la fuerza de sus propios feelings. Uncannily, just like in 1982! Pero al parecer, ni tiene las agallas (to be polite) ni las emo-skills—even *now*, our second time around, 28 years later—como para reconocerlo. Fucking grotesque, *ek sê*. And what up con las insane ambiguities en su email de hoy? ¿Qué hace esa ridícula final (contradictory) sentence, sino sugerir que I *keep* writing him (via caracol, *nogal*)? "Where we began" . . . WTF?

En casa

19-i-10

Hi Wimmie,

Gracias por leerme, y por esta hermosa reply:

*Dearest Soekie,*

*I am reeling with shock about these latest developments, can't imagine how you must be feeling! A horrible mixture of anger, irritation, disappointment, and sadness well up in me. How did all of this unfold? How could her seeing that SMS have led her to read your correspondence? I can only imagine that Roland had some sort of guilt-meltdown, probably precipitated by the fire and his feelings for you raging out of control. He probably couldn't manage to just gloss over the SMS because of this and confessed, showing her everything. She reacted in what I see as a normal way, demanding that he cut off all communication with you. He then tried for the drastic ending, but couldn't manage it, asking you to revert to snail mail. She may or may not have seen that one, but I doubt it. He then wrote a second letter under her supervision, terminating all contact.*

*With this Roland has proven, in my eyes, that he is still the coward he was in 1983, clinging then to the security of his family, his privilege as a white man in South Africa, his country club sporty life. Now he flees back into the security of a "happy" marriage, a northern-suburbs wife, regretful but perhaps relieved not to have to continue to deal with the extreme challenges you represent in so many ways. And yet, he doesn't want to let you go. He manages to leave the door open, longing for you, for the excitement, emotion, the life and true love that lies behind it.*

Como te puedes imaginar, heme aquí, drafting responses to R.'s bombshell. Me ha sobrevenido una avalancha de emociones encontradas: rabia, disbelief, llanto. There's been kind of a . . . progression, supongo. In the end, though, ni la rabia ni la venganza prevalece. Not this time. Me pregunto si estaré loca, I mean, porque siento tal affinity for Madiba's way, for *ubuntu*. Not that I would presume to compare my individual *hartseerheid* (new coinage, para variar) al sufrimiento de las TRC victims. O los 'Tines, por ejemplo, después de la Dirty War. *Maar* (she says now, como jamás habría dicho back then, en mis Little Miss Bolshevik days) no se trata de comparar, de jerarquizar las oppressions and afflictions, ¿o no?

Conmigo, creo que Roland experiences a self that he could not—cannot—con nadie más: intellectual, politically aware, juguetón, tender. Y sobre todo, *erotiese*. Y sin embargo, he's willing to sacrifice this Montenegro self en el altar de "Rand Club Rolo" (as you brilliantly baptized him): lo familiar, la seguridad. And DUTY, quizás su *primum mobile* . . .

Me tienta decirle que I'd been planning to make it easier on him (bueno, on *us*), contarle que hasta contemplaba no ir a verle en Nevada . . . Para mí, the *plek* of our love is less important. Tiene más que ver con . . . el reconocimiento. Con la aceptación de las mixed (are we seeing un motivo recurrente here?), often painful y no obstante (para mí, anyway) productive emotions it stirs up. I'm off to a health walk, bajo un cielo de plomo. Sé que parece una pavada, pero se me hace que we are lucky, me and you. Fully present a nuestras strange, cracked-open, *muti*-full vidas.

22-i-10

Montenegro (or should I say, Rand Club Rolo),

The pain of what you've done has been immense. Ese ridiculous, chick-enshit, ambiguo primer email, seguido del even *more* ridiculous, esposa-dictated one. This last hellish week, apenas me he permitido imaginar que you'd have the balls to pull yourself out of your tailspin and write me. Digo, *really* write, not some robotic, scripted *kak*. De hecho, casi me había resignado a la narrative de que you are *exactly* the same emo-coward as you were in 1982. Casi, pero not quite. Porque me dije, he has changed, he *must* have: si no, you would not love him (de nuevo). (Y)our correspondence is the proof. Y tu carta de ayer, flustered and self-protective as it is, es también la prueba.

An allegory-worthy incendio has swept through your life. Pero OJO: tú sabes que yo fui—I am—the "lightning strike" in your vida. No que la N. viera some innocuous text from Wim about me. I am (según me pediste) sending you a snail al despacho. For now, sigue este intertexto.

*Dear Shug,*

*I have failed to convince Nora that we were exploring the past—but in the present.*

OB-vio que no te cree—porque it ain't true! I wrote that *kak* (mintiendo sobre el "context" de nuestra renewed *relasie*), pa' cubrirte las nalgas. I knew full well que la N. would read it. Te di un fucking script, carnal. Confieso que es medio . . . touching que no seas un practiced philanderer, que tu default "cool hand Luke" persona cracked cuando la N. confonted you about Wim's text. OB-vio, tu panicked *reaksie* refleja tu guilt. E irónicamente (para *doble* Capricornio *nogal*), your inability to compartmentalize or control your feelings.

*In the heat of her anger I said that you knew that I was married to her. I said that neither you nor I were having or planning to have an affair—that our correspondence then (and revisited now) is the catalyst for your latest writing.*

That's rich . . . .

*So here's the rub. I told her that I didn't say that I love you. I simply can't say I did. English has only one word for love—there is no gradation.*

Montenegro, me dijiste que me amas, because you do. Y punto. OB-vio you can't admit you told me that—ni mucho menos que that's what you *feel*—a tu wife. Pero, ¿cómo coño te atreves a escribirme—to *me*, of all people—that Engels o cualquier lengua has only one word for love? That is *sommer kak*. Pero el matrimonio (any conventional relationship) no autoriza feelings of love or desire para otra persona. *There's* the fucking rub, *meneer*.

*I don't want to lose you and I don't want to lose what N. and I have now. If I may be so bold, could I suggest a shorter text that I can forward to N.? The possibility exists that she may wish to correspond directly if I forward your words to her. I understand that you may not be willing to proceed down this path.*

You know me well enough by now como para saber que en la puta vida estaré in touch with your wife. Y en todo caso, why should the woman (women?) in your life do your emo-*werk* for you?

*She did say that if our correspondence was innocent, why did I not tell her about it in the beginning?*

You know why.

*I am trying to convince N. that our relationship (yours and mine) is innocent and does not represent an attack or deceit upon what we (me & N.) have built up these last 13 yrs or so.*

Well, good luck with that. Porque si hubiese sido así (an "innocent"—*of vriendelike*—correspondence), you'd have had no problem dissimulating

cuando ella vio ese SMS de Wim. You could've said (deberías haber dicho),
—*Oh, this is from my former guhlfriend from the US, we've kept in touch over
the years, she was just worried about me and my family after the house fire.* Lo
cual, ironically, is true-ish. Why the fuck *didn't* you just say that? Porque
me amas.

And about your request (que te escriba algo "shorter," pa' mandarle a la
N.)? *Jy's mal:* como te dije, I won't do your bloody dirty *werk!*

## 25-i-10

Montenegro,

Vaya alivio hablar contigo hoy, from my *kantoor.* Looking out the window mientras hablábamos, listening to your voice, low and urgent, mientras
miraba hacia un snow-capped Mt. Baldy. Me sorpendió conseguirte. Era
pasada la mediaoche, your time, wasn't it? I love you too.

## 4-ii-10

Montenegro,

Tu silencio me friqueá. Did you forward my "serviceable" email to
N.? ¿Piensas en mí? How could you not be writing me en estos cold, dark
early February days que nos significan tanto? En este día, 28 years ago,
you turned that Dodge van around, pulled by a tidal lure (¿o relámpago?),
dragging your semi-incredulous, probably grouchy amigos *terug*, patrás a
San Francisco. Back to me.

Heme aquí, writing you, como me pediste. In one gorgeous, poignant
voicemail que guardo en el cell; hasta en ese stupid first email, de hace un
par de semanas, cuando me dijiste que la N. had seen some random SMS,
you *still* asked me to keep writing to you. Next week, estaré de vuelta en
nuestra city, *ons hart plek.* New Orleans.

Wim wrote me que le robaron el cell, right out of his house. Un teenager
que pertenece a un youth prayer group que él supervisa en Manenberg.
Montenegro, I'm worried about Wim. Y por ti. I wish you were elsewhere.
Closer. Working at some mine, or . . . Muchas veces rebobino. I wish we'd
been able to make a life. Somewhere. En alguna parte *otra*. Ya sé, ya sé:

you are (S'th) Effrican. Que tus hijas. *Jou werk.* Your ma (más que nada ella, *miskien*). You belong there. But I (also) belong with you. Y tú me perteneces.

15-ii-10

Montenegro,

Back late last night—a zillion e-machos en mi inbox. Pero not one of them from you. Record-breaking cold in New Orleans! A grim, sleeting rain los dos primeros días que cedió a ese milky southern midwinter sun el sábado y domingo. Mardi Gras (mañana) vino early en este Year of the Tiger, a week earlier than when we were there, en 1982. Todo, pero everything in that city me hace acordar de ti. Driving up St. Charles, recordaba cuando hicimos ese antebellum recorrido por primera vez, rubber-necking *uit die vensters* del Dodge van as we passed mansion after mansion, y todos esos incongruously glittering, bead-strewn trees. *Onthou jy?* We were on our way to some silly Tulane rugby game! Y ni hablar el Quarter. Allí, no hay nook 'n' cranny que no me remita a ti. My 15th time in New Orleans y todavía te siento aquí.

Vimos el Endymion parade (you and I missed it, *onthou jy?*) la noche del sábado, in mid-City. Pretty rowdy! Y la amiga de Miss Elaine, Michelle (a local parole officer), nos llevó al Lower 9th Ward. La devastación es palpable, still. Almost 5 years after Katrina (yo estaba en Cape Town cuando el hurricane, weird, *nê*). Muchos empty fields filled with low scrubby grass, de vez en cuando una foundation, unas cuantas vine-covered shells of houses, varias incongruous, bargelike, PoMo "eco" homes, sponsored por esa foundation del Brad Pitt. Well intentioned, pero kinda ridiculous. En un campo desolado, a lone white heron turned its orange-beaked profile and took flight, *whoosh*, hacia el río.

La Katrina destruction me puso en un mood sombrío. Y las faux-tanned Britney Spears clones and drunk, hulking Floridian frat boys (median age 20) didn't really do it for me either. I don't remember it being like that cuando estuvimos. Was it? Por otra parte, I don't reckon we'd have noticed: todo, todo infundido de nuestra private radiance. Todo nos parecía beautiful, mysterious, *exotiese*. Casi nos follábamos en la calle, *onthou jy*, pressing up against any wall, twining round each other in Pat O'Brien's, en el Riverwalk, on lower Bourbon Street.

Montenegro, my love. Feb. 18th is a Thursday again: el mismo día que concebimos nuestro little zygote in Houston, the crushing memory of which I'd suppressed for years, hasta que mi sojourn en el Montalvian Emerald Forest took me—shook me—right down to my foundations y lo desenterró.

Escuché un poco de ese famous cassette, BTW, of "The Last Night" (as we called it then). Damn, eras un cocky hijoesumaire at the time (pero con la voz más sexy del planeta). And I loved you anyway (or because of?). Your silence wounds me. Intuyo que you're doing some kind of . . . penance con la N. She whose name you didn't mention, ni una sola vez, en año y medio de impassioned letters, texts, phone calls. Capaz she's keeping a close eye on you, capaz you're keeping a close eye on yourself. Sé algo de tu Capricorn penchant for guilt. Y, sobre todo, for propriety. Pero, I also know your heart. Me pediste que no dejara de escribirte, and I haven't. Pero ese request sugiere que letters back are forthcoming . . .

26-ii-10

Montenegro,
One month of "total silence" from you. Bitter little risilla. Porque estas eran las mismísimas palabras que decretaste once upon a time, en un stage whisper, en muy otro context. HiLEH-rious, poignant, remember? Cuando los landlords en Chestnut Street, los Forte, were banging on the ceiling con su broom to hush our too-enthusiastic "Last Night" revelries.

Something is going on inside you, lo intuyo. I sense a struggle, entre tu emo-self y tu Bok Boytjie penchant for boundaries, duty, convention. ¿Tengo razón? So much of you (si bien no todo) is about containment. You contain *me* in fundamental ways, aunque no podia ver—ni apreciar—esto en S. Africa.

Ahora, después de tus horrid, completely unexpected and uncalled-for e-machos de mid-January, yo estaba a punto de resignarme. Ready to relinquish you in total disgust, rendirme ante la evidencia de tu cowardice. Release you to absolute containment. Y de hecho, me parece que this *is* where you "belong"—most of the time. Digo, en el diario a diario. La Gran Costumbre (*pace* Cortázar). But then you wrote me, y te me disculpaste. Hasta encontraste las agallas—y la elocuencia—para articular otra versión del amor. Deeper, more nuanced than I'd have expected, dado tu huffy, *uitgefreek* and *histeries* mind-set. Por eso tu silencio, now, es tan frustrating.

Como te escribí en el caracol (mailed to your *kantoor*, per your request): I'm not interested in permanently taking you away from your daughters, ni de tu país. Ni siquiera—much as it lacerates me to write this—de tu *vrou*. Weird, *ek weet*. Pero es verdad. Nor am I interested (en un "real life" sense) in uprooting myself de mi propia vida, de mi lugar en el mundo. Been there, done that (bitter little jaja). Me imagino que te costará entenderme. *Maar* te escribo esto aquí, ahora, because of the way I love you now.

Y sin embargo, sé que nos encontramos, que I was put in your life (twice, *nogal*) to embody for you, para mostrarte algo . . . más allá. Algo más allá de la contención, something else, something *more*. Nos pertenecemos. We are—en un nivel primordial—essential to one another.

*16-iii-10*

Rolo,

Las cosas han estado tan *kak* at my work que I haven't even been able to focus on the fact of my book's release. Y *natuurlik*, también está . . . esto. No puedo creer que me hayas escrito—right from the get-go—con ese casi shocking level of intimacy. Digo, considering your generally *verkrampte* fall-back mode. For a year and a half, y de repente, puf: *niks*.

My life (si bien mos def no la chamba) is mostly good. California is going broke; han congelado mi salary y mi hijo no tiene clue what he wants to do with his life. Pero hay colibríes and small skittering mini-legavaans all over the show, hay snow-capped peaks y los tortilla-scented plum trees florecen. And in about 6 weeks estaré libre, pa' enfocarme en mi writing. Y más que nada: cuando nos conocimos yo soñaba con ser escritora, and I have become one. Este libro (whose pages bear the secret, coded imprint of your body, your laugh, nuestro amor, my anger, el llanto amargo, our yearning, our forgiveness, nuestra unbroken connection), is hatched now, out en el mundo.

Montenegro: *dis so baie* strange, difficult and wrenching, sometimes, to "be" in two places at once (aun cuando uno es mostly a heart-*plek*, conjured by our words). Creo que esta dislocation es más natural para mí. Bueno, OB-vio. Y sin embargo, you went there. Habitaste este in-between place with me, hasta me retaste when I called you emo-laconic, *verkrampte* y un emo-cobarde. Don't be such an asshole! *Skryf, hoor.*

*31-iii-10*

R.,

Me pregunto dónde estás, down there en tu hemisferio, as autumn takes hold of the highveld. I wonder if you're sodo-mining en alguna parte (somewhere *not* Nevada . . . supongo), deploying ese soft-blasting Regalo thingie que inventaste. Me pregunto si piensas en mí *elke dag* (no obstante domestic injunctions to the contrary), as I do you.

*Ja*, soft blasts. Except for this one: la inmensa falla you've blasted open between us estas últimas semanas. Por tu fucking emo-cowardice. Disguised to yourself, quizás, como moral rectitude. Pero you ain't fooling me, *bokkie*. Tu silencio (per la N.'s edict) puede ser "the right thing to do" en cuanto a la Gran Costumbre. *Maar* hay otros moral imperatives, whether you (currently) acknowledge them or not. There's another place you hunger to be. Y tú lo sabes.

*15-v-10*

Montenegro,

Hoy día, looking for an address, scrolling around mis e-macho carpetas medio randomly, encontré emails de ti. From 2003. I'd written you, según, y te mandé foties, a la casa de tus *ouers*. You emailed me a massive, hella *lank antwoord*! Un huge update de como la A. te había divorciado, de tu remarriage con la N.—tu "varsity friend" from Wits, me escribiste. You told me about your hijas, de como vivían en Durban con tu ex-wife y su new husband. The one she'd left you for. You were *not* happy con este arreglo, leí entre líneas.

Por lo que me escribiste, I must've written you de los problemas con el Juvenil (Etienne, mi hijo). They were off the charts para entonces, and you were empathetic. We'd been out of touch for a few years, parece, antes de retomar el hilo en 2002. El mero año cuando te casaste con la N. (Hmmm . . . odd?), after living together "for a long time," me escribiste. Fittingly (ya sabes: no creo en la casualidad), me contaste que tu hermana la Shirlie (my former Little Girl) had just been asking you about me, y de Etienne. Se me había olvidado, completely, de que she'd visited us when he was a baby, cuando yo estaba en la UC–Davis.

En abril de 2003, cuando me escribiste, I was headed to Madrid, donde daría la primera international performance de mis crónicas. Jaja, I must've invited you for a rendezvous (I *would've* done that!), porque me explicabas que Madrid would be a bit difficult . . . After years of working for "luxury safari camps" (as a wilderness guide? As *what*, me pregunto), me contabas que you'd recently returned to mining. Funny: recuerdo que jamás se me había ocurrido que hicieras otra cosa. I admit, the idea of you as a *delwer* still seems—o ahora más que nunca—completely fitting to me. Según tu letter, ahora trabajabas en una "entrepreneurial capacity." *Vertaling*: you were working your nalgas off y estabas bien broke. En agosto de 2003 you wrote me again, cuando te conté que había muerto mi mom:

*Dearest Chávez,*

*I am very sorry to learn that your mother has gone. It is no salve, but it brought back to me a sunny day in SF when you and I enjoyed a lunch with both your mum and dad in Chinatown. My clearest memory of both your parents is that lunch and that is how I will always remember them. May they both rest together now and always. With Love, RF*

Ese email (it *was* a salve) landed up in a SPAM folder, ni idea cómo, pero somehow I *vissed* it out. Y luego, only intermittencies for the next few years, hasta, bueno, you know hasta cuando. Nothing, *nothing* could've prepared me for the intensity of your response, en mayo de 2008. Ni para lo que pasó entre nosotros, over the next year and a half. Nada excepto . . . el (recovered) recuerdo de nuestro comienzo. Y nada, tampoco—tras ese passionate interludio—podría haberme preparado para ese repentino, brutal withdrawal en enero. Nothing, that is, salvo este *otro* recuerdo incómodo, vestigial: sickeningly similar, familiar feelings inside me, cuando me tuve que encarar con la realidad de tus self-protective, emo-*verkrampte* ways once you'd reeled me in, una vez que me tuviste en tu turf, en Joburg. Somehow, lograste desprenderte de este fallback mode en 1983, cuando me pediste que me case contigo. Pero by then it felt too little too late. Especially tras el mythical San Francisco and New Orleans comienzo. This is *still*, Montenegro, hasta ahora (hasta en este raro, insólito, segundo . . . después), el amor de mi vida.

I allowed myself to hope—hasta creer—que habías cambiado. Y de hecho, you had. You *have*. Te me abriste un chingo más—in this current iteration or avatar of you—que lo que jamás te atrevías a hacer la primera vez. Simón, you were (still) lacónico. Pero al menos you recognized—y hasta te burlabas—de esta quality in yourself. Y por eso tu cowardly silence now (por más que lo intentes disfrazar de propriety) me confunde y me enfurece. And yet it shouldn't, capaz. I was in *such* agony in late '82, early '83. Ni sé bien a bien cómo sobreviví esos early months en South Africa. Y esa angustia, esa sensación de emotional betrayal es el único modo de explicar—if not excuse—lo que te hice. How I left you.

Ah, pero I too am different now. Less Manichaean, más paciente. Mucho más, la verdad. And more realistic, aunque no lo parezca, *miskien*. To wit, my unorthodox superpower: vivir con un alto nivel de ambigüedad.

23-vi-10

Montenegro,

Si esto te llega: hay Full Moon lunar eclipse en tu signo el 26. I've been in *diep* communion con Wim. Este verano (*winter vir julle*) será la primera vez, desde . . . 2005 sin extended annual *besoek*, and I'm already missing him. El otro día, fishing though my archivos (one of my fave passtimes, como sabes), I came across a letter he wrote me el 9 de julio de 2005. Era el día antes de la muerte de mi Granny Eunice (Chávez). Le había mandado mi "In My Country Crónica" (got me thinking of you, el proceso de escribir). Un par de semanas después I'd return to S. Africa for the first time since I'd left, justo antes de tu cumple, en 1984. Wim's letter tan moving, tan prescient. Hasta escribe la palabra *Ubuntu*! I had no memory of this letter, *natuurlik*, cuando elegí el título, hace poco, de mi book-in-progress: *Our Ubuntu, Montenegro: Del Balboa Cafe al Apartheid and Back*:

*Cara Susana,*

*I am praying for your Granny Chávez . . . I hope that they can restore her to health. The London bombs seem surreal, like a movie again, just like 9/11. Thank you for the crónica. Of course, it made me cry. I love the book [Antjie Krog's* The country of my skull*] and therefore decided not to see the film. The title is a bad translation of an Afrikaans sentiment. I think that country of my bones or skeleton would have been a better expression, but nou ja, she's an Afrikaner writing in English this time.*

*I have grown to like the title because it expresses my own profound connection to this mad place, something that is embedded in my skull too. I love you so much for your tears and reaction. You came here as a woman with powerful convictions and tried to live according to them, a heroic effort, but Africa always triumphs over our preconceptions. You didn't do anything wrong, you challenged us in our entrenched lifestyles and that was a good thing, especially then when there was nothing to shake us awake sotto il volcano. Your advent in my life was an awakening to conscience that changed my whole being.*

*We were all living as best we could and you couldn't be expected to react differently . . . if you had stayed, you would regret that (as I sometimes do). The most important thing is that you really connected to this country. It entered your bloodstream and your heart so that you are still part of it now. Come and see what has happened, come and see ubuntu (imperfect and flawed) instead of smoking ruins and stacked skulls. And know that in your own way you contributed to what has happened by coming here, living here, and loving us all.*

*Remember how you asked a black lady at the door of your flat whether her collection (ostensibly for a church) was going to the ANC and when she said no you refused to give her any money!!*

*I am also dreaming of your visit every few nights and of Joey, laughing with us and listening to township music.*

8-viii-10

R.,

He estado struggling these past months (well, todo 2010 en realidad), with such a conflicting brew of emotions, para intentar entender y simón, even to forgive your actions. Pero siempre vuelvo a esto: how *could* you just . . . fall silent? No solo the *way* you did (tan ugly, tan cowardly), sino—given the nature of our relationship—at all. Is it because I left you, once upon a time, hace tantos años? Pero eso no me tiene sentido: you exhibited no anger, cero deseo de revancha, no recrimination, *niks*, desde que te escribí en 2008, from Montalvo. And never since then. And your last words to me (por teléfono, el 24 de enero)? —*I love you, Shug*. Entonces, *hoekom*?

¿Por qué este going underground, especially after Rip van Winkle—como tú mismo te apodaste—was awakened by Sleeping Beauty's beso? Y en un sentido mayor, ¿qué significa (para la overarching narrative of our lives) nuestra reconnection, nuestro renovado amor? Este es el temita (jaja) que me preocupa: mi tarea (como ser humano, como escritora) es explorarlo, as fearlessly as I can.

# After the Lightning
## II

9-ix-10

Mnr. M.,

   ¿Dónde coño estás? Can you not defy domestic edicts, cambiar tu stoic and dutiful (and guilty) heart for that other one, el que era—es—mío? Anyway, ¿te acuerdas del lightning strike que hablamos (when your daughters' Durban home burnt down)? Bueno, now I've had my own: I've asked Pierre (quien ha compartido mi casa 17 años) to move out. Las razones, OB-vio, son muchas y . . . it's complicated (trillado as that sounds). Esto lleva gestándose muuuchos años. Or, quizás no sea tan complicated. Maybe it comes down to this: es una persona twisted, abusive. No exagero: he used that very word about himself en una dizque apology letter que me escribió en Buenos Aires, *kan jy dit glo?* Nine years ago! Pero apparently, I didn't fully "see" it hasta ahora. Algo pasó (es banal y anecdótico and I'll spare you los detalles) and I finally saw clearly—and reacted. *Finally.* En todo caso, digamos que mi writing—the fact of it y (a partir de mi second *boekie*, which I mailed to you) el contenido, too—has been a factor. No me arrepiento. And I won't—can't—give up my writing. Es mi lifeblood.

   Anygüey, quite by serendipity (ya conoces mis feelings on la casuali-dad) I opened a small cabinet in the garage hace unos días. One of those old wood cabinets que le decíamos las rabbit cages in SF, *onthou jy?* And out tumbled a cache of cartas, diarios, etc. Stuff from right before South Africa, durante y hasta years later. Rolo Babee, ¡yo no había abierto esa rabbit hole/ruby slipper-click en 15 o 20 años, I promise you! Pero the timing is oddly apt: everything's unraveling, las cosas están falling apart, y ahora me toca rehacerlo. Rehacerme. Like after an earthquake (para usar una Califas image) or a lightning strike (en tu tierra). Créeme, it's tremendously un-settling, pero . . . you know me. I'm managing to roll with los truenos.

Encontré amazing letters from you de los late '80s and early '90s, en los death throes del apartheid. Y hasta foties que me mandaste *uit* Namibia *en* Cullinan, *nogal.* Vaya kick-nalga corresponsal que eras, Rolo. Eloquent testament to a deep bond, un amor duradero. Even in the face of your *first* wife's celos y apprehension. She'd "intercepted" our correspondence! Sound familiar? Déjà vu, much? Anygüey, en una carta te me disculpabas por el lapse in contact, y escribiste que in the face of la A.'s *probleem* (ejém), you'd "gone underground" for a while. I promise you, your exact words. Me escribiste que you were now "surfacing," impelled by an intimacy difícil de definir o poner en palabras, forged in the Balboa Cafe almost a decade earlier. Una intimidad que había sobrevivido—despite what you called, bien quaintly, "inclement weather." Ah, Montenegro, surface again. Our love was—is—the most passionate, palpable thing I've ever known. Y sé que para ti es lo mismo.

¿Te acuerdas que follamos en el Vasbyt van, y en ese walk-in closet in Chicago, solo días después del miscarriage? In our last hours together en mi país, against all common sense, and much to the consternation de nuestros compinches (el Ken, el Du Preez, Miss Zooloo). We could not *not* make love. Heme aquí de repente, pierced por el recuerdo—visceral, olfactive—de nuestros cuerpos tristes pero deseantes, entrelazados. I remember now, suddenly: habernos dormido (when we finally fell asleep for a bit, esa much-needed winter's siesta). Despertarnos desorientados en esa late afternoon fading Midwestern light, tan cruel y snow-dim después de las lush New Orleans skies under which we'd peacocked our love, just that morning. Nos pareció criminal, I remember. Oh, Rolo.

También encontré esa letter que les mandé a mis *ouers*, in February 1983, donde intentaba explicarles por qué. Why I had to leave you. En cuanto vi esa more than 25-year-old UNISA stationery, las typed pages, me aplatanó todo el long-buried impacto de esa letter. Me caí al hot dusty garage floor y lloré. La carta es clear-eyed, pero rebosante de frustración y dolor. You loved me, les explicaba. Even after what I'd done. Y sin embargo you could *not* take a stance—to mitigate (ni siquiera encararte, head-on) ese intractable disconnect entre tu mujer y tu mundo. Yo era tu foreign, wild, intellectual, politicized love. —*You are the most fascinating woman I've ever known*, me habías dicho. ¿Y tú? Head Boy en Michaelhouse, ese tony English boys' prep school en Natal. Scion of Bedfordview. Top mining engineering student en Wits. El black Mercedes y el Rand Club y todos los demás perks all lined up, waiting for you.

Yo le caía bien a tu pa; tus hermanitas las twins were wild about me. Pero your ma, oh, I did a helluva lot more than "unsettle" her, Montenegro, seamos honestos. Esa *verkrampte* Scottish prig no creía que I'd make an appropriate wife for you, hey? Hasta con mi Harvard degree, y todo. Le aterraba la idea de que I might somehow derail your brilliant career. Pero su peor miedo era que te secuestrara, spirit you off to the States. *Yebo*, tu ma hizo todo lo posible para separarnos. And you stood by, Rolo. You let me go. Bueno, I'm still here.

*22-xi-10*

Montenegro,

Last year at this time me escribías passionately. Proponías venir a trabajar a los States. Habías conseguido chamba en la Hollister mine in Nevada, *nogal*. OJO: *you* dreamed up this plan yourself, to my shock—yo no tuve nada que ver. *You* were champing at the bit for us to be together, hasta a bit *uitgefreek* cuando te propuse que nos viéramos en otra parte, *anywhere* else but that windblown and homophobic Califas-adjacent estado. Somewhere like New Orleans, te dije. Anyweg, está claro (*ahora* está claro) que you spooked yourself. Pero all this was before the Cold Seisoen: antes del house fire, before you "let" your *vrou* find that—entirely innocuous—text de Wim en tu cell. El que no hayas podido explain away ni siquiera un harmless text como ese me parece bizarre hasta más no poder. Y luego, since late January, tu silencio.

Meanwhile, Roland, I've been through my own terremoto this year. Tiene que ver contigo, and yet it also doesn't. Pierre's trip to New Zealand en agosto, pa' visitar a su sister (su único viaje sin mí—in 17 years) precipitated a break with reality. Su desorden came to light in such a bizarre, violent way que I could no longer ignore or rationalize it. Or live with it.

Fíjate, Rolo, I'd almost become . . . another person los años que viví con él: cowed, dimmed, somehow, siempre pussyfooting around, trying not to "set him off." Ya sé que this strains credibility, for you who knows me from before "the Great Settling," as Wim calls my years with Pierre. *Maar* notice, dije *almost* (que *casi* me transformé en otra persona). Porque con mi book this year, *Scenes from la Cuenca de Los Angeles*, I effectively wrote him out of my life, aunque no me daba cuenta (consciously) mientras escribía. Pero rereading my book now, it's shockingly obvious. Y muchos readers han confirmado este insight.

23-xii-10

Mr. M., *my liefie*,

Por los strange, invisible linksy twists of fate que gobiernan mi vida, resulta que una amiga, Sandy Briggs (alumna of Pomona College, egresó en los '60s) y su husband, Peter, were graduate school friends de los Biehl (los padres de la Amy). No me acuerdo, or not exactly—details are fuzzy— how this connection came to light, pero I *can* tell you this: at *precisely* the same moment I learned this en un email de la Sandy, Wim conocía a Linda Biehl en Cape Town. Esto fue last week: ella visitó su parish in Manenberg, and then le invitó a una *partytjie* for la Amy Biehl Foundation. None of this would be happening, Montenegro—esta perfect tormenta of invisible links entre California and S. Africa—had you not sauntered by la vitrina del Balboa Cafe on that wintry San Francisco Thursday night hace tantos años. Y si yo no me hubiese lanzado, thrown myself off the cliff that was my vida (mi Bay Area disco girl/punk rocker crossed with wannabe Sandinista, semi-stalled grad student vida) and followed you to S. Africa. *Ag, my bokkie*, I would've followed you al fin de la tierra . . .

Y abrazo ahora—as this bitter, life-altering year draws to a close (en tu *verjaarsdag*)—I embrace, ay tan tenderly, esos nuestros earlier selves. Esos young selves that didn't know how to bend, compromise, wait. Tú eras más patient que yo back than, fo' sho. Y además: you could *see* (us), way farther into the *toekoms*, que yo. Pero to be fair to me, you acted like *such* a prick in Joburg! Way too *verkrampte* for even my passionate, *swart springbokkie* ways to be able to blast you free de esas northern suburb conventions. I didn't know how to GIFT back then. No soft blasts for me. Pero ni tú tampoco, bebé. Anyway, I embrace you now, again, con otro (y el mismo) amor.

*15-i-11*

R.,

Hace un año que me mandaste ese gelid, *vrou*-mandated (dictated?) email about Wim's SMS. A "lightning strike" of your own, me dijiste, and . . . well, you know the rest. You retracted ese *kak* several days later, por teléfono y por e-macho. Que te siga escribiendo, you asked me. Pero what the fuck for? No me cierra. Y ni mus ever since. I have no way of knowing—en el reino de (este) mundo—if you've received anything I've sent you. Debo confiar, I reckon, en las polisémicas posibilidades del silencio.

The new semester begins next Tuesday. Hace un año estuve en New Orleans, for an uncharacteristically (if appropriately?) cold Mardi Gras. New Orleans y San Francisco (aunque ésta, sadly, ever less) so much our cities. Pero New Orleans felt weirdly icy and lonely esta última vez. Sentí agudamente tu absence allí, since I'd been warmed by—come to rely upon—your presence, desde que te me regresaste.

2010, ¡vaya añito! No obstante la publicación de mi *boekie*. And even with my inclusion en la mere mere *Norton Anthology of Latino Literature*, 2010 felt, overall, fraught y banal a la vez. Tu repentina, shocking ausencia *really* fucked me up, my bru, I'm telling you. I fell into a kind of numb lull (en mi daily life, digo), which reached its shocking apex en septiembre. Pero I'm no longer reeling. En vez (como dicen mis Raza students), me estoy sanando. It's painstaking, often painful. My dreams, la escritura, mis amigos—this is the way I get through it. Como siempre.

*7-ii-11*

Montenegro,

Heme aquí, patrás de un writers' conference in Washington, DC. Me daba muuucha flojera ir, pero my friends (y la therapist) thought it would do me good. So I lanced myself, con mi poet friend, Ramón. Te sentí conmigo en un panel on Paul Celan's correspondence con Ilana Shmueli. Su amante, mos def not his *vrou*. ¿Ves? It's a thing, un objeto de estudio: las cartas. The way they wrote to each other me hizo acordar, in a peculiar, piercing way, de nuestras cartas. Then and now.

I've been trying to assuage this strange, bitter loneliness de tu silencio. Strange porque habían pasado dos décadas, coño, since we first loved each other, antes de este fresh burst, este reconocimiento. Bitter, tras tus reiteradas declaraciones de amor y hasta invitations (también reiteradas) to meet you.

Tomorrow, el 8 de febrero, was our dizque "Last Night," 29 years ago. The night we stayed up casi toda la noche hacienda el amor y llorando, *onthou jy?* Esa jangly, tender, coca- y Remy-fueled night. Esa noche que pensamos sería la última. Te rajaste la mañana siguiente, after driving me over to Berkeley, y pensé que that was it, I'd never see you again. Adiós destino, *tot siens*, amor de mi vida. I got *lank* wasted ese día, con Miss Zooloo, I remember. Ella también destrozada, pining for el Sea Lawyer. We smoked and drank everything in sight, y nos atendió, bien patiently, bien indulgent, la Tina. Las Tres Mosqueteras de la Marina. But then you called. And called. Me convocaste. And soon we were *saam*, in the south, nuestro sur. The American south. On the road to New Orleans.

*18-iii-11*

Montenegro,

Hoy, hace 29 años, on a warm, damp Houston morning, nos follamos tan fuerte—y tantas veces—that no amount of "tasteless, colorless, odorless" gel could prevent our little zygote from coming into being. OJO, hay que reconocer que we *were* pretty careless! Pero, was it really carelessness, o más bien al contrario, reckless, stubborn desire? Hace tiempo me escribiste que tu "emo-laconicism is not a terminal condition." Y me dijiste que you want to do and be with me everything I want you to do. So OK, *lekker*. Surface, for fuck's sake.

*7-iii-11*

R.,

Mañana es Mardi Gras. It's late this year. Last year en New Orleans vino antes. Cayó en febrero, just like in 1982. I was driving around the Lower 9th Ward, bajo ese low, leaden Netherlandish sky and unusual chill.

Miraba los Katrina-ruined spaces, esas almost obscenely abundant lianas tropicales que trepaban, growing up over las empty shells of little clap-board homes. Casi todas llevaban pintados unos harrowing, dispassionate hieroglyphs. Shorthand para indicar who or what had been found inside after the storm—una persona, un gato, nadie—and in what condition. Pensaba en ti. It had only been a couple of weeks, yet to me (my impatient ways) ya me parecía eterno tu silence. Pasado mañana: Ash Wednesday. 29 years ago, ese unstaunchable bloodjet. —*Poor little bugger*, dijiste, *gave himself up for Lent*. I cannot—will not—forget again. *En jy?*

*21-ix-11*

Montenegro,

Genius, según Nabokov, es el arte de encontrar el "invisible link" be-tween ostensibly unrelated, disparate things. Bueno pos I reckon I'm off the charts, then, *my bokkie*... Este es mi credo, en la vida y la escritura: to acknowledge, explore, and illuminate estos links. The deepest in my life is the one between you and me. Forged, como me has recordado tantas veces, en el Balboa Cafe en una blustery noche invernal in January 1982.

Y hablando de deep, what's the likelihood de que esto sea "only" a coincidence? En el *Los Angeles Times* hoy leí una larga nota about—now just check this—the once-again booming gold mining industry around... Elko, Nevada. I promise you! Era Hollister, north of Elko, ¿que no? That wild west mining town al que me invitaste, back in fall 2009? Poco antes de cortar, abruptly, nuestras comms. *Ag nee*, man, nada es casual, bebé. So, was it Barrick Gold or Newmont Mining donde conseguiste la chamba? Y: ¿qué onda con esos "mine concept" *plannetjies*?

*3-x-11*
Header: *Bodie, perhaps?*

Rolo,

El header quiere decir: *miskien* en vez de Elko (Hollister) you'd rather be *'n bietjie* closer to our old stomping grounds? En tal caso, the gold-mining boom around the "ghost town" of Bodie, CA, might pique your interest. O capaz las hills of Transylvania, más cerca de nuestras (Monte-negran) ancestral roots? Erase una vez me escribiste (in your dedication of Gordimer's *Burger's Daughter*), —*I know where you live; now transport yourself to where I live.* So, I did. I moved to your country para estar contigo, 29 years ago. And we know how *that* worked out: a spectacular desastre. Especially al considerar nuestro spectacular beginning.

All these years later, Montenegro, ya no te culpo por ese disaster. Or not entirely, aunque you've copped to your down-shutting emo-laconicism, y hasta tu miedo del amor, back then. Pero OJO, I don't blame myself entirely either: my fiery impatience, mi intransigencia ideológica, my pride. Ese orgullo que me hizo rechazar tus apologies (oh, how *interminable* 6 months seemed to my 26-year-old corazón), tu marriage proposal, en 1983.

Como te he dicho, a estas alturas I blame apartheid, mostly. Aunque ese term (loaded, overdetermined, contested) is and isn't just a kind of short-hand. Apartheid: esa soul-squelching, injustice-authorizing, all-pervading racist pesadilla. In nalgavista, these days—ahora que Rip van Winkle y la Sleeping Beauty han despertado—I *specifically* indict its more intimate trickle-down, too. O sea: the outrage, horror, and guilt que experimenté a diario (and projected onto you). Y en tu caso, the Bedfordview privilege y las rutinas que habías sacudido en mi país pero that settled right back upon you like an inherited mantle (or curse), una vez que te habías vuelto a casa. You were too inexperienced, demasiado habituado (¿cómodo?) para recha-zarlo, dice Wim—or even to negotiate with it.

So OK, pero nuestro desastroso breakup *wasn't* "the end" of us. El "continuing link"—que tú mismo has observado (as have *both* your wives) a lo largo de casi 30 años, especially desde 2008—es testimonio. Así que I'm thinking it's only fair that *you* now "transport yourself to where I live." My darling, perhaps *any* tejado we both were to live under 24/7 se volara de todo el heat que generamos (*onthou jy*, my Frida and Diego propuesta). Pero what about a compromise? How 'bout we take turns: *'n bietjie* here, *'n bietjie* there?

Regreso a S. Africa next year, Montenegro. Pero why don't you come see where and how I live, now, por mientras? ¿Te atreves? Se me hace que it's about a 2-hour flight desde LA a Elko, NV, o a Bodie, CA. Or one helluva rock 'n' road trip.

*16-x-11*

R.,

I'm with Nabokov. O sea, I'm all about noticing—and exploring—esos invisible (to most ojos) links. To wit: una breve pero nevertheless front-page *LA Times* article, "Opening into the Past." And especially la fotie que la acompaña, tomada como si fuera from *within* the mysterious Blombos cave, unas 180 millas al este de Cape Town. Esa rara perspectiva—opening out onto a limitless horizon and ocean—parecía interpelarme. This definitely bizarre article (para front-page item in LA) spoke to *me*, directly. *Miskien* el descubrimiento de los "oldest paint containers ever found" has also spoken to you?

Pero hablando de paint: I'm having a bit of a rough time lately. Mi hogar has been lately invaded by painters and contractors—de *muy* variados niveles de competency. Sigh. La casa se va a ver bien different, muy *me, en baie mooi*, soon. Pero at the moment está todo bahtante chaotic. Hideous artefactos de los 17 años con un disordered abuser keep popping up, en los lugares (y momentos) más inesperados.

Leí una gorgeous nota en el *LA Times* yesterday, by Latino writer Héctor Tobar. De la onda en Wall Street, and our own homegrown version, "Occupy LA," Tobar dice: "Art can be like that: a beacon, a celebration of possibility. In California, there are still people who believe in its power." Soy una de ellas. *Kom besoek my, hoor*, ven a ver mi casa. Come see my own private Emerald City, mi "Amazon Moss"-painted study. And most particularly, mi "Evening Blue" *slaapkamer*.

*23-i-12*

Montenegro,

Hoy—5 días antes del 30th anniversary of our meeting en el Club—comienza el Year of the Dragon. Auspicious para nuestro Chinese sign (Chango). We buried our love, alive, in 1983. Lo desenterramos en el Emerald Forest in 2008. —*I don't want to lose you*, me escribiste en enero 2010 (almost two years ago, coño). —*And*, agregaste (casi como afterthought me parecía, and *yet*: este default, esta nonchoice has defined your vida these past two years, para ni mencionar los últimos treinta), *I don't want to lose N.—what we've* built.

"Building" ha sido tu MO these past three decades, ¿que no? Pero el Bok Boytjie Capricornian sure-footedness de tu (former) wilderness-guide persona sure as fuck no se aplica a tu love life. Allí tu doble-capricornio caution, your straight-up *fear* (of vulnerability, of change, of risk—de la emo-*verdad*) reina. No estás enamorado de tu *vrou*. Yet you've capitulated to her. Eres cobarde. And your defeat, tu frustración y resentimiento es visible—en cada (ridiculously undercurated) foto que te he visto, from 2010 on.

No quieres perderme, you say? Y sin embargo, your day-to-day life, tu (in)acción: ¿qué es sino precisamente un concerted effort to lose me—to bury again (y de nuevo, alive)—"what we have"? Wouldn't it be more honest to just cop to your inability to instigate change (por culpabilidad, duty, habit—whatever) *without* capitulating to the silence que la N. te exigió? You may be able to "immure" your feelings (tu palabra), pero eso no quita nada. Más bien al revés. Wouldn't you feel, qué sé sho, más en paz con tu consciencia if you at least *acknowledged* your heart's truth, aun si no puedes vivir de acuerdo con esta verdad?

30 years ago allí estábamos, en el Año del Perro Chinese New Year's parade. Acurrucados en esas magic North Beach streets. The lunar New Year illuminates truth. Y yo aquí, ahora veo claramente que algo en tu daily life made you—*makes* you—renounce or bury ese "otro" you. The *real* you, dicen Wim and Joanna (mi astróloga): bold, intelligent, peleonero (I didn't mind that *ever*, al contrario), funny, cachondo as hell, apasionado. Thirty years of denial and suppression te ha hecho rusty, Rip van Winkle. Pero asleep ain't dead. Despierta, Montenegro. Do it for you. Para nosotros. Aun si este "us" isn't destined to live under the same (norther suburbs) tejado. Te escribo hoy, on Chinese New Year, 30 years into the future de nuestra entonces-nasciente love story. All has not been written.

*28-i-12*

Montengro, amor,

Dondequiera que estés, bush-whacking or soft-blast *geskenking*: I *know* you do not forget, oh, immured one. On that score, checa lo que dice un "ancestro" tuyo, Scottish theologian William Jonas Barkley: "Forgetting is an involuntary act. The more you want to leave something behind you, the more it follows you."

Today, especially, me parece que debemos enfocarnos más bien en la life-changing passion de nuestra early season. The night we met, hace 30 años. Because *everything*, todo lo que te aterraba y confrontaba en S. Africa was—is—*also* el amor de tu vida. Este es el nudo: te permitiste la maravilla, the emotional boldness of love in *my* country, *my bokkie*. *And* in that other, more unheimlich geography: en nuestra correspondencia. First in 1982 y de nuevo durante 2008–9. When that magical, off-the-grid latitude de Montalvo—el vortex, como le decíamos—connected us again. You haven't *lived* there in a long time, Rolo Babee—if ever. Pero dale, no te niegues una return visit. Especially not tonight.

8-ii-12

Montenegro,

Hace un mogollón de tiempo, months and months ago, you implored me not to "fall silent"; me aseguraste de que tu "emo-laconicism" no era terminal condition (con toda la irónica polisemia de esa expresión). Well, WTF? Tu silencio no obstante, I trust that somewhere down there en el *delwer*'s grotto of your immured corazón, you did not forget, yes? Hoy hace 30 años, *presies*, de esa famous "Last Night." Of course, hubo otra *real* "last night" weeks later, en Chicago. Pero el 8 de febrero de 1982 . . . that was the night we knew—*acknowledged*—our love. Y si bien tuvimos muchas otras noches, on balance I'd say *this* night, 30 years ago, fue la más passionate de mi vida.

Lately lloro un chingo, just as I used to hace 30 años. En los días que nos separaban. It's healthy, creo. Me siento electric, crispada, sobrecogida por un profound sense of loss. Este es, precisamente, el trauma que Leslie (mi therapist) says we both buried 29 years ago en S. Africa. Cuando nos perdimos. O nos . . . abandonamos. Pues bien, Rolo: we *began* to excavate all that en 2008. Para mí, ahora, the blinders are off. All bets are off. My jailer (Pierre) is no more. And I'm *not* going to rebury it all solo porque tú hayas vuelto a tu Rip van Winkle *slaap*, skulked back a tu fucking undermundo.

*20-ii-12*

Montenegro,

Today, on this very Monday hace 30 años, we headed due north out of NoLa hacia Chicago, where we'd say our final good-byes (en mi continente). ¿Te acuerdas de ese van ride? Se me hace que you were more open, más raw en ese van ride than *ever* in your life (antes, y mos def, since). Wouldn't you say? Do you remember all the blood? Do you remember us fucking, no obstante la sangre? And talking, murmurando tan urgently mientras nos follábamos. Desnudos, el Ken al volante y el Sea Lawyer ridin' shotgun, tú y yo follando en ese musky, slithery green sleeping bag, ese thin cocoon el único refugio entre nuestros cuerpos y el icy metal del van floor.

Mañana es Mardi Gras. Yesterday, on the Sunday hace 30 años, vimos el Bacchus Parade, *onthou jy?* I still have esas purple commemorative beads you caught for me. Me parece imposible que te hayas olvidado de tales cosas. Sabemos que you've long had a penchant for emo-repression, pero eso no equivale al olvido. Al contrario.

*6-iii-12*

Montenegro,

El archivo histórico constata que hoy—hace 30 años—you left my continent. You left the Montenegro-mundo, donde nuestro amor era posible, and returned to yours. Check this: Wim has lately devised un framework . . . folklórico, o mitológico, for our story. The one we've lived, la que yo ahora me he puesto a escribir. He likens you to the selkies, esas half-seal criaturas of (your ancestral) Scottish lore. ¿Ves? Invisible links deluxe, bebé. Did you ever see that Colin Farrell filum *Ondine*? Or *The Secret of Roan Inish*, de John Sayles? Te darán una idea. Anygüey, los selkies only have *one* true (human) love, pero the lure of their under(water)mundo casi siempre, inevitably, overpowers that love. *Dis baie tragies*, la verdad.

You succumbed. Desde el momento que regresaste al Africa—on this very day hace 30 años—creo que our love was doomed. Aunque we didn't know it yet. Al contrario. Tú me amabas. And I was already set on my course; tú mismo me habías encaminado. You drew me to you to *confirm*, me dijiste (en Pretoria, in our little Sunnyside flat), tus feelings. Tu amor. Something you'd never felt before. Pero si bien no underwater (more like 50 leagues bajo *tierra—in die myne*), una vez patrás en Bedfordview, casi al tiro you began the process of (re)immuring your too-vulnerable heart. Porque apartheid aparte (could it, *can* it ever be?), the deepest, darkest *underwêreld* is of your *own* making: fortressed inside yourself. No estoy loca, remembering, *reinhabiting* our love, a 30 años de su comienzo. Eliot says it best, en su "Little Gidding":

> We shall not cease from exploration
> And the end of all our exploring
> Will be to arrive where we started
> And know the place for the first time.

For me, tú eres el lugar. Te perdono, Montenegro. Y te amo, still. Pero OJO: here, not there.

*5-w-12*

R., my *liefie*,

Más invisible links. Abrí un scholarly journal el otro día (apenitas los leo, these days; my work, como sabes, has taken me in another direction estos últimos 10 años) and was electrified to read, donde el journal se abrió dizque al azar: "What is past is not dead. It is not even past. We cut ourselves off from it; we pretend to be strangers." *Natuurlik*, al instante I recognized el epígraph que había elegido de Faulkner, de *As I Lay Dying*, para encabezar el "Montalvo Diary" chapter. From my last book. Tellingly, mira como Faulkner leaves *off* the last sentence. Y al hacer esto, he transforms Christa Wolf's psychoanalytic *observasie* into something more folksy, más Southern goth, o casi. Pero ahora, it's this *last* sentence, *presies*, la que me interesa más. Cuando leo esta *restored* quote, I'm pierced by memory. And truth. Porque, isn't this *exactly* what you're trying to do? ¿A mí, a nuestro amor?

Estoy convencida de que como dice mi pana el Tinker Salas, te va a salir el tiro por la culata. Porque I'm remembering one of your last letters to me, la de Crestview, on Christmas Eve 2009. Te había mandado la Mt. Baldy crónica, for your *verjaarsdag*. —*It's not that they're forgotten [memories/feelings]*, me dijiste, —*it's just that we've forgotten to remember them.*

So *remember* already (como dijera mi dad).

23-v-12

Montenegro,

Four years ago today (después de que Sarita me recuperó el memory of our little zygote) I emailed you pa' preguntarte si recordabas. Y simón, you did. Pa' mi everlasting shock, it was (all) immediately accessible to you. That and everything else, me escribiste. Also *vandag*: A Wim le confirmaron su transfer to Stellenbosch. Le cambian de Manenberg a Stellenbosch just before my arrival in S. Africa, para asumir el cargo de parish priest of three churches, *nogal*, as well as chaplain to Stellenbosch U. ¿No estudia allí una hija tuya?

There are culture wars deluxe en tu país, I see: la gente toda *uitgefreek* about U'Showa being represented w/ his *jaloga* hanging out en una art gallery! Gang wars, *ook*. Just recently, Wim was *instrumental* in broker-ing a peace entre las two main warring clicas—los Americans y los Hard Livings—en Manenberg, esa colored township en los Cape Flats where he's been living for the last 6 years. All in all, things in S. Africa parece que están hopping: vital, intense—y más que un pelín dangerous. Sound familiar?

I spent hours and hours yesterday releyendo mis cartas a Lee W. (and hers to me). Me las había devuelto years ago, *onthou jy*, pero antes de nuestra *rekonneksie*, I'd never felt compelled to look at them closely. Se quedaron allí, tucked away en un closet, durante mi 100-year *slaap* . . . I also reread esa epic letter, la que encontré hace unos meses en el dizque rabbit cage en el garaje, the one I wrote my parents en febrero de 1983. You know the one. Strange: aunque OB-vio I'd retained the vague outlines of your mother's disapproval of me, te confieso, Rolo, que I'd obliterated some of the *hyperbolically* offensive things she said. *To* me: how bad it looks que los blacks cojan el teléfono en el "lounge" if one's entertaining guests, por ejemplo. And *about* me, too. Tu ma se preocupaba—y se quejaba, quite openly—de que I'd "spoil your career chances" al no ser "the right *sort* of wife." Pero su biggest obsession era que yo te convenciera a rajar, to "*give it all up* and move to America."

Now, leo estas palabras and I see (mostly) FEAR. Miedo de perder su hold on you. And I weep, lentas lágrimas sucias (*pace* Neruda) for the girl I was back then, a los 26 años, cuando tu ma brought down that indictment. I was defiant mos def, pero sobre todo I was *overwhemingly* alone, vulnerable. Can you imagine how I felt, escuchando esas palabras? *You* were my home, Rolo—*my enigste huis*—in Africa. Y ahora tiemblo de frustración retroactiva, de regret. No me cabe en la cabeza que aceptaras, tan passively, el bigoted small-mindedness de tu ma. You allowed *her* to control and determine (y)our future, ¡coño!

Pero por el milagro balsámico del tiempo—and my own contemplative nature, *and* my writing y los insights de Wim y otros crooch friends (not to mention therapy)—ya no siento la scorched-earth rage toward you que sentía entonces. Esa self-righteous rabia que no me permitió tomar en serio tu "anagnorisis" (your word). Cuando me dijiste, a couple of months after I wrote that letter to my parents, que habías tenido un huge breakthrough mientras yo estaba en Londres. Que te habías dado cuenta de que I was right: you *had* put your family, your privileged milieu between us. Que te habías resguardado de la intimidad—de mí, *nogal*, tu amor—weekend after (never-alone) weekend. *Braai* after *braai*. Pero lo veías todo claro ahora. You still loved me, me dijiste. More than ever. Aun después de mi betrayal. You *still* felt that Balboa Cafe spark. And you asked me to marry you. Pero I couldn't hear you anymore by then, Rolo. Un rugido de outrage me llenaba los oídos. Where the fuck was the man I'd fallen in love with hacía solo un año? Why did it take him so long to surface? ¿No veías el daño que me habías hecho?

Desde aquí, ahora, I wish I'd been able to forgive you *then*. Open my heart to you de nuevo. Ay, ojalá no te hubiera tomado esos excruciating 6 months to "come to your senses," as you put it back then. Porque checa where we've landed up *now*: your life the *embodiment* of everything que tu ma mapped out for you desde el momento que naciste. Can you deny it? ¿Estás contento? I can read it in your eyes, *die antwoord*.

And yet: *look* where we are now. Está esa Montalvo-spawned fissure in your foundation. Or a love-*assegai*, *miskien*, cual flecha del mere mere Cupido (versión Zulu), aimed toward the very heart of *our* foundation. It undeniably happened; it is here. No obstante esa ridiculous, trout letter you showed your *vrou*. Y no obstante tu silencio.

27-*vi*-12

Montenegro,

En tres semanas I'll be on your doorstep. *Passop, liefie!* Me han dado una visiting scholar *posisie* en la U. of Cape Town. Pero you know what I'm (really) going for. So clear your calendario. Y OJO: no te estoy hablando de "ir a tomar un café" (the catch-all, multipurpose term for a date en Buenos Aires). Noooo, nuestra marca particular, our comfort zone siempre ha sido horizontal. That always worked for us, no obstante las circunstancias, no matter *die plek*.

*Moenie* scared *wees nie*, ¡coño! My Montenegro sure as shootin' nunca lo estaba. ¿Qué no eras tan "rough, rugged, and independent"? You may be rusty as hell, Rip van Winkle. Tú mismo lo has dicho. Pero like I've said, asleep ain't dead. Wake up. Ya era hora. This is the longest you've spent underground, me parece, since I've known you. No cuento ese hiato— a few years—during your matrimonio #1. Porque LITTLE EYE: yo me rendí al silencio también, back then. Enacting my own version of domestic "bliss." Um, yeah right . . . Pero anygüey, whether I've "unsettled" or even terrified you (no me corto: we're *way* past that, no?), siempre pero siempre has estado mesmerized, in equal measure, by me.

¿Encontrarás el valor? Will you act on your heart's truth? Llego a tu país el 18 de julio, about a month earlier than I did the first time, hace 30 años. Esta vez, I'm going for me. Para ver a mis amigos. Para conocer Starwood (mi faux-*vertaling* of Stellenbosch) y Cape Town, el interior. To reconnect with Pretoria, Mamelodi. Todos mis lugares, y algunos nuevos. Pero no te confundas, Montenegro: I'm going for you. Digo: for us.

# *Bloedruiwe* Crónica

## *A CODA IN TWO PARTS*

There's a love you can't survive
**Richard Thompson**

Forever hasn't happened yet
**John Doe**

Maybe that's just the price you pay
For the chains you refuse
**Richard Thompson**

## After *Bride Flight*

Heme aquí—para variar—ponderando en mi ponder heart (*pace* Joanna Woolfolk). Musing about that *mooi* Dutch filum *Bride Flight*. It's *'n bietjie*—OK, muy—melodramático, pero los actores give it a kind of gravitas, hasta urgencia, te diría. Y (OB-vio), it's very *us*. Hasta tiene un invisible linksy casting twist: my idol, el Rutger Hauer, returned to Dutch cinema tras 30 años en Hollywood pa' hacer el papel de Frank (the older version), el Dutch emigré vineyard owner en New Zealand.

Se basa en la realidad: a famous post-WWII vuelo de 1953, que llevaba a muchas Dutch future brides a sus waiting grooms en New Zealand. En el flight, los protagonistas, Ada y Frank, son seatmates y su química burns off the screen, aunque she's engaged to another Dutch oke—a quien solo ha visto una vez. By the time they land in Christchurch—37 hours later, *nogal*—están perdidamente enamorados. Se separan en full-on tearjerker mode y . . . cada uno hace su vida.

Heme aquí, thinking about Ada. Después de años de unhappy but dutiful family life, se escapa en autobús, buscando a Frank (who's been writing her letters). She allows herself *one* passionate interludio with Frank, el sexy, canchero, earthy amor de su vida. Esta escena en el film es breathtakingly direct, urgente, powerful. *Baie erotiese*. Ada struggles mightily, caught entre la consciencia y la pasión. She *tries* to envision, to create a life with him. Pero al final she can't—she doesn't *allow* herself to—*stay* there with Frank. Le tira demasiado el deber o la culpa. O las dos cosas, fatally intertwined. Ada vuelve a su dizque life—filmed, tellingly, in dour, sepia tones—con ese *verkrampte*, Calvinist *dominee*-in-training husband y los tres kids. Pero we've seen her heart is elsewhere: está con Frank.

And it hit me over the *kop*: you are like Ada, Montenegro. One can make choices—oh, this film brings it home to me—one can *choose* to live one's life, or end up living one's life (el resultado es el mismo, *nê?*) *for* others.

At the expense of one's own happiness, love, passion. Imagínate. Vaya novedad (bitter little jaja) . . .

En una hermosa *briefie,* you said you were having a hard time finding a "best fit" home for me in Africa. Me llamaste una black springbok, *onthou jy?* Point taken, bebé. It's true we didn't fare so well en Sudáfrica. En Joburg. In Bedfordview, precisamente. Y las razones del *why* vengo explorando en estas cartas, in these e-males y sueños y recuerdos que constituyen nuestros working papers, como quien dice, o sea *Our Ubuntu, Montenegro.* So, OK, quizás no en los northern suburbs. Too close to home—for *you,* al menos! Pero elsewhere? Elsewhere, we are a perfect fit. En otras latitudes, we belong. Together.

—*You speak of impossibilities,* escribe la Fanny Browne a John Keats, referring to one of her poet-amante's letters, en la cual Keats describe su fatally impecunious (not to mention tubercular) state! ¿Te acuerdas, Montenegro? I wrote you after seeing that film *Bright Star* de la Jane Campion en octubre del 2009. I was a living dead, una zombie en mi vida cotidiana when I saw that film, sentada en el darkened theater al lado de aquel stranger, el enjuto, Grant Wood-ish automaton que vivía conmigo. Pero pa' mis adentros I was swooning over you, canalizando nuestra vexed pero renewed love story through la adorable Abbie Cornish as Fanny y el soulful, sexy (si bien consumptive) Ben Wishaw as Keats.

*Completely* in love with you de nuevo, 25 años después de nuestro epic breakup, our star-crossed South African sundering. Y sin embargo no quise aceptar—not right away, not right then—tu propuesta de estar juntos, en Nevada. Tu chamba en la Hollister Mine, ¿te acuerdas? Remember how cross you got? —*If not Nevada, then* where? you wrote me grumpily. —*There* are *no mines in New Orleans, Shug,* me escribiste, half-laughing, half-desperate.

Quizás haya sido fatal mistake, not to take you up on Elko, Nevada. Pero no. No creo. If I'd accepted, si tú y yo nos hubiéscmos lanzado a un US-based affair, capaz I'd have been lured—lulled—into believing my life was OK. Quizás habría seguido así, sleepwalking, quién sabe cuántos años más. Como dice la Joanna Woolfolk, mi astróloga, if I'd had you close by, I might not have broken free of the abusive clutches of el Dorian (Pierre), como le decimos Wim y yo. The horror, the horror (*pace* el Brando in *Apocalypse Now*). Esos 17 años de Bella Durmiente almost reduced me to cenizas. *Casi*, I said, pero no cigarro. I'm still here. Still alive. Mucho *más* alive que antes, in fact. Pero anygüey, yo temía que it would bring down the whole house (of cards), nuestra reunión. And I wasn't sure we were ready. Especialmente tú.

Pero it's ironic. Yo era la impossibility-monger, la primera vez: *I* dealt the death blow to us in South Africa. Tú me pediste que te perdonara, you asked me to wait, to reconsider. You asked me to marry you. And you *never* spoke to me of impossibilities. You always thought us one limitless posibilidad no matter what, no obstante dónde: las calles de San Francisco o New Orleans; a walk-in closet floor in Chicago in the dead of winter; acurrucados—gimiendo, susurrando—on the metal floor of the Vasbyt Dodge van, inside our green sleeping bag. Y hasta en el highveld, (y)our Transvaal, after I'd begun to fade and falter, to recoil—del apartheid y sus tentáculos, de tu ma-induced parálisis—even then, we were *still* all possibility for you. If we could only wait till Europe, o New Mexico. O Napa. If we could only get through this rough patch. If, if, if . . .

And now? Esto es lo que sé de ti, Montenegro: your heart is true, but your hands are tied. Este film *Bride Flight* me abrió los ojos. Or, let's say, me lo confirmó. Y la empatía que sentí hacia Ada me provocó, unbidden, un repentino rush of tenderness hacia ti. You and your fucking cobardía emocional. Tu default mode: choosing safety. Back-pedaling from the abyss—el peligro de la pasión—con la excusa (¿inconsciente?) de lo familiar. Being dependable. Dutiful. Y ahora, experimenté sensaciones extrañas, tiernas y conflictivas, feelings I was immune to in 1983, cuando me pediste que tuviera paciencia, que te diera otro chance. Simón: este *Bride Flight* invisible link me abrió los ojos—to what ails you (and sustains you?)—and yet, como ves, esta vez *no* me cerró el corazón. So this is love, now.

—*Who do you love?* pregunta Frank, en la climáctica love scene de *Bride Flight*. —*I love* you. —*And I* you, responde Ada, holding his gaze, si bien sentimos (even as they make graphically passionate love, stare soulfully into each other's eyes) que algo—otro—le tira. Y . . . ella regresa. She doesn't stay with her love. Después de probar con Frank el first harvest's wine en Druiwebloed—el biblically named vineyard de Frank en su nuevo país, New Zealand—Ada regresa al *verkrampte*, dead-eyed, preacher-in-training marido.

Pero *ek wil jou hê*. I want our *bloedruiwe* moment. A Frida and Diego drawbridge, como hemos hablado. And so I spar with you, as is our wont, aquí en esta página en blanco, as on our lion-lechos de antaño. Don't make me wait, para tocarnos de nuevo, hasta que estés en la tierra, coño. Like poor Ada. Se queda en esa su sleepwalking, *dominee*-dominated vida, pero she finally defies him pa' ir a ver al Frank. Tras recibir una invite, regresa al Druiwebloed wine farm. Se inclina para tocarle, tenderly, la cara: at his fucking funeral. No te atrevas a hacerme una jugada así, Montenegro. Ya sabes: la paciencia no es mi strong suit.

## Después de Pretoria
### Our *Ubuntu*, Montenegro

First, I heard you. Tu misma voz de siempre: low murmurs, a jovial greeting. Del otro lado de la puerta I heard you making small talk con Wim mientras manejaban, second-nature, toda la South African security que es otro planeta pa' mí: electric gates, razor wire, clanging interior metal gates, double y hasta triple deadbolts. Yo te esperaba dressed to kill: esas Ultrasuede pants que me habías admirado en una foto, una vaguely safari-print V-neck tank top. Esperaba, jittery as a bride, que abrieran el último deadbolt a la casa de Lynette, Wim's sister, mi South African *sussie*.

And there you were, de repente, 30 years after the first time. And again — según la déjà vu, wormhole logic de nuestro lifelong love — I was transfixed. Era algo así como esa famous scene en *La casa de Barnarda Alba*, con el caballo garañón. Tall, short hair, canoso (como en esa melancholy selfie que me habías mandado), dark-eyed, wearing a ridiculous off-white fleece pullover. Pero it *was* winter, after all. And you'd just driven nine hours through that highveld cold pa' verme, en un semi beat-up red *bakkie*, de una mine visit way up north en el Limpopo (oh, visions of leopards and baobab trees and bushveld), cerca de la Zimbabwe border.

Our eyes locked, en un casi idéntico frisson al de esa *otra* winter night, en el Balboa Cafe. De reojo vi que Wim — overwhelmed por esa lava flow mirada inter nos — se esfumaba hacia el adjacent condo de su mamá, murmuring supportive pleasantries. — *You're still smoking, Rolo?* balbuceé, al ver la cigarette pack que traías en la mano, eye drops (endearingly, intimately) en la otra. — *You're not, Shug?* — *Who still does, in this day and age?* te pregunté, riéndome. Y no nos dijimos más na', porque en dos pasos you crossed Lynette's small lounge, me cogiste en brazos y nos tambaleamos hacia el bedroom.

What we learned en la cama: we still fit. Instant combustion, deseo arrollador. Bajo tu mirada, tus manos, tus labios, I lost all sense of time.

*Bloedruiwe* Crónica

No noté el frío, my body all long-slumbering, reignited yearning, yielding. Humedad. Instinct. Esa strange-familiar urgencia. Cuando volví en mí, the wintry August full moon was rising. Y esa pale golden light, streaming through Lynette's huge picture window desde el jardín, emboldened me. Quería que me resolvieras muchas incógnitas. Todas las preguntas que either you'd sidestepped en tus emails o yo no me había atrevido a hacerte. —*What's with the old* bakkie? I teased you gently. *I thought you'd be rockin' a black Merc. I thought you'd be rich by now, Rolo* (la discreción, I admit, nunca ha sido mi fuerte). Lo del *bakkie* se explicaba por el rough Limpopo terrain, *natuurlik*. Pero then, a flash of your famous *buffel* temper. —*Well he's not rich* (te referías al marido de la A., tu ex-wife, con quienes viven tus hijas), *so I'm not.*

Luego, me diste una larga, algo arcane explanation de tu strangely meandering career path: you left la mining industry en los late '90s (when the gettin' was still good for a white engineer, musité, pero me quedé callada) para meterte en la luxury safari business. Pero you'd sold your interests in that, creo recordar. Luego te meriste de CEO para no sé cuál eccentric billionaire que quería fundar eco-resorts en no me acuerdo dónde. Mozambique, I think. Eso tampoco te fue muy bien. Y ahora you'd returned to mining, pero como independent contractor. Y en la new, postapartheid South Africa, well . . . you were hustling.

Detecté un disconcerting strain of bitterness, resentimiento. Cuando te mencioné al Ian McCallum, former Springbok rugby player, plus—incongruously—poet, psiquiatra y wilderness guide, me dijiste, warmly, que you'd known him, desde tus días en ese tony prep school, Michaelhouse. I remembered, with a wrenching start, cuando Wim me había mandado su hermoso poema "The Rising" (hoping it would spur you to *aksie*). I'd forwarded it to you, only a few months earlier. Durante tu Great Silence. —*That's what I imagined Roland would become, something of a Renaissance man, like this guy*, me había dicho el Mike Chip, cuando le platiqué del McCallum. Yo también lo había pensado. Pero now, me quedé callada. Y cuando te pregunté de la Hollister gold mine, en Nevada, —*My* buffel *temper hasn't served me very well in my work, Shug*, me dijiste medio wryly, mientras me acariciabas el brazo. And then, almost under your breath, me murmuraste, —*I'm basically a miserable git.*

Cambié de tema medio abruptly, taken aback por esa naked—if elliptical—confesión (aunque al pensarlo, I shouldn't have been, *miskien*: you've always been able to bare your alma to me). Sería hasta después— months later—cuando se me ocurrió preguntarle a una English prof colega que qué corno significaba "git," exactly, that the full horror would sink in. A lame or crippled race horse, me dijo ella, going way back en la Brit or Scottish etimología, as she's prone to do. Anygüey, I got the point. So, te platiqué de mí. De los *anni terribili* del Juvenil, ahora thankfully on the wane. Y del Dorian. —*I know, Shug*, me dijiste con infinita ternura, nailing the baroque angst (that I *really* didn't want to get into) con una sola palabra, frighteningly apt: *your tormentor.*

Entonces, hice de tripas corazón and I asked the question preying on me desde ese oscuro día de enero 2010: why the hell didn't you just tell la N. que some random former guhlfriend had been worried about you, tus hijas, ese bizarre housefire, etc. —*Are you mad, Shug?* me exclamaste, *Nora knows* exactly *who you are. She's always known! If the conversation even veers to the US she gets cross.* And with that, ocurrió lo impensable: *you* stunned *me* into silence . . . si bien solo temporalily.

The sky was now inky black, star-studded. You were famished, te diste cuenta de golpe. Te sentías "a bit gritty" after the long drive me dijiste, adorably, y te pegaste una quick shower tras saludar a la Mami B., Wim's mom, en tu correctísimo Afrikaans. Yo me vestí de nuevo, while you showered. Me sentía glowing desde adentro, awakened desert bloom. Desorientada pero at home a la vez. A la luz de esa now-chalky, enorme full moon, Pretoria se veía uncanny, fantasmal. With a start, me di cuenta de que this was *not* your cuello del bosque y también: you expected me to find us a restó. Me reía pa' mis adentros, incrédula, as we bounced along en ese aging red *bakkie*, cigarrillo entre tus labios y my hand nestled be-tween your thighs. I summoned my 30-year-old GPS y de milagro (siempre he tenido espectacular sense of direction); we ended up in the News Cafe en Hatfield, al lado de nuestro antiguo barrio, Sunnyside.

You gripped my hand mientras caminamos del parking al restó y menos mal: me sentía desanclada, floating. The altitude, ese dry Pretoria winter chill, your broad shoulders, our long legs swinging in tandem (como habíamos caminado 30 years ago en New Orleans, en San Francisco), me dejaba sin aliento, dizzy. As we entered the dim, hip restó, celebré mi buena elección. It was late, pero the News Cafe serves hasta altas horas de la madrugada. It was packed, y todo el mundo nos miraba mientras nos acomodaba un dreadlocked mozo. Y no era solo porque we were the only nonblacks en el restó—despedíamos endorphins o pheromones o algo, sin lugar a dudas. El mozo hovered expectantly, su half sonrisa reconocía nuestro besotted aunque clearly non-teenage estado. You scooted your chair close to mine y me cogiste de la mano, me hiciste leerte de la carta— habías dejado tus reading glasses en el *bakkie*. ¿Por vanidad, por los nervios? My heart swelled with tenderness. Te pedí una huge salad, tú nos pediste una botella de noble *rooiwyn* (à la Castells). I couldn't eat a bite.

Como en ese golden light *slaapkamer*, earlier, perdí toda noción del tiempo. I only know que te pude decir, finally, everything I'd been wanting to tell you, cara a cara, for 30 years. As you ate and I drank, no me quitabas los ojos de encima. Love- (and Pinotage-) emboldened, I tamped down my misgivings, mi aprehensión de tu *buffel* temper, tu knee-jerk defensiveness around this loaded subject, y te dije esto: —*I need you to know, Rolo, that what your ma did to us, the way she treated me, nearly killed me.* Me mirabas wide-eyed, pero—por primera vez en la vida—you didn't leap to her defense. — *Why didn't you tell me?* was all you said. —*I did. Over and over. You couldn't hear me back then.* I pressed on: —*I need you to know something else. Remember London? I lied to you . . . to both of you. That baby . . .* Your face went dark then, pero no era la ugly mueca de self-righteousness, jealousy, betrayal de hace 30 años. — *You mean to tell me,* me interrumpiste gently, *that we could've been the parents of two and instead we're parents of none?* I nodded. Para entonces, yo lloraba openly. El mozo, who'd been milling about solicitously (y no sin curiosdad), refilling our wine glasses, backed away—clucking sympathetically, me parecía—cual si se hubiese topado con un radioactive forcefield.

Tears filled your eyes then, too. Los dos llorábamos nakedly, silently, como en la famosa "Last Night," 30 winters before. Me sentía, en ese momento, cual si rompiese la superficie de un sueño, o de un fairy tale, like la Little Mermaid when she breaks through the waves y ve al príncipe, su destino humano, pero . . . —*I love you, my darling,* te dije. *But I don't want to marry you.* — *Why not?* me preguntaste, angustiado. *What do you mean?*

*What* do *you want? —I don't need to live with you. I don't even* want *to live with you. Not here. I can't.* En eso, you took my two hands in yours, pulled them to your heart. —*I only know . . . I just love you, Montenegro.* You turned your palms up, cual si me ofrendaras el corazón, en un gesto oddly transcultural y timeless, entre Zulu y Aztec. —*I love you too, Shug.*

We drove back to Queenswood cracked-open y exaltados, no space between our *bakkie*-jostling thighs, my head on your shoulder. And you pulled me to you en esa rumpled, moon-bathed bed y así dormimos toda la noche, your arm encircling my breasts, dedos entrelazados.

I'd never understood it—esa outsized *reaksie* de la N. al innocuous text de Wim. Until Pretoria. And so, as is my wont (ever Daddy's girl), I reach toward making—articulating—meaning mediante el cine. *45 Years,* dirigido por el brillante Brit, Andrew Haigh, y starring la spellbinding, enigmática Charlotte Rampling, me agudizó la mirada. En una entrevista con Mary Gaitskill, hablando de Kate (whom she plays), la Rampling dice, "There are things Kate has compromised on . . . that's what people do, because they don't want to rock the boat. Then this thing happens, it all comes up to the surface, and she doesn't want to face it. She doesn't even know what she's got to face."

Pero según me contaste, Montenegro, en nuestra Pretoria reunion, la N. knows *exactly* "what she's got to face." Esa ostensibly invisible, ínfima falla—esa verdad subterránea—soy yo. Our love was too true and too painful (in its loss) como para que me incorporaras a tu daily life. Como hizo el Geoff en *45 Years,* you buried us, and went on with your life. Me desterraste. Pero unlike la Katya, Geoff's glacier-entombed love from 50 years earlier, me enterraste viva.

Y así como todo comienza a desmoronarse cuando la Kate—following an atavistic, long-suppressed instinct—hace su forensic foray al attic y encuentra la foto de Katya, con todo y su gently swelling tummy, para tu *vrou,* Wim's slight, offhand text was analogous to that photo. Small flaw deviene devastating crevass en un abrir y cerrar de ojos. O, en las inmortales palabras de Mercutio, "Ay, ay, a scratch, a scratch. Marry, 'tis enough." Cuando la N. vio ese text (mise en abyme de nuestro amor viviente), she found out—o más bien confirmó—what she's always known (but lives denying): es una substitute wife. No el amor de tu vida. Hence: su arrebato de rabia, sus threats. Hence, también, your retreat into cowardly compliance. Y ahora, even after Pretoria, after you summoned the courage to inhabit conmigo—oh, enchanted full moon ecotone—nuestra verdad, again te has vuelto cómplice de un entierro.

Falling in love with me fue una desviación de la norma para ti. I'm a spanner en los works de tu northern suburbs, "reach for the remote," Southforky lifestyle. Una aberración tan stark como el black springbok en el lion-colored veld. Falling in love with you, on the other hand, fue un hecho igual de decisivo pero constitutivo para mí. Ironically, not *during* our love story sino en el después. Porque después del falling in love y el falling apart, el reensamblaje—picking up los pieces in South Africa under apartheid—me hizo quien soy.

Unlike la glacier-buried Katya, I'm not frozen. Embalsamada yo—and our lost little zygote(s)—en amniótico ámbar viviente más de 25 años, I'm alive. Viva para recordarte, para constituir la constante falla en tu fundamento. Alive para contar esta nuestra gran—si *tragies* y utópica—love story.

# AUTHOR'S NOTE

In this book, I'm working the edge beween memoir and fiction. Y este ragged edge—this in-between, ecotonic amalgam entre memoria e imaginación—es el sweet-spot of life writing, for me. In other words, mi patria. Herein you'll find black holes, sudden anagnorises, competing versions of (hi)story. In exploring these painful, joyful, sometimes discomfiting knots, I've sought to respect—even to foreground (rather than attempting to soften or mitigate)—their irresoluble nature.

The way Wyatt Mason describes Norwegian writer Linn Ullmann's project in *Unquiet* resonates powerfully for me. "What she was putting on the page," Mason writes, "wasn't repertorial evidence . . . Even if she was writing a scene based in what she could recall, she allowed herself to . . . see with the imagination. . . . She gave herself the freedom to imagine what had been forgotten, not in an attempt to establish facts . . . but to find the truth" (*New York Times Magazine*, 13 January 2019, 47).

In *Heartthrob*, I've changed the names of some of the characters, but they—we—are all real. No composites, no substitutes. The dialogue throughout has been reconstructed and edited from memory (itself at once laser-sharp—my fabled *olifant* memory—and black hole-ish), and also from diaries and letters. Correspondence has long been considered a minor art and is now (gracias, internido y social needia) a dying art. Pero like both my parents, I've been an avid correspondent—and archivist—since childhood. One of my chief aims (both ontological and artistic) is to highlight the vitality, the possibilities (productive, pleasurable, provocative) of correspondence.

A word (*of twee*) about my language(s): I'm always striving for that *other* sweet-spot: entre natural-sounding orality and a heightened, (hopefully) incantatory lyricism. My longtime friend, Tania Bester (a South African native Afrikaans speaker), has described my language as Afri-Spanglish, y creo que she nails it, ¿que no? Tania's felicitous trilingual coinage succinctly captures the mix of English and Spanish (y ahora con un sprinkling of Afrikaans) I created for *Heartthrob*. I know it's challenging, gente. Pero oso conmigo, ¿sí?

# ACKNOWLEDGMENTS

I'm very grateful to the following people for their apollo [*sic*!] during the long gestation and writing period of *Heartthrob*.

To former UWP acquisitions editor Gwen Walker, for her astute suggestions, y a su assistant, la Anna Muenchrath. To art director Jennifer Conn, who helped make the cover magic happen, y al design-whiz, senior editor/compositor Scott Lenz. To my longtime compinche, la sublimely bilingüe senior editor Sheila McMahon, project editor on this and my last book, whose meticulous copyediting and probing questions (about characters, situations, and words—including Afrikaans arcana) challenged and strengthened my writing. A tus pies, carnala. A los anonymous readers of this book in manuscript form—Reader #1: my deepest thanks for joining me en el crisol. Reader #2: I'm raising a Balboa Cafe martini to you. Bien dirty (si virtual), por supuesto.

To these friends and colegas all over el mundo, for inviting me to perform and discuss my work: Paul Allatson (U. of Technology, Sydney), Pilar Ara (Pasadena City College), Ksenija Bilbija (U. of Wisconsin–Madison), Elaine Brooks (U. of New Orleans), Carlota Caulfield (Mills C.), Deb Cohen (Slippery Rock U.), Sergio de la Mora (UC–Davis), Adam Demaray (Tulane U.), Roshawnda Derrick (Pepperdine U.), Epicteto Díaz Navarro (U. Complutense—Madrid), Evelina Galang (U. of Miami), Ramón García (Cal State-Northridge), Ramón González (U. de Valladolid), José Ignacio Guijarro (U. de Sevilla), David Kipen

(Libros Schmibros), Cristina Martínez Carazo (UC–Davis), Azila Reisenberger (U. of Cape Town), John Carlos Rowe (USC), Meghan Skahan (UCSB), John Max Zemke (U. Missouri–Columbia).

To friends and colegas at Pomona College: Denis Recéndez, cyberhoncho supreme, whose (information technology) skills, creativity, and imagination facilitated—indeed, made possible—the techno-hatching of this book, especially part III. Also to Jack Abecassis, José Cartagena-Calderón, Grace Dávila, David Divita, Virginie Pouzet-Duzer, Sheri Shepherd, and Miguel Tinker Salas, and to my research assistants, Frances Sutton and Aalia Thomas.

To Chris Sadiq, my longtime masajista, for everything you do to sustain and nourish the mind-body conecte, sine qua non.

To these friends, for your presence since the San Francisco comienzo de esta love story: Mike Chiappetta, Marianne (Breidenthal) Franco, Tina Schiller, Suzinn "Lee" Weiss, and James Zike.

To my dear ones: Marian "Pink" Williams, for your extraordinary visual and emo-insight and sensitivity, and for your love and support; Zachary "Sireno" Mirman, for patiently and thoroughly reading every word of this book (en sus múltiples avatares) and for your love and support; to both Marian and Zack, for your timely, skillful, and creative translation of *Heartthrob*'s corazón into the LionLovers design element used thoughout the book; to Paul "el Austra" Allatson, for your multiple rereads, invaluable editorial and formatting skills, and generosity; to Wim "Wu" Lindeque, Pretorian partner-in-crime, foil and Muso, lifelong compañero without whom this book would not have been possible; to my sister Sarita "Eva" Chávez Silverman, for obliging me to open la caja de Pandora de esta love story and, thus, kick-starting this book.

To my South African friends and *familie*: Tania Bester; Xavier Nagel; Mmome Neppe Selabe; and Beatrice, Lynette, and Mauritz Lindeque. And to my US familia: my sister Laura Chávez Silverman; mi primo Chuck "Jamón Gris" Graham y su esposa, la Jeannie; mi hijo, Etienne Joseph Strauss, y su hijo, Jeremiah Joseph. To my literary familia: my former editor at UWP and longtime compinche Raphael Kadushin, I owe you my (he)art.

To Etienne "Curé" Kapp and Lydia Vélez, gone too soon, always remembered (QEPD).